PROCESS VARIABLES
FOUR COMMON ELEMENTS
OF COUNSELING AND PSYCHOTHERAPY

PROCESS VARIABLES

FOUR COMMON ELEMENTS
OF COUNSELING AND PSYCHOTHERAPY

FREDERICK S. WALBORN

WITHDRAWN

Brooks/Cole Publishing Company

I(T)P™ An International Thomson Publishing Company

Pacific Grove • Albany • Bonn • Boston • Cincinnati • Detroit • London • Madrid • Melbourne
Mexico City • New York • Paris • San Francisco • Singapore • Tokyo • Toronto • Washington

A CLAIREMONT BOOK

Sponsoring Editor: *Claire Verduin and Eileen Murphy*
Marketing Team: *Nancy Kernal and Romy Fineroff*
Marketing Representative: *Mark Francisco*
Editorial Associate: *Patricia Vienneau*
Production Editor: *Laurel Jackson*
Production Assistant: *Mary Vezilich*
Credits continue on page 357.

Manuscript Editor: *Bernard Gilbert*
Permissions Editor: *Catherine Gingras*
Interior and Cover Design: *Laurie Albrecht*
Typesetting: *Joan Mueller Cochrane*
Cover Printing: *Quebecor Printing Fairfield*
Printing and Binding: *Phoenix Color Corporation, Inc.*

For more information, contact:

BROOKS/COLE PUBLISHING COMPANY
511 Forest Lodge Road
Pacific Grove, CA 93950
USA

International Thomson Publishing Europe
Berkshire House 168–173
High Holborn
London WC1V 7AA
England

Thomas Nelson Australia
102 Dodds Street
South Melbourne, 3205
Victoria, Australia

Nelson Canada
1120 Birchmont Road
Scarborough, Ontario
Canada M1K 5G4

International Thomson Editores
Campos Eliseos 385, Piso 7
Col. Polanco
11560 México D. F. México

International Thomson Publishing GmbH
Königswinterer Strasse 418
53227 Bonn
Germany

International Thomson Publishing Asia
221 Henderson Road
#05–10 Henderson Building
Singapore 0315

International Thomson Publishing Japan
Hirakawacho Kyowa Building, 3F
2-2-1 Hirakawacho
Chiyoda-ku, Tokyo 102
Japan

Printed in the United States of America

10 9 8 7 6 5 4 3 2 1

Library of Congress Cataloging-in-Publication Data

Walborn, Frederick S., [date]
    Process variables : four common elements of counseling and psychotherapy / Frederick S. Walborn.
        p.   cm.
    Includes bibliographical references and indexes.
    ISBN 0-534-20874-6 (alk. paper)
    1. Counseling.   2. Psychotherapy.   I. Title.
BF637.C6.W274   1996
158'.3—dc20   95-40446
                                                                    CIP

*I dedicate this book foremost to Rachel, a rare person
who openly expresses compassion and honesty.*

*I dedicate this book to our sons, Drew and Holt, who
have given me a fresh and vital perspective on life.*

*It is befitting that, at the core of my dedications,
I recognize and appreciate the love of my mother,
who provided me with the strength to be myself.*

*I dedicate this book to the memory of my father, who
displayed and provided me with the gift of questioning tradition.*

*I dedicate this book to Macie and Meriam, who
displayed for me the tenacity of love.*

*Finally, I dedicate this book to my supervisors, supervisees,
students, colleagues, professors, and, of course my clients,
from whom I have learned so much about life and living.*

CONTENTS

CHAPTER THREE

Supervision   45

PART TWO

RESEARCH AND PROCESS VARIABLES   77

CHAPTER FOUR

Outcome and Comparative Studies   79

PREFACE

Many students who are entering graduate school feel excessively anxious about doing counseling and psychotherapy. Many students are overwhelmed by the variety of styles of therapy and feel they would prefer to just "wing it." Upon graduation, some therapists question the utility of counseling and psychotherapy. Some students and experienced therapists accept that counseling and psychotherapy can alleviate people's emotional suffering, but they wonder what makes the process of therapy effective.

This book addresses those questions and anxieties. At the same time, it explores the dramatic changes now underway within the profession. With the rise of technical eclecticism, some therapists contend that there is no reason to work from an orientation. The rise of managed health care brings new demands for therapists to be accountable. Within the academic community and within the private sector, the need to blend the art of therapy with science is becoming increasingly clear.

This book examines the ingredients that account for the majority of change in counseling and psychotherapy—the process variables. Four process variables are presented: (1) the therapeutic relationship; (2) client expectations; (3) cognitive insight; and (4) emotional expression and experiencing. In addition, Part One is devoted to therapist factors that affect the implementation of the process variables of change.

Purpose of the Book

This book serves five major purposes:

1. To reduce the detrimental anxiety of some students and practicing therapists—that is, the anxiety that interferes with their ability to learn the process variables of change—by highlighting common struggles of becoming and being a therapist.

2. To integrate the practice of therapy with relevant research. A consistent theme throughout the book is that therapy is both an art and a science.

3. To introduce the reader to the various theories regarding process variables and to the research on four major process variables.

4. To provide numerous citations from leading authors of the major styles of therapy on methods of implementing these four process variables.

5. To convince, or remind, students and therapists that they are ultimately responsible for their own education.

This book is at the forefront of a major change occurring in the mental health field—an overt acknowledgment of the role of process variables of change that are common to all the major styles of therapy. Theorists and empiricists have been suggesting for a number of years that common features—process variables—make the various styles of therapy equally effective.

Comparative research—for example, the NIMH Treatment of Depression Collaborative Research (Elkin, Parloff, Hadley, & Autry, 1985)—has been unable to demonstrate that one form of therapy is generally more effective than another. Some therapists have interpreted this finding as support for technical eclectic therapy. However, the position taken in this book is that it is important for therapists to adopt theoretical orientation. Having developed an orientation, therapists will be more effective if they understand the implementation of the fundamental process variables of change.

Intended Audience of the Book

This book is written for academic and nonacademic readers. For the academic audience, the book is designed to be used in graduate-level courses. The student must already be acquainted with the various styles of therapy; an undergraduate course in theories of psychotherapy may suffice.

Because the idea that there are fundamental process variables of change has only been accepted relatively recently, the book does not easily fit into a traditional program of training therapists. It can be used as a main text or as a supplemental text.

Graduate students. This is not solely a theoretical text, nor is it a technique book. It is unique in that it provides a much-needed bridge between theory courses and courses on the techniques of a specific style of therapy, both of which are crucial facets of learning therapy.

Students often have difficulty in relating their theoretical courses to the practice of therapy. Likewise, as they learn the specific techniques of a therapeutic orientation, many students feel bewildered about the essence of the change process. When therapists develop an appreciation of the process variables of change, they are more likely to be able to juxtapose the various styles of therapy and apply their theoretical and technical knowledge.

What are the appropriate courses and training experiences for this book? Because it does not describe a specific style of therapy, and it does not include concrete case studies regarding the implementation of techniques, the book does not fit neatly on either side of the traditional division between theory courses and technique courses.

The problem is that presently there are no graduate courses that focus specifically on the process variables, or at least none that I am aware of. In this book, I argue that the process variables of change can no longer be dismissed as uncontrollable placebo effects and instead must be explicitly taught in the training of therapists. The ideal course would be exclusively devoted to the fundamental process variables of change and would be taken by students when they meet with their first client. However, because process variables are fundamental to counseling and psychotherapy, this book could be used in a variety of traditional courses.

Used in a theoretical and methods course on counseling and psychotherapy, the book helps students to appreciate the similarities between the approaches and to understand that many of the differences between the approaches are a matter of the degree to which the various process variables of change are emphasized. Used in teaching a specific approach, such as humanistic/existential therapy, the book allows students to build their specific approach on the foundation of process variables. Finally, the book is appropriate for practicum/internship courses in which therapists in training are applying the process variables of change in their work with clients.

Experienced therapists. This book is also appropriate for therapists already in practice. It can help to reduce some of the confusion and anxieties that even experienced therapists sometimes encounter. Because the increased appreciation of process variables as the foundation for change is so recent, many experienced therapists do not have a background in the relevant literature.

Use of Citations

A strength of this book is its extensive use of citations, in support of the contention that the major empiricists, theorists, and therapists of the differing styles of therapy largely agree on the role of the process variables. Because I feel it is important to emphasize that the process variables of change are fundamental to the major forms of therapy, I have taken the risk that the reader may feel overwhelmed by so many citations.

Terminology

The process variable literature is relevant to the work of clinical social workers, counselors, psychiatrists, and psychologists. The term *therapist* is used throughout to emphasize that process variables are applicable to most training programs. The term *client* is used instead of *patient* because this book focuses on people's strengths and on their movement toward increased autonomy during therapy.

The Three Major Orientations

For reasons of space, and to avoid confusing the reader, I have limited the book to the individual verbal therapies used with adults, although the process variables are appropriate to the application of other forms of therapy—for example, behavior therapy, family therapy, and hypnotherapy.

I have classified the various styles of individual verbal therapy into three categories: cognitive, humanistic, and psychodynamic. Some readers may find this grouping unsatisfactory, because there are so many differences between the types of therapy within each category. However, for the sake of clarity and ease of presentation, I have chosen to take the risk of overgeneralization.

Organization of the Book

The book is divided into three parts. A thread that runs throughout the book is that, if we are to be effective as therapists, we must engage in a difficult and never-ending struggle to be honest with ourselves and to accept that people are ultimately responsible for themselves.

Part One: Common endeavors of therapists. The three chapters in Part One examine the reasons people enter the helping profession, the process of selecting an orientation, and supervision. Numerous citations from graduate students and experienced therapists are included. A goal is to help readers realize that some of their anxieties about therapy are common among therapists. My hope is that, fortified by this knowledge, readers will continue their struggle to learn the process variables.

Part Two: Research and process variables. Some therapists are still not acquainted with the extensive research on therapy, although, in the past decade, research has become more relevant for the practicing therapist. In Part Two, the findings of the outcome and comparative research are summarized.

To date, no style of therapy has been found to be generally more effective than another style. I suggest that this is partly because all forms of therapy are based on common process variables. A chapter is devoted to the writings of numerous theorists on what these process variables might actually be. On the basis of this review, I identify four fundamental process variables of change: (1) the therapeutic relationship; (2) client expectations; (3) cognitive insight; and (4) emotional expression and experiencing. A chapter on the research findings regarding these four process variables concludes Part Two.

Part Three: Implementation of the four process variables. Although this section does provide some concrete examples of the implementation of these variables its main aim is to convince the therapist that all styles of therapy are founded on these common variables; that is, that the differences between the three major styles are substantially based on the differences in the degree to which they emphasize the various process variables. Comments by the leading proponents of the three major styles of therapy are included.

Even though the three parts of the book are interrelated, the reader may read only one or two of them and still gain a thorough understanding of the information within those parts. This flexibility may be helpful in academic settings in which time constraints do not permit the instructor to assign the entire book for study. However, the chapters within the parts are written to be read sequentially.

Acknowledgments

The writing and publication of this book has been the work of many people. Foremost, I am indebted to the honesty of the students and therapists who completed the survey and allowed me to use their words in Part One.

Now I understand why authors acknowledge the typist in books; without Patsy Wilson's time, knowledge, and patience, the book would not have been completed in this decade. I appreciate the help of Roger Cunningham and Leon Sullivan in dealing with a computer error. I am indebted to the librarians at the Trover Clinic Foundation for their expedient retrieval of books and journal articles.

Lively discussions with Paul Andrews, Tom Muehleman, and Gary Schultheis provided much of the inspiration for this book, and Bob Brooks and Dan Martin of the Trover Clinic Foundation provided time and enthusiastic support. Loman L. Trover's prophetic insight into the role of mental health in health care provided me with a work environment in which to learn and practice the teachings of this book.

I thank the following reviewers for their comments and suggestions: Alan Basham, Eastern Washington University; Kent M. Christiansen, Arizona State University; Arthur J. Clark, St. Lawrence University; Joshua Gold, Fairfield University; Barbara Herlihy, University of Houston–Clear Lake; Wayne Lanning, University of Nevada, Las Vegas; Tom McGovern, Arizona State University; and Nancy Murdock, University of Missouri–Kansas City.

I would also like to acknowledge the staff at Brooks/Cole who guided me through the publishing process, including Claire Verduin, Eileen Murphy, Romy Fineroff, Laurie Jackson, Kelly Shoemaker, Mary Vezilich, and Patricia Vienneau. Finally, I wish to thank designer Laurie Albrecht, manuscript editor Bernard Gilbert, and permissions editor Catherine Gingras for their work on this book.

Frederick S. Walborn

PART ONE
COMMON ENDEAVORS OF THERAPISTS

This book is devoted to process variables—those factors common to different styles of therapy that are essential to the process of change. Part Two will consider research related to process variables, and Part Three will discuss their implementation.

A major thesis of this book is that an understanding of process variables is critical to therapists' effectiveness. Part One addresses factors that are equally important to therapists' development: the experiences that they bring with them when they enter the field and their experiences in training and supervision. Part One is included because the experiential factors of learning and practicing therapy have a direct relationship with the therapist's ability to implement the process variables of change.

Chapter 1 advocates that therapists must recognize and accept their motivation for entering the profession if they are to help clients effectively. Chapter 2 emphasizes the need for therapists to acknowledge and develop their own therapeutic orientation. Chapter 3 describes how therapists contend with their anxiety in supervision and how their handling of anxiety has a direct impact on their ability to be an effective therapist.

Throughout Part One, I quote comments made by graduate students and experienced therapists in a survey conducted for this book. A copy of the survey form is reproduced in the Appendix.

Let's begin with a question that is central to therapists' effectiveness: Why do counselors and psychotherapists decide to enter the helping professions?

CHAPTER ONE
REASONS FOR ENTERING THE HELPING PROFESSION

In the late night Doc might be working at his old and battered microscope, delicately arranging plankton on a slide. . . . And there would be three voices singing in him, all singing together. The top voice of his thinking mind would sing, "What lovely little particles, neither plant nor animal but somehow both— the reservoir of all the life in the world . . ." The lower voice of his feeling mind would be singing, "What are you looking for, little man? Is it yourself you're trying to identify? Are you looking at little things to avoid big things?" And the third voice, which came from his marrow, would sing, "Lonesome! Lonesome! . . . Thought is the evasion of feeling. You're only walling the leaking loneliness."

(STEINBECK, 1954/1987, P. 25)

This passage about Doc, a respected character in John Steinbeck's novels, serves as a focal point for the present chapter.

When I initially read Steinbeck's words, they not only suggested a man's dilemma with his work, but also offered a depiction of why people pursue a career in the helping professions. This chapter focuses on three reasons that people enter counseling, psychology, or social work as a career. Therapists need to be aware of their motivations for entering the field so that they do not meet their needs at the sacrifice of practicing effective therapy.

THE THREE VOICES

I have grouped the reasons that people decide to enter the field of counseling and psychotherapy into three major categories. In keeping with the Steinbeck passage, I refer to these as the three motivating voices that therapists hear; they are similar in content to the three voices heard by Steinbeck's Doc.

Doc clearly heard the first voice singing a benign song about the life-giving particles of the plankton that he observed under his microscope. This was a sweet, reassuring voice: he felt fortunate to be in a career where he could appreciate such life-sustaining qualities.

Likewise, most therapists initially cite an altruistic reason for entering the helping professions. Like Doc, they desire to sustain and enhance life. This voice is easily accessible to the therapist's awareness; loud and clear, it says, "I want to help people."

However, Doc also heard a second voice: "What are you looking for, little man? . . . Are you looking at little things to avoid big things?" To therapists, this voice says: "What are you looking for? Are you looking toward others to avoid yourself?" This second voice arises from the needs of the therapist: People enter the field not only to help others but also to get their personal needs met. Quick to note that they entered the field for others, many therapists fail to mention what they gain from the profession.

Like Doc, many therapists hear a third voice, which comes from the marrow. It is the substance that life is made from, the stuff we try so desperately to avoid throughout our existence—our loneliness and aloneness. By examining other people's lives, therapists can ultimately avoid their own lives. Some therapists want to help others so they do not have to face the responsibility of their own aloneness.

I do not suggest that all therapists have the same voices—that is, the same needs, desires, or motives for entering the field. Some readers will be able to readily identify with all three of these reasons; others will not. My hope is that, after reading this chapter, readers will be able to reflect on their own reasons for selecting therapy as a career. Such knowledge, in the end, will aid the therapist in the process of providing sound counseling and psychotherapy. The idea that people enter counseling, psychiatry, psychology, or social work solely because they desire to help people is simply untrue. Pretending that it is true can leave all parties involved feeling empty and frustrated.

The remainder of this chapter is a discussion of these three major voices—the reasons that many therapists decide to enter this profession.

VOICE ONE: TO HELP OTHER PEOPLE

Just as Steinbeck's Doc heard his top voice singing of the life-giving properties of plankton, therapists hear their benign voice very clearly: "I want to help people." Odds are, if you were to ask counselors, psychologists, or social workers why they entered the field, their quick response would be that they wanted to nurture others; they wanted to help.

A Common Voice

In a survey that I conducted for this book (the survey form is reproduced in the Appendix), the majority of therapists commented that they entered the field because they wanted to nurture people. These are some of the responses by graduate students:

- I thought it would be a good field for me because I enjoy helping people find their strengths.

- I feel that people who enter the field really care about people and want to help them with their problems.

- While, undoubtedly, some enter the field for the wrong reasons (prestige, money), I feel it is likely that most do so because they are highly nurturant and have much to offer their fellows, this being the area in which they feel they can make the most positive impact.

One student noted that the major reason that he entered graduate school was to help others of his ethnic background.

- Being a black male I wanted the degree in psychology to strengthen my credibility within the black and white community. And also to assist other people of color to move beyond their particular problem(s) within the community in which they lived.

Certainly, the desire to be of service to others is an admirable professional goal.

It has been my experience that people enter the fields of counseling and psychotherapy to a great extent because of their strengths. Many therapists are simply good listeners. Even if they did not enter this profession, they would be sought out for their ability to provide emotional comfort and guidance. Many people enter the field because they have a history of helping troubled friends and relatives. They may have been told that they have the innate skills to be a therapist. Even before they enter graduate school, many beginning therapists have developed some of the skills necessary to help people change.

This altruistic motivation of therapists is the cornerstone of counseling and psychotherapy. It provides the basis for the all-important supportive relationship between therapist and client. It helps therapists to endure the sometimes painful process of change with their clients. The desire to help others is the foundation on which is built the therapist's understanding of techniques and process variables of change.

It is difficult for me to imagine a therapist who could be effective in therapy without having an intense and pervasive yearning to be of help. In other professions, people may be effective without having altruistic motivations. However, in counseling and psychotherapy, the therapist's motivation to be helpful to others is a fundamental requirement.

I have little doubt that many, if not most, people enter and stay in this field out of a deep respect for others. Unfortunately, some therapists do not give this respect for others an opportunity to mature into a deeper understanding of the change process, because they do not fully accept their other motives.

Only the Call to Help?

Do people really want our help? Can we really help people? In the blunt words of Paul Goodman, "The very worst thing you can do for people is to help them" (cited in Patterson, 1985, p. 357). The major goal of therapy, no matter what orientation, is to provide clients with an environment, a therapeutic relationship, in which they have the opportunity to become more responsible for their lives. However, many therapists block their clients' movement toward autonomy. Because they are overly nurturing, they are not able to provide the arena in which their clients can struggle to become more autonomous.

Prominent therapists have acknowledged that they are in this field not only to help others but also to meet their own needs. In his book *In and Out of the Garbage Pail*, Fritz Perls (1972) earned notoriety by a candid examination of his reasons for practicing therapy.

> Does this mean that I am a do-gooder or that I want to serve mankind? The fact that I formulate the question shows my doubts. I believe that I do what I do for myself, for my interest in solving problems, and most of all for my vanity. (p. 2)

Many would expect such a caustic comment from the individualistic writings of Perls. However, other writers have been equally honest about their reasons for entering the mental health field.

In *The Road Less Traveled*, Peck (1978) admits that, although his desire to help and his love for his clients are necessary ingredients for effective therapy, the therapeutic interaction is not a one-way street; the therapist also gets something from this relationship.

> The more I love, . . . the larger I become . . . Genuine love is self-replenishing. The more I nurture the spiritual growth of others, the more my own spiritual growth is nurtured. I am a totally selfish human being. I never do something for somebody else but I do it for myself. (p. 160)

When therapists can only hear the altruistic voice, they risk becoming care-givers and impeding the growth of their clients. Recognition and acceptance of other, perhaps narcissistic reasons for entering the profession ultimately enhances therapists' ability to create a relationship that is conducive to change.

VOICE TWO: TO MEET PERSONAL NEEDS

In recent years it has become popular to discuss the process of becoming and being a therapist. A number of books (Corey & Corey, 1989; Dryden & Spurling, 1989; Kottler, 1993; Noonan & Spurling, 1992; Sussman, 1992) analyze therapists' reasons for entering the profession.

Kanfer and Schefft (1987) propose that there are three self-oriented motives, or "three devils sitting on the shoulder of the therapist": (a) voyeurism; (b) power motive; and (c) self-therapy. They warn that, unless addressed by the therapist, these motives can lead to errors in all phases of therapy.

In *Becoming a Helper*, Corey and Corey (1989, pp. 2–6) list eight typical needs of helpers.

1. The need to make an impact.
2. The need to return a favor.
3. The need to care for others.
4. The need for self-help.
5. The need to be needed.
6. The need for money.
7. The need for prestige and status.
8. The need to provide answers.

The reader may recognize some of these reasons for entering the profession. The major point, however, is that it is not wrong to have these needs; in fact, it is healthy to acknowledge personal motives. When therapists are not aware of self-interested motivations, they risk sabotaging the client's growth in order to get their own needs met.

The personal needs that prompt individuals to become therapists may be grouped into two broad categories. First, they may enter the profession in part because they have experienced emotional suffering in their own lives; such a therapist is said to be a *wounded healer*. Second, therapists may be attracted to the field in part because of power issues. In the early stages of the client-therapist relationship, the therapist is granted considerable power.

I now review these two aspects of voice two.

The Wounded Healer

Some people desire to help other people because they have themselves suffered; they have been wounded. This wound can be a virtue, because wounded therapists are more likely to understand the suffering, confusion, and loneliness of their clients.

However, some people inside and outside of the field interpret this wounded healer concept to mean that therapists unobtrusively enter this helping profession because they seek therapy for themselves. In a skeptical appraisal of altruism, Skynner (1990) confronts people on their motives for entering the field.

This is the goose that lays the golden eggs. Many of us "sneak" into caring or therapeutic agencies by the staff door to get psychological help without acknowledging the need for it. Solutions to this kind of dilemma are not necessarily to be found in some new recruitment drive to attract different personnel to these professions. Altered organizational structures and better conditions of pay and service, and even more advanced training, will not necessarily provide a solution, or if they do they will only solve part of this problem. For the goose to lay its golden eggs it must be fed and this involves some acknowledgment amongst "care-givers" of the motives that draw them to their work. (p. 158)

My thesis is that to be a wounded healer can be a virtue or a vice, depending on therapists' level of self-awareness. When therapists are not aware of their motives for entering the profession, they risk moving the focus from meeting the client's needs to meeting their own hidden needs.

What, in fact, is the mental health background of therapists? I consider that question next.

The mental health of therapists.   Research supports the contention that the childhood development of many therapists has been plagued by turmoil and trauma—parental discord, parental separation or divorce, personal illness, or parental death (Hafner & Fakouri, 1984; Henry, 1966; Henry, Sims, & Spray, 1971). In a recent study, approximately one-fourth of psychologists surveyed (28.6% of women and 17.9% of men) recalled physical or sexual abuse as a child (Feldman-Summers & Pope, 1994).

An experienced doctoral-level therapist reported in my survey that she originally entered the field "to deal with my questions and feelings about my own family's distress and my personal reactions to these stressors." Note that this experienced therapist is clearly aware that her past familial problems were related to her entering the profession. This is a positive reason to enter the field; it is a strength. She has accepted the trials of her life and is willing to confront her reactions to past trauma. She is actively moving forward with her life.

Many therapists report an enmeshed relationship with their mothers (Norcross & Guy, 1989). One graduate student in my survey briefly described how she adopted a caretaking relationship with her mother.

I grew up in a single parent family and I suppose I kind of learned to "take care of" my mother. I've always tried to nurture people. Now, I sometimes have to restrain myself from trying to take care of people who don't require it.

Many therapists have learned their nurturing skills at an early age.

Therapists who have learned to be caretakers in childhood, at the expense of their own needs, come to the field with the ability to subordinate their own needs to their clients'. This can be positive in that it allows therapists to provide the supportive environment necessary for the client to feel safe and to take risks. However, many effective therapists have to go through a stage of their professional and personal development in which they learn not to center their relationships on the other person.

Some therapists with a background as a familial caretaker overidentify with their clients; they suffocate clients and fail to provide an environment that allows clients to take risks of change and become more autonomous. Also, therapists who take their caretaking role to an extreme, by severe and prolonged subordination of their own needs, may themselves develop emotional and interpersonal problems.

As adults, most therapists have emotional and interpersonal problems. One survey of 264 therapists, who differed in their levels of training and in the types of graduate programs they had undertaken, found that they had experienced pronounced personal problems: relationship problems (82% of respondents), depression (57%), substance abuse (11%), and suicide attempts (2%) (Deutsch, 1985). These numbers are not necessarily that astounding; a survey of accountants or teachers would reveal similar experiences. The major point is that therapists are not immune to problems.

Are the problems so pronounced that therapists seek therapy for themselves? Yes. In fact, 75–76% of psychologists, 67% of psychiatrists, and 65–72% of social workers seek counseling and psychotherapy services for themselves (Henry, Sims, & Spray, 1971; Norcross, Strausser, & Missar, 1988). In another survey, 47% of experienced therapists had sought therapy for relationship problems and 27% had sought therapy for depression (Deutsch, 1985).

These high rates at which therapists seek therapy for themselves may be interpreted to mean that the field attracts people who have emotional and relationship problems. Another way to view these figures is that therapists believe in what they do.

However, the high suicide rates for professional therapists are particularly disturbing. Psychiatrists commit suicide at a rate approximately twice that of practitioners in other medical specialties (Rich & Pitts, 1980). While male psychologists commit suicide at a rate slightly lower than the general male population, female psychologists commit suicide at twice the rate of the general female population (Steppacher & Mausner, 1973). The suicide rate for female psychiatrists is 47 times that of the general population (Moore, 1982).

Most likely, these high suicide rates reflect both the emotional instability of people who enter the profession and the extreme demands of the job. The higher rate of suicide among female therapists could perhaps be attributed to the persistent patriarchal character of our society and the frustration that women face even in pursuing a career based on nurturance.

Thus, research indicates that many therapists have come from homes where they were forced into caretaker roles; many come from broken homes; most have personal and relationship problems at times in their adult lives; and the majority seek therapy for themselves. Clearly, there is support for the notion of the wounded healer. How does this wound affect the ability of therapists?

The wounded healer as therapist.   Many therapists have learned to be caretakers who act as emotional buffers for family struggles, fighting, and pain (Norcross & Guy, 1989). Many have learned to put their own needs in the background for the good of others.

A graduate student in my survey commented on the development of her caretaker role.

> I grew up in a dysfunctional family. As the oldest child and female in a traditional gender role household, I learned very early to be very sensitive to others' needs, to be autoplastic, empathic, and a leader. I was a surrogate parent from a very young age and my identity and worth hinged on making others feel better.

What therapists have learned in childhood necessarily affects their relationships with clients. Thus, therapists who assumed a pseudoparental role in their family have learned that their support and dependency needs will be met only after they have met the needs of others. This pattern of denying their own dependency needs may lead some therapists to insist that their clients become more assertive and more autonomous, without a full appreciation of the appropriate timing of interventions.

> Many therapists are heavily defended against dependency needs by means of denial and reaction formations. Thus, they tend to be largely unaware of their own dependent longings, and may even exhibit a counterdependent defensive stance. (Sussman, 1992, p. 135)

Sussman (1992) cites the example of therapist Albert Ellis, who came from a traumatic childhood: he nearly died from tonsillitis and was in and out of the hospital for a number of years; his mother was self-centered; and his father was frequently absent and left the home when Ellis was at the critical developmental age of 12. Though Ellis discounts the role of his childhood in the selection of his career, he acknowledges that it has influenced his therapeutic style.

> My difficult childhood helped me do one important thing: become a stubborn and pronounced problem solver . . . So I figure out how to become my nutty mother's favorite child, how to get along with both my brother and sister in . . . spite of their continuing warring with each other, and how to live fairly happily without giving up my shyness. (Ellis, 1991, p. 3)

Sussman (1992) suggests that "Ellis's background, in fact, reveals many of the circumstances that are typical of those who develop an interest in psychotherapy" (p. 136).

It is my experience that the majority of therapists who come to the field as wounded healers tend not to be confrontive in their approach. Having learned as children to give precedence to the needs of others, they may grow up to be an adult who is not only sensitively oriented towards what others are feeling, but who also has a tendency toward self-abnegation and putting others first . . . This attitude also has the effect of encouraging repression of the child's aggressive feelings; since self-assertion is forbidden, and self-assertion cannot be separated from aggression. I do not think that anyone can be primarily oriented toward the feelings of others without repressing considerable aggression. (Storr, 1980, p. 179)

Therapists' self-abnegation can go to an extreme when they allow their clients to abuse them—for example, by making frequent phone calls to their home.

Experience and research support the wounded healer concept. We now come to a critical question: Can a person coming from a traumatic past truly be an effective therapist?

Wounded but not disabled.   Many therapists have developed empathic skills because they know what it is like to hurt emotionally. Dryden and Spurling (1989) make the point, however, that this emotional wound should not be too severe.

A persistent sense of having been hurt or wounded does indeed pervade [therapists'] accounts . . . But one's suffering is such, or is conceived as such, as to become a resource in that it sensitizes one to the suffering of others. For this to happen, for one's own suffering truly to become a source of strength and a means to understanding the plight of other people, the therapist must probably not have been too deeply wounded . . . or [must have been] wounded but also healed. (p. 195)

Research suggests that there is a modest positive relationship between emotional well-being and effectiveness as a therapist (Beutler, Crago, & Arizmendi, 1986). Thus, the school of hard knocks may be useful to a therapist, but not if the injuries are permanent.

Bugental (1987), a humanistic therapist, acknowledges that many therapists enter the profession because of concerns about their own traumatic life experiences, but argues that they should recognize this as a strength: "That is not a shameful admission; rather, it is closer to a proud boast. We chose to do something about our distresses" (Bugental, 1987, p. 271).

Issues of Power

Once again, therapists' power issues can either be a strength or a weakness in their professional lives, depending on the therapist's self-awareness. A fundamental aspect of effective therapy is the therapist's awareness of the oscillation of the distribution of power in the therapeutic relationship. Therapists who have an understanding of the role of power in the change process are more able to help their clients gain control and power over their own lives—that is, to help their clients assume more responsibility and autonomy.

Because the evolution of the power distribution is a key aspect of therapy, therapists need to be aware of their own desires for power and control over other people's lives. A therapist's quest for power over others can impede the client from becoming more autonomous. This facet of the second voice, the power issue, is presented in the following three sections: (a) the therapeutic relationship and power, (b) the therapist's quest for power, and (c) power and responsibility.

The therapeutic relationship and power.   There is no question that the therapist is in an extremely powerful position, at least during the beginning and middle stages of the therapeutic relationship.

> The therapist's office is an unreal world in which distractions are minimized and rituals are carefully observed. The therapist controls most of the show. Although the client chooses the content, the therapist directs the script and the interpretation of the lines. (Kottler, 1993, p. 28)

The client is immediately in a dependent position. The client pays money; the client usually does not know the ground rules of this type of relationship; there may be rituals that infantilize the client; and the client may feel vulnerable when he or she openly expresses emotions. Therapists, however, already know the ground rules of therapy and rarely lose control over their emotions. Simply put, to be the helper means to be in a position of power. As Horner (1989) notes, "The relationship is lop-sided by its very nature. This imbalance sets the stage for the emergence of power issues in the relationship" (p. 146). Therapists who do not recognize this initial imbalance of power within the therapeutic relationship are more likely to prove useless or even harmful to their clients.

Beginning therapists often believe idealistically that they will practice in a manner in which the power distribution is equal from the first session. However, even if therapists have the stamina to insist on an equal power distribution with their clients from the very first session, they may lack the empathetic ability to accept their clients' experiential world when clients first enter therapy. Clients are people who are feeling stuck; they have tried everything within their power to get on with their lives. They frequently feel confused, overwhelmed, and powerless.

The question is not whether there should, or should not, be an equal power relationship; it depends partially on the phase of therapy. In the beginning, as we have seen, the distribution of power tends to be unequal. As therapy evolves, the power distribution shifts; it wanes and waxes. A goal of therapy is to ensure that, by termination, the power of therapist and client is approximately equal. Part of the art of counseling and psychotherapy is to facilitate that power shift.

The therapist's quest for power.   As we know, therapists often state that they entered this profession to help others. They are less likely to admit the personal power issues that have drawn them to the field.

Guggenbuhl-Craig's (1979) description of the social worker applies equally to counselors and psychologists:

> In his own consciousness and to the world at large, the social worker feels obliged to regard the desire to help as his prime motivation. But in the depths of his soul the opposite is simultaneously constellated—not the desire to help, but lust for power and joy in depotentiating [taking power from] the "client." (p. 10)

Some students enter the field out of the desire to know what makes people tick. A number of respondents in my survey mentioned their curiosity about people. A graduate student reported:

> Initially, I was drawn toward the helping professions because I sensed an intellectual challenge, that of solving the unique puzzle that each client presents. I was drawn to the challenge of seeking to understand that which will probably never be truly understood: human behavior.

That desire to understand has its positive aspects, but it may coexist with a more hidden yearning: the desire for the power that knowledge brings. One experienced therapist in my survey gave this account of her reasons for entering the field:

> I thought then that "helping" other people would make me feel good or better about myself. I was young and idealistic. I also held a notion about "helping" that really meant my knowing something they didn't and thus having more power and control.

Patterson (1985) contends that

> the desire to be an expert, to feel knowledgeable and influential—if not omniscient and omnipotent—to be an authority, to be looked up to, is widespread and strong [among therapists]. There are those who have a need to control others, or who gain satisfaction from feeling superior, or who need even to be in control of the therapy relationship. Many, besides George Burns, would like to play God. (p. 224)

Strong as these impulses to dominate may be, therapists are often unwilling to acknowledge them, as humanistic therapist Rollo May (1982/1989) has pointed out:

> We are the "nice" people and, like the cultivated citizens of Athens
> in Socrates' time, we don't like to be publicly reminded, whether
> we secretly admit it to ourselves or not, that we are motivated even
> in our love by lust for power, anger, and revenge. (p. 248)

However, when therapists are not aware of their own power issues, they are more apt to foster a dependent relationship. The therapist who acknowledges power issues is more likely to establish a therapeutic setting in which clients can not only change their symptoms but can also become more autonomous.

Some people who enter the field have the fantasy that, by taking classes, they can learn what makes people behave in the way that they do. Then, as therapists, they will be able to dispense this wisdom to their clients, who will be eternally grateful, and all will be well with the world. However, there are times when the therapist does not have the answers; there are times when clients get worse instead of better; and there are times when clients get frustrated with the therapist. When things are not going smoothly or as planned, therapists who are not aware of their own power issues may inappropriately prioritize their need for power and control over their clients' autonomy.

We have already seen that many therapists have learned, in childhood, how to be caretakers. These individuals have acquired a skill that is fundamental to therapy: they can readily identify with other people's life situations. However, that strength can also be a weakness.

> The fact that people who are attracted to the practice of psycho-
> therapy tend to relate to others by identification rather than by
> mutual self-affirmation on equal terms has the consequence that
> the desire for power which they share with others is somewhat
> muted, and may not be obvious either to their patients or to
> themselves. (Storr, 1980, p. 181)

Therapists who deny the power inequality during the opening and middle phases of therapy need to check their motivations for entering the field. They risk taking the caretaker role to an extreme; they risk overidentifying with the underdog; and they risk being a rescuer. Rescuers usually are out to make themselves feel stronger, rather than to help people stand on their own two feet.

The question is not whether an equitable power distribution is right or wrong; it depends. What gets many therapists into trouble is that they get stuck in demanding to have all of the power and control in therapy, or they deny having any power no matter what the phase of therapy or demands of the situation are. Therapists who are flexible, who appreciate the oscillating nature of the power distribution in the therapeutic relationship, are more likely to be effective and to actively hear the needs of their clients.

Power and responsibility.   In the beginning of therapy, many clients want someone they can trust and lean on, someone whom they can work with on getting unstuck, someone who makes them feel safe enough to try new things and to struggle. As the relationship evolves, the client moves from a dependent role to a more active, independent role.

> As the child must break away from parental power, the patient should be able to emerge from the mantle of the therapist's power, challenging it if necessary, gradually establishing the self as an adult in the therapist's adult world. By the end of treatment, the sense of power differential should be gone, or well on its way to being gone. (Horner, 1989, p. 147)

To sum up, therapists are in a powerful position. Most people who enter the field are aware that the therapist has more power than the client at the beginning of any therapeutic relationship. Those who appreciate the role of power in therapy are more likely to become effective therapists—that is, to use their talents to help their clients gain more control over their own lives.

Voice Three: Loneliness and Aloneness

Recall what Steinbeck said about Doc:

> The third voice, which came from his marrow, would sing, "Lonesome! Lonesome! What good is it? Who benefits? Thought is the evasion of feeling. You're only walling the leaking loneliness." (Steinbeck, 1954/1987, p. 25)

Many people enter the field of counseling and psychotherapy to wall their own loneliness.

There is comfort in numbers. If we listen to others, then maybe this sense of loneliness will dissipate. Theodore Reik (1948) seems to know exactly what Doc meant:

> And this is the blessing of such loneliness: he who is always listening to the voices of others remains ignorant of his own. He who is always going to others will never come to himself. (p. 507)

As it applies to people entering the mental health profession, Reik's comment can be taken literally or figuratively.

Literally, some therapists enter the field because they are socially inept and lack interpersonal skills (Henry, Sims, & Spray, 1973). Being a therapist provides a relatively structured and supposedly safe meeting ground.

Figuratively, Reik's comment is representative of how some therapists avoid their own sense of aloneness, by looking to others for the answers. Yes, professors, supervisors, and books can give a jump-start and provide knowledge. They also can highlight trends that we might not have otherwise seen or experienced. However, the ultimate decision is our own. Other people can make learning more palatable, just as therapists can make the process of change more palatable. In both instances, the final decision lies with the individual. With the realization that the final decisions are our own comes a sense of aloneness.

Many therapists enter the field both to dispel their social loneliness in their daily lives and to dispel the aloneness that comes from the realization that they are ultimately responsible for their lives. In the following two sections I review these two aspects of the third voice which brings some people to the field—social loneliness and aloneness.

Social Loneliness

Many therapists have felt a sense of estrangement in their relationships with others. Spurling and Dryden (1989) relate the traumas of the wounded healer to therapists' social loneliness or isolation from others.

> What is the nature of the wound with which the therapist is afflicted, and from which he or she derives strength and understanding? Rather than any particular event or constellation of occurrences, the wound seems to consist of, or express, a sense of *isolation* or division from others. (p. 196)

Spurling and Dryden cite a number of leading therapists who recall a sense of social loneliness: Heppner (1989) notes that "a predominant feeling for me growing up was of being an outsider and being different in some way" (p. 70); Strupp (1989) describes a "persistent feeling of self-consciousness and alienation" (p. 102); and Mahoney reports a feeling of being an "outcast" (Mahoney & Eiseman, 1989, p. 19).

Sussman (1992) reports Hammer's opinion that some students, especially those from isolated childhoods, are drawn to the profession by their loneliness and intense hunger for companionship. Hammer wrote that these students "envision a career as a therapist as providing them with a constant source of interpersonal relationships to relieve their panic of being lonely and isolated" (cited in Sussman, 1992, p. 157).

Some people enter this profession because they have a background of feeling lonely. They imagine that the opportunity for the therapist to be in a relationship with a client will meet this social need. However, therapy, even though it consists of constantly working with people, can be a lonely job.

> Many therapists have entered the profession with hopes of dispelling loneliness by constantly working with people. But, because of the "work parameters" of psychotherapy, therapists are instead

often left with the loneliness of an extreme type of narcissism that imposes an enforced solitary existence of the self. (Welt & Herron, 1990, p. 321)

Among the work parameters that can leave the therapist feeling alone at the end of the day are the long periods of time in which the client does most of the talking and the constant demands on the therapist to attend to other people's needs and help them find a means to express themselves. Therapists are prey to endless doubts and uncertainties, always wondering if they are doing the right thing. Sometimes, sessions last too long and the therapist must play catch-up for the rest of the day. Clients don't say thank you as often as beginning therapists might expect. Sessions can be emotionally intense; people hurt. For all those reasons, times to just sit back and talk with a colleague are so welcomed.

Doing therapy can be a lonely job. Therapists should not get into the profession to be less lonely.

Aloneness

Besides the social loneliness, there is a basic sense of *aloneness,* which also makes up the third voice that draws many people to the field of counseling and psychotherapy.

As humans, one of our major goals is to take responsibility for our own lives—whether in the selection of a professional career or as a client in therapy. However, the acceptance that we are essentially responsible for our lives brings us face to face with a dreaded sense of aloneness.

In our daily lives, we hold that sense of aloneness at bay by means of duties, rituals, deadlines, and other contrivances. However, it is only when we can muster the strength to bathe in our aloneness that we have the opportunity to fully experience life. The accompanying sense of autonomy allows us to relate to others on the basis of a mutual desire for growth rather than out of unmet emotional needs.

Individuals can find areas of autonomy even in circumstances where their options are limited. Imprisoned in a concentration camp during World War II, Frankl (1963) acknowledged that, although he could not change the brutal conditions of his confinement, he was fully responsible for his own actions—for the manner in which he related to his environment.

Some therapists enter the field as a rather fanciful defense against the basic aloneness that accompanies autonomy. Specifically, they believe that they will learn the tricks of the trade in graduate school, and then they can go forth and cure people of their maladies. Underlying this yearning for a bag of tricks is the hope that, if they can be responsible for another, then someone else could be responsible for them.

Some people who enter the helping professions are attempting to evade their aloneness by waiting for books, professors, and supervisors to give them the knowledge of change. Yes, these resources can train students in the techniques, some of which are very powerful. However, the true change agent is how the therapist and client approach each other. The more thoroughly therapists have come to grips with their own issues of responsibility and aloneness, the more likely it is that they will be able to help their clients come to grips with their sense of autonomy. Some learn the tricks of the trade, and others learn the trade.

We must always keep in mind, as therapists, that we cannot control others; we can only set up conditions to make behaviors more likely to occur. The choice remains with the client.

Our fear of aloneness is ultimately a fear of our finiteness, our mortality. To contend with that fear, we tell ourselves that we won't really start living the life we choose until graduation, until we have a five-figure salary, until the kids are grown. Once we accept that our life is finite, we must also accept that we alone are responsible for how we use our time on earth; no one else can tell us what we should do.

Denial of finiteness is part of the human condition, as Becker (1973) made plain in his Pulitzer Prize–winning book *The Denial of Death*. More recently, Goldberg (1993) took up the theme:

> Human suffering arises from our awareness of vulnerability to pain and from our mortal status. Most of our daily roles and activities are designed to deny and buffer us from our dreaded aloneness, casting the shadow of our eventual non-being. Throughout our lives we seek a fund of knowledge and a place in the world that we magically hope will forestall, if not defeat death. (p. 160)

Given that aloneness issues are a human predicament that we all share, why is this understanding of aloneness so important for the therapist? For therapists, these issues are fundamental not only to their personal well-being but also to their professional effectiveness. Unlike a carpenter, who works with inert wood, a therapist works with people, in the shared pursuit of greater responsibility and autonomy. Therapists must face their aloneness issues if they are to function professionally.

The acceptance of our aloneness cannot be a superficial acknowledgment; it comes from the marrow. Next, I turn to a case example in which a client and I try to find this acceptance.

Case Example

In my journey of learning to actively listen, to acknowledge, and to accept my limitations as a therapist, one client was particularly memorable. This client's struggle and eventual acceptance of her own aloneness helped me to discover and begin to accept my aloneness in life.

The client was a 58-year-old woman, whom I shall call Dessie; this is not her real name. Dessie had a history of severe depression over the past year and had been on antidepressant medication throughout that period. She presented with all of the classic symptoms of depression (hopelessness, decreased appetite, insomnia, inability to concentrate, social withdrawal, and decreased energy) and had been hospitalized for depression eight months prior to our first session.

Within the first five minutes of our initial session, Dessie said that she was coming in for therapy only because of her constant concerns and fears about the welfare of her 27-year-old daughter. During the initial session, Dessie frequently referred to her daughter as if her daughter were an infant. The relationship between the client and her daughter was symbiotic. Dessie would not leave her house for fear that her daughter might telephone her. No time of the day went by without Dessie worrying about her daughter. While some of the client's fears were legitimate, the daughter's situation did not demand the attention that the client was giving her.

Dessie and I rather quickly developed a supportive but not a therapeutic relationship. When I mentioned my concern that our age difference (I was 24 years younger) might interfere with my working with her, she replied that she only needed help in ending her obsession with her daughter. I was satisfied that the age difference was only my concern.

Interventions were made to no avail. Dessie quickly rejected my attempts to discover whether there was any basis in reality for her anxieties. The daughter was a symbol for something, but I did not know what. I was missing something and could not hear beyond Dessie's protestations that her only problem was her daughter, that she only needed to let go of her daughter.

At the beginning of the third session, I began to hear what Dessie was attempting to say. It took a risk on my part. Dessie sat down in the chair and blurted out, once again, "I have to let go of my daughter." After a brief pause, in which we looked at one another, I replied in a quiet, affirmative voice, "That's not true; you cannot let go of your daughter, because you never did have her in the first place." She had a look of horror on her face. The client needed no clarification of my statement. Dessie had been defending herself from her own sense of aloneness by shifting the focus from herself.

Dessie became tearful and then began her therapeutic work. She volunteered that she had retired early, that her friends were dying, that she had no meaning in her life, and that she was aware of her remaining years slipping away. Though we had discussed each of these changes in her life previously, she had denied their import.

The truth was that retirement had brought a new awareness of her increased physical limitations and eventual death; nobody could die for her.

These thoughts and feelings were too much for Dessie. She had opted to die a slow, imprisoned death rather than to have to face her own finiteness, her own aloneness, and her accompanying responsibility for life. By attempting to assume the responsibility of another, she clung to the hope that someone could take responsibility for her, and make this nightmare of death go away.

Over the next few sessions, her agoraphobic symptoms began to dissipate, and she went out with her friends once again. Her depressive symptoms subsided, Dessie was tapered off her medication, and we then said our good-byes. Remarkably, she did fine with the separation of terminating therapy.

Some therapists are similar to Dessie. They inappropriately attempt to assume the responsibility for other people's lives, in the belief that, if they do, they will not have to face their own responsibilities—that someone else may come and rescue them. One graduate student in my survey hinted at this motivation.

> I can see some of the caretaker in me. Disclosing a little, I can see also that I would have rather been taken care of. Perhaps some-where I was feeling that if I could take some pain away for others, I may learn to take away some of my own.

And, if we can take away the pain of others, then maybe someone else can take away our pain. We won't have to be alone; there may be someone out there who can make everything all right.

Many clients want others—particularly their therapist—to assume responsibility for them. Ultimately, people seek to avoid the stark naked-ness of being alone. Therapists who have not adequately worked through their own responsibility and aloneness issues are bound to fall prey to their clients' needs, which nobody can meet. To not recognize and accept our own motives and needs, no matter how ugly they may be, can only hinder us in helping people to change.

> Only to the extent that one has had an experience or a feeling will he be able to understand it in others. It is in this spirit that Goethe once remarked that there exists no crime of which he could not imagine himself capable. Understanding is real only to the extent to which it is possible for one to project from his own life experi-ence such elements as he recognizes in the other person into the act of understanding. (Schachtel, 1966, p. 202)

Regardless of therapists' orientation, their major task is to help the client to not need help—to assist the client to become more responsible. How can we help others become more responsible if we have not confronted our own aloneness and responsibility issues?

We can help others to accept what is their own responsibility and what is ours. With this acceptance of boundaries, true life-giving therapeutic relationships develop.

WHAT'S A PERSON TO DO?

In this chapter, I have summarized three major reasons that therapists enter the counseling and psychotherapy fields: (1) the desire to help other people; (2) personal reasons—the wounded healer and power issues; and (3) escape from the loneliness of life. These three reasons—voices, as I have called them— are more relevant for some people than for others, and they do not exhaust all of the motivations that prompt individuals to take up therapy as a career.

Therapists need to know why they enter this field and why they stay in it. When therapists are not aware of their motivations, they are much more likely to get their own needs met at the expense of their clients'.

When therapists question their motivations for entering the profession, they are apt to feel vulnerable and insecure. These feelings of insecurity and doubt are an important part of becoming and being a therapist. It is from this self-doubt that we continue to struggle and to develop new approaches to working with each of our clients.

As a professor and supervisor, I have been fortunate to witness and be a part of students' struggles. Their feelings of doubt and anxiety, hard as they are, are an important part of the students' growth. Support groups, honest colleagues, and supervision can help students to use this anxiety in a positive manner.

Self-doubt and anxiety do not necessarily stop at graduation. In studying therapists with an average of more than 30 years of experience, Goldberg (1992) found that

> one of the central sources of disillusionment for mature practition- ers has to do with their fantasy as beginners of the skillful ease of practice as one becomes "seasoned." As beginners, they expected their clinical endeavors to be difficult, unsure, and often unsuc- cessful. But few anticipated that after years of experience it would continue to be difficult. (p. 24)

Doing therapy is a difficult job, for beginners and veterans alike.

In the professions of counseling, psychology, and social work, learning is a life-long endeavor. This is one of the virtues of the field; it is ever changing. Only those who have the persistence to withstand the ongoing struggle of self-honesty will reap the rewards of the field. Strupp (1991), in an autobiog- raphy, offered the following words of advice for aspiring therapists:

> If you are intent upon pursuing a goal, don't give up easily! I am a firm believer in persistence, and am often reminded of a quota- tion that is etched in my mind. It goes something like this: "Bright ideas are plentiful in science, but there are relatively few people who have the persistence to do the hard work of following one of them through." (p. 303)

The persistence of self-honesty is a particularly difficult challenge.

CHAPTER TWO

SELECTING AN ORIENTATION

*When Pharaoh had a dream he called in the experts
and they told him how it was and would be in the
kingdom . . . Like most modern people, I don't believe in prophecy or magic and then spend half my
time practicing it.*

(STEINBECK, 1961/1986D, P. 318)

My contention in this chapter is that therapists need to develop an orientation as a foundation for their practice, although the development of a workable orientation is frequently a struggle. I also suggest that learning the process variables of change can provide therapists with a foundation upon which to build their orientation.

However, some contemporary therapists refuse to develop a therapeutic orientation; they regard working with an orientation as an irrelevant ritual in the learning and practice of therapy. It has been my experience that, with the rise of the eclecticism movement, more therapists are openly questioning the utility of learning a therapeutic orientation.

WORKING WITHOUT AN ORIENTATION

In the survey I conducted for this book, many therapists described themselves as eclectic in their approach. Here's a sampling of comments from graduate students:

- I favor an eclectic approach, fairly grounded in anthropology. I view human beings as being *interactive* with a wide range of behaviors and responses available to them, to meet the demands of their environment. Psychology has to be broad. Future therapists should be exposed to a wide range of treatment experiences and/or techniques. The more tools within their clinical bag, the more likely they will be to respond and to recognize certain problems.

- I learned the humanistic approach as a nurse using basic reflection without much conversation. As a graduate student, I was able to use a psychodynamic approach with an eating disorders population. I also utilized a cognitive-behavioral approach with a variety of stress disorders population. I believe I have integrated my approach to use cognitive-behavioral approach to reduce specific maladaptive behavior and utilize psychodynamic approach to deal with underlying core issues.

- I truly believe that a therapist's orientation should reflect his or her work setting. My early training was in crisis intervention. The immediacy of the problems that clients faced in that arena meant a problem solving approach, perhaps cognitive-behavioral. However, with my clients in my practicum I've tried to practice an interpersonal approach.

- I feel that an integrative approach is the most functional approach. All therapies have something to offer. Through picking and choosing among operating procedures from the different therapies, the therapist will best be able to tailor the treatment to the individual client.

And here are some comments by experienced therapists:

- I am integrative in my approach. Utilizing one approach exclusively limits too much how I think about a client's issues and how I choose to get in there and work with them.

- It seems to me that many of the basic skills of a therapist are atheoretical.

- I am eclectic in my approach generally, and especially when I work with a client long term.

I vividly recall when it was a taboo to even hint at an eclectic approach. For example, prior to taking the oral exam to become a licensed psychologist, I was warned by colleagues not to say that I was eclectic in my approach. Such an admission was interpreted to mean that the therapist did not know what she or he was doing.

Surveys on the Eclectic Movement

The survey responses by experienced therapists and graduate students are interesting, but do therapists actually practice a diversity of approaches in their work? The following summary includes surveys conducted since 1945 on therapists who actively practice some form of eclectic therapy. In the majority of the studies, the subjects were clinical psychologists, and so the data may not accurately portray the history of eclecticism for counselors and social workers.

Date	Percentage of eclectic therapists	Research studies
1945	0	Thorne (1972) (cited in Patterson, 1986)
1961	41	Kelly (1961)
1973	55	Garfield and Kurtz (1974)
1978	58	Kelly, Goldberg, Fiske, and Kikowski (1978)

Date	*Percentage of eclectic therapists*	*Research studies*
1982	41	Smith (1982)
1982	30	Norcross and Prochaska (1982)
1983	30	Prochaska and Norcross (1983)
1989	32	Young, Feller, and Witmer (1989)
1989	75+	Zook and Walton (1989)

Because the studies varied with respect to the levels of training of the therapists, the settings, and the definitions of eclecticism, it would be difficult and erroneous to compare their results. However, it is at least safe to say that a minimum of one-third of therapists are presently working from some form of blending of approaches.

In Smith's (1982) survey of clinical and counseling psychologists, 41% of the psychologists described their approach as eclectic. What is particularly noteworthy is that, out of the 415 respondents in this survey, 98% believed that some type of blending of systems was the future of counseling and psychotherapy. My experience has been that this prediction was correct: blending, integration, and eclecticism became steadily more popular in the 1980s and 1990s. Increasingly, therapists graduating from school are openly declaring themselves eclectic in their practice.

There has been a major movement in the profession toward an appreciation of similarities among the various approaches and the need for flexibility on the part of the therapist. Strupp (1992), a leading figure of short-term psychodynamic therapy, reports:

> In practice, few therapists today call themselves "purists"; instead, eclecticism (the selected best of all approaches) seems to dominate the scene. This movement reflects a decisive departure from orthodoxy, together with much greater openness by most therapists to adapt to changing circumstances and to tailor techniques to the changing needs of patients as well as the demands of our multifaceted society. (p. 25)

This movement toward eclecticism has not gone unquestioned.

Questioning Eclecticism

The eclectic movement has been subjected to a barrage of criticisms and stereotypes. According to Garfield (1982), critics of eclecticism perceive it "as the adherence to a nonsystematic and rather haphazard clinical approach" (cited in Patterson, 1986, p. 460). Norcross (1986), a leading proponent of eclecticism, has collected a number of unflattering definitions of the term:

A vague and nebulous term, its connotations range from "a worn-out synonym for theoretical laziness" to the "only means to a comprehensive psychotherapy" (Smith, 1982) . . . In other corners, eclecticism connotes undisciplined subjectivity, "muddle-headedness," even minimal brain damage. Robertson (1979) quotes colleagues who refer to eclecticism as the "last refuge for mediocrity, the seal of incompetency" and "a classic case of professional anomie." (p. 5)

Even with this bad press, a number of therapists refer to themselves as eclectic or integrative in their approach.

Is eclecticism a movement to embrace, or the downfall of our profession? The answer, obviously, will depend on how eclecticism is defined.

The Varying Definitions of Eclecticism

What is eclecticism? I have heard both proponents and opponents of this approach define it as being atheoretical and selecting techniques from whatever styles of therapy serve their clients the best. Such a simple definition of eclecticism is not adequate, however.

Norcross and Saltzman (1990) have suggested two major types of eclecticism: the first type they term *eclecticism*, and the second they term *integration*. This is a common division made in the field. The term *eclectic* is frequently reserved in the literature for therapists who are atheoretical, who do not work from a theoretical base, and who combine a variety of techniques from differing approaches. By contrast, the integrative therapist does not deny the role of theory as a necessary base, a structure to work from. The integrative therapist attempts to synthesize differing theoretical approaches into one systematic theory. A representation of the integrative approach is Dollard and Miller's (1950) merging of behavioral and psychoanalytic approaches.

Other authors have suggested three major divisions of eclecticism: common-factors eclecticism; theoretical eclecticism; and technical eclecticism (Daldrup, Beutler, Engle, & Greenberg, 1988). The supposition of *common-factors eclecticism* is that factors common to all forms of therapy make therapy effective. Even though proponents of the various schools dictate differing techniques, there are common underlying factors that are the true change agents. For example, one common factor is the therapeutic relationship. Proponents of common-factors eclecticism suggest that all therapies are equivalent in efficacy and there is no need to be teaching the various schools of therapy; we only need to research, learn, and teach those fundamental factors common to all interventions that foster positive change.

Theoretical eclecticism is similar to the integrative approach. Therapists of a theoretical eclectic background believe that having a consistent theoretical framework is important; however, they blend the theory and techniques of different approaches to create a new coherent system.

Technical eclecticism, like Norcross and Saltzman's (1990) eclecticism, is atheoretical; the therapist chooses techniques at will from differing approaches.

If a therapist is eclectic, does this mean that she or he tends to be a proponent of common-factors, theoretical (integrative), or technical eclecticism? How do eclectic therapists describe their actual practice?

In Norcross and Prochaska's (1982) study, 30% of the psychologists surveyed referred to themselves as eclectic. These eclectic therapists defined their practices in three discrete manners.

In the first group (29% of the sample), the eclectic therapists worked from a specific orientation, but also incorporated a variety of other techniques. For example, they might refer to themselves as humanistic, and yet also use techniques from the cognitive and psychodynamic schools. This type of flexible approach is common in the field.

The majority of eclectic therapists (61%) attempted to integrate the theoretical and therapeutic approaches. Like the first group, they would use techniques from various approaches, but they developed their own unique style by integrating the foundations of two or more approaches into a single coherent system.

The third group (the remaining 10%) in the Norcross and Prochaska (1982) study were atheoretical in their approach and would use techniques from the various schools. This small minority of technical eclectic therapists did not work from a consistent framework.

Thus, of the 30% of psychologists practicing from an eclectic approach, only 10% practiced technical eclecticism. That is, only 3% of all of the psychologists studied by Norcross and Prochaska were practicing without a theoretical base; 97% of the therapists in their sample practiced from a single theoretical approach or an integrated theoretical approach. However, it is my experience that, in the late 1980s and the 1990s, more than 3% of therapists are practicing technical eclecticism.

If eclecticism is understood to mean that therapists must be flexible, it is definitely a requirement of any therapist. However, a major position taken in this book is that some therapists who refer to themselves as eclectic are probably technical eclectic therapists: they have refused the risk, and the eventual struggle, of adopting, integrating, and/or creating their own therapeutic approach.

> It is not uncommon to hear counselors who have no articulated orientations whatever describe themselves as practicing within an eclectic orientation. More correctly, they should call themselves "weathervane" counselors because their orientations change with the winds in the field. Developing your own approach to counseling requires you to pick and choose, but to do so in a knowledgeable

and defensible way. Developing your own approach also requires that you actively pursue perceptive criticism of your own approach and seek to make it better. (Scissons, 1993, p. 22)

With the rise of the eclectic movement, it is easier for therapists to refuse the struggle of developing their own orientation. However, the vast majority of therapists still work with a therapeutic orientation, for a number of reasons.

STRUCTURE WITH FLEXIBILITY

In the survey conducted for this book, a number of respondents discussed the need for therapists to work from a specific orientation, in order to have some structure in their practice. These are some of the comments made by graduate students:

- Unless well-grounded in a particular approach, one cannot critically examine the approach to retain those aspects and discard others that in the end do or do not blend with your unique integrative approach and philosophy.
- As long as an orientation is used to provide structure and facilitate learning and not to be used as an excuse for not helping a client whose problem doesn't fit with your orientation.
- Only if you're flexible.
- As long as those teaching and supervising the trainees aren't *rabid* adherents to their own orientation. Students need to appreciate the learning process in approaching an orientation. A "transplanted" orientation from therapist to student may be useful in the short term, I think. But, I think it holds less meaning than one sought "out on" one's own.
- I think it's good as a starting base. However, I think each person should be able to develop their own style, regardless of their supervisor's orientation.

Experienced therapists made similar points:

- An orientation is vastly important for conceptualizing and understanding client problems. However, I worry that students who bind themselves too firmly to an orientation inhibit their learning.
- As novices, I think we need to start with a particular framework of theory and practice.
- Know one system to provide some structure during confusing times.

- I think one must find the orientation that is a good "fit" between who they are and thus how they perceive their role as a therapist (i.e., orientation). This serves to ground trainees and from there they can branch out.

Notice some of the trends in the preceding comments: beginning therapists particularly need a coherent structure; supervisors should not dictate their approach to supervisees; therapists must remain flexible with their approach; an orientation can help through the "confusing times" or times of resistance; and a therapeutic style facilitates finding out what works and what does not work.

The Call for Structure

Whether carpenters, housecleaners, teachers, or therapists, we all need a framework to work from. With experience, therapists no longer notice their working frameworks. Experience breeds patterns—patterns of knowing what works and what does not work.

Many of the people in the survey emphasized that the beginning therapist, in particular, needs to adhere to an orientation. However, a coherent framework is also important for the experienced therapist.

Beginning therapists, experienced therapists, and neighbors across the street all have ideas about why people behave the way they do and ideas on how to help people to change during times of need. A goal of the effective therapist is to make these beliefs—their orientation—available to their awareness. When therapists notice the trends in their beliefs and actions, they are more likely to mature and to help people change in a positive manner.

Therapists do not simply learn someone else's orientation. We adopt our own approach. The approach that we choose is a reflection of what we already believe; it should not be something foreign to our experience. A workable therapeutic orientation encourages and builds upon the beliefs that we already have.

> Practicing counseling without an explicit theoretical rationale is somewhat like flying a plane without a map and without instruments. We do not see a theoretical orientation (or a counseling stance) as a rigid structure that prescribes the specific steps of what to do in a counseling situation. Rather, we see theory as a set of general guidelines that counselors can use to make sense of what they are doing. (Corey, Corey, & Callanan, 1988, pp. 102–103)

To illustrate the value of a therapeutic orientation, Bellak and Faithorn (1981) tell a comic anecdote about an old village smith who was requisitioned by the military to repair a general's car.

He lifted the hood, examined the engine, and then gave the distributor cap a sharp blow with his fist. Immediately, the motor started up. The general asked, "What do I owe you?" The village smith replied, "A hundred bucks." "A hundred bucks for one bang?" asked the general. "No," replied the smith, "one buck for the bang, ninety-nine for knowing *where* to bang." (p. 3)

Developing an orientation helps the therapist to know where to bang, where to look. If a therapist does not know where or how to look, then what is therapy all about? Does the therapist simply provide a supportive environment in which the client changes? Or does the therapist just go banging around and then, after a number of unnecessary failures, say, "I learned by experience." Well, we all learn by experience; why not put some form to that experience?

Structure to Enhance Intuition

Some therapists believe that the development of an orientation interferes with their intuitive process, their "third ear." Even though a keen intuitive ear is a critical therapeutic tool, it can be misleading if the therapist does not have a workable theoretical orientation.

> Although personal experience, common sense, and intuition are useful, they alone do not prepare one to negotiate an affect-laden therapeutic relationship. In order for a therapist to be effective with a wide range of people and problems, these valuable human qualities must be wed to a conceptual framework. Therapists must understand very specifically what they are trying to do in therapy—where they are going and why—in order to be consistently helpful to clients. Every therapist needs a conceptual framework as a guide. (Teyber, 1992, p. 4)

The therapist's theoretical orientation should not be just an abstract collection of terms. Rather, it should be a reflection of the therapist; it should make sense to the therapist at a human level. Therapists need not feel that they cannot borrow techniques from differing schools, or that they cannot experiment. In fact, flexibility and experimentation are key aspects of developing a theoretical orientation.

The development and maintenance of an orientation actually frees therapists to actively listen. Contrary to what many therapists believe, I suggest that the flexible application of an orientation aids the therapist in being intuitive. This works in at least three ways.

First, the therapist's struggle to develop an orientation itself promotes the expression of intuition. Intuition is often imagined to come from gut feelings; it's as if these creative expressions simply come out of the blue.

This is rarely the case. As May (1975) wrote in *The Courage to Create*, creative moments, which seem to arise almost magically, are actually preceded by times of deliberate struggle. In *Listening With the Third Ear*, Reik (1948) describes a dazzling array of intuitive interpretations and then explains their origin; these masterful interpretations did not just happen. Intuition is usually the result of a struggle to develop form. In counseling and psychotherapy, intuition is frequently preceded by the therapist's struggle to develop a workable orientation.

Second, working with an orientation frees the therapist to be flexible. Without structure, there is no structure to be flexible with. In the absence of a conceptual framework, what the therapist perceives as an intuition may actually be a laggard discharge of the therapist's transient moods or a response to a client's defensive, growth-stunting desires. Working from an orientation provides essential structure; it spawns rather than inhibits intuition.

Third, the adoption of a therapeutic orientation also fosters intuition because therapists feel more secure when they have a guide, a map to work from. They are not aimlessly wandering around.

> It is quite possible that knowledge of theory permits the therapist to view the patient's behavior in terms of an integrated framework and thus permits him to feel more secure. This, in turn, may allow him to pay more attention to the patient's needs. (Fiedler, 1951, p. 444)

To sum up, if a therapeutic orientation is to promote intuition, it must be a living reflection of how therapists view people, and therapists must be flexible with their orientation. A therapeutic orientation that is a sterile intellectual exercise will impede intuition.

Structure to Enhance the Relationship

The humanistic therapists have been particularly outspoken about the need for therapists to work from an orientation. They assert that an orientation not only provides the necessary structure to therapy, but also aids the therapist in developing a therapeutic relationship. Following are three humanistic therapists who have emphasized the need for therapists to have an orientation to work from.

Humanistic therapist Carl Rogers was questioning the utility of the technical eclectic movement back in the 1950s. He attacked this movement as "a superficial eclecticism which does not increase objectivity, and which leads nowhere. Truth is not arrived at by concessions from differing schools of thought" (Rogers, 1951a, p. 8). Rogers believed that a therapeutic orientation was necessary to provide therapists with a structure that could be used in developing hypotheses for change. He referred to the haphazard blending of approaches as "confused eclecticism [that] has blocked scientific progress in the field" (Rogers, 1951a, p. 24). Recall that Rogers was writing in the 1950s, before the eclectic movement gained strong footing.

Yalom (1980), another humanistic therapist, argued that a therapeutic orientation is essential because it provides (a) a sense of security for the therapist; (b) an "intellectual bone" for the therapist and client to gnaw upon together; and (c) consistency in the therapist's interventions. Together, these three factors will enhance the therapeutic relationship, which, as Yalom stressed, is ultimately the major change agent of therapy.

Rogers and Yalom issued a clear call for therapists to adopt a therapeutic orientation as a basis for their work. However, the development of an orientation is not a simple process.

Bugental (1987), a third humanistic therapist, characterizes the adoption of a therapeutic orientation as the third stage in therapists' development. In the first stage, the beginning therapist needs to learn the fundamentals—the techniques and relationship variables of conducting sessions. (This is akin to learning the process variables of change.) In the second stage, therapists actively listen to their clients; the dialogues move from the chit-chat of neighbors to conversations with increased emotional content. During Bugental's third stage, the therapist comes to appreciate the living aspects of theory and the application of the various approaches to practice, and is able to develop a coherent therapeutic orientation.

Unfortunately, many therapists superficially learn the techniques of the first stage and proceed no further; they become technicians and, in so doing, stifle the growth of the therapeutic relationship. Developing a therapeutic orientation is a creative yet difficult process, and depends on the therapist's willingness to meet the challenge.

Summarizing, a therapeutic orientation provides structure for the therapist to work from. It provides the therapist with knowledge and correspondingly with confidence. Applied in a flexible manner, an orientation can liberate the therapist's intuition and ultimately strengthen the therapeutic relationship.

Risks of Working with an Orientation

An orientation is a tool for the therapist. As with any tool, it may be applied in a constructive or a destructive manner. Particularly when people first learn to use a new tool, they may do more harm than good. Unfortunately, some then discard the tool.

Therapists who apply their orientation in a dogmatic manner may stunt the therapeutic relationship, in several ways. First, therapists may develop tunnel vision: they then only see aspects of the client's situation that fit neatly into their paradigm. The full repertoire of human experiences becomes constricted; clients become things to be manipulated according to a plan.

Second, therapists may limit the resources available to them. Having learned the major theoretical tenets and the accompanying techniques, such therapists fail to expand their knowledge base as they grow in the profession and as new applicable research emerges.

Third, when therapists adhere dogmatically to an orientation, they may stop their professional growth prematurely, by always looking outside of themselves for the answers. There is no question that outside resources—textbooks, instructors, and supervisors—are of substantial aid to any therapist; however, ultimately it is only the therapist and the client, two people in a room, that can address the client's problems. Likewise, when therapists are fanatical about their orientation, they risk impeding their client's growth by sending the message that therapists have all of the answers.

Fourth, working from an orientation may shield the therapist from the emotional aspects of therapy; therapy may become an intellectual exercise.

Just as working from a therapeutic orientation may provide necessary structure, enhance the therapist's intuition, and ultimately foster the development of a therapeutic relationship, the misapplication of an orientation may lead to too much structure, result in the intellectualization of the sessions, and interfere with the development of a therapeutic relationship. A therapeutic orientation is a tool that can be used constructively or destructively.

You Are Your Style

When they enter the field, students already have a distinct personality theory and a therapeutic style. All people, not just graduate students or experienced therapists, have their own ideas about why people behave as they do, and have their own ideas on how to help people to change. Of course, the ideas of the layperson are not as systematic as a specific orientation and usually are not readily available to the person's awareness.

Therapists are drawn to orientations that reflect their own ideas and personality. In the words of Zastrow (1993), "Counselors soon become aware that their personality partially determines which therapy approaches they are more comfortable in applying" (p. 601). This is no eye-opening statement. Of course our personality directs us to the style of therapy that we feel most comfortable in applying.

Because of their life experiences, some students are inclined to be cognitive therapists, others to be humanistic therapists, and still others to be psychodynamic therapists. Why do some people so adamantly refuse to develop and enrich an orientation in the process of developing their own unique style of therapy?

In my experience, there are two major reasons why some therapists have a distaste for admitting their orientation to themselves: inadequate training and a refusal of the associated risks. In regard to inadequate training, some institutions teach personality theory in a format that is so abstract (or so structured) that students cannot relate the readings to their subject, to living human beings.

In my view, however, the major reason that some therapists do not work from an orientation is that they refuse to make a commitment and to take the risk of being wrong. It is so much easier, at least superficially, for therapists to claim that they do not want to pigeonhole their clients.

When therapists develop an orientation, they must be willing to take on a number of risks. A common risk is that they may be ostracized and stereotyped by peers and supervisors. A second major risk is that they may become increasingly aware of how difficult it is to foster change; it is so much easier to be a passive listener. A third risk is that they are going to discover how ignorant they are and how different and complex people truly are. Students who do not study for an exam adopt a similar rationale: if they do poorly on the exam, they argue, it is not because they didn't understand; the poor grade is because they didn't study—because they didn't try. Likewise, therapists who do not struggle with the development of an orientation cannot be wrong. They can tell themselves, "The client did not change because the client did not want to change, not because I misapplied the approach." If therapists do not have an approach, they cannot misapply an approach.

Summarizing, it is my belief that every therapist needs to have structure and yet to be flexible. An experienced therapist in my survey put it this way:

> I find it makes for a more consistent structure for my part of the therapy process if I have a basic, consistent manner of conceptualizing what is happening. Techniques used may be from other orientations, but I make an attempt to remain true to the basic structure in determining how to work on specific issues. It is my experience that this also works for clients.

Those eclectic therapists who do not adopt a basic therapeutic orientation or integrate approaches into a meaningful whole are refusing the challenge of commitment to themselves, commitment to their clients, and commitment to their profession. They risk stunting their growth as effective therapists. These atheoretical or technical eclectic therapists are more likely to become a technician or a passive listener rather than an active participant who is there to help people through the struggle of change.

THE STRUGGLE OF SELECTING AN ORIENTATION

Like the development of a unique personality, the development of a distinct therapeutic approach is a struggle and a never-ending process. In many cases, however, the struggle of selecting an orientation is given little attention in graduate school; it is as if instructors do not want to impede students in their search. At the other extreme, a few professors and supervisors dictate only one style of therapy, neglecting all the other orientations.

As we have seen, personal circumstances may prevent therapists from developing a therapeutic orientation. However, other factors complicate the process of selecting and developing an orientation: the vast number of styles of therapy, the stereotyping of the various styles, and the recent blending of approaches. In the following sections I review these factors.

There Are So Many Styles

The range of therapeutic approaches is overwhelming. Harper (1959) listed 36 differing styles of therapy. Since then, the number of styles has increased steadily: from more than 60 in the early 1960s to 130 (Parloff, 1976), to more than 250 (Corsini, 1981; Herink, 1980), and finally to more than 400 (Kazdin, 1986)! How are therapists supposed to wade through all of this information and find the orientation that best fits their personality and experiences?

In practice, selecting an orientation may be easier than these figures suggest. Courses in personality theory, counseling, and psychotherapy usually focus on three major modalities of therapy; in this book I refer to them as the cognitive, humanistic, and psychodynamic camps. This classification helps therapists to find their bearings in searching for the approach that best reflects their personality. However, once they move beyond the general introductory texts of these three major schools of therapy, they discover that the diversity of approaches within each orientation is daunting.

For example, Mahoney and Arnkoff (1978) divided the cognitive-behavioral therapies into three major categories: (a) cognitive restructuring; (b) coping-skills therapies; and (c) problem-solving therapies. However, the cognitive restructuring category, for example, can be further subdivided into at least five differing styles of therapy (for example, Beck, 1963; Ellis, 1990; Guidano & Liotti, 1983; Maultsby, 1984; Meichenbaum, 1977).

Likewise, Pine (1990) divided the psychodynamic camp into four different categories, focusing on drive (Freud, 1895/1958b), ego (Arlow & Brenner, 1964; Blanck & Blanck, 1974; Hartmann, 1958), object (Fairbairn, 1952; Kernberg, 1980; Klein, 1948), and self (Kohut, 1971). As with the cognitive camp, each of these four psychodynamic categories may be further subdivided in terms of the techniques applied. Does the psychodynamic therapist adhere to the techniques of classic psychoanalysis, psychoanalytic therapy, psychodynamic psychotherapy, or supportive therapy?

Finally, humanistic therapists can choose between the approaches of Bugental (1987), Frankl (1963), Fromm (1955), Maslow (1968), May (1969), Perls (1969), Rogers (1951a), or Yalom (1980), and others.

Thus, the selection of an orientation can be a struggle simply because of the vast number of approaches available. However, the struggle is made harder by the varying stereotypes about therapeutic approaches that students bring to graduate school.

The Stereotyping of Approaches

Therapists of different orientations emphasize different aspects of human behavior and different helping techniques. Within the profession, these differences of emphasis are sometimes reduced to crude stereotypes: psychodynamic therapists are too cerebral; humanistic therapists are too wishy-washy; cognitive therapists are too cold. What therapist wants to be referred to as cerebral, wishy-washy, or cold? This section offers a brief synopsis of the often unspoken stereotypes regarding the three major orientations.

A stereotype regarding psychodynamic therapists is that they want to be detectives and analyze people. According to Nichols and Paolino (1986), "Psychodynamic treatment has been stereotyped as cerebral" (p. 123). Psychodynamic therapists are sometimes seen as narcissistic judges who place an overemphasis on transference and interpretation. That image underlies the rebuke issued by the psychodynamic therapist Greenson (1971/1990b) to his psychoanalytic colleagues: "I believe that 'only interpreting' or 'only analyzing' is insufficient for most of our patients" (p. 96).

The stereotype of humanistic therapists is that they lack direction: they sit there and passively listen, parroting when required, and pride themselves on being able to sit out their clients during prolonged silences. Humanistic therapists give the client nothing except some warm fuzzies and a bill.

The cognitive camp has been stereotyped as being just too cognitive. Cognitive therapists are seen as unfeeling managers who are scared of developing a relationship. Gutsch (1990) noted the opinion that "the cognitive approach lacks personal sensitivity—that is, feelings of empathy and warmth between therapist and client" (p. 154).

Therapists need to break free of these stereotypes if they are going to find a working framework for themselves. I'm amazed that opponents of approaches can be so critical without having read the original authors or without having training or course work on the approaches. Therapists who go through the struggle of developing a working framework will probably encounter many erroneous stereotypes, even within themselves.

The Blending of Approaches

The recent blending of approaches can also complicate therapists' search for a working framework. The differences between the three major camps seem so pronounced and clear in the introductory textbooks. (This clarity, of course, helps foster stereotypes.) However, the differences between the camps are less pronounced in books written by the original authors of the approaches. In practice, it's becoming more difficult to differentiate the approaches.

Even the major proponents of the three major schools of therapy have noticed a recent blending of the approaches. For example, Raimy (1980), a cognitive therapist, observes that "even the Freudians often concentrate on cognitive modification in treatment" (p. 154). With the rise of short-term psychodynamic therapy, psychodynamic therapists are behaving less like distant surgeons and much more as directive and active participants. They are developing a heightened appreciation of the role of irrational thoughts and of recent events in the client's life. Indeed, the case studies of some short-term psychodynamic therapists cannot easily be distinguished from writings of the cognitive camp.

The blending of approaches has given rise to some distinctive new therapeutic styles. As just one example, consider Albert Ellis's comparison of rational emotive therapy (RET) and Carl Rogers's client-centered therapy:

> Unlike Carl Rogers and other existential therapists, who believe that unconditional positive regard can be given by the therapist's modeling it and accepting clients unconditionally, RET practitioners try to give this kind of acceptance to all clients but also teach them how to give it to themselves. In this way, RET is both humanistic-existential and didactic and active-directive. (Ellis, 1993, p. 200)

Ellis is not alone in blending a specific style of therapy with the humanistic tenets. In general, the trend in all three major camps is to be more humanistic, in the sense that the critical role of the therapeutic relationship is acknowledged. Safran (1993) calls this a movement toward a social-constructivist perspective: the emphasis is on the interaction between the therapist and the client rather than the search for interpretive insights or the confrontation of irrational thoughts.

The diversity of approaches within a single camp of therapy is enormous. The similarities between approaches in different camps are sometimes greater than the similarities between approaches within a single camp. For example, a recent study found that the implementation of Meichenbaum's cognitive style of therapy differed as much from Beck's cognitive approach as from Strupp's psychodynamic approach (Goldsamt, Goldfried, Hayes, & Kerr, 1992).

In some cases, it can be difficult to assign a specific approach to one of the three major camps. Does Frankl's logotherapy belong in the humanistic or the cognitive camp? Does Kohut's self-psychology belong in the humanistic or the psychodynamic camp? Does Erich Fromm's approach belong in the humanistic or the psychodynamic camp? This categorization of approaches is not just a nosological exercise. It has practical consequences for a therapist in search of an appropriate working framework.

As we have seen, the distinction between cognitive therapy and short-term psychodynamic therapy is becoming less pronounced. Some people have argued that the cognitive and psychodynamic approaches are different only in the labels that these therapists use for their techniques: the phenomena described by cognitive and psychodynamic therapists are actually very similar; they just give them different names. For example, Beck (1993), a cognitive therapist, points out that the cognitive approach includes

> many concepts derived initially from psychoanalysis (e.g. the emphasis on identifying the meanings of pathogenic events), and the conceptualization of separate modes of cognitive processing (the relative rational vs. the automatic nonrational), corresponding, in part, to Freudian notions of primary and secondary processing. (p. 197)

Wessler (1990), in his cognitive appraisal therapy, has taken the psychodynamic term "unconscious" and replaced it with "nonconscious algorithm" or "personal rules of learning." The emphasis of his approach is to discover these hidden personal rules of learning and to help the client to consciously adopt alternatives. "Where id was, there shall ego be" (Freud, 1933/1964, p. 80).

Mahoney, a cognitive therapist, has noted an increased appreciation of unconscious processes in cognitive therapy and sees a convergence of the cognitive approach with the psychodynamic approach.

> Whereas early cognitive therapies were relatively more introspective, individualistic, ahistorical, and inattentive to the emotional relationship between counselor and client, the opposite of each of

these is more characteristic of contemporary cognitive psycho-therapies. (Mahoney, 1993, p. 190)

Robins and Hayes (1993), leading cognitive therapists, have identified a number of psychodynamic concepts that are gaining increasing acceptance by the cognitive camp: defensive functioning; interpersonal relationships; the therapeutic relationship as a key change agent; emotional arousal; and the exploration of past phenomena to gain insight into present thoughts, feelings, and behaviors.

Note that these comments about the convergence of the cognitive and psychodynamic approaches are coming from leading figures within the cognitive style of therapy.

Richard Lazarus (1980) (not to be confused with Arnold Lazarus of multimodal fame) has commented, in a spirit of "friendly irony," that the adoption of psychodynamic concepts in cognitive therapy

> brings to mind a joke I was told as a child: "When is a door not a door?" The answer was: "When it is ajar." I cannot escape the feeling that, similarly, the answer to the question "When is it okay to be psychodynamic?" is: "When the word 'psychodynamic' is changed to 'cognitive.'" (p. 122)

To sum up, therapists who decide that working from an orientation is worth the associated risks will face a struggle. The selection of an orientation is complicated by the vast quantity of varying approaches to select from, the stereotyping of approaches, and the recent blending of approaches.

The development of a personal orientation is never complete. In their first years of practice, therapists tend to oscillate between the various camps, as they attempt to find an approach that matches their personal style. With the passing years, the struggle usually becomes easier, but it never ends.

Fundamental Process Variables

It can be difficult to differentiate flexibility and eclecticism. What a number of people in the field refer to as being eclectic, I refer to as being flexible. If therapists have chosen a specific therapeutic orientation—or have integrated two or more approaches into one coherent system—but then adopt techniques from varying schools, they are not eclectic; they are being flexible within their approach. Egan (1990) argues that an effective practice requires

> more than a random borrowing of ideas and techniques from here and there. Helpers need a conceptual framework that enables them

to borrow ideas, methods, and techniques systematically from all theories, schools, and approaches and integrate them into their own theory and practice of helping. (p. 13)

To incorporate techniques from other schools is a sign of flexibility.

Being flexible does not mean that all therapeutic styles are the same. Some proponents of common-factors eclecticism and some proponents of process variables of change insist that the blending of approaches is so pervasive that we no longer need to learn the various styles of therapy. However, even with the recent blending, it is too soon to discard the diversity of approaches that are available to us. In practice, the different styles are different.

The Implementation of Styles Is Different

I vividly recall that, at the beginning of my internship, my fellow students were trying to figure out the orientations of the various supervisors with whom we would be working. (Naturally, we only wanted that information so that we could learn the most from our supervisors; we had no intention whatsoever of using it to win a positive evaluation.) One intern, because of circumstances beyond his control, had returned a second year to complete his internship. He was already acquainted with the therapeutic styles of the supervisors. He told us that supervisor A boasted of his cognitive approach, while supervisor B boasted of his psychodynamic approach. However, the intern was quick to assure us that in practice there was no difference between these supervisors.

Everyone in the field has encountered this idea—that, behind the closed doors of their office, all therapists do the same thing. We might talk about differing processes in the classrooms and during supervision but, when it comes down to it, are the therapists of the three major orientations actually doing the same thing?

In the previous section, I discussed the recent blending of approaches; the idea that therapists in different camps simply call the same phenomena by different names; the increased emphasis on the therapeutic relationship outside of humanistic therapy; and the growing similarity between the psychodynamic therapy and cognitive therapy. If therapists of differing camps are actually doing the same thing, then why bother with the struggle of finding and developing an orientation?

In practice, do therapists of varying orientations actually differ behind closed doors? Yes.

Strupp (1958) found that client-centered therapists tend to summarize the client's feelings, whereas short-term psychodynamic therapists tend to be more inferential. In another study, judges were able to determine whether individuals had undergone psychodynamic or cognitive-behavioral drug counseling with over 90% accuracy (Woody, McLellan, Luborsky, & O'Brien, 1981)!

After reviewing the verbatim transcripts of 30 short-term psychodynamic sessions and 32 cognitive-behavioral sessions, Jones and Pulos (1993) concluded that, even though there were similarities between the implementation of the approaches, there were indeed differences. For example, the cognitive therapists tended to control negative affect by the use of intellectual and rational measures, whereas the psychodynamic therapists emphasized the expression of emotions, made more past-present linkages, and tended to use the therapist-client relationship significantly more frequently as a major change agent. Experience and research support the conclusion that the implementation of the three major orientations is different, despite the recent blending of approaches.

I have changed my style of therapy over the years. As my style changed, so did my behavior in therapy. Cognitive therapists as a group tend to be more directive; the humanistic therapists tend to do less talking and to be more reflective; the psychodynamic therapists tend to actively foster the expression of emotions and to make past-present linkages. Of course the implementation of the differing styles is different.

When therapists say that the theoretical underpinnings and the implementation of the three major camps are equivalent, they are examining the question at too high a level of abstraction. When therapists say that all the styles are the same, and so there is no need to take on the task of developing a therapeutic framework, they are wrong.

Process versus Specificity

How can the therapy approaches be so different in content and yet be equally effective? As an example, just consider the *process* of labeling a person's depression versus the *content* of the label. A humanistic therapist may label a client's depression as a means of avoiding ontological anxiety; the cognitive therapist may label the depression as the result of irrational thoughts; and the psychodynamic therapist may label the depression as a consequence of developmental traumas. This serves as an excellent example of one process variable of change that is common across approaches: the act of labeling is the process variable, the content of the label is the specific orientation. The specific labels may vary; however, the *process of labeling* a person's maladaptive behaviors would be the process variable.

The act of labeling itself may be therapeutic; given a name for the condition, the client may feel less confused. This has been called the principle of Rumpelstiltskin.

In the children's story "Rumpelstiltskin," the evil dwarf is vanquished when the princess is able to discover and to state his name.

In a similar way, naming a particular problem and specifying what it relates to may have a significant detoxifying effect for the patient. (Budman & Gurman, 1988, p. 84)

The idea is to find the right label, the label the client can believe in. "Underlying the principle of Rumpelstiltskin is an important assumption—that the therapist knows the right name to put on the disorder" (Torrey, 1986).

The principle of Rumpelstiltskin does not take anything away from specific interventions. I believe that, in time, with continued research and enhanced therapeutic records, we will find that specific techniques and interventions are more appropriate for specific classes of problems and clients. That day has not yet arrived, but work toward this goal continues.

As therapeutic approaches are blended, interest in process variables— the common factors across approaches—is increasing. Prior to the 1980s, process variables were regarded merely as placebo effects. Now, they are gaining increased respectability. Respect for process variables, however, does not mean that therapists need not develop their own unique style of therapy.

SUMMARY

A therapist seeking to develop a personal orientation faces a challenge. The task is complicated by the seemingly endless variety of approaches, the stereotyping of approaches, and the recent blending of approaches.

A few therapists opt to foreclose on this struggle by becoming technical eclectic therapists: their approach is atheoretical and they borrow techniques from the various approaches. In this chapter, a number of criticisms of this strategy have been presented. Even Frank (1973), a leading author on process variables who has been cited by eclectic therapists as supportive of eclecticism, contends that "the advance of both knowledge and practice is probably better served by members of different schools defending their own positions, while being tolerant of other schools, than by being uncritical [technical] eclectics" (p. 342).

To adhere to a therapeutic orientation is to emphasize some phenomena over others. Having adopted that emphasis, therapists exercise flexibility. To some degree, all effective therapists utilize elements of a humanistic approach (for example, empathy); a cognitive approach (for example, the client's cognitive construction of events); and a psychodynamic approach (for example, patterns not readily available to a client's awareness). Effective therapists emphasize some phenomena over others in order to have a framework to work from; however, this emphasis is not a dogmatic code. I usually say that therapists develop a theoretical *leaning*; they do not contract tunnel vision.

A working framework provides structure to therapists' work. It promotes consistency, and therapists are less likely to fall prey to their clients' resistance to change. The structure provides a sense of security for therapists and, if aptly applied, frees therapists to actively listen to their clients and to use their intuition. All of these positive features enhance the therapeutic relationship.

Recognition that certain process variables are common across approaches does not eliminate therapists' responsibility to develop a therapeutic orientation. However, an appreciation of process variables can remind therapists to be flexible in the application of their approach.

CHAPTER THREE
SUPERVISION

The gods are fallen and all safety gone. And there is one sure thing about the fall of gods: They do not fall a little; they crash and shatter or sink deeply into green muck. It is a tedious job to build them up again; they never quite shine . . . It is an aching kind of growing.

(STEINBECK, 1952/1988A, P. 25)

This passage by John Steinbeck aptly describes the client's search for autonomy. Clients frequently enter therapy enthusiastically looking for the god, the therapist, who will provide them with the wisdom of change. The culmination of this search for autonomy arrives when clients realize that therapists do not have all of the answers and that change is a personal, often painful, venture. Therapy is a journey in which clients learn to assume more responsibility for themselves.

All forms of therapy, whether cognitive, humanistic, or psychodynamic, work toward the ultimate goal of helping the client to become more autonomous. It is an aching kind of growing. The gods—counselors and psychotherapists—frequently fall in the process and never quite shine the same again. Clients' discovery that their therapist cannot live their lives for them is not the end of a search but a new beginning.

Many, if not most, beginning therapists go through a similar process in their search for a professional identity. Therapists are required to go from the relatively safe days of being instructed on what to do, from textbooks and lectures, to the challenge of taking their first client and beginning supervision. Supervision is a bold step in the therapist's journey toward the development of a professional identity.

Frequently, therapists entering supervision expect answers to make their confusion and anxiety go away. Some neophyte therapists expect the all-knowing supervisor to come riding into their lives with magical power.

> In this deep yearning for magical power, the resident [or intern, or practicum student] is bound to be disappointed. The disappointment will be extremely intense if the supervisor pretends to have such power or has not worked through such yearnings in his own psyche. The shock of discovery that even if he slavishly imitates the supervisor, his patients do not get well, is often very difficult for the resident to accept. (Chessick, 1971, p. 277)

Like therapists with their clients, supervisors can provide a setting in which neophyte therapists develop increased autonomous functioning. However, just as the ultimate change agent in therapy resides in the client, the ultimate change agent in supervision resides in the supervisee. The process of helping the supervisee become more autonomous is the foundation of supervision.

This process of working toward autonomous functioning is rarely smooth or painless. The gods must fall. This critical step is not learned from textbooks or lecture notes. It is a change in how the therapist approaches life.

> It is common that trainees idealize their supervisors as benevolent, omnipotent mentors. When, however, supervisors fail to give supervisees what they crave, the supervisors are seen as harsh and critical withdrawers. The feelings of admiration are replaced by anger, rage or devaluation. (Olsson, 1991, pp. 513–514)

Supervisees are frequently ill-prepared for the heightened ambivalence that can emerge from supervision.

The purpose of this chapter is to introduce the reader to many of the vicissitudes of supervision that can have a profound impact on the development of an autonomous professional identity. The chapter is divided into seven main sections.

Some therapists, particularly beginning therapists, do not realize that acceptance of their anxiety in supervision can be an important facet of their professional growth. The first section outlines how some of the supervisees' anxiety is related to their motivations for entering the field and their development—or lack of development—of a therapeutic orientation.

The second section offers four common styles of coping with anxiety during supervision, and the third section summarizes common developmental stages that supervisees pass through. The fourth section reviews an important debate: Is supervision didactic training or a form of personal therapy?

The fifth section summarizes the research on supervision that is applicable to this chapter, and the sixth section suggests ways that supervisees and supervisors can make constructive use of anxiety during supervision sessions.

The seventh, and final, section discusses process variables of therapy as related to supervision and serves as a transition to the remainder of the book.

ANXIETY OF THE SUPERVISEE

Anxiety is the threatening, unknown future—fear of doing something different, of changing. Supervision, being a change process, is usually anxiety-provoking. Typically, supervisees fear that their supervisors will discover they are incapable. Supervisees

> often feel that they are expected to demonstrate the expertise that they are there to learn. Anxiety is heightened not only by the unknown, but by the stakes trainees have in their future professional lives. The question: "Can I become a competent therapist?" looms large. (Berger & Buchholz, 1993, p. 86)

Much of the anxiety stems from such questions as: Am I competent? Will the supervisor discover that I am a charlatan? Worse yet, will I be told that I'm sitting in the wrong chair during the therapy hour?

In the survey, I asked graduate students and experienced therapists to recall the thoughts and feelings that accompanied their first experience in supervision. Anxiety is pervasive throughout their responses, as these comments by graduate students make clear:

- I remember that when I first began supervision I was afraid to admit my uncertainties to my supervisor. I guess I feared that she would tell me that I wasn't fit to be a therapist.
- I suppose, as is probably inevitable, that initially my thoughts and feelings were those of trepidation. Happily though, my fears were quickly allayed so I learned that my supervisors were there to help me, and that any criticisms were not character assaults but rather attempts to show me how to be a better therapist.
- Oh shit! I hope I didn't do anything wrong!
- I was *very* nervous. I was afraid I was going to say something totally wrong and the client would get worse. Once things got going, though, I relaxed and it got easier.

Experienced therapists reported similar experiences:

- I felt completely artificial and self-conscious, doubting my every word.
- I remember feeling very vulnerable. My supervisors expected us to bring up countertransference issues and if we didn't, they did! Being in therapy myself was critical or I would have really felt like I was lost in a huge blind spot. I also early on wanted supervisors to tell me what to do. That didn't work too well.
- I felt very intimidated and generally tried to keep a low profile.
- I was frightened of my supervisor and afraid of being rejected, humiliated, and finally told I "couldn't make it."

Many beginning and experienced therapists know the fear of being told, "You can't make it."

Numerous factors can heighten and maintain the supervisee's self-doubts: the supervisee's and supervisor's differing expectations of supervision (Berger & Buchholz, 1993; Rubinstein, 1992); the style of supervision (Bartlett, 1983); the supervisee's maturity level (Ronnestad & Skovholt, 1993); the means of recording the therapy sessions (Aveline, 1992); and the means of evaluating the supervisee (Borders & Fong, 1991; Greenberg, 1980; Marshall & Confer, 1980; Patterson, 1983; Robiner, 1982).

One factor that is rarely mentioned is that the various reasons for which people enter the helping professions have a direct impact on their experiences and anxiety in supervision.

Anxiety and Reasons for Entering the Helping Professions

In Chapter 1, I described three possible reasons why therapists enter the helping professions: the desire to help; personal motives (being a wounded healer and power issues); and the avoidance of aloneness. In the following three sections I outline how these motives may have an impact on supervision.

Supervision and the desire to help. Most therapists readily acknowledge that they entered the helping profession because they wanted to help people. As noted in Chapter 1, the majority of people who enter the profession would probably have been sought out by friends and family for guidance even if they did not choose the helping profession. Many people who choose counseling and psychotherapy as a career have developed an ability to be sympathetic to the emotional pain of other people.

The problem arises when these desires to help other people take the form of caretaking tendencies. Instead of actively helping people to change, caretaking therapists fail to take risks. (To be active does not mean to be directive.) They may have learned as children that, if they were emotionally supportive of their caretakers, the support would then be reciprocated.

> Ordinarily those who want to help others have somehow acquired a rather powerful need to nurture others. What has usually not been acquired as well is the way in which the need can be actualized in fruitful help to others. (Mueller & Kell, 1972, p. 64)

When therapists have learned to take a more passive approach, they are not effective. A goal of supervision is to help the therapist move from a passive, supportive stance to a more active focus on helping the client to change.

Note that many of the students and therapists in my survey mentioned that, when they began supervision, they were afraid of being discovered, of being exposed as charlatans. Barnat (1977) described similar experiences in supervision:

> Intense anxiety was due to the feeling that I was an empty-handed bumbler, hiding behind a popular image. I was a sham. The client was a sham—except that the client was on firmer ground than I. He was "really" a client but I wasn't "really" a therapist. I felt quite vulnerable because of a lurking fantasy that the client might ask me to justify my presence: I have a neurosis; what brings you here? (p. 309)

Is this fear just performance anxiety, or is it also linked to the reasons why people enter the helping professions?

In fact, therapists with passive caretaking tendencies are more likely to experience anxiety in supervision. Students taking undergraduate and graduate courses can easily conceal their fear of rocking the boat, their tendency to remain passive. However, with admission into supervision, they fear that the supervisor will discover that they have learned not to take risks, that they don't really want to help people to change, that they only want to nurture and to be liked.

I propose that, to a considerable degree, this feeling of being a sham or a charlatan is not a fear of not knowing the various techniques of doing therapy; rather, beginning therapists know at a gut level that they are going to be exposed as caretakers. The desire of the supervisee to nurture comes into conflict with pressure from the supervisor to help people to change. Usually, change wins out (Mueller & Kell, 1972).

How does this desire of the supervisee to remain in a passive nurturing role impact supervision? Frequently the passive supervisee will view the active supervisor as too cold and distant. The supervisor wants to know where the supervisee is going with goals and hypotheses; the supervisee wants to keep things vague.

> The becoming therapist just "likes" people and wants to help them. The determination to help is often accompanied by a remarkable lack of specificity or concreteness about ways to go about achieving this lofty social goal. (Mueller & Kell, 1972, p. 89)

Therapists who have a keen appreciation and acceptance that their caretaking, nurturing stance has pulled them into the helping profession are more likely to use their anxiety of supervision in a constructive manner. Supervisees who have caretaking tendencies and continuously deny such tendencies are likely to meet supervision with conflicting desires, much resistance, and little professional growth.

Supervision and personal motives.   As noted in Chapter 1, some therapists enter the field because they have been emotionally wounded.

The goal of training programs is not to keep out the wounded; the goal is to keep them and to produce effective therapists. Therapists who deny their personal wounds are more likely to overidentify with their clients and/or turn supervision into therapy for themselves. By exposing personal issues, they may entice their supervisor to not wound them further. While supervisees' emotional well-being is crucial to their professional development, supervision is not intended as therapy for the supervisee. When clients' needs are being neglected, supervisees should consider continuing their own personal therapy.

Many who enter the helping professions say that they want to understand why people behave as they do and to find out more about themselves. Again, this is an admirable goal. It is a strength to pursue a career that is founded on personal growth. However, life is rich with double-edged swords, in which strengths are also weaknesses.

As we saw in Chapter 1, this quest for knowledge can conceal the desire for power over others: "I know what makes you tick, and in my omnipotent wisdom I will convey this knowledge to you." Some therapists enter the field because they want to be in a position of power over others.

Some students who are unaware of their power motives learn techniques with an insatiable appetite. Once they move from the classroom to the practice of therapy, and realize that techniques alone are not enough, they throw up their arms in disgust and insist that there is no rhyme or reason to doing therapy: "Why not just be a technical eclectic?"

Others are disgusted when clients and supervisors do not hear their pearls of wisdom. Many therapists with hidden power motives become sullen when their clients fail to change. Such hidden power motives often become evident in a hostile (even if passive) conflict with a supervisor. The finger of blame is pointed outwards.

I believe that most therapists go through times in their education when they become disgruntled with the impotency of many techniques, become narcissistically wounded when others do not appreciate their pearls of wisdom, become sullen when clients do not readily change as expected, and become involved in power-play maneuvers with their supervisors. However, these experiences are apt to be more pronounced when therapists have hidden power motives for entering the helping professions. As a result, supervision is not only anxiety-provoking but also very frustrating.

Many supervisees all too readily place their supervisors on pedestals. It is only appropriate to remind supervisees that their supervisors are human and may also have power issues.

Many supervisors state that they originally wanted to do supervision because they wanted a break from doing therapy and they wanted to share their years of wisdom with their supervisees. Sound familiar? Being the supervisor is a powerful position; some supervisors are not aware of their own power motivations and how this can enter into supervision (Gorkin, 1987; Lower, 1972; Salvendy, 1993).

Many supervisors are not prepared for the vicissitudes of supervision. As a result, they want to keep everything at a nurturing level, or else they want to teach therapy at a didactic level (Olivieri-Larsson, 1993; Swift &

Wonderlich, 1993). Supervisors who have not worked through their own power issues—who have not recognized and accepted them—are more likely to fall into a spurious relationship with the supervisee, in which all participants may superficially be satisfied but no true change and professional growth occurs.

Supervision and aloneness.   Very few therapists voluntarily state that they entered the helping professions as a way to work with their aloneness issues. However, as outlined in Chapter 1, this is a powerful motive for many people.

Practicing therapy and being in supervision confronts the supervisee directly with aloneness issues: How responsible am I for another? To what degree is another person responsible for my life? What can I do to really help people to change? Is this whole thing of doing therapy one big sham? Am I a charlatan?

The need to nurture others and the need to control others can be seen as attempts to shirk aloneness issues. For example, supervisees' search for power over others

> is not only related to the individual personality of each [therapist] but is also stimulated by feelings of emptiness and diminished self-esteem . . . Sharaf and Levinson [1964] state that, "To fill the void, [the therapist] turns to his supervisor whom he imbues, at an unconscious level, with magical omnipotent powers." (Book, 1973, p. 490)

When therapists have not adequately recognized their aloneness issues, they are more likely to imagine that their supervisors have "magical omnipotent powers."

I cannot overemphasize that respect and liking for a supervisor are conducive to effective therapy. Therapists—and people in general—fare well when they have a mentor to go with them through the vicissitudes of learning and life. However, when therapists consistently deny their darker, less benevolent reasons for entering the profession, they risk giving their supervisor too much responsibility for their own professional development.

For both supervisees and clients, the acceptance of aloneness is a key step in the quest for autonomy. Kaiser (1965) was a pioneer of this viewpoint.

> He [Kaiser] maintained that the inability of individuals to tolerate feelings of alienation and isolation from others formed the basis of all psychopathology, regardless of symptoms. We can either learn how to commune with each other as separate autonomous individuals, or resort to what he called a fantasy of fusion in order to avoid intolerable levels of anxiety at those times when our individuality

gives us heightened awareness of our differentness or separateness from others. To face a decision which can only be made by ourselves or experience reality in a distinct way from others may threaten us with intolerable isolation. (Frantz, 1992, pp. 42–43)

Fear of this intolerable isolation or aloneness drives supervisees to look outside of themselves for the answers. Accepting their own responsibility means facing the dread of being alone in the world. Some therapists give their supervisors too much power out of their own dread of aloneness.

Therapists' personal issues may enhance or deter the client's growth. At some point, effective supervision requires therapists to examine how their personal thoughts, feelings, and behaviors have an impact on the development of the therapeutic relationship and ultimately on helping the client to change.

To sum up, therapists' denial of their motivations for entering the helping professions can explain much of their intense anxiety about supervision. Many therapists who need to passively nurture others will feel vulnerable, exposed, and anxious when confronted with a supervisor whose focus is change. Unresolved power issues can provoke a frustrating and never-ending search for the one answer that will make people change. Supervisees' avoidance of their aloneness can create a supervisory relationship of pretended superficial mutual respect.

When therapists are more accepting of their own motivations, they are more likely to enter supervision with realistic expectations and manageable anxiety. This does not happen overnight; growth in these areas is a part of learning the art of therapy and a significant part of supervision.

Anxiety and Working with an Orientation

Much of beginning supervisees' anxiety is related to their lack of a consistent therapeutic orientation from which to work. As noted in Chapter 2, most experienced therapists have adopted, developed, and/or integrated an approach to working with their clients. This therapeutic orientation does not appear overnight but is the culmination of a prolonged struggle.

Theory is crucial in the preparation of counselors and its value is particularly evident in the work of the supervisor. That is, the supervisor works from a theory that simultaneously serves as a guide to supervisory goals and behaviors and as a resource from which supervisees can draw for their own developing theories. (Goodyear & Bradley, 1983, p. 59)

Goodyear and Bradley (1983) found agreement between the authors of five leading therapeutic styles (behavioral, client-centered, rational emotive therapy, cognitive-developmental, and psychoanalytic) that students and therapists should eventually learn one style of therapy.

When therapists entering supervision are not aware of their own style of working with people, they are more likely to feel threatened by supervision and anxious. Some therapists are fortunate in that they have discovered their therapeutic orientation by the time they meet their first client. Having a leaning, some structure, serves to make the supervision process less daunting. Therapists who have no idea what their preferences are when they begin supervision can lessen the anxiety inherent in supervision by openly discussing with their supervisor their struggle to adopt an orientation.

Since a goal of effective supervision is for the supervisee to become more autonomous, supervisees have the right to ask what their supervisor's orientation is—not only the supervisor's style of therapy but also his or her style of supervision. Supervisors' styles of supervision are partially determined by their therapeutic styles. Unfortunately, as Yogev (1982) noted, "Many supervisors do not have a clear idea of their style of supervision and have difficulties when they have such discussions with supervisees" (p. 239). Obviously, this can increase supervisees' anxiety.

Summarizing, therapists are more apt to be anxious unless they have an orientation to guide them. If a therapist has not begun to develop a therapeutic style, then supervision is a good place to seek help in doing so. Even when therapists do have a preference for a style of therapy, supervision can help. The practice of therapy is far removed from the world of textbooks. Supervision can provide a bridge between theory and practice.

FOUR STYLES OF CONTENDING WITH ANXIETY

Supervision is usually anxiety-provoking. There are numerous sources for this anxiety: just starting out in a new venture; not knowing what is expected with a particular supervisor; the risk of evaluation and how it may impact on graduation or job ratings; and performance anxiety, with the knowledge that each and every movement is captured on tape. Anxiety is to be expected in these circumstances.

As we have seen in the previous sections, supervisees who are unaware of their motivations for entering the profession ("I only want to help people") and who lack a therapeutic orientation feel a heightened sense of anxiety. Unable to use their anxiety in a productive manner, they may retreat to old, maladaptive patterns. They are then particularly likely to foster dependent relationships with their clients and supervisors.

Supervisees deal with their anxiety in many ways (Yerushalmi, 1992). For insights into this process, we may look to research on identity.

Marcia (1966, 1967) suggested four basic styles in the attainment of a sense of identity—diffusion, foreclosure, moratorium, and achievement. These basic styles differ in regard to the degree of crisis and commitment in the individual's striving for an identity. Overall, Marcia's basic assumption is that the individual has gone through some degree of crisis, some degree of struggle, in achieving an identity.

The following sections examine Marcia's four basic styles as they relate to supervisees' progress toward a coherent sense of professional identity. These styles can have a positive or negative impact on their supervision, on their growth as a therapist, and on their personal growth.

The Diffuse Supervisee

According to Marcia (1966, 1967), identity-diffuse individuals do not go through a crisis period, and they have not made a commitment to their values, ideologies, or occupation. Likewise, the supervisee may opt to take on a diffuse role and refuse to go through the crisis, or struggle, of attaining a coherent sense of professional identity.

Some identity-diffuse supervisees enter their supervision with little knowledge of what motivated them to enter the field; some believe that all the talk and writings on developing a therapeutic style are senseless, and prefer to just wing it. These are the supervisees who get frustrated that their supervisor doesn't understand how they want to help people. Some diffuse supervisees tend to be foxy in their approach to supervision.

> The foxy student avoids going counter to the suggestions of the supervisor. He does not present difficult cases and does not antagonize or confront the supervisor. Such students make relatively small effort to assert their individuality. (Bush, 1969, p. 162)

Diffuse supervisees make little progress. Because they tend not to rock the boat, either with their clients or with their supervisors, they may continue this mimicry, while not knowing what they are doing and silently believing that this whole thing of counseling and psychotherapy is just a ruse. If therapy is a sham, then they must be a fraud.

When the supervisor is not aware of any active struggling on the part of the supervisee, that may be an indication of trouble. "A good supervisory alliance is not necessarily a harmonious one. As with the therapeutic alliance, resistance is expected and its absence is suspect" (Jackel, 1982, p. 9).

Of course, any therapist at the beginning of a career can expect some sense of diffusion. I am not suggesting that supervisees should immediately disclose all their anxieties to their supervisors. Like any relationship, supervision evolves. In such a personal encounter, it is often healthy to begin cautiously. Supervisees get into trouble, however, when they avoid risks throughout supervision and their career.

The Foreclosed Supervisee

Marcia's second style of identity is the identity-foreclosed individual. In supervision, these foreclosed supervisees, like the diffuse supervisee, refuse to go through a time of crisis. Unlike the diffuse individual, the foreclosed supervisee does have a therapeutic orientation, but it does not come from a personal struggle; rather, it is borrowed from someone else—for example, a charismatic writer or supervisor.

Sometimes supervisees foreclose on a style of therapy simply because it is described in an unpretentious, practical manner. For example, I have worked with therapists who, after reading a book on rational emotive therapy (RET), claimed to be die-hard RETs. Many of these foreclosed RET therapists are actually passive therapists, who confront their clients as the need arises with the declaration that the clients are only hurting themselves by thinking irrationally. These pseudo-RET therapists lack a full understanding of the richness and flexibility of the approach.

Likewise, I have worked with supervisees who have adopted an arduous and enigmatic approach, such as object relations. In their practice, they tend to be passive therapists who have learned to talk the talk but have refused to learn the fundamentals and the actual application of the approach.

Finally, Abramowitz and Abramowitz (1976) suggested that some therapists foreclose on the humanistic style of therapy to avoid their own conflicts about the expression of aggression. Again, these therapists insist, "I only want to help people." Abramowitz and Abramowitz believe that therapists foreclose on a humanistic style of therapy because of unresolved family-authority struggles. These people are difficult to work with in supervision. "The message to the supervisor is essentially this: 'The more you insist on forcing me to shed my cocoon of dependency and try on new skills that require mature decision-making, the more complicated your life is going to be'" (Abramowitz & Abramowitz, 1976, p. 588).

The bottom line is that foreclosed supervisees, like diffuse supervisees, do not want to go through a struggle; they do not want to feel the anxiety. Unlike diffuse supervisees, however, foreclosed supervisees are not open to the supervisor's suggestions and can be very difficult to work with.

When therapists do struggle to develop a style of therapy, they are likely to foreclose briefly on different styles, to see how they fit. Such brief foreclosure does not interfere with the therapist's growth. However, premature foreclosure on an approach, out of a refusal to face anxiety and conflict, stunts the therapist's development. As with the diffuse supervisee, therapy becomes a silent sham, even though these therapists profess to know what they are doing.

The Supervisee in Moratorium

Marcia's third type of identity formation is the individual who goes through a time of moratorium. In this case, the supervisee accepts the anxiety of becoming and being an effective counselor or psychotherapist. These supervisees accept that anxiety is an important aspect of growth.

> The ability to tolerate and even welcome anxiety in order to interpret accurately the information it contains is an important skill for individuals and systems that are in the business of guiding the evolution of others. It also demands that they learn to function in its paradoxical vortex. It demands that they learn to be challenged by situations that feel threatening and embrace with curiosity experiences of anxiety, uncertainty, surprise, emptiness, disorientation, lostness, dread or discouragement. (Frantz, 1992, p. 37)

For the supervisor, this is the ideal individual to work with, whether the supervisee is about to meet the first client or has a vast amount of experience. Practicing therapy is linked with the unknown; the unknown is linked with anxiety. The therapist who has developed a personal style is more likely to accept the anxiety as a part of the process of therapy and feels less overwhelmed.

Therapists in a state of moratorium approach their anxiety instead of denying it.

> The anxiety approacher is aware of his anxiety, able to label it and admit it, and to begin to search inside self and outside for its cause. Putting a therapist and supervisor together who share this tendency can lead to an open-consultative relationship as they search and wonder. The student learns that the supervisor is not omnipotent—all-knowing—but rather willing to explore and learn and face the anxiety. (Moldawsky, 1980, p. 128)

Note how much of an achievement it is just to get to the state of moratorium. First, the gods—the books, the professors, and even the supervisors—must fall.

The diffuse and foreclosed supervisees eventually also attempt to disparage the gods. The key is that the supervisee in a state of moratorium *accepts* the anxiety.

> I told a supervisor that I had doubts about being in my profession, that I was overwhelmed by all the pain I saw around me, and that I was concerned that I was not helping anybody. I remember being very emotional and feeling extremely discouraged. My supervisor's smile surprised me. "I would be very concerned about you as a helper," he said, "if you never asked yourself these kinds of ques-

tions and were not willing to confront yourself with these feelings."
In retrospect, I think he was telling me that he was encouraged for
me because I was acknowledging my struggles and was not pretending to be the all-competent counselor who was without fears.
(Corey & Corey, 1989, p. 11)

Therapists go through stages in order to reach a state of moratorium.
On entering supervision, many students have the idea that the supervisor
will tell them what they need to do. With time, supervisees discover that
they are mainly responsible for their actions as therapists.

> At the beginning, the student is inexperienced, uncertain, and
> seeking of approval. He is likely to have difficulty in openly and
> directly expressing his reactions to the supervisor as a person and
> as a teacher. Consequently, over-compliance [identity diffusion]
> and passive-aggressive negativism [identity foreclosure] are more
> typical of the student in the early phases. (Bush, 1969, p. 161)

All too frequently, the personality-theory courses and the therapeutic-
approach courses are taught in a manner that leaves students even more
confused.

A state of diffusion appears to be an integral part of students' progress
toward a state of moratorium. Gradually, students begin to become aware of
how important they are as participants in the therapeutic change process.
When therapists begin to stop looking outside of themselves for the
answers and begin to question their motives for being in the field and their
style of therapy, they are more apt to enter moratorium. The supervisee

> finds himself in a position somewhat similar to that of an adoles-
> cent. He is tired of being told what to do. He feels that he has a
> mind of his own, and sufficient knowledge and experience to be
> able to make his own decisions and exercise his own judgement.
> When this occurs, there is likely to be more open conflict between
> the candidate and his supervisors. (Bush, 1969, p. 162)

It is no easy road for the supervisee to reach a state of moratorium. There
are many risks involved. Supervisees must admit all their anxieties—not
only those brought on by their supervisor but also those that focus on
themselves. "The gods are fallen and all safety gone. And there is one sure
thing about the fall of gods: They do not fall a little; they crash and shatter
or sink deeply into green muck" (Steinbeck, 1952/1988a, p. 25).

Identity Achievement of the Supervisee

Marcia's (1966) fourth, and final, phase of identity formation is identity
achievement. In this final phase, therapists have gone through morato-

rium; they have recognized and accepted their anxieties about supervision. Therapists who approach this stage have a more realistic acceptance of their capacities and limitations. They have committed to an underlying ideology, a style of therapy that is an extension of their personal beliefs.

Supervisees with a sense of identity achievement have a realistic concept of their goals in therapy and the possibility of their attainment. They are likely to be less susceptible to authoritarianism and less vulnerable to anxiety. A sense of identity achievement does not come solely from experience; it derives from the struggle of becoming and being a therapist.

Learning and practicing therapy is a growth process from the beginning. As with any growth process, this means change and anxiety. In the end, people who accept the challenge are more likely to help their clients change and to enjoy their endeavors.

DEVELOPMENTAL THEORIES OF SUPERVISION

The goal of developmental supervision is to provide a supervisory environment that facilitates the optimal growth of the supervisee. Specifically, developmental supervision enhances the supervisee's growth in the areas of therapeutic techniques, theory, self-awareness, and the ability to create a therapeutic environment conducive to change; it culminates in a heightened sense of professional identity. A key to developmental supervision is an appreciation that supervisees' motivations and needs change over time.

> The trainee is viewed not just as a counselor lacking specific skills but as an individual who is embarking on a course of development that will culminate in the emergence of a counselor identity. This end point constitutes the integration of skills, theory, and a more complete awareness of oneself and others. This process is placed in a developmental framework that takes into account the different motivations, needs, and potential resistances of counselors at different levels or stages of development. The premise is that there are qualitative differences in addition to, and not accounted for by, mere quantitative differences in skill level and the knowledge of theories. (Stoltenberg, 1981, p. 59)

Supervision is not solely a growth in the knowledge of techniques and theory, but also a qualitative growth of the therapist's sense of professional identity.

Some Developmental Theories of Supervision

Although the theoretical and empirical fields of supervision are relatively new, there are already numerous theories regarding the content and the vicissitudes of the stages that a supervisee and supervisor encounter (Ard, 1973; Blocher, 1983; Ekstein & Wallerstein, 1972; Fleming, 1953; Fried-lander, Dye, Costello, & Kobos, 1984; Gaoni & Neumann, 1974; Grater, 1985; Hess, 1986; Hogan, 1964; Littrell, Lee-Borden, & Lorenz, 1979; Loganbill, Hardy, & Delworth, 1983; Stoltenberg, 1981; Thorbeck, 1992; Watkins, 1992; Yogev, 1982). This idea that supervisees go through a number of stages during supervision is becoming more accepted. Super-visors also go through various developmental stages (Watkins, 1993).

As with therapeutic orientations, most developmental theories of su-pervision emphasize the movement from dependency to increased auton-omy.

For example, Stoltenberg (1981) stated that, as therapists move into a second developmental stage of supervision, supervisees are primarily confronted with dependency/autonomy conflicts.

> The individual is attempting to find himself or herself in the practice of counseling while still having rather strong dependency needs. Self-awareness is increasing as the trainee struggles with insight into his or her own motivations and behaviors. There is a constant oscillation between being over confident in newly learned counseling skills and being overwhelmed by the increasing respon-sibility. (p. 62)

While some developmental supervision theorists place a greater emphasis on dependency/autonomy issues than others, all agree on this movement toward increased autonomy.

Drawing from the adolescent literature, Watkins (1992) identified four types of dependency/autonomy issues that supervisees frequently confront: functional, attitudinal, emotional, and conflictual. It is beyond the scope of this book to review these four issues. What Watkins points out, however, is that the supervisee may be functioning in an autonomous manner in one area, but functioning at a dependent level in another area.

In the following section I review one of the developmental theories in more detail.

Loganbill, Hardy, and Delworth's Developmental Stages

Of the numerous developmental theories on supervision, Loganbill, Hardy, and Delworth's (1983) is one of the most detailed and comprehensive to date. I briefly review here the stages they outlined because their work is frequently cited in the literature; their stages closely parallel Marcia's (1966) stages of identity formation; and their theory is consistent with a focus on the underlying process of change.

As with many cogent theories, this one did not emerge fully formed. The developmental stages first proposed by Hogan (1964) were further expanded by Stoltenberg (1981) before being adopted and further clarified by Loganbill, Hardy, and Delworth (1983).

Stages as times of crisis. Developmental theories of supervision suggest that the supervisee may pass through times of crisis—stages of increased stress and anxiety. "Although some of the stages and processes may be very painful, it is developmentally important for the supervisee to experience them fully" (Loganbill et al., 1983, p. 4). If supervisees embrace the anxiety, they are more likely to use their supervision in a productive manner.

Like Marcia's (1966) developmental stages of identity formation, Loganbill, Hardy, and Delworth's (1983) stages were based on the writings of Erikson (1968). The idea is that stages of development, whether toward personal identity or professional identity, may be emotionally painful and may serve as an opportunity for "turning." That is, individuals may feel more vulnerable during a stage of crisis but, on emerging from the disarray, they have an enhanced opportunity for positive change.

> No significant human relationship progresses without conflict, without stress, without regression or stalemates. These conflicts within the relationship, rather than being seen as barriers, can themselves serve as a focus for promoting growth in the supervisee. (Loganbill et al., 1983, p. 29)

There may seem to be an unnecessary emphasis in this book on the conflicts and crises of supervision at the expense of its supportive aspects. Of course, supervision needs to be a place in which supervisees feel safe and emotionally supported. However, receiving support does not usually impede supervisees' professional growth. Rather, how supervisees contend with their anxiety in supervision can potentially be destructive to their growth.

Both supervisees and their supervisors must accept that anxiety is a natural aspect of the process.

> Such thinking allows us not only to use, but to welcome, conflict and confusion as an opportunity for growth, and to make significant interventions with faith in the resiliency, adaptability, and infinite capacities of our supervisees. (Loganbill et al., 1983, p. 15)

Therapists who accept the inherent anxiety of practicing therapy and being in supervision are more likely to be able to use their anxiety in a productive manner.

Loganbill et al. (1983) summarize three major stages that supervisees typically encounter: (1) stagnation, (2) confusion, and (3) integration. These three stages are similar to Marcia's (1966) stages of diffusion, moratorium, and achievement, respectively. They then go on to discuss eight issues that supervisees confront.

Eight recycling issues of the supervisee. A feature that makes the Loganbill et al. (1983) article particularly enticing is that they list and describe eight recycling issues that supervisees encounter. Seven of these issues are expanded from Chickering's (1969) developmental issues of the adolescent/young adult. They added the eighth issue, professional ethics.

Loganbill et al. (1983) did not assign any particular chronological order to these issues. However, Sansbury (1982) suggested the following sequence: (1) competence, (2) purpose and direction, (3) theoretical/conceptual identity, (4) emotional/awareness/confrontation, (5) respect for individual differences, (6) autonomy, (7) professional ethics, and (8) personal motivation. The reader is recommended to read the original article for a more detailed account of these eight issues.

A good way to differentiate the three stages—stagnation, confusion, and integration—from the eight issues is to consider that the issues describe the content areas that supervisees encounter, while the stages characterize the manner in which supervisees work with the issues. For example, a therapist may be in the stage of diffusion on the issue of respect for individual differences, in the stage of confusion on the issue of theoretical identity, and in the stage of integration on the issue of emotional awareness. In other words, therapists do not one day function in an autonomous manner with respect to all the various issues in the practice of therapy; they tend to be more advanced in some areas than in others.

Two of the eight issues are particularly relevant to this book: theoretical identity and personal motivation. Theoretical identity denotes the process in which the therapist develops a therapeutic orientation. During the first stage, stagnation, therapists frequently do not even know that it is necessary to have some form of structure in their work. Or, during the stage of stagnation, they may have foreclosed and adopted a blind adherence to an orientation. During the second stage, confusion, therapists try on a number of theoretical approaches to find the best fit, until they have developed and/or accepted their own style, which constitutes the third stage, integration.

What does the therapist get out of therapy? Why do people enter the helping professions? These are questions of personal motivation. Noting a number of reasons that therapists enter the field—for example, intimacy (social motives, loneliness), power, financial motives, personal growth, intellectual issues, and altruism—Loganbill et al. (1983) recommend that supervisees go through the three stages in recognizing and accepting their own motivations for becoming therapists.

For example, they suggest that, during the first stage, stagnation, it is common for supervisees to completely deny any power issues that may have brought them to the field. "The power motivation—even in its constructive form—is one that is often repressed or denied" (Loganbill et al., 1983, p. 26). In the second stage, confusion, supervisees recognize some of their power motivations and may be fearful that other dark forces may be lurking in the shadows. By the time supervisees reach the third level of supervision, achievement, they recognize and accept their personal motivations for doing therapy. "Stage three supervisees are aware of and accepting of both potentially destructive and constructive motivation factors with themselves, and able to control or utilize these in the best interests of the client" (Loganbill et al., 1983, p. 26).

Becoming aware of personal motivations for entering the helping professions is an integral facet of a therapist's training, and supervision is an appropriate arena in which the supervisee can discuss and become aware of the reasons that they entered the profession.

Recycling through an issue: A personal account. Loganbill et al. (1983) noted that therapists usually *recycle* through the eight issues. Rarely do therapists simply go through a few weeks of struggle during supervision and then come to a final level of integration on developmental issues. They continue to address them throughout their careers. Each pass, each time of struggle through an issue, is an opportunity to move toward a higher level of integration.

Personally, I have recycled through the issue of my motivations for entering and staying in this profession numerous times throughout my career. The following is a condensed account of just a few examples. Of course, some of the examples I cite are common developmental issues for many therapists. One reason that these issues are so common among therapists, I believe, is that therapists have similar motivations for seeking out this profession.

Initially, when I decided to go to graduate school, I was only aware of my desire to help people. In my relationships I tended to be a peacemaker and was not assertive. My job was to be nice, to only give positive emotional strokes with all of my clients, and to minimize any frustrations or times of emotional hurting.

When I began doing therapy in my training, I was passive and would sit for hours doing my parroting technique, with periodic reframing for the sake of variety. During my practicums and internship, I was frustrated with my supervisors because they seemed so cold and uncaring about my clients. Looking back, I think that I chose to portray my supervisors as detached in part because I wanted to be more passive and to not take risks; whereas my supervisors wanted me to be more active in the therapeutic process. Definitely, my supervisors have helped me to question my passive stance.

I have recycled through this desire to be a passive helper at intervals throughout my career. During these phases, I would get overly emotionally attached with my clients; many times, I would get my boundaries confused and interfere with my clients' growth.

And then there have been the clients who have had the gall to get angry with me for not helping them to change. During supervision, I dreaded my supervisors and peers seeing the videotapes. Oh yes, the books say the client's anger can be healthy, but to experience this was a whole different story, especially when I did not want to rock the boat; I wanted people to just get better.

I could not understand why my clients did not realize that I was helping them. When my clients were angry with me, I immediately believed that I had done something wrong. I would scurry around trying to find something (usually a more directive technique) to make them like me, to make them see that I wanted to help them. It has been an ongoing struggle for me to move from being a passive therapist ("I only want to help people") to being more active (not necessarily directive) in facilitating clients' process of change.

During graduate school, and particularly during my supervision, I began to become aware of my personal power issues around becoming a therapist. When I initially decided to enter the profession, I was one of those therapists who thought that, by taking classes and reading books, I would learn what makes people the way they are. I would then convey this information to my clients; they would have an "aha" experience, thank me, and go riding off into the sunset. Nowhere in this vision was anything about emotions, uncertainties, and struggles. In part, I entered this field in search of the power of knowledge over others.

Partially as a result of my clean, simplistic desire for the power of knowledge, I was not prepared for the emotional aspects of therapy. In time, I began to accept the necessity for people to be able to express their emotional pain in therapy. However, it did not come easy.

And then, there have been the clients whose symptoms got worse instead of better! Since I was supposed to be all-knowing, because I was supposed to harbor the knowledge to help them, the escalation of their symptoms threatened my powerful position in therapy: one of my reasons for entering this field was being tested. I have recycled numerous times through a situation in which the client's presenting symptoms have become more pronounced and I have then inappropriately become more directive and started dispensing homework assignments.

Among the most frustrating aspects of counseling and psychotherapy are the clients who prematurely stop their therapy, with no warning; they simply do not show up again. Wishing to keep my clients coming in for therapy, I have gone through periods when I tended to be overly directive with all of my clients, and then I have gone through periods when I have been overly nondirective with all of my clients. In different phases, I have developed a leaning toward each of the three major styles of therapy. All of these maneuvers, I believe, were directly linked to my aloneness issues. How responsible can I be for another person? How responsible can another person be for me?

There are a number of reasons for my changes in behavior. However, one factor is that my motivation for staying in the profession has changed since I first entered graduate school, and my behaviors in therapy reflect this change in my motivation.

During some phases of my career, I mainly wanted to passively nurture people; during other phases, I mainly wanted to learn the deep, dark secrets of people and to be in a powerful position. Throughout, I wanted to help people in order to learn to deal with my own aloneness issues. I now stay in the field because of an integration of these three reasons.

My motivation to help remains. However, I now have a deeper respect for people and their emotions; an acceptance of some of the weaknesses and strengths that I brought to the field; an attentive ear listening for the times when I meet my personal needs at the expense of my clients' growth; and a stronger acceptance of my limitations. I believe that, throughout these years of struggling, I have allowed myself to become emotionally closer with my clients, not so much out of sympathy, but in order to be with another human being during a struggle and to use my support and knowledge to help them with their growth.

It was during supervision that I began to question more intently my motivations for being in the profession. I have gone through similar recycling through the other issues outlined by Loganbill et al. With each pass, with each struggle, therapists have an opportunity to move up to a higher level in their development of a professional identity. Supervision brings to the foreground many of the issues that therapists will recycle throughout their careers.

PURPOSE OF SUPERVISION

Even if the supervisee and supervisor agree that therapists go through developmental stages throughout their training and career, the way in which they define supervision—its goals and the means to achieve these goals—has an impact on the developmental progress of the supervisee (Bascue & Yalof, 1991; Bordin, 1983). What is the purpose of supervision? Aveline (1992) suggests, "The purpose of training is to facilitate the exercise of natural abilities and acquired skills to best effect" (p. 347). In supervision, therapists learn to use the abilities and skills that they already have.

A problem with this definition is that many therapists who enter the field have acquired the skill of nurturing people in a passive manner, without the goal of constructive change, and they expect supervision to facilitate their passive nurturing style.

The nurturant motive is to reduce anxiety and conflict in others. Thus, the successful nurturer is usually well able to make his clients feel better temporarily. He is also quite capable of forming warm, close relationships with his clients. The relationships which are formed are not necessarily therapeutically changing, however. (Mueller & Kell, 1972, p. 95)

To enhance the supervisee's acquired skills of passive listening is not an admirable goal for supervision.

Many clients have developed maladaptive ways of coping with stress and anxiety in their lives. They usually suffer from emotional pain; however, they are invested in maintaining the maladaptive behaviors. To relinquish these behaviors is to face the anxiety of change, and it is much easier, or safer, to continue with the pain. One purpose of supervision is to help the therapist recognize the contradictory message of clients who want help to rid themselves of the emotional pain yet do not want help to change their maladaptive behaviors.

How does the supervisor help the therapist with this dilemma? Does the supervisor teach the supervisee techniques? Or does the supervisor work on a more experiential level with the supervisee, so that supervision is analogous to personal therapy for the supervisee?

Is supervision didactic training or personal therapy? Like so much of the counseling and psychotherapy literature, this question dates back to the days when psychoanalysis was the major form of therapy. The question was whether or not the supervisor should be the supervisee's analyst (Thorbeck, 1992). The proponents of Carl Rogers's humanistic approach have likewise noted this dichotomy in approaching supervision.

Supervision or training programs in the fields of counseling and psychotherapy have been formulated traditionally in terms of a didactic-intellectual approach which emphasizes the shaping of therapist behavior or the experiential-accepting approach which focuses upon therapist growth and development. (Truax, Carkhuff, & Douds, 1964, p. 240)

Whether the relationship between supervisee and supervisor is to be more didactic or more experiential is a key question in defining supervision. In the next two sections, I review some of the literature on these two approaches.

Supervision as Didactic Training

Particularly when they are starting out, many therapists want information on how to conceptualize counseling and psychotherapy. Many, if not most, neophyte therapists need a more didactic approach to supervision initially, and they fail to ask for this because they don't want to appear obsessive-compulsive, green, or stupid. Graduate school is sometimes unnecessarily competitive. Students who request a more didactic approach risk being ostracized and unjustly accused of running from personal issues.

An experience of mine in graduate school accents the risk of requesting a more didactic approach. Although the following scenario occurred in a classroom, it is equally applicable to supervision. It was the first class of an existential psychotherapy course. The seats were arranged in a circle and the instructor informed us that the emphasis of the class throughout the semester would be on a group exercise of experiential therapy.

On that memorable first day of class, we went around the room saying what we hoped to gain from the course. I was second to last in the circle. My fellow students were either more advanced in their professional growth than I was, or else had more quickly understood what the instructor wanted: they delivered appropriate buzz words and declared that they were there to "find themselves." Then came my turn. I said it and, once said, it was too late to take it back: "I want structure." Silence, dead silence, fell on the room. I got closer to my aloneness issues on that day.

It seemed as if everyone in the circle cast their nonjudgmental eyes upon me. I thought I was being honest. The instructor-therapist asked me to explain. I couldn't stop: I wanted to learn something from this course besides how I felt; I wanted some straightforward education; I wanted some structure; I wanted help with conceptualizing the change process.

The instructor let me off the hook. He seemed at least to respect the risk that I had taken. Looking back, I know that I was not talking just about doing therapy; I was speaking about my personal life. However, it's too easy to say that I was green, I was avoiding some personal issues, and I felt threatened by the group format. The fact is, I *was* green; I was just beginning to learn this approach, and I needed the structure not only on a personal level but also as an apprentice learning a craft.

Supervision is an appropriate place for didactic training, whether the style of therapy is cognitive, humanistic, or psychodynamic. Cohen and DeBetz (1977) take a strong stance in advocating a didactic approach to supervision:

> The supervisor's role is primarily that of a teacher, not a therapist, and the trainee comes to the supervisor to learn, not to be treated. It seems unfair to cast the trainee in a patient role while tacitly denying the freedom and rights that patients enjoy. (p. 59)

The supervisee does not enjoy the same rights of confidentiality that the client does. The supervisee is evaluated. If therapists want personal therapy, they should seek personal therapy.

Supervision as Personal Therapy

Opposing the didactic style of supervision, two therapists in the survey that I conducted stated that supervision is, and should be, similar to personal therapy.

A graduate student wrote:

Recognize that, in a sense, you are your supervisor's client. The goal of supervision, as in therapy, is to promote change and growth in you, both as a therapist and a person.

An experienced therapist agreed:

The first time in supervision, I thought the supervisor would be like a teacher and tell or show me what to do. I didn't see it as a parallel to the therapy relationship, in which my development as a therapist was the focus of the endeavor.

The adherents of an experiential style of supervision contend that, since doing counseling and psychotherapy is an emotional experience, the best format in the training of therapists is experiential. Recognizing that a didactic style of supervision is necessary to a degree, Altucher (1967) adds:

The emotional part is the most crucial. The important learning occurs in situations where one's feelings are engaged. A further assumption is that for emotional learning to be meaningful, some critical changes must occur within the counselor. These changes almost always produce discomforts. (p. 165)

Learning to be an effective therapist produces discomforts; it is anxiety-provoking.

Supervision is the place for the student and the experienced therapist to discuss their personal issues, anxieties, thoughts, and feelings about the practice of therapy. Those supervisees willing to take the risks are more likely to gain from their supervision.

Trainees who are able to explore themselves would be ones showing greatest positive change in their therapist behaviors. Trainees' self-exploration, is then, here posited as one of the critical elements in supervision, whether that supervision is aimed at producing analytic, client-centered or eclectic therapists. (Truax, Carkhuff, & Douds, 1964, p. 243)

Note that this comment was made in 1964, prior to the recent expansion of the cognitive approach.

Psychotherapy is a craft. However, it differs from most crafts in that its outcome depends on the therapist's personality and ability to develop a supportive and collaborative relationship with another person.

Psychotherapy . . . makes a greater demand upon those who would teach and learn it than most other occupations. To be a plumber or carpenter, one works under and with an experienced plumber or carpenter . . . Pipes and faucets could be successfully repaired by greedy, angry, hostile, insensitive, arrogant or uncaring persons.

> People cannot. Similarly, how to replace a washer can be learned
> from a manual. And how to position one's chair behind a couch or
> how to submit a bill to a patient can be learned from a textbook.
> But how to have those attitudes which must allow the therapeutic
> work to proceed, cannot. (Greben, 1979, p. 504)

Therapists bring to their practice many of their own personal issues, which
can hinder the therapeutic change of their clients. Where should those
issues be addressed? Should we subject all applicants to graduate school
to psychological tests or intensive soul-searching interviews, in an attempt
to ensure that they have no maladaptive patterns? If we took such a drastic
approach, as noted in Chapter 1, we would at best be left with only a
handful of therapists.

To describe the purpose of supervision as either didactic training or
personal therapy creates a problem. As the reader is probably aware, any
either/or question, whether posed in a book or by a client, is a setup. There
is always a gray area between the two choices. The real question is where
the emphasis lies between the two extremes. This will depend on ever-
changing variables, including the experience level of the supervisee and
the supervisor; the type of clients the supervisee is working with; and the
institution where supervision is done.

> Anyone who has taken part in supervision—either as a supervisor
> or as a supervisee—can recognize its uniqueness as an educational
> experience, which cannot be limited to the intellectual dimension.
> The emotional content inherent in the supervisory process makes
> it rather similar to the therapeutic situation. The dilemma as to
> how, and to what degree, one has to cope with the emotional aspect
> of supervision bothers supervisors as well as supervisees and
> evokes a great deal of tension. (Rubinstein, 1992, p. 97)

The question is not whether supervision is didactic training or therapy; the
question is to what degree and how.

How supervision is conducted poses another problem. Is supervision
the appropriate arena for the supervisee to undergo therapy? No. However,
rational-emotive therapists Wessler and Ellis (1983) offer a useful qualifi-
cation:

> The supervision sessions themselves are occasionally used for
> therapy purposes, as when the supervisee indicates that a personal
> problem interferes with working with the client. When this is so,
> and when therapists' beliefs and feelings interfere with their doing
> an effective job with clients (what some other approaches term
> "counter-transference"), the supervisor and the other supervisees
> in the small supervision group sometimes explore these beliefs and
> feelings. (p. 46)

Thus, when a therapist's personal issues interfere with working with a client, a more experiential approach may be taken. This is a key distinction.

Supervision is not the place for personal therapy. Supervisees' issues are brought to the supervisor's attention only as they relate to doing therapy.

> The supervisor needs continually to ascertain that supervisory activities are primarily aimed at professional and not personal development. The intertwining of these objectives necessitates differentiating focus and emphasis, which may be an aim in itself. The supervisor may assist the graduate student toward increased self-awareness as this relates to professional functioning. (Ronnestad & Skovholt, 1993, p. 401)

As we have seen, an issue that frequently emerges in supervision is supervisees' need to passively nurture their clients. Supervision is the appropriate arena to discuss this need, so that therapists can take a more active role in the change process; didactic teaching can only do so much.

Is supervision more effective if a less-threatening didactic approach is adopted or if a more anxiety-provoking experiential approach is pursued? According to the developmental theories of supervision, it would seem to depend on supervisees' level of experience. Beginning therapists tend to seek a more structured didactic approach, whereas more experienced therapists need a more experiential approach. However, supervision is always a blend of the two.

This seems to make sense, but does the empirical literature support this? Or, as with so many things that we take for granted, does a systematic evaluation of this question lead to a different conclusion?

RESEARCH ON THE DEVELOPMENTAL STAGES OF SUPERVISION

Some studies have suggested that a didactic approach to supervision is more effective (Payne & Gralinski, 1969; Payne, Winter, & Bell, 1972); others have found that the didactic and the experiential approaches are equally effective (Austin & Altekruse, 1972; Silverman, 1972). One reason for the discrepancy in the results is that different raters use different criteria. In one study, for example, supervisees rated supervision as superior when it was more didactic, whereas supervisors rated it as superior when it was more experiential (Worthington & Roehlke, 1979).

Research has indicated that beginning therapists are more likely than experienced therapists to depend on their supervisors to provide the answers on how to do therapy (Reising & Daniels, 1983); beginning therapists expect supervision to be more didactic and want to learn the techniques of therapy (Delaney & Moore, 1966; Stoltenberg & Delword, 1987; Worthington & Roehlke, 1979); and beginning therapists prefer an authoritative supervisor who provides instruction (Fisher, 1989). Research also suggests that, when supervisors adopt a more didactic approach with beginning therapists, supervision is more effective (Cross & Brown, 1983).

While developmental theories and the empirical literature support the idea that supervisees and supervisors go through stages, even the earliest stages of supervision include an experiential component.

> The supervision process should probably represent some balance between the two aspects, depending upon the needs and the learning styles of the supervisees and the style of the supervisor. In really successful supervision the two seem to mesh and interact. (Rice, 1980, p. 145)

Even though neophyte therapists frequently seek a structured didactic format, there is still an experiential component in their supervision. The majority of the time may be devoted to the teaching of techniques and ways to conceptualize clients' presenting problems, but effective supervision requires supervisees to explore their own issues relating to the practice of therapy. As we have seen, therapists' motivations and issues have a direct impact on their effectiveness in helping people to change.

Even with an experienced therapist, a more didactic approach may be appropriate at times. It is an ever-changing balance.

> Bridging these polar [didactic and experiential] positions is a middle path with which, depending upon the special needs of the supervisee, the supervisor will integrate the didactic and self-awareness approaches so that both are attended to according to the needs of the supervisee at his or her particular stage of clinical development. (Taub-Bynum, Hersh, Poey, & Spring, 1991, p. 11)

Supervision is a mirror of therapy in this respect. The supervisor and supervisee must attend to the process as it unfolds.

Many beginning therapists enter their supervision wanting a more didactic approach. It is completely appropriate for them to request structure in their supervision.

CONSTRUCTIVE USE OF ANXIETY IN SUPERVISION

By recognizing and accepting that supervision is an anxiety-provoking venture, supervisees take a major step toward the constructive use of that anxiety. Denying the anxiety, although much easier to do, will impede their professional growth.

Learning the art of psychotherapy can be an anxiety-provoking endeavor. These anxieties are engendered by the loss of the medical model [the fall of the gods], with attendant feelings of anger, doubt and alienation . . . It is necessary for the [therapist] to deal with and, hopefully, work through these stresses so that he may learn and practise psychotherapy in a non-constricted, non-distorted manner. (Book, 1973, p. 492)

Supervisees must learn to view their anxiety in a positive manner, as healthy and growth-fostering.

Graduate student stress may be lessened through the positive values placed on self-awareness and affective and emotional expression (i.e., students are told that these demands are difficult and are encouraged to express their fears). Despite this, supervisors should be aware that many students have learned that it pays to conceal their self-doubts. Also, students in the helping professions are generally interpersonally skillful and are often able to conceal their anxiety. (Ronnestad & Skovholt, 1993, p. 398)

Supervisees who actively struggle to develop their own idiosyncratic style of practicing therapy are more likely to use their anxiety in a constructive manner.

Supervisees can also talk directly with their supervisors about their anxieties. For some supervisees, though, just the act of talking about their anxiety regarding supervision and therapy makes them even more anxious. All too often, it is left to the supervisor to discuss the anxieties of supervision.

Some students need to be re-educated to the fact that supervision has an interpersonal-learning aspect in addition to the didactic-cognitive learning and skill mastery aspects. These students are very surprised and sometimes reluctant to disclose personal issues, since their expectation was that only clients' material is discussed in supervision. (Yogev, 1982, p. 238)

Supervisees who take the risk of openly discussing their anxieties with their supervisors are likely to be met with a much-needed acceptance of their experiences. For supervisees, taking an active role in their supervision is a major step toward becoming more autonomous.

The supervisee and supervisor need to openly discuss the format of supervision and agree on a contract (Bartlett, 1983; Berger & Buchholz, 1993; Frantz, 1992; Greenberg, 1980). Is supervision going to be more didactic, more experiential, or a more even balance between the two? Unfortunately, some supervisors do not make a contract nor discuss what is expected in supervision. "It is our experience that supervisors differ highly on the degree to which they emphasize establishing a supervision contract or the degree of specificity if a contract is established" (Ronnestad & Skovholt, 1993, p. 402). When the supervisor fails to discuss the format of supervision, it is left to the supervisees to discuss what they want and need. In such vague situations, it is no wonder that supervisees are anxious.

An area of supervision that *is* frequently discussed is the medium for transcribing material for supervision—that is, whether supervisees' presentation of cases is based on mental recall, the client's chart, audiotapes, videotapes, or live supervision. Numerous articles and research data support the conclusion that supervisees are more likely to become effective therapists if taped or live supervision is the medium, rather than the supervisee's recall (Aveline, 1992; Bartlett, 1983; Kivlighan, Angelone, & Swafford, 1991; Wessler & Ellis, 1983). Supervisees can also ask to observe their supervisors providing therapy, and this can have a positive impact on the learning process (Rubinstein, 1992; Salvendy, 1993).

Unfortunately, an area sometimes not discussed at the beginning of supervision is the evaluation process and the criteria used. Supervisees have the right to know the criteria on which they are being evaluated (Bartlett, 1983; Borders & Fong, 1991; Cohen, 1980; Newman, 1981; Salvendy, 1993). If, in the beginning sessions of supervision, the supervisor does not discuss with the supervisee the means for measuring progress or the formal evaluation procedures, then it is left to the supervisee to ask. "The supervisor has criteria, whether he or she admits it or not, and the student has a right to know what they are" (Patterson, 1983, p. 23).

To summarize, supervisees are more likely to use their anxiety in a constructive manner when they take responsibility for their own education. Having accepted that anxiety is a crucial aspect of supervision and that they must develop a personal therapeutic orientation, supervisees must also recognize that they are basically responsible for their progress in supervision. Ultimately, it is their responsibility to initiate discussion of the parameters of supervision: the balance between didactic and experiential content, the medium in which cases will be presented, and the means of evaluation.

PROCESS VARIABLES AND SUPERVISION

Process variables are the key elements common to all styles of change—to all theoretical orientations; they are not tied to any particular therapeutic style. The thesis of this book is that process variables account for the majority of change that occurs in counseling and psychotherapy.

The literature on process variables is also applicable to supervision. Loganbill, Hardy, and Delworth's (1983) developmental stage theory is a nonspecific process-variable approach to supervision that is appropriate to the three major camps of therapy: "The present model is based upon the assumption that a central core exists which characterizes supervision regardless of the particular theoretical orientation of the individual supervisor" (Loganbill et al., 1983, p. 21). Counselors and therapists are becoming increasingly aware of the process variables of change.

My contention is that therapists need to have a basic knowledge of the process variables of change. That knowledge assists them in integrating elements of various therapeutic orientations into their own personal style.

> Theory courses, which are usually taught as a prerequisite to practicum training, may best be delayed until initial instruction in nonspecific skills [process variables] has been accomplished [and] attention at the later stages of training and in postdoctoral training seminars would be focused more on the integration of diverse theoretical models and less on isolated skill development. (Guest & Beutler, 1988, p. 657)

In practice, the work of developing a personal style of therapy probably continues in parallel with the acceptance of the process variables of change. The process variables describe the process of therapy itself; the therapeutic style describes the therapist's degree of emphasis on each process variable and provides the content of the process variables.

Supervision is an arena in which therapists can learn the fundamental process variables of change. Patterson (1983), a proponent of client-centered therapy, has noted that, when a supervisee and supervisor have differing therapeutic styles, an emphasis on the role of the process variables of change allows them to work together effectively. Even when the participants agree on a style of therapy, failure to address the process variables during supervision poses the risk that the supervisee will simply become a skilled technician.

It should be emphasized that effective implementation of the process variables of change requires that the supervisees recognize their motivations for entering the field and actively develop their own style of therapy.

SUMMARY

During my doctoral graduate training, I had a two-semester course on becoming and being a supervisor. In the course, we had first-year practicum therapists as supervisees. I vividly recall thinking that I would have liked to have read those articles and books on supervision when I was a first-year practicum student. As a supervisee beginning therapy, I would have liked to have known that being anxious was all right, was expected, and was even a positive sign of my professional growth. It would have given me permission to take more risks with my supervisors.

The theme running throughout this book is that people must assume responsibility for their own lives.

> The student therapist, in his or her relationship to a supervisor, is very often contending with the issue of dependency and attempting to find some resolution for it. Insofar as the student is helped to be dependent, while necessary, but encouraged to grow towards a state of more independent thought and action based on solid theory and skills, supervision will be achieving one of its major aims and the supervisee will experience supervision as satisfying and rewarding. (Cohen, 1980, p. 82)

Therapy, like any change, means taking risks. If therapists refuse to take risks, their work with clients will suffer.

Supervisees are ultimately responsible for what they learn from supervision.

> It has been said that perhaps the most important outcome of supervision is for the trainee to be able to listen to him or herself, and that the supervisor's presence is ultimately not as important as it might initially seem (Rioch, 1980). The responsibility for gaining competence as a clinician rests, finally, on the shoulders of the trainee. (Berger & Buchholz, 1993, p. 91)

And it does.

Whether you are working as a carpenter, learning to play tennis, or entering a personal relationship, you are sure to make mistakes. The problem is not to avoid all pitfalls. Mistakes and anxiety can be both major deterrents and opportunities for growth; it depends on the manner in which supervisees deal with them. Elvin Semrad, a renowned training analyst in the Boston community, offered these sage words to his students:

> Every time you fall on your face and fail, if you learn something from it, you progress: if you don't, you go down the drain. You're all young and maybe you have most of your failures still in the future. None of us likes to look at the failures in our lives. (cited in Rako & Mazer, 1983, p. 79)

As we have seen, how therapists deal with anxiety has a critical influence on their professional growth. Another key component of therapists' development is an understanding of process variables, which form the major subject of this book, and to which we now turn.

PART TWO
RESEARCH AND PROCESS VARIABLES

Research in the areas of counseling and psychotherapy has become relevant for the practicing therapist. The contemporary therapist needs to stay abreast of the empirical literature; the results of research studies are having an impact on the management of health care. Part Two is divided into three chapters.

Chapter 4 is a review of the outcome and comparative research literature. That is, the findings of the empirical literature are reviewed in regards to answering two questions: Is therapy effective? Which of the three major styles of therapy is most effective? As the art and science of therapy continue to evolve, it is inevitable that the results of the research findings on these two questions will also change over time.

In Chapter 5, the concept of process variables is introduced. Four process variables—fundamental variables of change that are common to the three major styles of therapy—are identified on the basis of a review of the theoretical literature.

In Chapter 6, the empirical literature is reviewed, to answer the question: Does research support the existence of these four process variables?

CHAPTER FOUR

OUTCOME AND COMPARATIVE STUDIES

Disease, you say? Infection? Down almost to non-existence? But tell me, are not neurotic disturbances on the increase? And are they curable or does the cure spread them?

(STEINBECK, 1954/1987, P. 169)

This chapter reviews classic and current outcome and comparative studies of psychotherapy research. Outcome studies attempt to answer the question: Are counseling and psychotherapy effective? Comparative studies, on the other hand, attempt to answer the question: Which style of therapy is most effective? This review of the outcome and comparative studies is not exhaustive, and the ardent reader is referred to Bergin and Garfield (1994) for a more comprehensive summary of the clinical research.

IS THERAPY EFFECTIVE?

At one time, therapists had the luxury of needing only devotion and faith to testify regarding the efficacy of counseling and psychotherapy. However, the honeymoon is over; times have changed. The public is psychologically more sophisticated; a wider array of different styles of therapy is now available; policymakers are demanding accountability; and third-party payers want results.

The counselor, psychiatrist, psychologist, and social worker of the 1990s need to stay abreast of clinical research. The archaic assertion of therapists that "research has nothing to offer the clinician" is no longer tenable, and research has indeed shifted to "studies that are more relevant to clinicians" (Piper, 1988, p. 1055).

With the increasing demands of society and the increasing availability of clinically relevant research, practicing therapists cannot afford to neglect the growing body of research on therapy. Therapy is both an art and a science. If sagaciously applied, the science component of therapy can be a valuable tool for the therapist.

Negative Critiques of Therapy

The potency of therapy has long been questioned. Fuerst commented on the questionable legitimacy of therapy in 1938: "Unfortunately there exists a great deal of confusion and contradiction about what really can be accomplished by psychotherapy" (Fuerst, 1938, p. 260). Doubts about therapy continued to surface. Mirroring Fuerst's comment, Colby (1964) found that the conclusions of empirical studies on the effectiveness of therapy were in a condition of "disorder, confusion, and impasse" (cited from Atthowe, 1973, p. 34).

Negative critiques of therapy have been made by individuals outside of the field (Gross, 1978) and even by practicing therapists (Tennov, 1975; Zilbergeld, 1983). In *Psychotherapy: The Hazardous Cure*, Tennov (1975) strongly questioned the utility of psychotherapy.

> If it is in fact damaging or ineffective, or if he [the therapist], individually, personally, and unlike what he believes to be the case with his colleagues, is ineffective, then his life has been a failure. Expressions of doubt have grown more pervasive over the last two decades, since scientific evidence of ineffectiveness has begun to accrue and therapists have been urged to subject their techniques to criticism based on considerations other than whether or not they followed the proscriptions of traditional practice. (p. 106)

Tennov was a practicing behavioral consultant when she wrote this critical essay.

Has the scientific evidence truly shown the ineffectiveness of therapy? In 1972, the executive officer of the American Psychological Association conceded that "our credibility is in doubt" (Little, 1972, p. 2). The next year, a psychologist made the following charge:

> Since World War II there has been a growing concern about mental health and a greater acceptance of psychotherapy as a means of treating "mental illness." . . . There is no agreed-upon, objective evidence based on experimental studies that use appropriate measures and control groups which indicate that any school or method of psychotherapy based on psychodynamic principles, theories, or concepts helps people to overcome disordered, inappropriate, or deviant behavior that is presumed to have a psychological basis any better than any other school or method or any more than their own life experiences . . . Testimonials are not evidence—whether they are offered on behalf of psychotherapy, prayer, or voodoo. (Hurvitz, 1973, p. 232)

Should psychotherapy be ranked with prayer and voodoo?

The practice of counselors and psychotherapists is frequently compared with that of ministers, pastors, and rabbis. All operate on the principles of self-disclosure and confidentiality and define themselves as helpers. In *Witchdoctors and Psychiatrists*, Torrey (1986), a practicing psychiatrist, presented a convincing argument, from a social perspective, that the similarities between a Manhattan psychiatrist and a bush shaman are greater than the differences.

Does the effectiveness of psychotherapy exist only in the mind of the therapist? Is the animosity of the authors quoted here, some of whom are trained and experienced therapists, a reflection of their personal biases and their own poor results in the delivery of psychotherapy services? Is there any empirical research to support their thesis? Yes.

Negative Outcome Studies

In this chapter, I use the term *negative outcome studies* to refer to research that has not supported the value of psychotherapy.

Counseling and psychotherapy services in this country underwent considerable expansion after World War II. "The war and its aftermath, with the large number of veterans in need of psychiatric and psychological care, were largely responsible for the tremendous changes and expansion that were to characterize the postwar period" (Garfield, 1992, p. 10). Veterans Administration hospitals were overwhelmed, and psychiatrists' time was taxed. To meet this increased demand, psychologists began to undergo training as therapists (Garfield, 1992). Prior to World War II, psychologists had confined themselves largely to research and psychological testing. As psychologists moved into the field of therapy, they brought with them their research-oriented attitude, and the result was a substantial increase in the number of studies designed to assess the efficacy of counseling and psychotherapy. In 1952, Eysenck declared war, with his review of outcome studies, "The Effects of Psychotherapy: An Evaluation."

Eysenck's review of the literature.   Eysenck (1952) reviewed the results of 24 outcome studies and compared the success rates of these studies with a nontreatment control group. He summarized his findings.

> Patients treated by means of psychoanalysis improve to the extent of 44 per cent; patients treated eclectically improve to the extent of 64 per cent; patients treated only custodially or by general practitioners improve to the extent of 72 per cent. There thus appears to be an inverse correlation between recovery and psychotherapy; the more psychotherapy, the smaller the recovery rate. (p. 322)

Needless to say, the results of Eysenck's review rocked the foundations of therapy. People with neurotic symptoms had an overall better success rate if they received no therapy! This conclusion was not based on one study; it was based on a review of 24 outcome studies.

Eysenck appeared to be thorough in his review: he excluded studies that were poorly planned, lacked follow-up, and/or failed to indicate the type of treatment. Those included were considered to be the best studies of the day. Regarding the degree of experimental rigor in the design of the outcome studies, Miles, Barrabee, and Finesinger (1951) commented:

> When the various studies are compared in terms of thoroughness, careful planning, strictness of criteria and objectivity, there is often an inverse correlation between these factors and the percentage of successful results reported. (p. 88)

In other words, studies that were well designed were less likely to support the effectiveness of psychotherapy!

Likewise, Foulds (1958) showed that poorly designed studies over-represented the efficacy of psychotherapy: Foulds found that in the poorly designed studies the estimate of success was 83%, whereas in the well-designed studies the estimate of success was only 25%. It is no wonder that practitioners and others have questioned the effectiveness of counseling and psychotherapy.

The tentative conclusion is that we have been training people in a field that is ineffective. Based on his 1952 article, Eysenck came to a similar conclusion:

> But even the much more modest conclusions that the figures fail to show any favorable effects of psychotherapy should give pause to those who would wish to give an important part in the training of clinical psychologists to a skill the existence and effectiveness of which is still unsupported by any scientifically acceptable evidence. (p. 323)

Eysenck's forbidding words were warnings not only to psychologists but also to others in the fields of counseling and psychotherapy. Why would anyone want to offer services whose effectiveness is not supported by research?

Eysenck's 1952 study is still frequently cited in textbooks and by opponents of psychotherapy. However, critics of psychotherapy also base their conclusions on current research, to which I now turn.

Paraprofessionals versus professionals. Opponents of therapy habitually quote studies that compare the success rates of paraprofessionals with those of professional therapists. If training in the techniques of therapy is necessary for a person to be an effective therapist, then it would be expected that people with little or no training would not be as effective as experienced trained therapists. However, research has indicated that paraprofessionals are frequently just as effective as experienced therapists, and sometimes more effective.

Medical students with no therapy training or experience had an impressive success rate in counseling psychiatric outpatients (Heine, 1962, Uhlenhuth & Duncan, 1968). Homemakers who went through an intensive training program similar to a graduate program have been shown to do effective therapy (Rioch, 1963).

A powerful study conducted by Carkhuff and Truax (1965) is still cited in the literature as evidence that paraprofessionals can do the work of professional therapists. Five trained, lay hospital personnel met with hospitalized patients in groups for a total of 24 sessions. Only one of the five paraprofessionals had a college education. The training program consisted of 100 hours, much less than a formal graduate program. The emphasis in the training program was on the process variables of therapy, rather than training in a specific style of therapy.

Carkhuff and Truax (1965) concluded that the ward behavior of the patients treated by the paraprofessionals improved significantly in comparison to a control group who received no group therapy. The authors emphasized that the results could not be attributed to the paraprofessionals' high status, because the ward personnel of the hospital openly criticized the lay therapists. The ward personnel feared that the group therapy conducted by the nonprofessionals would upset the clients and be harmful. It is also interesting to note that on a measure of empathic understanding, often considered to be a critical variable of effective therapists, the lay therapists performed at higher levels than postinternship graduate students.

Although the Carkhuff and Truax (1965) study is dated and is limited to hospitalized patients, it was a well-designed study for its time and has continued to be cited as evidence questioning the need for intensive training. A weakness of the Carkhuff and Truax (1965) study, however, is that ward behavior, the dependent variable, was assessed on the basis of subjective pre- and posttreatment ratings by the ward nurses and ward attendants.

This methodological shortcoming was corrected in a similar study conducted by Poser (1966). This study was also done in a hospital setting; the lay therapists were undergraduate students with no training or experience in therapy. In Poser's study, however, the results of objective psychological tests were used as the criterion measure of change. The patients in group therapy with the paraprofessionals showed significantly more improvement than a control group with no group treatment. More importantly, "the lay therapists achieved slightly better results than psychiatrists and psychiatric social workers doing group therapy with similar patients" (p. 283). The results of these studies (Carkhuff & Truax, 1965; Poser, 1966) question the need for intensive formal training in counseling and psychotherapy, at least in the case of group therapy with hospitalized patients.

Not all of the studies comparing paraprofessionals and professionals have been limited to an inpatient population. Gomes-Schwartz (1978) compared the therapeutic effectiveness of experienced psychotherapists and academic professors. The professional therapists consisted of four psychiatrists, with a mean of 23.5 years of experience, and four doctoral-level psychologists, with a mean of 15 years of experience.

The therapists definitely had the years of experience to qualify as professionals. The paraprofessional college professors were affiliated with the departments of mathematics, English, history, and philosophy. The dependent variable consisted of three global measures—including the Minnesota Multiphasic Personality Inventory (MMPI)—and three individualized measures of outcome (patient, therapist, and clinical-observer ratings). Gomes-Schwartz (1978) concluded that "untrained professor/therapists generally [effected] as much improvement as experienced psychologists and psychiatrists" (p. 1032). The reader may want to refer to the original article for a more detailed description of this well-designed study, which has definitely brought into question the appropriateness of traditional training programs.

Empirical research comparing nonprofessional and professional therapists expanded as funding increased. Durlak (1979) reviewed 42 studies that contrasted the effectiveness of nonprofessionals and experienced therapists. The results were not overly welcomed by the counseling and clinical community.

> Overall, outcome results in comparative studies have favored paraprofessionals . . . In only one study were professionals significantly more effective than all paraprofessionals with whom they were compared. In terms of measurable outcome, there were no significant differences among helpers in 28 investigations, but paraprofessionals were significantly more effective than professionals in 12 studies. (pp. 84–85)

In only one of the 42 studies were the professionals more effective than the paraprofessionals! In 12 of the studies the paraprofessionals were more effective than the professionals! Durlak's conclusion that paraprofessionals are more effective than professionals has fostered further reviews.

Nietzel and Fisher (1981) countered Durlak's review by reexamining 39 of Durlak's original studies and four recent studies. They state that Durlak's review was confounded by inadequate internal validity, inconsistent and inappropriate definitions of paraprofessional and professional, and the problem inherent in accepting the null hypothesis. They concluded:

> When the quality of the experimental evidence is carefully considered, the most accurate conclusion is that the question of the comparative effectiveness of professionals and paraprofessionals treating bona fide clinical problems has not been adequately addressed . . . Poor data may be worse than no data at all, because poor data can mislead. (Nietzel & Fisher, 1981, p. 564)

Even in the objective field of empirical research, such differences between studies and interpretations of findings are common. Researchers often derive divergent results and contradictory conclusions from the *same* data.

For example, Hattie, Sharpley, and Rogers (1984) reaffirmed Durlak's original conclusion by examining Nietzel and Fisher's data via an objective statistical measure (meta-analysis). On the basis of Nietzel and Fisher's critique, Hattie et al. limited their review to 39 studies.

> Our conclusion is supportive of but not as strong as Durlak's (i.e., that paraprofessionals achieve clinical outcomes equal to or significantly better than those obtained by professionals) . . . There appears to be evidence demonstrating that paraprofessionals must be considered as effective additions to the helping services, and in many cases are more effective than professional counselors. (p. 540)

These results may be disturbing to therapists in training, who have invested much time and money in their education. Why seek formal training in a craft if nonprofessionals are just as effective as professionals?

Other challenges to the efficacy of therapy.   "Don't bother doing therapy; clients get better anyway." I've heard that advice myself. Many people believe that therapy appears to help because of a "regression to the mean" (Thompson, 1983, p. 23)—because, over time, people get better anyway.

Some people even believe that therapy makes people's symptoms worse. There is empirical research to support this conviction. Reviews of the literature (Bergin & Lambert, 1978; Lambert & DeJulio, 1978; Lambert, Shapiro, & Bergin, 1986) have concluded that approximately 10% of treated clients do become worse, as compared to 5% of untreated clients. Sometimes, therapy may have a detrimental effect.

Evaluation of Negative Outcome Studies

Many authors and researchers seem to believe that the effectiveness of psychotherapy is merely anecdotal. They proclaim that evidence on the efficacy of counseling and psychotherapy must be based on hearsay, because there is little empirical research to support it. People who make these claims have simply not done their homework.

There is no shortage of outcome studies. Even in 1952, when Eysenck did his classic study, over 24 studies were available for analysis. In 1986, Lambert, Shapiro and Bergin summarized 14 outcome review studies. The number of studies considered in these 14 reviews ranged from 9 to 474! The argument that the effectiveness of psychotherapy hinges on a few studies is, at best, hearsay, or, at worst, absolutely false.

Critique of Eysenck's original study.   There are a number of major faults in the Eysenck (1952) study. One problem with Eysenck's study is that the control group of patients apparently did receive some form of counseling or psychotherapy while hospitalized. Eysenck's control-group data were taken from Landis (1938), who noted that all patients did get some degree of psychotherapy while hospitalized. This definitely weakens Eysenck's conclusion that individuals who receive psychotherapy respond less well than do individuals who receive no psychotherapy. In fact, all of Eysenck's subjects received some psychotherapy.

A second problem with Eysenck's classic study is the type of population included. He reviewed studies that consisted of patients with a diagnosis of "neurosis," including individuals suffering from "organ neurosis, psychopathic states, and character disturbances" (Eysenck, 1952, p. 321). Counseling and psychotherapy tend to be less effective with certain diagnostic categories—in particular, with people who have organic problems or long-term characterological problems. The treatment of choice for individuals with severe, chronic problems is usually training in independent living skills or placement in a structured setting such as a hospital. Eysenck's control treatment condition, hospitalization, was probably the primary treatment of choice for the population in his study.

A third objection to the Eysenck study concerns the way in which he measured therapeutic success. Was it on the basis of an objective test, systematic ratings of the therapist, systematic ratings by the patient, and/or systematic ratings by an objective observer? No. The measure of success for the criterion group was simply the impression of the attending physician—not a very objective measure! However, Landis (1938), upon whom Eysenck based his two-thirds recovery rate for the control group, made the following comment in regard to this unit of measure.

> The only unit of measure available is the report made by the physician stating that the patient has recovered, is much improved, is improved or unimproved. This unit is probably as satisfactory as any type of human subjective judgment, partaking of both the good and bad points of such judgments. (p. 156)

Therefore, the determination of whether a hospitalized patient improved was based solely on the physician's self-report. Such ratings are not always reliable. Even Eysenck (1952) made the comment that his figures for control-group recovery "are very probably more lenient" (p. 322) than the figures for the experimental groups. The 72% success rate for the nontherapy group seems to have been very lenient.

Recent studies with objective measures have found the average spontaneous improvement rate to be around 40% (Bergin, 1971; Bergin & Lambert, 1978; Lambert, 1976). In a brief review of the literature on people who tend to get better over time without therapy, Lambert (1986) concluded that "the median spontaneous remission rate for all available studies was 43%, with a range of 18% to 67%. This figure is far from the original estimate of two-thirds suggested by Eysenck (1952)" (p. 438).

It appears that people do tend to get better on their own in approximately 40% of the cases, not Eysenck's conclusion of two-thirds.

The fact remains that, in Eysenck's study, only 44% of the individuals in psychoanalysis improved. However, it is important to note that approximately one-third of the psychoanalytic patients stopped treatment prematurely. Eysenck admitted that, if premature termination was taken into account, then the "chances of improvement under psychoanalysis are approximately equal to his chances of improvement under eclectic treatment" (p. 322). The rate of improvement in the eclectic treatment was 64%. In other words, after correcting some of the flaws in Eysenck's study, it does appear that therapy is more effective than a true nontreatment group and also that there may be no difference between the different styles of therapy.

Critique of paraprofessional studies.   The studies comparing paraprofessionals and professionals definitely raise questions regarding the need for traditional training programs in counseling and psychotherapy. Carkhuff and Truax (1965) and Poser (1966) concluded that lay therapists are effective with an inpatient population. This finding alone is not a severe blow to the adherents of counseling and psychotherapy. Almost any supportive and teaching interventions would be expected to help older individuals suffering from severe and chronic pathology, as were the subjects in these two studies. Simply the added attention and the focus on independent living skills can be helpful for these individuals.

However, the finding by Gomes-Schwartz (1978) that college professors were as successful as experienced professionals in conducting therapy with an outpatient population does indeed bring the need for therapy training and experience into question.

Who were these college professors? In the Gomes-Schwartz study, the college professors were not randomly selected! Rather, professors who were frequently approached by students for personal help were selected to be included in the study. In other words, even though these professors did not have any formal training, they probably exhibited the basic qualities of an effective therapist—in particular, the ability to foster a trusting therapeutic relationship. In such trusting relationships, a person is more apt to disclose and confront emotional problems that he or she has been attempting to avoid.

A second point concerns other personal qualities of these professors. Given that all of the professors had 17 or more years of postdoctoral experience, they were very likely to have achieved one of their career goals—tenure. As such, they were apt to have a healthy degree of self-confidence and self-esteem. Finally, these professors were probably in their

40s or older and undoubtedly accumulated a number of life experiences (marriage, children, etc.) and the wisdom that can accompany such experiences.

Overall, these college professors appear to be individuals who had already exhibited skills in developing trusting relationships, had a history of being able to help students with stressful life situations, and were likely to have a healthy degree of confidence. What the authors may have found is that some people have the qualities of an effective therapist and can do therapy with no formal training.

Durlak's (1979) review of 42 articles comparing the effectiveness of paraprofessionals and professionals raises serious questions regarding the need for training and the efficacy of traditional therapy. Recall Durak's (1979) conclusion that "paraprofessionals achieve clinical outcomes equal to or significantly better than those obtained by professionals" (p. 80). As discussed earlier, Nietzel and Fisher's (1981) reevaluation of the same data modified some of Durlak's conclusions, but still indicated that the two groups appeared equally effective. Then, Hattie, Sharpley, and Rogers (1984) reexamined the data using an objective statistical measure and reaffirmed Durlak's basic finding that, in many cases, paraprofessionals are more effective in counseling and psychotherapy than professionals.

However, Berman and Norton (1985) reevaluated the Durlak data and identified various flaws in 11 of the original studies: the professionals had no formal training; the distinction between paraprofessional and professional appeared arbitrary; or the treatment was not actually a standard form of therapy. Once they excluded the 11 faulty studies from their review, they stated, "We found no evidence that paraprofessional therapists are more effective than professional" therapists (p. 404). However, they did find, once again, that paraprofessionals and professionals are equally effective.

However, common sense dictates that not everyone has the basic personality characteristics to be a therapist. The point that needs clarification is that, in some of the paraprofessional studies, the lay counselors were working in a hospital setting and were probably effective because they were caring individuals and provided much-needed support and guidance; in other studies, the lay therapists were not randomly selected, but were individuals who possessed skills conducive to creating a therapeutic environment. In my opinion, what we are seeing in these studies is that some people possess skills that can be beneficial when working with some clientele. A truly random study that included people from a wide array of professions (for example, accountants, maintenance workers, farmers, administrators, and chemists) would not give these equivocal results.

Critique of other challenges.   Later in the chapter, I discuss followup studies addressing the belief that therapy is not effective, and is only a regression toward the mean. What about the charge that psychotherapy makes people worse? Studies have found that 10% of treatment clients tend to get worse, as compared to 5% of nontreatment clients. These figures have often been interpreted as support for the power of therapy: if therapy is a powerful factor in the change process, it's not surprising that it can sometimes exert a negative influence.

Does surgery ever have adverse effects? Does a physician's misdiagnosis ever have adverse effects? Does a miscommunication between staff and support staff ever have adverse effects? If counseling and psychotherapy are powerful change agents, they would be expected also to have the potential to exacerbate symptoms.

Summary.   The negative outcome study of Eysenck (1952), the findings of paraprofessional studies, and the findings of other negative outcome studies all raise questions not only about the appropriate type of training, but about the need to train therapists at all. However, the poor design of many of these studies limits the validity and application of their findings.

The conclusion that therapy is ineffective is based on biased and limited information and is wrong. I now turn to current outcome research that supports the efficacy of therapy.

Positive Outcome Studies

If the research consisted only of negative findings on the effectiveness of counseling and psychotherapy, the mental health field would no longer exist. Third-party reimbursements would have come to a halt a long time ago. Literally hundreds of studies support the efficacy of therapy. In this section, I summarize positive outcome studies that have supported therapy, examine reviews of the literature on positive outcome studies, and conclude with a synopsis of the classic Smith, Glass, and Miller (1980) meta-analytic study.

Individual positive outcome studies.   To review even a fraction of the research articles that show therapy to be more effective than no treatment is beyond the scope of this book. Instead, a few intriguing studies that compare psychotherapy to pharmacotherapy are discussed.

It is well documented in the field that psychotropic medications have a curative success rate well above that of no treatment (Klerman, 1986). As a consequence, antidepressants are considered in some circles to be the treatment of choice for people suffering from major depression. If it could be shown that psychotherapy is as effective as medical treatment, this would provide strong support for the efficacy of therapy. Let's now consider two studies that compared the results of therapy and medication in the treatment of depression.

Rush, Beck, Kovacs, and Hollon (1977) compared the symptomatic-improvement rate and the treatment-completion rate of clients treated with either medication (imipramine hydrochloride) or cognitive therapy. In both cases, treatment lasted 12 weeks. The population for this study consisted of outpatients who had been diagnosed as suffering from major depression, without psychotic or bipolar symptoms. The results showed that the people treated with cognitive-behavior therapy displayed greater symptomatic relief and had a higher treatment completion rate than did the medication treatment group. The results of a one-year followup with these patients indicated that both groups generally maintained their progress; and on the basis of self-ratings, the cognitive-behavior sample had less depressive symptoms than did the medication group (Kovacs, Rush, Beck, & Hollon, 1981).

Weissman et al. (1979) conducted a similar study using four treatment groups. In one treatment condition, clients received pharmacotherapy with amitriptyline hydrochloride as the medication. The second treatment condition was interpersonal psychotherapy, a form of psychodynamic therapy. In this approach, the techniques of a psychodynamic orientation are used, but the emphasis is on current social relationships rather than on making a link between current symptoms and past relationships. A third group was included for control purposes. This control group was referred to as the nonscheduled supportive psychotherapy group. In this nonscheduled condition the patient could call on an as-needed basis and meet with a psychiatrist for 50 minutes. The fourth treatment group was composed of people who received both psychotherapy and medication.

As in the study comparing cognitive-behavior therapy with medication, the subjects were ambulatory, nonbipolar, nonpsychotic, acutely depressed clients. The study was designed to consist of 16 weeks of treatment. Overall, the findings were that interpersonal psychotherapy and medication were equally effective for the treatment of depression; people in both of these treatment groups showed a higher success rate than people in the control group (nonscheduled supportive therapy). Apparently there was also an additive treatment effect: the combination of psychotherapy and pharmacotherapy was more effective than either treatment alone. The rates of completion for the 16-week treatment plans were: 67% for the combined psychotherapy and pharmacotherapy group, 48% in the psychotherapy group, 33% in the pharmacotherapy group, and 30% in the nonscheduled group. A one-year followup study showed that there were no major differences of symptomatology between the medication and psychotherapy groups (Weissman, Klerman, Prosoff, Sholomskas, & Padian, 1981). Clients in the treatment groups maintained their improved status, in terms of significant reduction in the symptoms of depression. Interestingly enough, people in the interpersonal psychotherapy group scored significantly better on some measures of social functioning at the one-year followup.

I elected to cite these two studies because they dared to compare the success rate of psychotherapy to that of pharmacotherapy. They appear to indicate that talking therapy is at least as effective as medication in the treatment of depression.

Meta-analytic studies of therapy. The 1980s was the decade of meta-analytic studies in counseling and psychotherapy research. A meta-analytic study is a review of outcome studies that compares the average treatment effect of an experimental group to the average nontreatment effect of a control group. The comparison is summarized in the *effect size*, defined as $(m_1 - m_2) \div s$, where m_1 and m_2 refer, respectively, to the treatment and control group means, and s is the pooled within-group standard deviation. That is, to calculate the effect size, the average score on the criterion measures for a group of clients who receive no treatment is subtracted from the average score on the criterion measures for a group of clients who receive therapy, and this difference is then divided by the pooled within-group standard deviation of the scores. If the effect size calculated is significantly large, we can conclude that therapy is more effective than no treatment.

Numerous meta-analytic studies have supported the efficacy of counseling and psychotherapy (Bergin & Lambert, 1978; Lambert, Shapiro, & Bergin, 1986; Smith, Glass, & Miller, 1980). For example, Weissman (1979) reviewed 17 studies that had compared various styles of counseling and psychotherapy with pharmacotherapy. The conclusions reached were that talking therapy was more effective than no treatment and that talking therapy and pharmacotherapy were equivalent. Note that this conclusion was based on the findings not of just one study, but of 17 studies.

Steinbrueck, Maxwell, and Howard (1983) conducted a meta-analytic review in which they compared the effect size of psychotherapy (with respect to control groups) with the effect size of drug therapy (with respect to control groups). Reviewing 56 studies, they concluded that psychotherapy was more effective than drug therapy for the treatment of unipolar depression. Again, this meta-analytic study provides ample support for the effectiveness of psychotherapy.

Finally, Nietzel, Russell, Hemmings, and Gretter's (1987) meta-analytic study compared therapy with a control group on the basis of studies that utilized the Beck Depression Inventory as the criterion measure for change. By limiting the review to articles that used only one measure for the dependent variable, the authors increased the reliability of their results. In a meta-analysis, one of the studies considered might use a measure that is very sensitive to change (and, therefore, find significant results), whereas another might use a nonsensitive measure (and not find significant results). By using only studies with ratings based on the Beck Depression Inventory, this potential problem was eliminated.

In the Nietzel et al. (1987) meta-analysis, 28 studies were evaluated. The overall conclusion was that therapy does indeed have moderate clinical significance and that the improvement is well maintained at followup.

These meta-analytic studies strongly support the efficacy of psychotherapy over a nontreatment control group. Also, there is ample evidence in the literature that psychotherapy is at least as effective as drug therapy in the treatment of unipolar depression.

Smith, Glass, and Miller's Meta-Analytic Study

Smith, Glass, and Miller (1980) reviewed 475 controlled studies on the efficacy of psychotherapy. This review yielded 1,766 effect-size measures. (There are more effect sizes than studies because a separate effect size is calculated for each dependent variable and for each style of therapy.) On account of the wealth of data reviewed, and the controversy that surrounds the methodology and results of this study, I review this classic study in more depth.

The average of the effect-size measures was 0.85 (with a standard error of 0.03). That is, averaged across all outcome measures and styles of therapy, the mean for the treatment group was 0.85 standard deviations higher than the mean for the control group. What this means is that the average person in therapy was better off than 80% of the untreated sample! The average person in therapy will do better, on a variety of outcome measures, than 80% of people who receive no therapy.

This finding is based on a study that is not plagued by many of the faults of the original Eysenck (1952) study. In contrast to Eysenck's review of 24 studies, which included only psychoanalysis and eclectic therapy, the Smith et al. review was based on 475 studies that encompassed an array of 18 therapy styles (client-centered, Gestalt, psychodynamic, rational emotive, reality therapy, etc.). Whereas Eysenck compared individuals in therapy to hospitalized patients, who probably were given some form of talking therapy, the studies reviewed by Smith et al. compared the therapy group to a control group of individuals who received no treatment. Smith et al.'s (1980) basic finding was that

> published conclusions about the absence of benefits from psychotherapy are incorrect; they are based on unrepresentative samples of the research literature or unsophisticated methods for deriving meaningful information from it. (p. 88)

The authors did not stop there.

Many opponents of therapy have argued that claims of its effectiveness are based on the results of poorly designed studies (Miles, Barrabee, & Finesinger, 1951). In response to this charge, Smith et al. (1980) examined the experimental rigor of the studies that they reviewed.

> The allegation by critics of psychotherapy—that poor quality re-
> search methods account for the positive outcomes observed—can
> now be laid to rest. The degree of experimental rigor employed by the
> researcher was positively related to the size of effect produced.
> Greater controls were associated with slightly higher effects. (p. 126)

Yes, the better the design of the study and the more controls the researchers used, the more significant the difference was between the treatment and the control groups.

This finding is what one would predict if therapy is effective. Lambert,
Shapiro, and Bergin (1986) reached a similar conclusion in their review of
outcome studies.

> In sum, the overall finding that psychological treatments are in
> general effective cannot be "explained away" by reference to meth-
> odological weaknesses in the data reviewed or in the reviewing
> method. A large number of controlled studies reveal a positive
> therapeutic effect when compared with no treatment; and very few
> reviewers disagree with this basic overall observation. (p. 161)

As of this date, the vast majority of empiricists who have reviewed the
outcome studies would have to agree that counseling and psychotherapy
constitute a robust and sound form of treatment for emotional problems.
The average person in counseling or psychotherapy will be better off than
80% of people who do not get treatment. These data strongly indicate that
therapy works.

Critique of the Smith, Glass, and Miller Study

The publication of the Smith et al. (1980) findings did not go unchallenged.
One area of controversy is whether psychotherapy is more effective than
a placebo.

Despite the ample research that supports the efficacy of counseling
and psychotherapy, this question persists. For example, Rosenthal and
Frank (1956) leaped to a conclusion that was to become a major area of
debate during the 1980s.

> Improvement under a special form of psychotherapy cannot be
> taken as evidence for: (a) correctness of the theory on which it is
> based; or (b) efficacy of the specific technique used, unless im-
> provement can be shown to be greater than, or quantitatively
> different from that produced by the patient's faith in the efficacy
> of the therapist and his technique—"the placebo effect." (p. 300)

The opponents of therapy insist that therapeutic techniques cannot be regarded as effective unless they can be shown to be more effective than a placebo.

But what exactly is a placebo? In the medical arena, a placebo is simply a chemically inert substance, a sugar pill. In therapy research, however, the definition of placebo is more difficult. For example, whereas adherents of a directive approach to therapy often attribute the efficacy of the nondirective Rogerian approach to placebo factors inherent in the therapeutic relationship, nondirective counselors respond that these so-called placebo factors are actually the essence of their approach.

Researchers comparing treatment groups and placebo groups have identified conditions such as warmth, cajolery, hope, suggestion, attention, discussion, expectation, and relaxation as placebos. However, many of these conditions could be regarded as necessary variables for effective treatment. Empiricists sometimes circumvent this dilemma by defining a placebo as a form of intervention that does not include specific factors identified with a particular form of therapy (for example, psychoanalysis is associated with past-present links; cognitive therapy is associated with the confrontation of irrational thoughts). The findings of such studies have been mixed, at best. Like many of the clinical research findings, the outcomes have not established a clear difference in effectiveness between therapy and placebo effects.

The major study that questioned the Smith et al. (1980) research was conducted by Prioleau, Murdock, and Brody (1983). Prioleau et al. claimed that Smith et al.'s finding was biased, because the authors of the original studies had included placebo treatment as a part of the treatment group. To eliminate this bias, Prioleau et al. chose to compare formal treatment with placebo treatments.

They were able to find 32 studies that contrasted counseling and psychotherapy with placebo treatment. The authors used the following definition of placebo: "The patient is led to believe that the treatment is efficacious and the treatment does not contain any other therapeutic components" (Prioleau, Murdock, & Brody, 1983, p. 277). Instead of the 0.85 effect size of Smith et al. (1980), Prioleau et al. (1983) found an overall effect size of only about 0.40.

Prioleau et al.'s (1983) findings prompted the following commentary from Eysenck (1983):

> The effectiveness of psychotherapy has always been the specter at the wedding feast; where thousands of psychiatrists, psychoanalysts, clinical psychologists, social workers and others celebrate the happy event and pay no heed to the need of evidence for the premature crystallization of their spurious orthodoxies, the need to do so, emphasized by experimentalists and other critical spirits, has always threatened to upset the happy union. (p. 290)

Is the effectiveness of counseling and psychotherapy merely a phantom in therapists' minds? Are thousands of mental health workers fearful that experimentalists may expose the continued charade?

Eysenck's was one of 23 commentaries published along with Prioleau et al.'s study in the journal *The Behavioral and Brain Sciences*. Some were critical of the study's methodology; others were dubiously supportive of the methodology but questioned the conclusions; others agreed with Eysenck.

A major flaw of the Prioleau et al. study was that in their methodology they included some forms of questionable treatment in the placebo group. For example, two commentaries (Garfield, 1983; Rosenthal, 1983) noted that Prioleau et al. included an article (Gillan & Rachman, 1974) on phobic clientele that used hierarchy construction and muscle relaxation as a placebo treatment. However, these procedures are legitimate forms of psychological treatment for phobias.

Garfield (1983) also noted that, in another study (Jarmon, 1972), rational emotive therapy (RET) was the form of counseling, while the placebo was to read a RET book. However, RET is an extremely didactic approach, and reading its principles may confer some of the benefits of the therapy itself; this can hardly be defined as a placebo condition.

In another commentary, Glass, Smith, and Miller (1983) stated that the Prioleau et al. (1983) study "confirmed the fact" (p. 293) that the average person receiving psychotherapy was about 0.40 standard deviation units above the placebo groups. In other words, the Prioleau et al. study still indicates that persons receiving psychotherapy show improvement. Therefore, Glass et al. questioned Prioleau et al.'s (1983) negative conclusion:

> An effect of .40 sigma units is roughly the size of the gain that students in a graduate seminar in psychology would show from pretest to posttest on a comprehensive written exam over the contents of the course—and no one we know suggests that students cease to study or professors to teach. (p. 293)

Glass et al. suggested that Prioleau et al. (1983) were simply attempting to revive the old battle between verbal and behavioral therapy from the 1960s.

Brody (1983), one of the authors of the Prioleau et al. study, made the following response to the commentaries: "I believe that clinicians may have an inadequate understanding of the etiology of the conditions they treat" (p. 307). He cited research that attributes maladaptive behavior solely to organic and/or extrapsychic events that "the person or therapist may not be able to control" (p. 307).

Brody (1983) went on:

> I would like to make a public offer to these psychologists or to any readers of this *The Behavioral Brain and Sciences* treatment. I will publicly retract, with the editor's permission, any conclusions reached in our target article, if anyone can provide me with evidence of a study finding that psychotherapy leads to benefits

that exceed those obtained by placebo treatments for neurotic outpatients. (p. 304)

I do not know if Brody ever obtained the editor's permission to retract their conclusions. However, the results of other studies that also reexamined Smith et al.'s (1980) original data indicate that he should.

In one study, the investigators reviewed only those original articles of the Smith et al. (1980) review that involved individuals who exhibited typical psychiatric problems (such as neuroses, phobias, and emotional-somatic complaints) and who sought treatment for themselves (Andrews & Harvey, 1981). In other words, the authors excluded analogue studies—typically involving undergraduate students who volunteer for experiments in return for course credit—and retained the data most relevant to the typical situation faced by practicing therapists. After eliminating analogue studies, the authors found that clients showed more improvement than 77% of the untreated controls. This study refutes one of the findings of Prioleau et al. (1983).

A second reanalysis of the Smith et al. (1980) data focused on the comparison of therapy and placebo groups (Landman & Dawes, 1982):

When groups that received therapy were directly compared with groups administered placebo treatment, therapy emerges as superior. Although the placebo effect may contribute to some degree to successful outcomes of psychotherapy, the placebo effect constituted only a small fraction of the overall effect in the present set of studies that had both placebo and NT [no-treatment] controls. (p. 511)

Thus, research shows that subjects who are typical clients (rather than subjects in analogue studies) do improve with treatment and that psychotherapy is superior to placebo treatment. Placebo groups do, however, show some measurable change.

Bloch and Lambert (1985) noted that Smith et. al. (1980) actually did exclude placebo treatments and undifferentiated counseling in a second analysis of their data. In this analysis, the effect size increased from 0.85 standard deviation units to 0.93. Contrary to the accusations by Prioleau et al. (1983), the inclusion of placebo treatments in Smith et al.'s original analysis only served to dilute the effect size. As a result of their second analysis, Smith et al. (1980) commented that their initial conclusion—that the average client in psychotherapy displays more improvement across a variety of outcome measures than 80% of individuals without treatment—is actually a conservative estimate.

This whole idea of therapy as a placebo has received much attention. Kazdin (1986) suggested that the reason a placebo effect is noticed at all in counseling and psychotherapy may be that nonspecific factors within the placebo and within the formal treatments act as change agents. That is, all forms of therapy hold some common ground: the instillation of hope, a supportive relationship, a contractual agreement, cognitive insight, and so forth. Garfield (1990) argued

> that whatever general features placebo conditions may have, they tend to produce a positive result, even though it is less than that produced by a regular form of psychotherapy. Therefore, part of the positive effect secured by psychotherapy may be due to such hypothesized variables as seeing a therapist, the creation of hope, and the passage of time. These could be viewed as potential process variables, and perhaps they represent, or are related to, the therapeutic relationship in general. (p. 278)

These common nonspecific factors could account for the basic change that is witnessed in therapy and placebo treatments. Likewise, these same nonspecific factors may also help to explain the lack of a clear differentiation in the efficacy of paraprofessionals and professionals.

There were many flaws in the paraprofessional research. Most notably, the paraprofessionals were not randomly selected. Some had worked in a hospital setting and were trained in the process of therapy (or common nonspecific factors); others were homemakers who also received intensive training in the common factors of therapy; and some were college professors who had already exhibited their skills in helping others. The hypothesis advanced in this chapter, which remains only a hypothesis to this date, is that the literature comparing paraprofessionals and professionals is so mixed because the paraprofessionals selected in the studies already exhibited skills conducive to therapeutic change or else had been trained in the basics of the change process.

Likewise, the finding that placebo effects have a significant positive impact (although less than that of formal therapy) supports the idea of common process variables of change. Finally, if the various styles of therapy are equally effective, this would also support the role of nonspecific process variables in counseling and psychotherapy.

Is therapy effective? This question has now been answered in the affirmative. In the past two decades, attention has shifted to another question: Which style of therapy is most effective? It is to this topic of research that I now turn.

COMPARATIVE STUDIES

Considering the divergence of the various styles of counseling and psychotherapy, it seems reasonable to expect that some styles of therapy would be more effective than others. The discrepancies between the techniques of various schools are vast. The client-centered approach places an emphasis on therapists providing a trusting and genuine relationship; the cognitive-behavioral camp places an emphasis on clients accepting that their irrational thoughts impede their growth; the psychoanalytic camp places an emphasis on clients obtaining insight into the role that past relationships have on their current behaviors and problems. Given the variations in the specific theoretical perspectives and the resulting variations in technique, it seems logical that one approach would be more effective. For example, if insight into one's past is indeed necessary for change, then the efficacy of a psychoanalytic perspective would be expected to exceed that of approaches that do not utilize psychogenic insight.

In the remaining sections of this chapter, I summarize the major comparative studies; reviews of comparative studies; problems frequently encountered with these review studies; and results of a National Institute of Mental Health project.

The Dodo Bird Verdict

In 1975, Luborsky, Singer, and Luborsky published their findings from a review of comparative studies. Their review supported the results of the outcome studies—that counseling and psychotherapy are more effective than no treatment. They also found that one form of therapy did not appear to be more effective than another. Although the various schools of therapy attribute change to different specific factors and therefore use different therapeutic techniques, this classic study concluded that all styles of therapy appear to be equally effective. This information is disarming for many mental health workers, who have devoted so much time and energy to learning a specific style of therapy.

Luborsky et al. described their conclusion as the dodo bird verdict: everyone has won and all must have prizes. This phrase has gained great fame in this area of comparative research; it is taken from Lewis Carroll's (1865/1981) *Alice's Adventures in Wonderland*. In this fantasy, a race was held, and at the conclusion the dodo bird made the resounding exclamation, "Everyone has won and all must have prizes."

How can all the various forms of therapy be equally effective when they are so different? One explanation for these findings has been that the various forms of therapy are actually more similar than they are different. Perhaps it is the nonspecific techniques, the process variables, that are the true change agents. "These common ingredients of psychotherapies may be so much more potent than the specific ones that it is wrong to lump them together in the sense of giving them equal weight" (Luborsky, Singer, & Luborsky, 1975, p. 1006). If this is so, then, in our training programs, we have been placing too much emphasis on the specific techniques of the varying schools, and not enough emphasis on the nonspecific process variables of therapy. There are features inherent in the therapy process that promote change. It is these features that are most important, rather than the specific techniques of the various schools of therapy.

These common features include such variables as: providing a nonthreatening environment; developing a relationship in which the client and therapist work together as a team; and offering a plausible explanation for the client's suffering.

These common nonspecific factors will be discussed in Chapters 5 and 6. I now briefly examine the comparative studies that followed Luborsky, Singer, and Luborsky's landmark review.

Individual Comparison Studies

Since the publication of Luborsky, Singer, and Luborsky's (1975) study, there have been a host of studies comparing different forms of treatment; these studies have been of higher quality in terms of design.

Gomes-Schwartz (1978) compared psychodynamic therapy and client-centered therapy. Clients were randomly assigned to one of the two modes of treatment. The therapists were experienced in their respective mode of treatment; prior studies, by contrast, frequently used students in graduate training programs as therapists. The finding was that psychodynamic and client-centered therapies were equally effective.

The Gomes-Schwartz (1978) study also concluded that client involvement was a key factor in the client's change: the more active the client was in the therapy, the better the client did. Gomes-Schwartz (1978) suggested that preparing clients for therapy—letting them know what to expect—would encourage them to be more active in their treatment.

An interesting result was obtained in a study comparing interpersonal group therapy (a form of psychodynamic therapy) and cognitive group therapy (Shaffer, Shapiro, Sank, & Coghlan, 1981): the two styles of treatment were found to be equally efficacious in the treatment of depression, anxiety, and assertiveness.

What makes this study particularly interesting is that the authors openly admitted their allegiance to cognitive therapy in their article. Such an admission is the exception, not the rule. A common problem that has plagued counseling and clinical research is that individual universities and research centers tend to be devoted to a particular theoretical and therapeutic orientation, and publications from such centers tend to support their preferred style of intervention. However, Shaffer et al., who admittedly leaned toward a cognitive therapy perspective, concluded that the different types of treatment were equally effective. The authors suggested that one reason for their finding is that "all patients felt a sense of self-efficacy over their problems" (p. 155); that is, all the clients were given a plausible rationale for their suffering, whether that rationale was cognitively or psychodynamically based.

Another comparison study again found no significant difference between cognitive-behavioral and psychodynamic group psychotherapy in terms of the clinical variables (Steuer et al., 1984). However, the cognitive-behavioral group scored significantly better on the Beck Depression Inventory. This study serves to remind us that the method of measurement can have an impact on the results.

> Cognitive-behavioral therapy may "teach" the scale. The possibility of this type of measurement bias should be borne in mind when the BDI [Beck Depression Inventory] is used as an outcome measure in psychotherapy research comparing cognitive-behavioral therapy with other treatments. The other measures used in the present study did not show treatment differences. (Steuer et al., 1984, p. 187)

Researchers of different theoretical perspectives frequently discuss the notion of biased measures.

The psychodynamic camp insists that specific symptom measures tend to favor cognitive-behavioral styles of therapy. They believe that global measures may be a better method of measuring change. The study by Steuer et al. (1984) highlights the need to have several dependent measures. Along these same lines, Luborsky, Singer, and Luborsky (1975) noted that many of the comparative studies they reviewed used only clinicians' ratings of change as the dependent measure. This definitely increases the potential for biased results.

A well-designed study by Luborsky, McLellan, Woody, O'Brien, and Auerbach (1985) compared three modes of intervention for patients seeking methadone treatment: supportive-expressive therapy (a form of short-term psychoanalytic therapy), cognitive-behavioral therapy, and drug counseling. In all three treatment conditions, the clients had drug counseling; the drug counseling group therefore served as the control group. To control for variability and bias, a number of criterion measures were included.

A notable aspect of the study's design was that the authors controlled for therapists' variability in their delivery of therapy. In the vast majority of prior outcome and comparison studies, it was assumed that, if the therapists had a number of years of experience, they would be appropriately administering that specific mode of therapy that they said they practiced. However, experience has shown that, in therapy, therapists are not always doing what they say they are doing.

In order to control for this within-therapist variability, the psychoanalytic therapists were selected by Lester Luborsky (a leading proponent of the short-term psychoanalytic camp), and the cognitive therapists were selected by Aaron Beck (a leading proponent of the cognitive camp). The therapists also received some supervision from the leader of their respective fields. However, the major controlling element for therapist variability was that the therapists had manualized training in their respective areas: training for the cognitive therapists was based on a manual written by Beck, Rush, Shaw, and Emery (1979), which gives very specific guidelines for the practice of cognitive therapy, while a manual written by Luborsky (1984) was used by the short-term psychoanalytic therapists.

The therapy sessions were videotaped. This allowed an objective observer to rate preselected portions of the tapes in terms of the degree to which the therapists adhered to their orientation. This way, the examiners knew that the psychoanalytic therapists were indeed doing a form of psychodynamic therapy and that the cognitive therapists were indeed doing a form of cognitive therapy.

If there is indeed a difference between the efficacy of these two styles of therapy, it should have shown up in this study. However, the finding was that short-term psychoanalytic therapy and cognitive therapy were equally effective. Neither form of psychotherapy was more effective than the control condition of supportive drug counseling alone.

The results of comparative studies are sometimes questioned if no followup is conducted. Psychoanalytic therapists, in particular, claim that, in some studies, cognitive therapy may appear to be more effective initially, merely because of symptom relief. These dynamically oriented therapists believe that psychodynamic therapies may actually be more effective in followup studies, in which the criterion measures are implemented months or years after the treatment.

In response, a study was conducted with 91 elderly depressed patients (Thompson, Gallagher, & Breckenridge, 1987). There were three treatment conditions (behavioral, cognitive, and brief psychodynamic) and one control condition. As in the Luborsky et al. (1985) study, therapists were trained by leaders in their respective fields and were rated on the degree that they followed a manualized version of their orientation. The findings at the end of treatment were that: (a) psychotherapy in general was more effective than the control group; and (b) the three styles of therapy were equally effective. These two findings were replicated in a two-year followup study (Gallagher-Thompson, Hanley-Peterson, & Thompson, 1990).

Review Articles on the Comparison Studies

Smith, Glass, and Miller (1980) not only reviewed the outcome studies published prior to 1978, but also reviewed comparison studies that could have thrown light on the question of which therapy is most effective. Like Luborsky, Singer, and Luborsky (1975), Smith et al. concluded that the differing forms of intervention were equally effective. This review of the comparison studies was not passively received.

Shapiro and Shapiro (1982) did a meta-analysis of comparative therapy studies, including a number of design controls not fully taken into account by Smith et al. (1980). Their conclusion was "a modest but undeniable superiority of behavioral and cognitive methods and a corresponding relative inferiority of dynamic and humanistic methods" (p. 596). By including only well-designed studies in their review, Shapiro and Shapiro did find significant differences between therapies; their results favored behavioral and cognitive interventions.

The original Smith et al. (1980) data were again examined. A second review of the comparative studies found that cognitive therapy was no more effective than other therapies (Miller & Berman, 1983).

Another finding of the Shapiro and Shapiro (1982) review was that cognitive therapy was more effective than systematic desensitization. However, a rebuttal article that examined only articles in which cognitive therapy was compared with desensitization treatment found no significant difference between these treatments (Berman, Miller, & Massman, 1985). The authors concluded that Shapiro and Shapiro's (1982) review found a significant difference favoring cognitive therapy because they included studies that were done by investigators who had an allegiance to cognitive therapy.

> We discovered that in all but one of the studies reviewed by Shapiro and Shapiro, the investigators indicated a preference for cognitive therapy. In contrast, the allegiance of investigators in the larger group of studies we examined was more varied . . . Our analysis suggested that such theoretical allegiances may affect the outcome of a study. Results from studies in which the investigators favored a cognitive treatment indicated cognitive therapy to be superior, whereas results from investigators favoring desensitization indicated that desensitization was the better treatment. (p. 458)

The sophistication of the empirical literature has matured since the original Eysenck (1952) review, and is entering another stage.

Commentaries on the Comparative Studies

Does empirical research continue to support the dodo bird verdict? Is one style of therapy superior to the others? The answer still appears to be yes, no, or maybe. The articles I have chosen to summarize illustrate that, even within the objective domain of research, there is still much room for biases to enter.

Reviewing the then-current state of comparative studies, Stiles, Shapiro, & Elliot (1986) cited Lewis Carroll's description of the dodo bird's behavior at greater length:

> First, it marked out a race-course, in a sort of circle ("the exact shape doesn't matter," it said) and then all the party were placed

along the course, here and there. There was no "One, two, three and away," but they began running when they liked, and left off when they liked so that is was not easy to know when the race was over. However, when they had been running half an hour or so, and were quite dry again, the Dodo suddenly called out "The race is over!" and they all crowded round it, panting and asking, "But who has won?" (Carroll, 1865/1981, p. 165)

It was then that the cry of the dodo bird came forth: "All have won, and all must have prizes." Stiles et al.'s point is that much of the comparative research to date has been as haphazard and poorly designed as the race that preceded the dodo bird's cry. Thus, Luborsky, Singer, and Luborsky's (1975) dodo bird verdict may have been premature.

The at times dry, but humorous, anecdotes of the empirical investigators do not stop here. The metaphor of the dodo bird was reexamined by Shadish and Sweeney (1991), 16 years after Luborsky et al.'s review:

But the analogy has an obvious flaw: Dodo birds are not very smart, so it is not clear why we would let them award prizes to begin with. That only happens in Wonderland. The dodo bird conclusion is an artifact of the dodo bird's failure to look for plausible mediators and moderators. (p. 888)

They suggested that, in attempting to understand the therapeutic process, we need to look at moderators and mediators: *moderators* are variables that affect the relation between specific treatment factors and outcome measures; and *mediators* are those variables intermediate between the independent variable, the treatment, and the dependent variable, the outcome. In other words, instead of focusing so much on which approach is the most effective, we need to examine more closely the common process variables of the differing styles of therapy.

Some empiricists believe it is still too soon to conclude that all forms of therapy are equally effective. Kazdin and Bass (1989) called attention to the statistical power of the analyses used—that is, the ability to find differences that are actually present. They suggested that, although the analyses may have had enough power to determine a significant difference for the outcome studies, they lack the power to find the smaller differences between styles of therapy.

The power of an analysis can be increased by increasing the sample size; this would entail many more expensive comparative studies. However, another way to increase the power is to change the alpha level from the traditional 0.05 value. A 0.05 level of significance means that the differences observed would be expected to occur by chance only 5% of the time. Why not change the alpha level to 0.10? There would still be only a 10% probability that the observed differences in the study were due to chance. In comparative studies, increasing the alpha level in order to gain more power makes sense. However, we are working against years of tradition in the psychological literature.

Another way to increase the power is to design studies more stringently. Kazdin (1986) lamented:

> The power of a test of course goes beyond considerations of effect size, sample size, and alpha. Because effect size depends on within-group variability of the observations, any facet of the experiment that can reduce this variability can augment power. (p. 102)

The use of manualized treatments in which therapists are rated on the degree that they adhere to an approach is definitely a step toward this goal.

Even Smith et al. (1980), who got meta-analytic reviews of therapy studies underway, were prolific in their predictions and warnings concerning the dodo bird verdict:

> Ex post facto statistical equating of therapies is only partly satisfactory, since many potential confounding variables remain uncontrolled. The best solution for the reduction of the influence of extraneous variables is experimental; that is, for one researcher to study the effects of two or more therapies directly, using the same kinds of client, therapy of standard duration, therapists of equivalent training, and common measurements. In this way, all extraneous variables are controlled and differences in average effects between the two therapies reflect directly on their differential effectiveness. (p. 106)

Smith et al. acknowledged the limitations of review articles and suggested that a single, large scale, well-designed study be conducted.

Piper (1988) also suggested that a large-scale, methodologically powerful research project be funded to assess the state of affairs in comparative research. He recommended that, among other things, this research project should include the following:

1. The use of clinical trials (real clients and patients) instead of graduate students or anecdotal studies.
2. Random allocation of patients to two or more treatment conditions.
3. Manual training for the therapists.
4. Supervision for the therapists.
5. Data review for process variables (that is, common curative factors).
6. Experienced therapists instead of therapists in training.
7. Examination of the data for interaction effects.
8. The use of a battery of sensitive and reliable outcome measures.
9. Large sample size.

A study that included even a few of Kazdin's and Piper's major recommendations would provide some definitive information on the relative effectiveness of therapeutic approaches. Then we would no longer be misled by review articles that include poorly designed and often biased studies. Such a single study would require an astronomical sum of money, careful planning, and considerable time. In fact, such a study is underway, and some preliminary conclusions have been published.

The NIMH Collaborative Research on Treatment of Depression

In July 1980, three research sites were funded by the National Institute of Mental Health (NIMH) to do a large-scale comparative study (Elkin, Parloff, Hadley, & Autry, 1985). It was not until 1989, however, that the results of this massive study began to emerge. One of the purposes of the study was to compare the efficacy of four different types of treatment for major depression—pharmacotherapy, cognitive-behavior therapy, interpersonal psychotherapy, and a placebo condition.

The pharmacotherapy consisted of standardized treatment with imipramine. The cognitive-behavioral intervention followed the basic writings of Aaron Beck and his manualized version of this intervention (Beck, Rush, Shaw, & Emery, 1979). The interpersonal psychotherapy was based on psychodynamic techniques, but was characterized by a here-and-now orientation rather than attempts to make past-present interpretive links. A manualized version of this approach was employed (Klerman, Weissman, Rounsaville, & Chevron, 1984). In the placebo condition, patients were given a placebo pill, in a double-blind manner: neither the psychiatrist nor the patient knew that the pill was a placebo.

Thus far, the study does not seem much more noteworthy than some of the other comparative studies already cited. However, as a collaborative effort in which all four forms of treatment are conducted at three different sites, this project was able to limit the bias due to particular research centers' allegiance to a specific style of therapy. The study may be described as a 4 (treatments) X 3 (research sites) factorial design. This design means that an interaction effect such that one treatment is superior in only one or two sites will be detected in the analysis.

Other exceptional facets of this project are the selection and training of the therapists. All of the psychotherapists had at least two years of training following their doctoral internship. All of the psychiatrists had at least two years of experience following their residency.

The therapists were selected so that they adhered to the approach to which they were assigned even before the study began. They received intensive didactic training from the manual of their respective therapy approach. After training, the therapists were evaluated for 12–19 months during a practicum. The top candidates were selected for participation in the study and sent to one of the three selected research centers.

Trainers monitored videotapes throughout the practicum and the actual study to prevent *drifting*—that is, to ensure that the therapists were adhering to their orientation. During the study, all sessions were audio-taped and videotaped. The design of this project left little room for errors in terms of purity of therapeutic orientation.

All four treatments (pharmacotherapy, cognitive-behavioral, interpersonal, and placebo) involved meeting with the patient over a period of 16 weeks, with a maximum of 20 sessions. In response to the criticisms concerning inadequate, biased, and single-criterion measurement of the dependent variable, change, this study involved a battery of 22 outcome measures! The tests included specific symptom measures and global measures; rating was by independent clinical evaluators, therapists, clients, and significant others. This design might seem somewhat of an overkill response to the previous problems in assessment. However, it leaves little or no chance that the results will be biased on account of the therapists' or clients' ratings.

The assessment tests were administered prior to treatment and then at the fourth, eighth, twelfth, and sixteenth week of treatment. This will allow the researchers to examine how the process elements unfolded during the treatment. Another problem of comparative studies has been the failure to conduct followups. In the NIMH study, followup measures were administered 6, 12, and 18 months after termination.

By the end, the project included 155 patients, a relatively large sample size compared to past studies. An alpha level of 0.10 was employed, so that moderate differences would be detected. The therapists' training assured that they were doing what they said they were doing. This study has adequate power: it should be able to find significant differences, if they exist. Surely this study will bring some order to the chaos of the research literature.

For more details regarding the design of this study, the reader is referred to the original article (Elkin et al., 1985). Its long-awaited result is stated as follows:

> In the set of findings for the total unstratified sample of patients in our primary analyses, it is clear that there is no evidence of greater effectiveness of one of the psychotherapies as compared with the other and no evidence that either of the psychotherapies was significantly less effective than the standard reference treatment. All treatment conditions evidenced significant change from pretreatment to posttreatment. (Elkin et al., 1989, p. 980)

The dodo bird lives. As some of the researchers concluded, "Perhaps the most parsimonious interpretation of our findings is that there are core processes that operate across treatments, overriding differences among techniques, that is, the common factors" (Imber et al., 1990, p. 357).

Further support for the potency of the process variables of change comes from another summary study, which examined mode-specific effects (Watkins et al., 1993). It was hypothesized that some measures of change would be more sensitive to one style of therapy than to another— for example, that clients in cognitive therapy would show earlier changes in dysfunctional attitude measures than would clients in interpersonal psychotherapy; that clients in interpersonal psychotherapy would show faster change on social adjustment measures; and that clients in the pharmacotherapy treatment would show more rapid change on relief of endogenous symptoms. The authors did find more rapid relief of endogenous symptoms for the pharmacotherapy group, but there was no strong evidence for other mode-specific effects.

> The fact that mode-specific effects did not occur over time for the psychotherapies, when coupled with the similarity of the treatment effects at termination, suggests either that the target measures may not be specific enough or that some factor common to each of the psychotherapies may have played a major role in patient changes over time. That is to say, these data may indicate, similar to the conclusions reached by Imber et al. (1990), the presence of one or a few major curative factors with relatively little variance as a result of specific technique. (Watkins et al., 1993, p. 864)

The overwhelming conclusion of the NIMH project is that different styles of therapy are equally effective in the treatment of depression and that there are probably common curative factors—process variables—that make them equally effective.

The findings of the NIMH collaborative study are going to have a profound impact on the teaching and practice of counseling and psychotherapy in the years to come. How we view counseling and psychotherapy is undergoing a dramatic change. Undue emphasis on specific techniques of the various styles is giving way to an appreciation of the nonspecific variables—the process variables of change. Two leading authors of the NIMH project have made the following summation.

> Abandoning the specificity hypothesis and accepting the nonspecificity hypothesis on the basis of no difference findings would carry serious implications for the field. In addition to casting doubt on the value of current psychotherapy training, the findings regarding the nonspecificity hypothesis—as interpreted by many laymen—cast doubt on the credibility of the entire field. The concept of nonspecificity has been broadly interpreted as including everything that is not encompassed in the construct of specificity. It has been used to refer to placebo and to common elements

such as the therapeutic alliance, suggestion, attention, and hope. (Parloff & Elkin, 1992, p. 448)

The remainder of this book directly addresses the nonspecificity hypothesis, the process variables of change.

SUMMARY

The current research overwhelmingly supports the conclusion that counseling and psychotherapy are more effective than no treatment. However, the results of studies comparing the effectiveness of paraprofessional and professional therapists and the effectiveness of various styles of therapy may leave some in the field bewildered. For others, these results were to be expected. As has been highlighted throughout this chapter, factors that are common to all approaches operate in therapy. These process variables of change are crucial to effective therapy, whether one is a paraprofessional, a cognitive behaviorist, a humanistic therapist, or a psychodynamic therapist.

CHAPTER FIVE

THEORETICAL PROCESS VARIABLES

And, Merlin, I think you are a trickster and a fraud;
every time I have gone away from you it has been
with the conviction that you have said mighty
things, yet, on thinking, I could never recall any of
them. I think you work a subtle conjuring with the
soft voice of you, and your harps.

(Steinbeck, 1929/1986a, p. 136)

Clients often leave therapy feeling better, yet not knowing why. Unable to recall all the mighty things the therapist said, they sometimes come to feel that they are dealing with a trickster or a fraud. However, not only do clients have difficulty in describing what happened in therapy, counselors and psychotherapists also encounter trouble in recalling what happened within the 50-minute hour that was so beneficial.

THE VARIOUS SCHOOLS OF THERAPY

Many therapists who work from an explicit orientation attribute the client's change to the particular techniques within their specific approach to therapy. Asked why a client suffering from panic attacks made positive change in therapy, a humanistic therapist may reply that the necessary and sufficient conditions of change—unconditional positive regard, genuineness, and empathy—were provided (Rogers, 1957). Asked the same question, a cognitive therapist may respond that he or she confronted the client's irrational thoughts so that the client could achieve a satisfying life by "intelligently organizing and disciplining his thinking" (Ellis & Harper, 1961, p. 13). With a similar client, a psychodynamic therapist may emphasize the role of clarification, confrontation, and interpretation of past events (Glover, 1931).

Some adherents of a specific school of therapy insist that their approach harbors the true ingredients for fostering change and that the various other schools are effective only because they unwittingly incorporate the same techniques. For example, an ardent psychodynamic therapist may insist that the cognitive approach is effective only because, behind their closed office doors, cognitive therapists actually implement a number of psychodynamic techniques.

This argument has not been supported by research. During the past decade, as we saw in Chapter 4, a number of well-designed studies have compared the effectiveness of various styles of therapy (for example, Elkin et al., 1985). These comparative studies concluded that, even though the implementation of the approaches was different (Beutler, 1983), they all had equivalent success rates on a number of dependent variables.

Indeed, Luborsky, Singer, and Luborsky (1975) found that therapists who closely adhered to their specific style were *more* likely to be effective than therapists who strayed from the basic tenets of their specific approach. Shaw (1983) reached the same conclusion in preparing therapists for the NIMH collaborative project.

Psychodynamic therapists often argue that, while the client may change under a less depth-oriented style of therapy, the change is superficial. To date, however, there is no consistent finding that one particular school is more effective on symptomatic, global, client-rated, therapist-rated, independent-rated, or objective measures of change.

A GROWING APPRECIATION OF PROCESS VARIABLES

For a number of years, theorists have suggested that the commonalities among the various therapies play a greater role in promoting change than do the differences among them. These commonalities may explain, in part, why research has not found that one style of therapy is more effective than another.

The idea of factors common to all modes of therapy is not new. In 1961, Ungersma wrote:

> The present situation in psychotherapy is not unlike that of the man who mounted his horse and rode off in all directions. The theoretical orientation of therapists is based upon widely divergent hypotheses, theories and ideologies . . . Nevertheless, all schools, given favorable conditions, achieve favorable results: the patient or client gets relief and is often enough cured of his difficulties. (Ungersma, 1961, p. 55)

Frank's (1973) summary is still applicable today.

> Despite decades of effort, it has been impossible to show convincingly that one therapeutic method is more effective than any other for the majority of psychological illnesses. This suggests that any specific healing effects of different methods would be overshadowed by therapeutically potent ingredients shared by all. (p. 2)

It is these *ingredients shared by all* that numerous theorists have suggested which are actually the major variables inductive to fostering change in therapy. If all styles of therapy are equally efficacious, then perhaps training programs need to emphasize the factors that are common to all modes of therapy.

Patterson (1974) argued that "the differences among [styles of therapy] are accidental, at best irrelevant or at worst detrimental. An approach may be effective in spite of, rather than because of, its unique variables" (p. x). This is the same Patterson whose book *Theories of Counseling and Psychotherapy* (Patterson, 1986) is a centerpiece of many introductory theory courses.

The fundamental question facing therapists in training is: Why do people change? What is it about the process of counseling and psychotherapy that creates change? With the growing acceptance that the effectiveness of therapy depends on ingredients common to all styles, which have variously been called curative factors, common factors, nonspecific factors, and process variables, perhaps training programs need to emphasize these factors.

In the following section, I examine theorists' hypotheses regarding the process variables of change.

. LITERATURE REVIEW

It was Rosenzweig (1936) who initiated the dodo bird debate, more than half a century ago. Prefacing his article with the now-famed remark, "Everybody has won, and all must have prizes (Carroll, 1865/1981), Rosenzweig (1936) suggested that three factors are common to all forms of therapy: implicit procedures and a psychological personality organization which allow for a synergistic effect. All forms of therapy do seem to possess these common factors.

Unfortunately, Rosenzweig was not specific in identifying the implicit procedures—the unverbalized aspects of the therapeutic relationship. He only noted that they include catharsis and the therapist's personality.

He was more explicit regarding the role of psychological interpretations:

> Whether the therapist talks in terms of psychoanalysis or Christian Science is . . . relatively unimportant as compared with the *formal consistency* with which the doctrine employed is adhered to, for by virtue of this consistency the patient receives a schema for achieving some sort and degree of personality organization. (Rosenzweig, 1936, p. 413)

In other words, the content of a confrontation or interpretation is not of primary importance. What is important is that therapists stick with an orientation, whether cognitive, humanistic, or psychodynamic. This would partially account for the paradoxical research finding (Luborsky, Singer, & Luborsky, 1975; Shaw, 1983) that therapists of all orientations tend to be more effective if they remain true to their approach.

Rosenzweig noted that, because people are so complex, the therapist can find a grain of truth in many different interpretations. This means that selecting an orientation is a difficult task, but it is necessary in order to ensure a formal consistency of interpretation. Conflicting interpretations leave the client feeling lost and confused.

Finally, Rosenzweig (1936) suggested that the synergistic effect arises because the personality is an interdependent organization: to create change in one area can result in change in other aspects of the client's life. A change in a person's thoughts can create changes in emotions and behaviors, or a change in emotions can create changes in the person's thoughts and behaviors, and so on.

A decade after Rosenzweig's article, Alexander and French (1946) concluded that the emotions are the fundamental change agent in counseling.

> In order to be relieved of his neurotic ways of feeling and acting, the patient must undergo new emotional experiences suited to undo the morbid effects of the emotional experiences of his earlier life. Other therapeutic factors—such as intellectual insight, abreaction, recollection of the past, etc.—are all subordinated to this central therapeutic principle. (p. 338)

In their view, the therapist must provide the client with a corrective emotional experience within the therapy hour that counters the inimical response of the client's parents. Thus, suppose that the client's independent behavior as a child was met by belittling and hostile comments from his critical parents. Then, to provide a corrective emotional experience, the therapist reacts to the independent behaviors of the client in a nonjudgmental manner and may even praise the client's strength in deciding to move on with life. Alexander and French viewed this corrective emotional experience provided by the therapist as the core that makes all forms of counseling effective.

Revitalizing the writings of Rosenzweig, Garfield (1957) suggested that the fundamental elements of counseling are that therapists are sympathetic and not moralizing; that a therapeutic relationship ensues; and that clients are provided with new cognitive understanding for their problems. Garfield also appreciated the role of emotions in therapy and believed that catharsis is a necessary condition for change.

The dodo bird walked back onto the scene with Frank's (1973) classic book *Persuasion and Healing*. Frank prefaced every chapter with a quote from *Alice in Wonderland*. He identified four common features of all forms of therapy.

1. Relationship. The key for a therapeutic relationship is that the client must have confidence in the therapist and a desire to be helped.

2. Locales. The setting suggests psychological help. In our society, it may be a therapist's office, a hospital with its credentialed staff and dignified hallways, or the university health clinic.

3. Cognitive insight. Like most process theorists, Frank suggests that the content does not matter as much as the actual encounter. He states that all psychotherapies are based on a myth that provides an explanation of illness or normalcy.

4. Prescription or procedure. The client is provided with a specific avenue of relief.

If these four process variables are in place, then the following necessary conditions for change automatically ensue.

1. The client has an opportunity to learn at cognitive and experiential levels.

2. There is an increase in the client's sense of relief; that is, the client has an expectation of hope and faith in the treatment.

3. Success experiences give the client renewed hope, which expands into other areas of life.

4. The client is pulled toward emotional engagement with the larger society.

5. The client becomes emotionally involved in life.

Like previous writers, Frank stressed the role of the relationship and of cognitive insight in eliciting change.

The therapist must empathize with the client and persist in trying to help through difficult times. Some therapists may find it disconcerting that Frank describes cognitive insight in terms of a myth that explains the behavior. This myth must be consistent with the culture of the client: thus, in mainstream U.S. culture, panic attacks may be attributed to irrational cognitive cycles, whereas in other cultures, panic attacks might be attributed to demonic possession. The key factors are that the cognitive input comes from someone whom clients trust; that they gain a new understanding; and that the input is both socially acceptable and acceptable to the particular client.

Frank also commented that sessions must be emotionally arousing in order to produce change, although he was unclear about the specific role that emotions play. Finally, he insisted that clients' positive expectation of therapy—their faith in therapy—is fundamental to change. Client confidence is reinforced by the locale, which presents the therapist as a skilled helper.

Thus, the studies we have reviewed so far suggest that effective therapy should include the following features: a therapeutic relationship, cognitive insight, emotional arousal, and positive client expectations.

Strupp (1973) concluded that the factor that bonds the various styles of psychotherapy is the therapeutic relationship—an "emotionally charged affectional relationship" (p. 6). To be effective, therapy cannot be a stale intellectual exercise; the client's emotions must be engaged.

Garfield returned in 1974 and stressed the role of the therapeutic relationship and of cognitive insight in the change process. Like Frank, Garfield (1974) also noted that successful therapy is dependent upon the client's positive expectations. Client expectations of psychotherapy have increasingly been recognized in the literature as an important process variable.

Applebaum (1978) suggested six necessary conditions for change.

1. Explanation
2. Therapeutic relationship
3. Client expectations
4. Corrective emotional experience
5. Emotional release
6. An altered state of consciousness

We are already familiar with the first five factors. The last variable is new. The role of an altered state of consciousness may be readily apparent with some techniques—for example, hypnosis, meditation, progressive relaxation, systematic desensitization, and imagery. This subjective variable may also be associated with the emotional aspects of the process and the therapeutic relationship.

Goldfried (1980) suggested two common process variables: "(a) providing the patient/client with new, corrective experiences, and (b) offering the patient/client direct feedback" (p. 994).

After his famed dodo bird review of the literature (Luborsky, Singer, & Luborsky, 1975), Luborsky returned to the scene in 1984, with the statement that there are three *central curative factors* or process variables underlying change: self-understanding, a helping alliance, and the incorporation of gains. The third variable is necessary because cognitive understanding is not enough for behavioral change: clients must utilize their new insight to foster change.

Recently, Torrey (1986) identified four common process variables of psychotherapy, which he claims also underlie the effectiveness of the shaman or witchdoctor:

1. A shared worldview between therapist and client. Any worldview will do; it can be articulated in terms of irrational thoughts, oedipal concerns, or demonic possession.
2. Personal qualities of the therapist. Torrey emphasizes the Rogerian qualities of the therapeutic relationship.
3. Expectations and emotional arousal.
4. A sense of mastery.

As we have seen, the theory that common process variables underlie the various therapies is not new. However, as relevant research data become more available and as therapists come to terms with the demands of increased accountability in a managed health care environment, the importance of process variables in therapists' training and practice is finally gaining wider recognition.

FOUR PROCESS VARIABLES OF THERAPY

Most of the authors reviewed in the previous section concluded that at least four process variables are necessary for change: (a) a therapeutic relationship; (b) cognitive insight; (c) affective experience; and (d) appropriate client expectations. The remainder of this chapter presents a brief discussion of these four process variables.

The Therapeutic Relationship

Numerous theorists have contended that the therapeutic relationship is the major reason people change in counseling and psychotherapy. However, books on the various approaches to counseling and psychotherapy focus on techniques specific to that style of therapy and often take for granted the importance of the therapeutic relationship. Nevertheless, therapists from all three major camps have noted the key role of this process variable.

Despite the stereotype that cognitive therapists create a dictatorial relationship, Beck, Rush, Shaw, and Emery (1979) note that "the cognitive therapist applies the specific techniques in the context of a particular kind of interpersonal relationship" (p. 45). Specifically, Beck et al. suggest that the cognitive therapist must be able to provide the Rogerian conditions of warmth, accurate empathy, and genuineness.

A stereotype regarding psychodynamic therapists is that they are aloof and distant and that, like a plumber, they adopt a mechanical this-piece-fits-that-piece approach. Nevertheless, hidden within Freud's 24-volume search for the "gold of interpretation" are his comments on the role of the therapeutic relationship. Indeed, Freud (1912/1990b) described the unconditional conditions and friendly aspects of transference as the "vehicle of success in psychoanalysis exactly as it is in other methods of treatment" (p. 105). Other psychoanalytic authors have noted the role of the therapeutic alliance as the key process variable in their practice (Greenson, 1965/1990c; Kohut, 1984/1990; Zetzel, 1956).

Perhaps Freud's emphasis on the therapeutic relationship was lost in the English translation (Bettelheim, 1982). Perhaps Freud, the man, was overly mechanistic (Lewis, 1981). Or perhaps the history of psychoanalysis prefigures what is now occurring in the field of mental health as a whole.

Alexander (1935) chastised the proponents of the various schools of psychoanalysis for their bickering and their neglect of the common elements of psychoanalysis (catharsis, intellectual insight, and the appearance of repressed childhood memories). He accused the diverse analytic theorists of not giving due attention to the fundamentals of change. Alexander hinted in his essay that some analysts were failing to integrate the common elements and were placing too much emphasis on one element (for example, intellectual insight) in an attempt to create something new. Sound familiar?

The experiential therapists—Gestalt therapists (Polster & Polster, 1973; Zinker, 1977) and existential therapists (Laing, 1967; May, 1975)—have consistently noted the critical role of the therapeutic relationship. The writings and teachings of Carl Rogers are central to the literature on the therapeutic relationship.

Rogers's three conditions of change. Carl Rogers (1980) has gained notoriety in the mental health field for his insistence that there are three necessary and sufficient conditions for fostering change in therapy: the genuineness of the therapist, empathic understanding, and unconditional positive regard. According to Rogers, if the therapist is able to embody these three conditions in therapy, the client then spontaneously makes positive changes.

In his first condition, genuineness of the therapist—also referred to as *realness* or *congruence*—Rogers was reacting against the old surgeon/patient type of relationship, in which the therapist was a distant, matter-of-fact expert. Rogers suggests that the effective therapist does not hide behind a veil of professionalism. Therapists are themselves; they are real in the relationship.

Congruence also means that the counselor's thoughts, feelings, and behaviors are consistent. Rogers commented that therapists must be aware of their own feelings in the therapy hour; these feelings, even if negative, can be used in a positive manner. Rogers noted that, when the therapist is feeling annoyed or bored, "it is preferable for the counselor to be real than to put up a façade of interest and concern and liking which he does not feel" (Rogers & Stevens, 1967, p. 91). This does not imply that therapists should always blurt out their feelings; rather, therapists need to attend to their feelings and to express them whenever it is appropriate. This idea has been incorporated more recently in the concept of countertransference (Epstein & Feiner, 1983; Gorkin, 1987).

To be genuine is an overall attitude toward life. It is a willingness to be transparent, to be able to take risks and to not hide behind a shield of techniques. The therapist who is being real is not trying to fix someone. If a therapist can be genuine, then all the other factors of therapy can perhaps fall into place. "I have sometimes wondered if this is the only quality which matters in a counseling relationship" (Rogers & Stevens, 1967, p. 92).

Rogers's second necessary condition is for the therapist to be empathic. Empathy is the ability to sense the private world of another. The essence of an empathic moment is captured in a picture reproduced by Allport (1937): in the picture, a pole vaulter is barely clearing the pole; the onlookers are lifting their own legs as if to clear the bar themselves. It is this as-if quality of the therapeutic relationship that is so important for therapists. What the therapist experiences is not exactly the same as what the client experiences. It is this as-if quality of the relationship—this ability to keep the boundaries intact—that enables therapists to be of help. Counselors in this mode are attempting to find within themselves what the client is experiencing at that moment.

Rogers's third condition of effective therapy is for the therapist to provide unconditional positive regard. He also referred to this as acceptance, caring, or prizing. It is an acceptance of the other as a complete person. For example, therapists are well on their way to being genuine, empathic, and accepting when they fully appreciate, in a nondefensive manner, that clients are at times angry with therapists for not fixing them.

Rogers's three conditions of the therapeutic relationship have been accepted as core conditions for change in many therapeutic approaches. The reader is referred to Rogers's (1951a) book *Client-Centered Therapy*, which provides a humane and practical account of the supportive relationship in fostering change in therapy.

Experiential and collaborative aspects of the therapeutic relationship. This section on the therapeutic relationship was included for the following reasons: for the reader to gain at least an elementary experiential definition of a therapeutic relationship and to define the role of the *collaborative* relationship as a key component of the therapeutic relationship. A therapeutic relationship begins to emerge when a client feels understood. I have had clients tell me behaviorally and explicitly after the initial session that someone finally understands what is going on with them. By this, they mean emotional rather than cognitive understanding. If clients do not believe that you understand their predicament, the sessions may become stale and full of conflict.

Clients feel safe when an emotional holding environment develops in the therapist's office. Clients can tell the therapist things about themselves that they have never told anyone. Think of the numerous clients who come into a therapist's office and report an incident of sexual abuse that they had never mentioned to anyone before. Think of the clients who say that they never show their emotions but then break down in tears in the therapist's office.

These are the rich times of counseling and psychotherapy. Clients are able to say things in the therapist's office that they could not previously admit to themselves. On such occasions, the therapist is trusted even more than clients trust themselves. In time, clients are able to internalize this relationship and trust their own thoughts, feelings, and behaviors.

The therapeutic relationship matures from a sense of acceptance to a stage of mutual exploration. Even Rogers (1951a) noted the natural evolution from the holding environment that the therapist provides initially to a collaborative relationship.

> In the emotional warmth of the relationship with the therapist, the client begins to experience a feeling of safety as he finds that whatever attitude he expresses is understood in almost the same way that he perceives it, and is accepted. He then is able to explore. (p. 41)

Only when clients believe and feel that they are understood will they begin to take the risk of exploration.

In this stage of exploration, the therapist and client work together as a team. Horney (1942), in her pragmatic approach to psychoanalysis, wrote of the collaborative relationship between client and therapist:

> Psychoanalysis in its very essence is co-operative work, both patient and analyst bent on understanding the patient's difficulties. The latter tries to lay himself open to the analyst and, as we have seen, the analyst observes, tries to understand, and, if appropriate, conveys his interpretation to the patient . . . And as long as such a co-operative spirit prevails it is comparatively easy for the analyst to understand the patient and to convey to him his findings. (p. 138)

When the therapist actively listens, client resistance lessens. The client becomes more active and verbal. The collaborative relationship matures.

All the leading styles of therapy now have an appreciation of the first process variable, the therapeutic relationship. However, the various approaches do not agree on the role of the second process variable, cognitive insight.

Cognitive Insight and Change

Do clients require some type of new understanding—some insight—as a necessary condition to change? The psychoanalytic and cognitive camps would readily answer yes; although their interpretations differ.

Freud regarded insight as a necessary condition of psychoanalysis. No psychoanalysis could be complete without the "pure gold of analysis, interpretation" (Freud, 1919/1955b, p. 22). Sifneos (1987), a contemporary short-term dynamic therapist, makes a similar assertion.

> Problem solving [interpretation] has been repeatedly mentioned by our patients as having been a crucial aspect of their STAPP [short-term anxiety-provoking psychotherapy] . . . contrary to the

belief by some investigators that nonspecific factors such as empathy and support are the only effective therapeutic components
of psychotherapy. (p 149)

As its name implies, cognitive therapy identifies cognition, in which
the client gains new insight into his or her life, as the primary change agent.

However, Carl Rogers's (1957) client-centered approach asserts that
the communication of genuine warmth, empathy, and unconditional positive regard by the therapist are necessary and sufficient conditions for the
client to change. Rogers denies that cognition within the therapy hour is
necessary for effective therapy.

Is it part of the therapist's role to help clients gain a new insight into
their problem? Or is it enough to provide Rogers's three conditions of a
supportive relationship? All therapists must address these questions. As
we have seen, many process-variable theorists believe that some form of
client insight is necessary for change. What matters, from a process-variable
viewpoint, is not the content of the insight but the client's belief that the
new perception can help resolve his or her problems. Current empirical
literature on cognitive insight as a process variable of change is reviewed
in Chapter 6.

Emotions in Therapy

Counseling and psychotherapy are, by their nature, emotional experiences.
Emotions are the fuel for change, as Freud (1913/1958a) noted: "The
primary motive force in the therapy is the patient's suffering and wish to
be cured that arises from it" (p. 143). Emotional (affective) experience is
a third process variable common to all forms of counseling.

Clients usually enter therapy because they are hurting. They feel
confused and alone; nobody seems to understand. They want someone to
help make the pain go away. Without emotional understanding, clients
continue to feel "empty, confused, and often fragmented [and they will
not have] the impetus from the action tendencies to motivate action"
(Greenberg & Safran, 1989, p. 720). When therapists evade their clients'
emotions, it only adds to their clients' suffering. But, by providing a secure
and safe environment in which feelings may be expressed, therapists
supply the much-needed motivation for change.

Of course, emotional sessions can take a toll on the therapist. "The
work itself is draining . . . There is an affective participation that can mean
that every therapy session is an emotional experience" (Welt & Herron,
1990, p. 38). When therapists are genuine, they are actively involved in the
sessions. Some sessions can bring a therapist to life; others are exhausting.

All of the major approaches to counseling respect the necessity of
emotions in therapy. "Even the last bastion of the emphasis on the rational

in interpretation, Albert Ellis's theory, has moved toward the affect and signals this in its name change from *Rational Therapy* to *Rational-Emotive Therapy*" (Hammer, 1990, p. 19).

Client Expectations

The role of the client's expectations in effective therapy is the fourth factor common to all styles. The client who comes to therapy with few misconceptions and much hope has a much better prognosis than someone who is sent to therapy by court order or someone who demands to be fixed right away. The client who has realistic expectations of what to expect from therapy is more likely to change. The client who trusts the therapist and accepts the therapist's competence is more likely to change. The client who is hopeful is more likely to change.

However, many clients bring a number of misconceptions about therapy to their first session. Some believe that the therapist is going to tell them what is wrong with them and will fix them, as in the physician/patient relationship that they are used to. Some clients seeing a cognitive therapist may expect to lay on a couch and to talk of childhood memories. Some clients going to see a psychodynamic or experiential therapist may be distraught at the lack of input from the therapist. Many people seeking counseling for the first time fear that they will become a totally different person whom friends and relatives won't know. Others expect the therapist to completely change their lives; they want to become totally different people.

People have different expectations regarding the length of treatment. Some expect one, maybe two sessions. Others expect that effective therapy will take years. Some people sabotage their therapy at the very beginning because they secretly think they must be crazy to see a therapist. Honest clients will sometimes admit that they do not want to tell the therapist what they truly think and feel, because they fear that their therapists may hospitalize them. A few people silently believe that therapy makes people crazy and makes them commit suicide: "Pastor Smith went to see a shrink and he killed himself."

Such misconceptions of therapy may reflect people's personalities. Therapists can try to address them in an educational manner, so as to allow the work of therapy to go forward. Certainly, clients' expectations regarding therapy—not least their faith in its effectiveness—have an impact on how much they will change.

SUMMARY

Research has not substantiated any of the claims that one style of therapy is more effective than another. Following Rosenzweig's introduction of the dodo bird's verdict in 1936, numerous theorists have suggested that certain process variables are common to the various approaches and may be necessary conditions for change in therapy. Four process variables were considered in this chapter: (a) a therapeutic relationship; (b) client expectations; (c) cognitive insight; and (d) an affective experience. Most writers affiliated with the three main styles of therapy have at least recognized the necessity of these four factors in therapy.

Given that there is empirical support for the efficacy of therapy and for the dodo bird's verdict, does research support the idea that these four common process variables are key factors of change in counseling and psychotherapy? The following chapter is a synopsis of research on these four process variables.

CHAPTER SIX

RESEARCH ON PROCESS VARIABLES

I never had time to look at things, Mac, never. I never looked how leaves come out. I never looked at the way things happen . . . just once in a while you get that feeling—I never look at anything. I never take time to see anything.

(STEINBECK, 1936/1986B, P. 339)

Students in mental health frequently begin their training with a fresh outlook on the practice of therapy. As a field of change, we need to embrace the enthusiastic eyes of newcomers to the field.

All to often, however, training programs neglect and deaden these fresh viewpoints, which have the potential to mature into sound therapeutic skills. In many training programs, students are expected to learn an abundance of techniques. The client—the person—gets lost. Beutler (1986) commented:

> It has always intrigued me that although over 80% of the literature on psychotherapy theory is devoted to specific technologies and procedures, most of the effectiveness of psychotherapy can be attributed to factors that are common across approaches and that characterize most effective therapists and treatable conditions. Indeed, Lambert and DeJulio (1978) as well as Shapiro and Shapiro (1982) have suggested that only 10–15% of the variation in outcome can be attributed to specific approaches. Hence, over 80% of the literature is devoted to focusing on 10% of change. (p. 94)

These numbers are astounding! Plainly, many books and training programs overemphasize specific techniques at the expense of the common process variables of change.

Research on process variables is relatively new. "The empirical study of the psychotherapeutic process is a young discipline, primarily spanning the last 30 years" (Marmar, 1990, p. 265). However, in that 30 years a vast amount of research has accumulated. That information can be of great value, as Goldfried (1980) points out.

> To the extent that clinicians of varying orientations are able to arrive at a common set of strategies, it is likely that what emerges will consist of robust phenomena, as they have managed to survive

the distortions imposed by the therapists' varying theoretical biases. (p. 996)

In this chapter, I review research on the four process variables considered in Chapter 5: (a) a therapeutic relationship, (b) client expectations, (c) cognitive insight, and (d) an affective (emotional) experience. Some theorists suggest that there are more, or less, primary process variables. I selected these four on the basis of my experiences to date and because they appear in the writings of numerous other authors.

Students and therapists stumble through countless books, lectures, and seminars on techniques. This chapter is intended to give the reader time to look at the process of therapy in a broader way.

THE THERAPEUTIC RELATIONSHIP

The empirical literature on process variables includes an abundance of research on the role of the therapeutic relationship in therapy. Reviewing 26 studies conducted between 1954 and 1974, Gurman (1977) found a positive correlation between a client's perception of the existence of a therapeutic relationship and the client's perception of a positive outcome. Review articles have consistently found support for the therapeutic relationship as a key process variable in therapy (Gurman & Razin, 1977; Lambert, DeJulio, & Stein, 1978).

In the following summary of the empirical literature many of the authors reflect a psychodynamic orientation. This is not due to bias in the presentation of the information. Rather, the bulk of the current research on the importance of the therapeutic relationship has been conducted by psychodynamic empiricists, as noted by Garfield (1986a).

However, this does not mean that there has been no research on the role of the therapeutic relationship in other modes of therapy. For example, although behavior therapy is sometimes stereotyped as insensitive to relationship variables, a literature review on the effectiveness of therapy reached the following conclusion:

> Not only can one find support for the importance of relationship factors in the dynamic therapies, but, as in the Cross and Sheehan (1982) report, even some literature on behavior therapy suggests the importance of these variables. Morris and Suckerman (1974a, 1974b, 1975) and Wolowitz (1975), for example, discussed the place of therapist warmth in behavioral desensitization. (Lambert, Shapiro, & Bergin, 1986, p. 172)

In this section, I review articles on the degree to which change can be credited to the therapeutic relationship; the differences between novice and expert therapists in the development of relationships; the development of a therapeutic relationship early in therapy; the role of a supportive relationship; and the importance of a collaborative relationship.

The Therapeutic Relationship and Variability of Outcome

A fair amount of the variability between therapy and outcome can be explained by the degree to which a therapeutic relationship is established. Research has found a .50 correlation between the degree of a therapeutic relationship and the outcome, which means that the relationship accounts for 25% of the variance of various outcome measures (Morgan, Luborsky, Crits-Christoph, Curtis, & Solomon, 1982). If there were a direct cause-effect association between the therapeutic relationship and outcome, then 100% of the variability of the outcome measure could be explained by the degree that an ideal therapeutic relationship has been developed. In the empirical literature, to explain 25% of a phenomenon is a profound finding.

A second study found that 30–46% of the variance in outcome could be attributed to the degree that a client perceived that a relationship had been established by the second or third session (Greenberg & Webster, 1982). Reviewing 1,100 research findings on process variables, Orlinsky and Howard (1986) reported: "Not surprisingly, the overall quality of the therapeutic bond or alliance also was found to be consistently associated with good outcome" (p. 366), regardless of whether the outcome was evaluated by the client, the therapist, or an observer. The bottom line from the review literature is that, if a therapeutic relationship is achieved, then therapy is more likely to be a success.

Readers who seek a more intensive analysis can turn to numerous articles on the development of various contemporary measures of the therapeutic alliance (Alexander & Luborsky, 1986; Hartley & Strupp, 1983; Horvath & Greenberg, 1989; Marmar, Horowitz, Weiss, & Marziali, 1986).

There is ample research indicating that a therapeutic relationship is a necessary component of change. What is it about the therapeutic relationship that induces change? Research findings also address that question.

Experts versus Nonexperts

A rather intriguing area of process research compares the ability of experts and nonexperts to develop a therapeutic relationship.

In 1950, Fiedler conducted an experiment in which he compared the effectiveness of therapists of differing approaches but also of therapists with varying abilities to develop an ideal relationship with their clients.

The therapeutic relationship may be primarily a function of the theory and method which the therapist utilizes (this is the prevailing professional opinion), or it may be a function of the therapist's expertness. If, as this writer and others believe (for example, Shoben, 1949), the therapeutic relationship is the core of therapy, then we must expect that good therapists of any school will create an essentially similar relationship and that their relationships will differ less among each other than with the less expert within their own school. (Fiedler, 1950b, p. 436)

This fascinating study has a fair amount of internal and external validity, even by today's standards.

Specifically, Fiedler's hypotheses were that: (1) therapists who were considered experts in their field would develop similar forms of therapeutic relationships with clients; and (2) the difference in the therapeutic relationships formed by experts and nonexperts of the same orientation would be greater than the difference between the relationships formed by experts of different orientations. This second hypothesis echoes the dodo bird's cry.

Fiedler's study included therapists from the three popular schools of his day: psychoanalytic, nondirective, and Adlerian. Adlerian therapy is a directive form of intervention, in contrast to the other two schools. Fiedler's selection of experts in the three schools was based on the therapists' national reputation in that particular style of therapy. He did not clarify where the nonexpert therapists came from.

Sessions were electrically recorded (remember this was 1950), and four judges rated the tapes on 75 statements regarding the therapeutic relationship, by the Q-sort technique. Three judges were representatives from the three styles of therapy, and the fourth judge had no therapy training or experience. One of the items in the Q-sort was, for example, "The therapist usually maintains rapport with the patient."

Fiedler (1950a) found that expert therapists, no matter what their orientation, came closer to an ideal therapeutic relationship than did nonexperts. This finding is not remarkable.

The second finding of the study was that experts of seemingly contradictory orientations (directive and nondirective) create relationships that are more alike than experts and nonexperts within their own approach! However, the writings of the various schools describe the development of a therapeutic relationship in very different terms. A possible conclusion from this study is that therapists who are good at what they do learn to attend to the development of a therapeutic relationship.

What is this ideal relationship that Fiedler proposed? Fiedler (1951) noted

the greater ability of the expert to understand the feelings of the patient, his greater security in the therapeutic situation, and his capacity to show interest and warmth *without becoming overly involved* with the patient. [emphasis added] (Fiedler, 1951, p. 37)

Barrett-Lennard (1962) also compared experts and nonexperts on the degree of attainment of a therapeutic relationship. However, whereas observers rated the attainment of a therapeutic relationship in Fiedler's experiment, the clients and the therapists were the raters in the later study. Also, an outcome measure was implemented after only five sessions.

Barrett-Lennard found, even after only five sessions, that the expert therapists were significantly more skillful at developing a therapeutic relationship than nonexpert therapists. Clients of expert therapists also tended to score higher on the outcome measure.

These findings are unremarkable. Most people in the field would expect expert therapists to be more proficient in developing a therapeutic relationship and to foster therapeutic gains. However, another finding of this study is more interesting: the correlation between relationship and outcome was significantly more pronounced when the therapeutic relationship was rated from the client's perspective rather than from the therapist's perspective. Therapists' impressions are not the best gauge of whether a positive therapeutic relationship has developed.

This conclusion was supported in a recent review article by Horvath and Symonds (1991), who did a meta-analysis of 24 studies that had used one particular measure of the therapeutic relationship, the Working Alliance Inventory. They found, on the basis of a wide variety of outcome assessments, that client and observer ratings of a working relationship were more predictive of outcome than were therapist ratings. It is the clients' perceptions of the relationship that are critical to the outcome, not the therapists' perceptions of the relationship.

Mallinckrodt and Nelson (1991) compared therapists of three different levels of training in terms of their ability to develop a therapeutic relationship. The study was based on the writings of Bordin (1979), in which therapists and clients assessed the therapeutic relationship by completing the Working Alliance Inventory and rated the bond, task, and goal dimensions of the alliance.

A major difference from the Fiedler (1950a) study is that the expertness of the therapists was concretely defined in terms of their degree of training: (a) novices who were in their first practicum; (b) advanced trainees in their second practicum; and (c) experienced therapists and postdoctoral staff. A second major difference from the Fiedler study is that the more refined measure of the therapeutic relationship offered a stronger possibility of finding differences along one of the three dimensions of the therapeutic alliance.

The study found that there was no significant difference between the three levels of training groups on the ability to develop a bond. However, therapists at higher levels of training scored significantly higher on the task and goal dimensions.

> In relation to experienced counselors, trainees seem best able to form bonds but least able to set treatment goals or perform in-session tasks to achieve those goals. Thus some trainees may be able to offer necessary but not sufficient conditions for successful therapy. Perhaps teaching students, even earlier in their training than is common practice, to articulate a personal theory of counseling that guides case conceptualization, guides selection of treatment goals, and directs the tasks of counseling may help to significantly improve trainees' therapeutic alliances. (Mallinckrodt & Nelson, 1991, p. 137)

As we noted in Chapter 2, learning specific techniques is only one aspect of the development of an orientation. The importance of a theoretical leaning is that it helps therapists to not feel so overwhelmed by the volume of information that confronts them and to have some structure that may assist in the development of a therapeutic relationship.

We have already seen that the development of a therapeutic relationship early in therapy may be a necessary condition for effective therapy. To explore that issue further, let's examine the findings of studies conducted early in the treatment process.

Early Alliance and Outcome

Therapists I have been supervising have sometimes said to me, "I am working on the development of a relationship." I take this to mean that the therapist is adopting a passive form of supportive therapy, whether it be appropriate for a particular client or not. The underlying message is that, once the therapist has been supportive enough with a client, the client will make the expected changes.

The risk of assuming a passive role is that the sessions may become stale; there may be little change. Indeed, a constructive relationship may never develop.

Research data indicate that a therapeutic relationship must form in the early stages if therapy is to be effective. In the previous section, I noted a study that found a positive correlation between the development of a positive therapeutic relationship by the fifth session and eventual positive outcome (Barrett-Lennard, 1962). In a more recent study of 73 clients, statements from 10 clients who had improved the most and from 10 clients who had improved the least were used in the development of a relationship measure, the Penn Helping Alliance Rating Method (Morgan, Luborsky, Crits-Christoph, Curtis, & Solomon, 1982). The findings generally showed a positive correlation between the relationship and outcome measures.

Where present, the therapeutic relationship appeared in the early stages of the process.

> The helping alliance was already present at sessions 3 and 5 and showed a modest degree of consistency in the early and late sessions. We do not know whether it is regularly evident in sessions 1 and 2 as well, or whether it formed at the patient's first sight of the therapist. For some patients, the alliance seemed to begin as soon as the patient and therapist met. (Morgan et al., 1982, p. 400)

Another finding was that, for the group of clients who improved most, the collaborative relationship tended to develop further as the sessions progressed.

Thus, these studies suggest that the development of a therapeutic relationship early in therapy is a necessary condition for a successful outcome. If a therapeutic relationship does not emerge early, the therapist may be working with someone who suffers from a long-standing personality disorder. In an intensive analysis of two clients in therapy, one who had a successful outcome and one who did not, Strupp (1980b) reached a similar conclusion:

> Results showed that the outcome of psychotherapy depends markedly on the patient's ability to form a productive working relationship with the therapist early in therapy. Conversely, deep-seated characterological problems, manifesting themselves particularly in negativism, hostility, and other resistances, may give rise to insurmountable barriers resulting in negative therapeutic outcomes. (p. 708)

The client may be chronically unable to develop relationships or to trust others. Therapists need to be aware of these possibilities.

However, this does not mean that the development of a therapeutic relationship depends solely on the client. Therapists can take steps to foster a trusting and collaborative relationship early in therapy. How the therapist approaches the client, particularly in the first sessions, partially determines whether a constructive relationship develops. What questions the therapist asks during the initial assessment; how the therapist goes about developing treatment goals with the client; how the therapist deals with emotions; how active the therapist is; and how flexible the therapist is—all of these factors have an impact on the emergence of the therapeutic relationship. The final chapters of this book focus on the development of a therapeutic relationship.

The Supportive Relationship

Two important aspects of the therapeutic relationship are now considered: the supportive relationship, which embodies Rogers's conditions of change—empathy, genuineness, and unconditional positive regard (or warmth); and the collaborative relationship in which the therapist and the client are working together as a team. In the next section, I review the literature on the collaborative relationship. First, I briefly review the empirical data on the supportive relationship.

Most graduate students are still keenly aware of Rogers's necessary and sufficient conditions of change, even though they were first introduced four decades ago. Rogers's long life in the literature may be partially attributed to the fact that he was himself an empiricist. Thanks to the research conducted on Rogers's three conditions of change, particularly during the 1960s, they are now familiar to therapists of all orientations.

There is ample empirical support for Rogers's three conditions (Braaten, 1961; Patterson, 1974; Tomlinson & Hart, 1962; Truax & Carkhuff, 1964; Truax et al., 1966; Whitehorn & Betz, 1954). These studies have been conducted in a number of settings, with therapists of differing levels of training, and with a variety of populations. One study, with resident psychiatrists as therapists, concluded

> that high levels of therapeutic conditions [empathy, genuineness, and warmth] not only tend to produce a greater degree of patient improvement but also seem to be an important factor in minimizing patient deterioration during psychotherapy: 50% of the patients treated by therapists offering relatively low conditions showed no change or deterioration, while only 10% of the patients receiving relatively high levels of conditions showed no change or deterioration on the patient global improvement scale. This latter finding is consistent with the hypothesis that psychotherapy can be for better or for worse, depending upon the levels of conditions provided during treatment. (Truax et al., 1966, p. 399)

However, a number of studies found no relationship between a supportive relationship (embodying Rogers's three conditions of change) and outcome (Bergin & Suinn, 1975; Beutler, Johnson, Neville, & Worman, 1972; Chinsky & Rappaport, 1970; Garfield & Bergin, 1971; Gormally & Hill, 1974; Mullen & Abeles, 1971; Shapiro, 1976). It now appears that to provide a supportive environment is necessary but not sufficient for change to occur. *"The recent evidence, although equivocal, does seem to support that empathy, warmth, and genuineness are related in some way to client change, but their potency and generalizability are not as great as some thought"* (Mitchell, Bozart, & Krauft, 1977, p. 483).

A supportive relationship appears to be necessary for change, but it is not enough (Hill & Corbett, 1993).

The Collaborative Relationship

Rather than overwhelm the reader with the profusion of research on the association between a collaborative relationship and outcome, I will focus on the major findings of Orlinsky and Howard's (1986) review of the literature. This account at least provides a springboard from which the more zealous reader can explore the original studies.

Orlinsky and Howard (1986) reported that situations in which the therapist encouraged client independence were associated with a positive outcome (across a variety of outcome measures) in 64% of 11 studies they reviewed. By contrast, none of the studies found a significant association between therapist directiveness and outcome. A weakness of these studies is that the therapist's degree of directiveness or collaboration was based on therapist ratings. That is, the therapists rated themselves on whether they were directive or collaborative. The validity of these studies is open to doubt, since therapists may not be the most reliable judges of their own behavior.

Therefore, Orlinsky and Howard also reviewed studies in which observers rated the degree to which therapists were directive or collaborative in their relationship with clients. In 17 distinct analyses, 65% of the findings supported a positive association between a collaborative relationship and outcome; none of the studies supported a directive relationship.

Finally, the review examined whether clients who are dependent on their therapist are more apt to change. Orlinsky and Howard reviewed 20 findings of studies that compared client dependency/collaboration (as the independent variable) and outcome (as the dependent variable). The 20 different comparisons varied on who rated the independent variable, the client's dependency (therapist-rated, client-rated, or observer-rated measures), and on the type of dependent variable, the outcome (therapist-rated, client-rated, observer-rated, or objective measures). Across these highly discrepant measures, 65% of the findings favored client collaboration; none of the studies favored client dependency.

The evidence is in: there is strong, consistent support for the role of a collaborative relationship between therapist and client in facilitating a successful outcome. This does not exclude the therapist's contribution as an expert in the field nor the importance of the therapist's active participation.

Overly directive therapists risk a lonely journey; their frustration is that their clients do not adhere to their directives. Their clients feel alone, because directive therapists do not seem to understand. Likewise, overly passive therapists risk a lonely journey; their frustration is that they must wait for their clients. Clients of passive therapists feel alone, because they are waiting for their therapists. In a collaborative relationship, when two people work together, they are no longer alone.

Summary

Research shows that there is a strong correlation between the attainment of a therapeutic relationship and a positive outcome. Experts—therapists with experience—tend to be more adept at developing a therapeutic relationship than nonexperts. It appears from the research that a supportive relationship is a necessary, but probably not a sufficient, condition for effective counseling and psychotherapy. Finally, an overwhelming number of studies have found a positive correlation between the attainment of a collaborative relationship and a positive outcome.

Research confirms that the therapeutic relationship is a fundamental process variable of counseling and psychotherapy.

POSITIVE CLIENT EXPECTATIONS

Even as early as 1963, Friedman suggested that the reason why the comparative literature had found no differences in efficacy between the various styles of therapy was because of a key process variable—client expectations.

> The consistent finding of lack of over-all differences in improvement rates of different therapies may be due to failure to understand adequately and take into account changes produced by the factor common to all therapies—the patient's expectancy that the treatment will help him. Any situation which mobilizes this expectancy may be capable of reducing his symptom intensity. Relief of this sort would be immediate and, with some patients, lasting. (Friedman, 1963, p. 66)

The role of client expectations in therapy is hard to deny.

> Because of certain properties of all therapeutic relationships, the therapist inevitably exerts a strong influence on the patient. This influence arises primarily from the patient's hope or faith that treatment will relieve his distress. This favorable expectation is strengthened by cultural factors, aspects of the referral or intake process, cues in the therapy situation which indicate that hope will be forthcoming, and the therapist's own confidence in his ability to help, springing from his training and his methods. (Frank, 1959, p. 37)

Of course clients' expectations have an impact on the effectiveness of therapy. I still do not like to work with court-ordered individuals who only want to serve their time with me. I prefer people who come voluntarily to my office and ask for help with their emotional pain.

As we saw in Chapter 1, the client's expectations of therapy can put the therapist in a position of considerable power. Therapists must be aware of the possibility of abusing that power.

Patients entering psychotherapy have various degrees of belief in its efficacy . . . We know that the authoritarian attitude of the physician can produce this conviction in some patients. (Rosenthal & Frank, 1956, p. 296)

Before I review some of the studies on client expectancy, it is appropriate to introduce a brief commentary on a related area—premature termination.

Premature Termination

We would expect that, when clients are not motivated or have misconceptions about therapy, they would be apt to drop out of counseling and psychotherapy prematurely. In practice, a large percentage of a therapist's clients choose premature termination. A study conducted during the 1950s found that 30–65% of clients drop out of therapy prematurely (Frank, Gliedman, Imber, Nash, & Stone, 1957). The situation has not changed that much over the years.

In a more recent review of the literature on clients' continuation in therapy, Garfield (1986b) concluded that the median length of treatment tends to be 3–12 sessions; the average is 6 sessions. That may not seem alarming, in light of the recent increase in short-term therapy. However, Garfield (1986b) commented that, in most of the 18 studies reviewed, this brevity of treatment was not planned.

> Contrary to many traditional expectations concerning length of therapy, *most clinic clients remain in therapy for only a few interviews*. In practically all of the clinics studied, this pattern was viewed as a problem and was not the result of a deliberately planned brief therapy, even in clinics that rely on brief therapy. Rather, in most instances, the patient failed to return for a scheduled appointment. (p. 219)

In one study reviewing the records of 17 community mental health facilities, 40.8% of clients failed to return after the initial interview (Sue, McKinney, & Allen, 1976)! A recent meta-analysis on therapy dropout rate concluded that 46.86% of clients prematurely terminate therapy (Wierzbicki & Pekarik, 1993).

Psychoanalysts generally meet with their patients over a number of years. What is their dropout rate? Aronson and Weintraub (1978) found that the premature termination rate of psychoanalysis is only 10–19%. They attributed this low dropout rate to intensive screening of patients and the patients' relatively high level of motivation.

Summarizing, research confirms that, when clients are not motivated or have misconceptions about therapy, they are apt to drop out of therapy prematurely.

Expectancy Studies

The lack of attention to the process variable of client expectations may partially account for the high premature termination rates in therapy. The research on client expectations may be divided into two basic categories. The first class of studies examines clients' level of motivation and their expectations of help. The idea is that clients who expect that therapy will help are more likely to benefit than are clients who are skeptical about counseling and psychotherapy. The second class of expectancy studies examines how educating clients about what to expect in therapy and socializing clients to therapy impacts attendance and therapeutic outcome.

In a critical review of the empirical literature on expectancy, Wilkins (1973) noted that

> expectancy of therapeutic gain has been treated as either (a) a trait characteristic of the attitude an individual brings into the therapy situation concerning how much benefit he will receive (expectancy trait) or (b) a state experimentally induced by instructions delivered to [subjects] about the effectiveness of the procedures to which they will be exposed. (pp. 69–70)

In the following two sections I review studies of client expectancy. I also include a third section on desensitization, because of the extensive debate in the literature on the role of client expectations in this intervention.

Expectations of help.   Considerable research on client expectations and therapy outcome appeared in the 1960s. When clients expect to be helped by therapy, are they more likely to report a reduction of symptoms or to perform better on posttests in comparison to clients who are skeptical about therapy? Yes. Studies based on a variety of outcome measures have indicated that clients who expect to get help from therapy are more likely to benefit (Friedman, 1963; Goldstein, 1960; Goldstein & Shipman, 1961; Tollinton, 1973).

However, not all studies agree. An experiment by Heine and Trosman (1960) did not find a positive correlation between the clients' expectations that therapy would help and outcome. What this study did find is that clients who expected a collaborative relationship were significantly more likely to benefit from therapy than were clients who expected a directive doctor/patient relationship.

Finally, some research suggests that individuals with lower socioeconomic status expect a doctor/patient relationship and that, because of these misconceptions, they do not benefit to the same degree as those with more appropriate expectations of therapy (Overall & Aronson, 1962).

The realization that many clients have misconceptions about therapy has prompted interest in the possibility of socializing clients to therapy—of explaining what to expect from therapy.

Socializing the client to therapy. During the 1960s, researchers began to examine whether clients of lower socioeconomic levels would have a better outcome in therapy if they were educated at the outset in what to expect from the process. It was believed that people from the middle and upper classes had an appropriate understanding of what therapy entailed. In this book, I will refer to such preparation as *socialization*.

In the original socialization study (Hoehn-Saric et al., 1964), the researchers prepared clients for therapy by means of a Role Induction Interview (RII).

> The RII, as it was carried out in this study, may be presumed to have had a variety of effects. (1) A rationale for psychotherapy was given to the patient. He was told in terms that he could compre-hend what to expect from his therapist and what would be expected of him . . . (2) The possibility of negative feelings about therapy was anticipated and explained . . . In this context the importance of regular attendance, especially at times when one is inclined not to come was emphasized. Not surprisingly, attendance discrimi-nates the experimental and control groups. To what degree atten-dance alone might have influenced outcome remains an open question. (3) Finally, the interview strongly communicated the expectation that the patient will improve with the type of treatment offered in four months. (pp. 276–277)

Overall, the literature suggests that socializing the client to therapy does not influence outcome directly, but rather operates as a mediator variable. For example, in many studies there is a significant difference between the experimental group (received socialization) and the control group (did not receive socialization) on outcome variables, but this difference may solely be due to the fact that the experimental group subjects had a greater attendance rate.

Even if socializing a client to therapy simply operates as a mediator variable, it still has a pronounced effect on outcome. One striking study found that the experimental group showed greater improvement than did the control group on 21 out of 23 outcome measures (Truax & Wargo, 1969)!

An interesting feature of the original Hoehn-Saric et al. (1964) study is that clients were told that they should expect improvement in four months. One possibility is that the experimental group showed more improvement in that study because the clients were told to expect improvement. In order to test this hypothesis, another study was conducted in which 36 clients were randomly assigned to four different treatment groups: (a) a control group with the usual referral process; (b) a group with the usual referral process who were told to expect improvement in four months; (c) a socialization group *without* the positive prognosis in four months; and (d) a socialization group who were also told to expect improvement in four months (Sloane, Cristol, Pepernik, & Staples, 1970).

This study found a slight improvement for the two socialized groups—in comparison to the two groups that did not receive socialization—on measures of social, sexual, and work adjustment. The key finding in this study concerned the effect of the prognosis.

> Suggestion that they would feel better in 4 months had no effect on outcome. Moreover, patients who received this suggestion were found by the therapists to be less likable than those who did not. (Sloane, Cristol, Pepernik, & Staples, 1970, p. 18)

Therefore, it appears that the key process variable is the socialization process rather than the making of prognoses.

A host of other studies have found that socializing clients to therapy has a positive impact on attendance and outcome measures (Bandura, Jeffrey, & Wright, 1974; Jacobs, Charles, Jacobs, Weinstein, & Mann, 1972; Strupp & Bloxom, 1973). Other studies have also found that periodically socializing the client—that is, socializing the client to therapy at intervals throughout therapy—has a positive impact (Eisenberg, 1981; Friedlander, 1981; Warren & Rice, 1972).

Finally, a study on socializing clients to group therapy did not find a significant effect on therapy outcome in comparison with a nonsocialized group (Piper, Debbane, Bienvenu, & Garant, 1982) but did find a significant and pronounced impact on attendance.

> The results also indicated that pretraining had a positive effect on attendance and possibly a positive effect on remaining. It will be contested here that the data about remaining represent a significant clinical effect, even if not a significant statistical effect. To experience two or three drop-outs out of seven or eight patients during the first four months of group therapy represents a serious clinical problem. To experience no drop-outs is rare. Yet one-half of the pretrained groups experienced no drop-outs. (p. 321)

The main therapeutic impact of socializing a client to therapy may be that it increases the likelihood that the client remains in therapy.

Systematic desensitization and expectations. Systematic desensitization is a technique developed on the basis of the principles of classical conditioning that is often used to reduce anxiety. Cognitive therapists have asked to what degree systematic desensitization is a result of the client's expectations. In a study by Wilson and Thomas (1973), one group of snake-fearful college students were told that systematic desensitization is "an established and highly successful method for the elimination of neurotic fears" (p. 282). A second group of subjects were informed that, "contrary to our expectations, studies we conducted the previous semester revealed our SSD [standardized systematic desensitization] procedure to be ineffective in reducing fears such as those we are currently studying" (p. 283). Under these conditions, subjects in the high-expectancy condition did show more improvement on self-ratings, but there was no significant difference on a behavior-avoidance test. Wilson and Thomas concluded that, since there was no significant difference between the groups on the behavioral measure, standardized systematic desensitization could not be attributed to expectancy on the part of the client.

However, reviewers of the research on systematic desensitization have not always been so kind. Among the least skeptical is Morgan (1973):

> While one cannot state that expectancy plays no role in the outcome of desensitization (one cannot affirm the null hypothesis), one can conclude that it most probably plays a minimal role at best in the achievement of obtained results. (p. 374)

By contrast, Lick and Bootzin (1975) concluded in their review article on expectancy factors in the treatment of fear that

> While methodological problems associated with subject variables, placebo credibility, and expectancy assessment make much of this research difficult to interpret, there are enough good studies to indicate that expectancy variables are important change mediators. (p. 928)

Finally, in a review article, Kazdin and Wilcoxin (1976) concluded, after considering possible methodological flaws of some studies, that systematic desensitization is based solely on the client's expectations of help.

> The few studies that do equalize client expectancy for success across conditions do not consistently support the efficacy of desensitization as having specific therapy components. In short, the present state of desensitization research allows for the rival interpretation that nonspecific treatment effects [process variables] rather than specific therapeutic ingredients account for change. Moreover, when this rival interpretation is ruled out, the evidence does not strongly support the efficacy of desensitization as a specific treatment strategy. (p. 753)

The essential point is that a client's expectations do have an impact on treatment, whether it be desensitization or psychoanalysis.

Summary

Clients who are motivated and have realistic expectations of what to expect from counseling and psychotherapy are more likely to benefit from therapy than are clients who are referred under duress and those who have misconceptions about the process. Research also indicates that socializing clients to therapy by explaining what to expect is a powerful intervention.

Socializing clients to therapy is probably a mediator variable, in that it fosters client participation and reduces premature dropout. However, simply telling clients that they will probably be doing better in time is not an effective form of socialization. Rather, socializing clients helps to eliminate a number of their misconceptions about the process of therapy. Chapter 9 provides a format for socialization that the therapist can adopt and adapt.

COGNITIVE INSIGHT

A third major process variable is cognitive insight. Many process-variable theorists have suggested that, if therapy is to be effective, clients must gain a new understanding of their condition. To provide such cognitive insight, therapists employ techniques including clarification, cognitive restructuring, confrontation, interpretation, reflection, and reframing. Does research confirm that these techniques are necessary for effective therapy?

In this book, I use the term *cognitive insight* to mean the act by which therapists provide the client with some information about his or her condition. In the empirical literature, this is usually called *interpretation*.

Definitions of Interpretation

Many therapists have the notion that interpretation is a psychoanalytic technique in which past-present links are made to foster further client understanding. In research, however, a more general definition of interpretation is adopted.

In a review article, Claiborn (1982) summarized the following definitions of interpretation in the empirical literature: direct input based on the therapist's theoretical position, anecdotes, metaphors, restatements, reflections, questions, and the Socratic method of leading the client. Indeed, all of these are methods for the therapist to offer new understanding to the client. They vary with respect to how directly the therapist offers this new understanding.

Even though the following information has been gleaned from the literature on interpretation, I prefer the term *cognitive insight*, which comfortably accommodates the variety of means by which the therapist may offer clients new information about themselves, as well as a wide range of content.

Direct Interpretation versus Reflection

Therapists may offer directive or nondirective interpretation. A directive interpretation might involve supplying information or commentary to the client, while a nondirective technique is, for example, to reflect back the client's feelings. Which of these techniques is more effective? As in the comparative literature on the efficacy of various forms of therapy, this research has found equivocal results.

A number of studies have found that reflection tends to be helpful, whereas questions and more direct forms of interpretations tend not to be (Frank & Sweetland, 1962; Kanfer, Phillips, Matarazzo, & Saslow, 1960; Snyder, 1945). An oft-cited study by Bergman (1951) concluded that reflection of feeling was significantly related to an increase in the positive aspects of therapy, whereas interpretation (such therapist responses as supplying information, stating conclusions about the material presented, and interposing the therapist's viewpoint) and structuring (in which the therapist described his or her theory of therapy or views on the therapist and client roles) were related to an increase in the negative aspects of counseling.

The results of this study were challenged by Claiborn (1982), who noted that Bergman "studied interpretation following client requests for evaluation or help; this sequence cast interpretations in the form of answers to client questions and, not surprisingly, closed off further discussion" (p. 441). In other words, Bergman's study was biased: given its design, interpretation would not be expected to lead to the client's continued self-exploration comments, which Bergman identified as the positive aspects of therapy, the dependent variable.

In a study similar to Bergman's, in which clients' responses to the therapist's comments were analyzed, the results were not so clear-cut. Frank and Sweetland (1962) found that, when therapists used clarification of feelings (a nondirective technique) and forcing insight (a technique similar to the more directive forms of cognitive therapy and short-term psychodynamic therapy), clients' understanding and insight responses markedly increased. If it is a goal of therapy for clients to obtain understanding about their condition, then this study indicates that both clarification of feelings and more directive forms of intervention are effective.

Auerswald (1974) compared restatement and interpretation. Restatement was defined as a paraphrase of the content of the client's statement, and interpretation as the therapist's expression of unverbalized client attitudes and of an alternative view of client problems. In this study, the dependent variable, the measure of change, was whether the client talked about his or her feelings following the therapist's restatement or interpretation.

The study found that restatement decreased the client's subsequent statements of feelings, whereas interpretation increased the client's statements of feelings. In other words, directive interpretation was more effective.

> In comparing restatement and interpretation, one aspect of their structures best explains their differential effect on affect. Restatement, in reiterating a portion of the client's previous response, in effect narrows the client's perceptions and offers no new data to his awareness. If he is not cognizant of or is denying his feelings, he can easily continue doing so if the counselor employs the restatement technique. Restatement demands that the counselor remain within the client's perceptual world. Interpretation, by comparison, opens new avenues to the client. (Auerswald, 1974, p. 14)

This conclusion is consistent with the hypotheses of this book. Cognitive insight is at least partially effective because it offers clients a new understanding of the predicament that has prevented them from getting on with their lives. Therapists' interventions of restatement may be more powerful in inducing change in the first few sessions, while interpretation may be more effective in the later sessions, after a supportive relationship has been established.

Auerswald (1974) contrasted "interpretation (a more difficult technique to master) . . . with restatement (a quickly learned and often used technique)" (p. 10). Indeed it does appear that interpretation is a difficult technique to master. In the previous section, we noted Mallinckrodt and Nelson's (1991) conclusion that, while therapists with varying degrees of training could establish a bonding relationship, therapists with more training and experience were more effective in developing the task and goal aspects of the therapeutic relationship.

In a 1982 review of varying therapist responses (advisements, interpretations, questions, reassurances, reflections, and self-disclosure) and their helpfulness, as perceived by the client and the therapist, "interpretations received the highest helpfulness ratings from both client and counselor. Advisements were rated as slightly more helpful than nonadvisements, and questions were rated as slightly less helpful than nonquestions" (Elliott, Barker, Caskey, & Pistrang, 1982, p. 354). In this context, interpretations meant providing the client with new information such as cause-effect relationships and labels. The client samples included analogue clients; that is, volunteers who underwent therapy purely for the purposes of the research.

Volunteer students were used in another study of helpful and nonhelpful events by Elliott (1985), who asked the students what responses they found to have been of benefit; 86 helpful and 70 nonhelpful counselor responses were identified. Cluster analysis of the data revealed two major superclusters that were characterized as beneficial—new perspective and understanding.

> Perspective cluster includes the psychodynamic notion of insight (Roback, 1974) as well as the contemporary notion of cognitive restructuring (e.g., Beck, Rush, Shaw, & Emery, 1979; Meichenbaum, 1977) . . . On the other hand, Understanding, the predominant Interpersonal cluster, corresponds to the client-centered empathy construct (e.g., Barrett-Lennard, 1981; Rogers, 1975). (Elliott, 1985, p. 318)

Note that, in this study, understanding means that clients feel understood by the therapist, not that they gain further understanding of their dilemma.

The conclusion of this study that both empathy and cognitive insight are powerful therapist variables is encouraging. Note, however, that numerous factors raise questions about the utility of Elliott's study. Most notably, it was an analogue study: the subjects were college students who were not active clients at a counseling center. Furthermore, the volunteers described what was and was not helpful after only one session with the therapist.

The intention of this brief review is not to wage again the old battle of directive versus nondirective counseling, Rogerian versus psychoanalytic, or reflection versus interpretation. Its main conclusion is that the comparative research data on these two techniques are equivocal.

Case Studies on Interpretation

Much of the research on interpretation (cognitive insight) has consisted of analogue studies, in which the clientele are undergraduate psychology volunteers. Analogue studies add much to our knowledge of the process of psychotherapy, but their external validity is weak. Perhaps in reaction, there has been a trend toward case studies with actual clients, which can provide an in-depth understanding of the process of counseling and psychotherapy. In their case study, Hill, Carter, and O'Farrell (1983) reviewed therapist responses over 12 sessions, which were audiotaped and then transcribed to written form for ease of rating. Three raters placed the therapist responses into 1 of 14 categories: "minimal encourager, silence, approval-reassurance, information, direct guidance, closed question, open question, restatement, reflection, interpretation, confrontation, nonverbal referent, self-disclosure, and other" (Hill et al., 1983, pp. 5–6). The raters achieved an agreement level of 80% on the placement of responses into categories. Therefore, if one judge believed the therapist made a particular response, there was a significant likelihood that the other two raters concurred.

Even within the confines of this single study, there were varying definitions of interpretation.

> In some interpretations, reasons were hypothesized for why the client behaved as she did within her context; others focused on the client's role in maintaining her conflicts; others made connections between various feelings and behaviors; and others connected present difficulties with past events. (Hill et al., 1983, p. 15)

If the therapist made a response that met this broad definition of interpretation, then it was categorized as an interpretation.

Four outcome measures were administered prior to therapy and at termination: Hopkins Symptom Checklist, Tennessee Self Concept Scale, Target Complaints, and a Likert scale of satisfaction with counseling. The Therapy Session Report was completed after each session by the client and by the therapist in order to obtain data on the "best" and "worst" sessions.

I will report only a few of the findings; the reader is referred to the original article for further details.

Hill et al. (1983) concluded "that interpretations were the most effective change agents" (p. 15). They consistently pointed out that their positive findings were within the context of a supportive style of treatment.

The authors of this study also made the following comments in regards to the content of their interpretations.

> Were the interpretations accurate or valid? Perhaps the absolute truth can never be determined. The most important issue seems to be that the client generally accepted them and was able to use them to change her behavior. (Hill et al., 1983, p. 15)

Once again, the content of the interpretation does not seem to be as important as the act of providing some cognitive input that the client otherwise was not aware of or dismissed.

A second case study of the same design strongly supported the conclusion that interpretations are a positive mechanism of change (O'Farrell, Hill, & Patton, 1986).

A weakness of case study research concerns the extent to which the findings can be generalized to a larger population—in the present context, to differing clients and to differing therapists. However, case studies are particularly useful in identifying areas for further research.

Interpretation as a Process Variable

As we have seen, a number of experimental, analogue, and case studies indicate that interpretation (cognitive insight) is an important process variable. However, other studies fail to substantiate its utility.

Another problem is that the degree of variability of outcome explained by the use of interpretation and other therapist responses is negligible, ranging from an all-time low of 1% (Hill, Helms, Spiegel, & Tichenor, 1988) to a high of less than 10% (Elliott, Barker, Caskey, & Pistrang, 1982). Even though the majority of process-variable theorists concur that some form of cognitive insight is a necessary condition for effective therapy, research does not always support this conclusion.

In reviewing the empirical literature on interpretation, it is an enormous task to compare the results of one study to another, because of the wildly different definitions of interpretation between and even within studies. Hopefully, as the quality and quantity of process-variable research increase, a more conclusive assessment of cognitive insight as a key variable of change will be possible.

Summary

Given the varying definitions of interpretation and the conflicting results in the empirical literature, the mechanism for cognitive insight in fostering change has yet to be established.

Claiborn (1982) listed three possible models that explain why cognitive insight is an important process variable for all forms of counseling: the relationship model, the discrepancy model, and the content model. Briefly, the relationship model argues that cognitive insight is a key process variable because it displays interest on the part of the therapist and is, in essence, a gift that the therapist provides to the client; this gift may foster further exploration by the client. The discrepancy model suggests that, by such methods as reframing, the therapist provides a different, more benign interpretation for the client's confusing and often chaotic behaviors, thoughts, and feelings. Finally, the content model attributes change to the specific wording of the therapist's interpretations. This model, if correct, would imply that different orientations would have different efficacy rates.

The role of cognitive insight as a process variable is still controversial. Claiborn's (1982) comments retain their force today:

> Interpretations differing greatly in content seem to have a comparable impact on clients. No one interpretive framework has proven superior to any other in promoting therapeutic processes, such as client exploration, or in leading to positive outcome, however that is assessed. Research indicates that providing the client with a new meaningful framework is more helpful than not doing so. Yet all counseling approaches supply the client with some discrepant meaning. Orientations differ only in the subtlety and indirectness of the counselor's discrepant communications. (pp. 450–451)

It does seem that all forms of therapy implement some type of interpretation (cognitive insight). A major difference of these approaches is in the directiveness with which the therapist provides new cognitions.

In a call for future researchers on interpretation to pay close attention to internal and external validity, Spiegel and Hill (1989) make an important point:

> We suggest that measuring and describing the nature of the relationship go hand in hand with describing the quantity and type of interpretations being offered, because the quality of the relationship is likely to determine the potential effectiveness of an interpretation. Practitioners and researchers have recognized that technique does not exist independently of the relationship. Rather the relationship serves as both a source of interpretations and is also enhanced by them. (p. 126)

The therapeutic relationship feeds the potency of cognitive insight; likewise, effective interpretations (that is, cognitive insights) strengthen the therapeutic relationship.

Emotions in Therapy

Are clients who express emotions during therapy more likely to benefit than are clients who do not express their emotions? To answer this, we must ask another question: How do we define and objectify the expression of emotions? For example, is the definition limited to somatic expressions such as laughing or crying, or does the definition include the emotional tone of the sessions?

To examine these questions, I review the research on emotions in this section. I adopt the basic format proposed by Greenberg and Safran (1989), who recommended that the research on emotions be classified according to its match with the three major theories of counseling and psychotherapy:

> (a) the role of emotional expression in catharsis [psychoanalytic and psychodynamic therapy], (b) the role of emotional arousal in anxiety reduction [cognitive-behavioral therapy], and (c) the role of emotion in experiencing [experiential and humanistic therapy]. These three areas represent the major empirical literatures on emotion that have been spawned by each of the three therapy traditions. (p. 21)

I will consider these three basic areas in turn.

Catharsis

Catharsis, or emotional expression, has a long history in the psychodynamic literature, beginning with Freud's (1895/1958b) *The Psychotherapy of Hysteria*. Although there are divergent theoretical views on the role of catharsis within the psychodynamic camp (Alexander & French, 1946; Rapaport, 1967; Sullivan, 1953), a central theme is that emotional expression is a crucial component of therapy. The classical position is that repression of affect is the antecedent of many maladaptive behaviors. A goal of therapy is for the client to express these repressed emotions.

I limit this review of the research on catharsis to four types of studies: (a) analogue, (b) physiological outcome, (c) physical arousal, and (d) emotive psychotherapy.

Analogue studies on catharsis.   Analogue studies are frequently carried out with undergraduate volunteer subjects; the studies attempt to simulate or at least approximate a therapeutic encounter so that conclusions in regard to actual therapy sessions can be made. Nichols and Zax (1977) reviewed a number of analogue studies: many supported the efficacy of catharsis (Dittes, 1957; Goldman-Eisler, 1956; Haggard & Murray, 1942; Levison, Zax, & Cowen, 1961; Martin, Lundy, & Lewin, 1960; Ruesch & Prestwood, 1949); others had ambiguous conclusions (Gordon, 1957; Grossman, 1952; Wiener, 1955); and one study did not support the efficacy of catharsis (Keet, 1948).

The considerable number of analogue studies that have supported catharsis suggests that catharsis is effective. However, the preceding studies are not current, and the design of analogue studies raises questions about the credibility of their findings:

> Analogue studies of expression are not very adequate tests of its effects. Subjects often lack the distress that motivates actual patients to change, and they lack the emotional blocks that make such changes difficult. Analogue studies thus cannot produce the veridical intense emotional discharge that occurs in emotive therapies. (Greenberg & Safran, 1987, p. 90)

I now turn to studies conducted with actual clients.

Physiological outcome measures of catharsis.   Researchers have assessed physiological measures of outcome following an array of cathartic approaches to therapy. Studies of primal therapy (Karle, Corriere, & Hart, 1973), feeling therapy (Woldenberg, 1976), and long-term feeling therapy (Karle et al., 1976) found that clients had lower pulse rate, blood pressure, and temperature following these emotive styles of therapy.

If you consider lower pulse rate and temperature to be measures of effectiveness, you might conclude that emotive styles of therapy can be effective. However, these physiological measures are remote from the actual goals of therapy. Are clients in a heightened state of arousal more apt to make the desired *psychological* changes in their lives?

Physical arousal and catharsis.   In two interesting studies, clients were physiologically aroused by ether. In the first study, clients were followed over four sessions (Hoehn-Saric, Frank, & Gurland, 1968). The clients were provided a suggestion for change in the first session. In the following three sessions, the same suggestions were made by a therapist prior to and following an administration of ether. The ether-administered sessions were the experimental situation. It was hypothesized that the clients would be more emotionally aroused in these sessions and would be more likely to display positive change on a Semantic Differential measure of attitude change. The conclusion of this study was that clients made more positive change in the arousal condition than in the nonarousal condition.

A problem with this study is that there was no control group of clients. In addition, because the nonarousal condition was the first session and the arousal sessions followed, it could be argued that the clients showed a higher change on the outcome measure simply because it was a later stage in therapy.

To address these concerns, a second study included a control group of clients, who were administered aromatic water treatment (Hoehn-Saric et al., 1972). The experimental group again received ether. The water and ether were administered during the middle two sessions of therapy that spanned three months. The researchers found that the positive attitude change of the ether group was greater than that of the water-treatment group. They concluded that, since both the control and the experimental groups experienced the dramatic and unusual circumstances of being administered a foreign substance in treatment, the influence of this factor could be ruled out, and the positive change could be attributed to emotional arousal.

Studies using ether are still remote from most therapists' style of intervention. Are there any studies in which psychological measures of change are applied when a therapist uses behavioral and verbal techniques to enhance the client's arousal? Yes.

Emotive psychotherapy.   Nichols and Zax (1977) outline a wide variety of cathartic techniques that a therapist can use to heighten the client's emotional state—for example, repeating emotionally toned statements, role playing, and expressive movements.

Three studies have examined the relationship between emotive therapy and behavioral and psychological outcome measures. Nichols (1974) found that, while clients in emotive therapy exhibited more emotional discharge than did clients in traditional psychodynamic therapy, the traditional psychodynamic therapy group showed more positive change on an objective measure (the Minnesota Multiphasic Personality Inventory). However, clients who were high emotional dischargers tended to show more improvement on behavioral outcome measures than did low emotional dischargers. Nichols concluded that this finding supported catharsis as a process variable.

In a second study on emotive techniques in therapy, Nichols and Bierenbaum (1978) compared clients who exhibited controlling emotional defenses (obsessives) to clients who exhibited emotional lability (hysterics). They found that the obsessive clientele benefited the most from cathartic treatment and suggested that catharsis served as a breakthrough for these clients, allowing them to make somatic-emotional discharge (to laugh, cry, yell, and so on).

In the third study, clients with hysterical styles exhibited more emotional discharge than did clients with obsessive styles (Pierce, Nichols, & DuBrin, 1983). However, the clients' improvement by termination was the same for those with obsessive styles as for those with hysteric styles.

In a review of the catharsis literature, Greenberg and Safran (1987) concluded:

> A more differentiated view on affect is probably necessary to tease out "with whom" and "when" expressive methods are helpful, rather than to assume that the general approach can be shown to be superior to some other general approach. (p. 94)

The various forms of research on catharsis—analogue, physiological, etc.—corroborate that catharsis can be an effective form of intervention. As research continues, perhaps the effectiveness of particular types of cathartic treatment with particular types of clients, at particular times in therapy, can be addressed.

Anxiety-Induction Techniques

There are two major types of behavioral anxiety-induction techniques; flooding and implosion. These two techniques heighten the client's anxiety. They have historically been used with avoidance behaviors, phobias in particular. Flooding is a learning technique in which the principle of extinction operates: the person is exposed to the feared object or situation while not being allowed to escape. The movie *Raiders of the Lost Ark* includes a scene with many snakes. An example of flooding would be to ask snake-phobic clients to watch this scene, without being allowed to leave the room or to close their eyes.

Implosion is more theatrical and anxiety-filled than flooding. It also operates on the principle of extinction, but the anxiety evoked is more intense. For example, in implosive sessions, snake-phobic clients have been told to imagine the following sequence: see the snake; pick up the snake; it is biting you; let it bite; feel the pain; it is crawling into your eye sockets and wiggling in there; now feel it wiggling inside your head (Hogan, 1968; Hogan & Kirchner, 1967). This technique is not used as frequently as it once was.

A review of the literature reached these conclusions:

> It continues to be difficult to provide an overall evaluation of the effectiveness of implosive or flooding procedures. Although there is a relatively large number of reports in the literature—a proportion of them continue to report either a failure of the basic technique or less therapeutic effectiveness in comparison with another form of behavior therapy. Although there seems to be dwindling interest in anxiety induction procedures, perhaps for humane or ethical reasons, a more conclusive evaluation may be possible in the future as research results accrue. (Masters, Burish, Hollon, & Rimm, 1987, p. 330)

For the purposes of this book, let it suffice to say that flooding and implosion presently have mixed results. No doubt, other techniques that are equally dramatic will be developed in the verbal therapies. The therapist must first judge the utility of the technique on ethical and humane principles, and then decide if less dramatic less intrusive emotive techniques may be equally effective.

Experiencing in Therapy

Of the various studies on the role of emotions, the research on experiencing is probably the most relevant to therapists of varying orientations in their day-to-day practice. Research on experiencing—also referred to as client focusing or self-relatedness—came into prominence with Carl Rogers's insistence on the role of the client's phenomenological experience of counseling (Rogers, 1951a; Rogers, 1958).

The idea is that the ideal client is able to focus on, and express, feelings and, on that basis, to integrate the affective and cognitive components of his or her experience.

The literature on experience differs from that on catharsis in that the catharsis research emphasizes a somatic-emotional catharsis—such as laughing, crying, or yelling—whereas the experience literature examines a cognitive-emotional catharsis in which the client displays involved talking (Nichols & Zax, 1977)—that is, the client is actively involved in therapy.

The Experiencing Scale has been extensively used in this line of research (Klein, Mathieu, Gendlin, & Kiesler, 1969). Recordings of sessions are rated on a seven-point scale in terms of the degree of client involvement in therapy. At the lower end of the scale, clients' discussions are superficial and impersonal; at the midpoint levels, clients engage in a more inward discussion of feelings; and, at the higher levels, clients are synthesizing their feelings with cognition for problem-solving purposes.

One review of process variables found that experiencing was the most frequently noted process variable related to outcome (Luborsky, Chandler, Auerbach, Cohen, & Bachrach, 1971). A second review article did not find such a drastic correlation but did note a positive relationship between experiencing and outcome (Klein, Mathieu-Coughlan, & Kiesler, 1986).

Finally, Orlinsky and Howard (1986) reviewed the research on self-relatedness, a concept akin to experiencing. Self-related clients are in touch with themselves, aware of their thoughts and feelings, and more accepting of their feelings. Orlinsky and Howard assessed this variable in terms of openness versus defensiveness. They concluded that, of the 16 findings reviewed, 14 noted a positive relationship between self-relatedness and outcome.

The research overwhelmingly supports experiencing as a key process variable in counseling and psychotherapy. It is not simply that clients gain cognitive insight or gain a release of their emotions. Rather, clients' full involvement in their therapy on an intellectual and emotional level appears to be critical to effective therapy.

Summary on Emotions

A number of studies of differing designs support catharsis as a key process variable. With regard to anxiety-induction techniques, the research findings are mixed; the use of dramatic techniques to heighten clients' emotional arousal may be inadvisable when less intrusive techniques are no less effective in fostering positive change. Finally, research on experiencing amply supports the contention that clients who are emotionally engaged in their therapy are more likely to benefit from it.

SUMMARY

Research resoundingly confirms that the early establishment of a therapeutic relationship in therapy is a powerful process variable. It further suggests that the therapeutic relationship consists of both supportive and collaborative components. The literature indicates that clients who are motivated and have appropriate expectations about therapy are more likely to benefit than are unmotivated, misguided people. Socializing a client to therapy is an effective means for a therapist to obtain a higher success rate of change, partially because clients are more likely to continue in their therapy.

The research on providing clients with some form of cognitive insight has been equivocal. Future studies with more specific hypotheses—regarding the degree of directiveness, the particular stage of therapy, and the particular type of client, for example—will help to clarify the importance of this variable. Finally, research on catharsis (somatic-emotional) and particularly on experiencing (cognitive-emotional) has supported the role of emotions as a key process variable.

These four process variables are interdependent. Socializing clients to therapy helps to build a trusting supportive relationship and prepares clients for the maturation of a collaborative relationship. With increased trust, therapists may be able to provide their clients with information that they have tended to avoid. This discrepant information may increase clients' emotional investment in therapy, which could increase their positive expectations of therapy, and so on.

A change in one process variable creates a change in the other process variables. However, the relationship between the variables is by no means linear. Part Three is a discussion of the implementation of these four fundamental process variables.

PART THREE
IMPLEMENTATION OF THE FOUR PROCESS VARIABLES

We have seen that there is research to support the four common process variables of counseling and psychotherapy: (a) the therapeutic relationship; (b) client expectations; (c) cognitive insight; and (d) emotional expression and experiencing. Part Three of this book focuses on the implementation of these four process variables.

Two themes emerge from these chapters. The first is the critical role of the therapeutic relationship. If there is a strong therapeutic relationship, then interventions are more likely to be effective. Likewise, when effective interventions are used, they serve to enhance the therapeutic relationship. My comments on the implementation of the four process variables could also be regarded as a discussion of methods to enhance the therapeutic relationship.

The second theme that emerges in Part Three is that all forms of effective therapy increase a client's sense of responsibility and autonomy. I include extensive citations from leading therapists within the three major styles of therapy in support of that notion.

Separate chapters address each of the four process variables. In addition, because the first session is so critical to the development of the four process variables, I have included a chapter on key interventions at that stage of therapy.

A final chapter is devoted to active listening and termination. Active listening is important for the implementation of the process variables of change. A person cannot learn and memorize hard-and-fast rules on the practice of therapy and then expect to be an effective therapist; active listening requires the therapist to tolerate some degree of uncertainty. The termination phase, like the initial session, is a critical stage of therapy for many clients.

I begin Part Three by discussing the most fundamental process variable of change—the therapeutic relationship.

CHAPTER SEVEN

THE THERAPEUTIC RELATIONSHIP

Here is the node, you who hate change and fear revolution. Keep these two squatting men apart; make them hate, fear, suspect each other . . . The danger is here, for two men are not as lonely and perplexed as one. And from this first "we" there grows a still more dangerous thing: "I have a little food" plus "I have none." If from this problem the sum is "We have a little food," the thing is on its way, the movement has direction.

(STEINBECK, 1939/1988B, P. 194)

The opening passage of this chapter is taken from *The Grapes of Wrath*, John Steinbeck's classic novel on the Great Depression of the 1930s. In Steinbeck's novel, the banks did not want the sharecroppers to gain a sense of "we." When the sharecroppers worked together, this meant change.

Counselors, psychiatrists, psychologists, and social workers seek change. Therapy aims to reduce the chaotic confusion in the client's life, to provide direction. When people are in a relationship in which they trust one another, they lose the sense of loneliness; they gain the strength that is needed to make changes.

THE THREE MAJOR ORIENTATIONS

Therapists of the three major orientations are fully aware that the therapeutic relationship is crucial for change.

> The foundation of counseling is the relationship between counselor and client. Different approaches emphasize the counseling relationship to varying degrees, but all practitioners understand that the client and the counselor must first make contact. (Meier & Davis, 1993, p. 2)

Among the humanistic therapists, Frankl (1960/1967b) is characteristically outspoken:

> The crucial agency in psychotherapy is not so much the method, but rather the relationship between the patient and his doctor [therapist] . . . This relationship between two persons is what seems to be the most significant aspect of the psychotherapeutic process, a more important factor than any method or technique. (p. 144)

This explicit emphasis on the therapeutic relationship is what attracts many students and therapists to the humanistic approach.

According to leading psychodynamic therapists, "the therapist's ability to form an alliance is possibly the most crucial determinant of his effectiveness" (Luborsky et al., 1985, p. 610).

Cognitive therapists have been stereotyped as neglecting the role of the therapeutic relationship, but that image is out of date. "One of the cardinal principles of cognitive therapy is instilling a sense of collaboration and trust in the patient" (Beck et al., 1990, p. 64). Gaston (1990) concluded:

> Although much of the theoretical and empirical work on the alliance [therapeutic relationship] has primarily come from psychodynamic and client-centered traditions, there has been recently a growing recognition of the role of the alliance in other psychotherapy approaches, such as cognitive and behavioral therapy. (p. 143)

I am not aware of a proponent of a major school of therapy who does not agree with Goldstein (1962): "There can no longer be any doubt as to the primary status which must be accorded the therapeutic transaction" (p. 105).

In *What Is Psychotherapy?* Zeig and Munion (1990) asked 81 therapists of widely varying orientations to describe their personal therapeutic styles.

> Many of the contributors explicitly, and all of the contributors implicitly, reference the importance of the therapeutic relationship. After all, the therapy process occurs within the context of an empowering empathic relationship between a designated therapist and a patient. (p. 6)

Note that the reference to the therapeutic relationship is sometimes implicit. This sometimes confuses students in graduate programs. Many students who enter a graduate program are already aware that the relationship between client and therapist is the foundation for growth. However, because many cognitive and psychodynamic authors do not explicitly mention the therapeutic relationship, students can easily accept stereotyped views of these approaches: cognitive therapists are locked in their heads; psychodynamic therapists want to solve a mystery. In actuality, effective therapists of the three major verbal therapies know that the therapeutic relationship is the fundamental change agent.

I am in full agreement with Bugental and Bracke (1992):

> In our view, an often unrecognized but important value common to many—if not most—psychotherapies is a subtle (and sometimes, even unconscious) allegiance to humanistic values. Also, experienced clinicians of contrasting orientations often operate implicitly within an existential framework. This evolution seems

to be a subterranean product of working with genuine engagement in this deeply human enterprise. (p. 32)

Therapists explicitly or implicitly appreciate the necessity of therapeutic engagement with their clients.

This chapter examines the therapeutic relationship as the fundamental process variable of therapy.

THE THERAPEUTIC RELATIONSHIP

As students know and regret, counseling, psychiatry, psychology, and social work use many different terms to describe the same or similar phenomena. Unfortunately, we have inherited numerous esoteric terms to describe the therapeutic relationship; I review some of them in the next section.

Terminology

In the early days of psychoanalysis, Freud regarded transference as the most important aspect of the relationship between the analysand and the analyst. The relationship was seen as an important change agent only because it was the avenue by which the analysand transferred thoughts, feelings, and behaviors from significant others onto the analyst.

As the years passed, other psychoanalytic authors placed increased emphasis on the real relationship that exists within the therapeutic hour, as opposed to the transferential relationship. In the words of Greenson (1965/1990c), psychodynamic writers increasingly began to appreciate the "nonerotic, rational rapport which the patient has with his analyst" (p. 280).

Terms coined by psychoanalytic authors to describe this rational rapport include: ego alliance (Sterba, 1934); rational transference (Fenichel, 1941); therapeutic alliance (Zetzel, 1956); mature transference (Stone, 1961); working alliance (Greenson, 1965/1990c); and helping alliance (Luborsky, 1984). These terms can still be found in the theoretical and empirical literature. In this book, the term *therapeutic relationship* (Garfield, 1990) is used to describe the nontransferential relationship.

Two Major Components of the Therapeutic Relationship

What is the therapeutic relationship? According to Stiles, Shapiro, and Elliot (1986, p. 173), it is "a positive emotional bond and a sense of mutual collaboration" between therapist and client. It is important for therapists to understand this distinction between the positive emotional bond and the sense of collaboration.

As we saw in Chapter 6, research indicates that beginning therapists develop the emotional bond as skillfully as do experienced therapists. However, experienced therapists are more adept at developing a task-oriented, or collaborative, style of relationship (Mallinckrodt & Nelson, 1991).

In all healthy relationships, there is a sense of trust. Even Freud wrote on the importance of a supportive relationship.

> It remains the first aim of the treatment to attach to it [therapy] and to the person of the doctor . . . If one exhibits a serious interest in him, carefully clears away the resistances that crop up at the beginning and avoids making certain mistakes, he will of himself form such an attachment . . . It is certainly possible to forfeit this first success if from the start one takes any standpoint other than that of sympathetic understanding. (Freud, 1913/1958a, pp. 139–140)

The second aspect of the therapeutic relationship, collaboration, is often neglected in therapy. However, as cognitive therapist Aaron Beck (1989) notes, "Until the relationship between therapist and patient is truly collaborative, little progress will be made on the central processes maintaining the disorder" (p. x).

To summarize, I use the following terms in this book. The *therapeutic relationship* refers to the relationship in general: a meeting of two people with the goal of helping the client make positive changes in his or her life. The *supportive relationship* is one aspect of the therapeutic relationship; in fact, it is the foundation of therapy. If the client perceives the therapist as trustworthy and helpful, the relationship is supportive. The *collaborative relationship* is the second aspect of the therapeutic relationship: if the client believes that therapist and client are working together as a team, the relationship is collaborative.

A therapist may be directive or nondirective and still be able to develop a supportive and collaborative relationship. Therapists often get into trouble when they become overly directive or overly nondirective, without attending to a particular client's needs at a particular point in therapy.

The Supportive Relationship

The supportive aspect of the therapeutic relationship is the bedrock for all forms of counseling, psychiatry, psychology, and social work. If the supportive relationship is not present, therapy has little chance of being helpful (Strupp, 1980a). Psychodynamic therapists Butler, Strupp, and Binder (1992) assert:

> This therapeutic bond far outweighs specific intervention, length,
> or type of therapy. In practice, this quality of the relationship is
> often based on the patient's feeling of being listened to and under-
> stood. This, above all else, impresses us as the essence of therapy,
> and the effectiveness of any dynamic therapist, brief or otherwise,
> is ultimately limited by his or her ability to establish this connec-
> tion with the patient. (p. 91)

This comment applies to any therapist, regardless of orientation.

Think of a relationship with a close friend when you were at a
crossroad in your life. When you were in a healthy relationship, the
relationship gave you the strength to face unwanted thoughts, feelings, and
behaviors. You became more tolerant and accepting of yourself. Being in
a supportive environment is liberating.

How will our clients respond if they believe the therapist is not
supportive, is not empathic to their present condition in life? Often, when
the supportive relationship is not present, clients drop out of therapy
prematurely.

In one recent study of 93 clients, only 26% remained in therapy; the
author concluded that the supportive relationship was lacking (Beckham,
1992).

> Early levels of rapport between patient and therapist are clearly
> related to the process of patients deciding to remain in treatment.
> It may be that greater efforts by therapists at establishing rapport
> would have prevented some of the dropouts in this study. (p. 181)

There are many ways to characterize the supportive relationship. I
have opted to examine the role of empathy and the role of the corrective
emotional experience.

Empathy.   With time, empathy has become a buzzword and has lost much
of its integrity. But the full meaning of the word is still very much alive in
the writings of Carl Rogers.

> To sense the client's private world as if it were your own, but
> without ever losing the "as if" quality—this is empathy, and this
> seems essential to therapy. To sense the client's anger, fear, or
> confusion as if it were your own, yet without your own anger, fear,
> or confusion getting bound up in it, is the condition we are
> endeavoring to describe. (Rogers, 1957, p. 99)

Cognitive therapists describe empathy as a key component of cognitive therapy and recommend that therapists "step into the patient's world
and see and experience life the way the patient does" (Beck, Rush, Shaw,
& Emery, 1979, p. 47). Psychodynamic therapists also acknowledge the role
of empathy: "We define it as 'vicarious introspection' or, more simply, as

one person's [attempt to] experience the inner life of another while simultaneously retaining the stance of an objective observer" (Kohut, 1984/1990, p. 464).

Empathy is stepping into another's shoes; it means abandoning judgment for acceptance. Empathy is experiencing the person's life as he or she does. It means accepting the other person's feelings, sense of helplessness, and frustrations. The therapist does not try to rob the client of these experiences. In an anecdote that therapists tell, a client asks what the therapist would do if she or he were in the same predicament. The therapist replies, "That's simple. If I were in your shoes, I would have done exactly the same thing."

Effective therapists embrace the client's experience, the confusion and fatigue. If the therapist can face the hurt, then perhaps the client can accept it. With the therapist's support, the opportunity for change emerges.

Many therapists who lack empathic skills, particularly those who are just starting out, do not want to experience the client's pain. All too often, beginning therapists fail to develop a supportive relationship because they fear intense emotions; they believe they must fix the client.

As Rogers noted, it is the "as if" quality of empathy that protects the therapist from becoming overwhelmed.

> The counselor becomes aware of the client's private feelings and meanings as if they were his or her own, without losing the "as if" quality . . . This condition has received a vast amount of research attention over the years and is probably the most important of the facilitative conditions. (Woody, Hansen, & Rossberg, 1989, p. 61)

For example, if a client feels rage toward a spouse, I may also be able to identify that rage and to feel it as if it were my own. Yet, as Rogers pointed out, my rage is not bound up in it, as is the client's. I do not live with the spouse on a day-to-day basis.

To be truly empathic, I must work with clients on helping them find their own way. I may have theory and experience as guides, but I still do not have their answers. Such a phenomenological stance brings up the therapist's own issues of isolation, responsibility for another, and lack of ability to truly fix another. I can only help people to help themselves.

Empathy is so much more than being sympathetic. As we have seen, beginning therapists often lack empathy because they cannot accept the client's emotional pain. Many experienced therapists, by contrast, have grown weary. As becomes apparent during case conferences, they can all too easily identify and solicit the client's emotional pain, but they neglect the client's strengths.

For a few years, I worked with a number of people most aptly diagnosed as cases of borderline personality disorder. Their lives were filled with trauma. Working with these people I learned to appreciate their strength to continue. So many times I felt their hurt and pain in my office. I wondered what kept them going.

Most therapists agree that it is difficult to work with individuals with borderline personality disorder. One of the major reasons that I was able to help these people was that I learned to appreciate and respect their fortitude. If you walk away from a session and are not aware of your client's strengths, you may be distancing yourself too much. The empathic posture cannot merely recognize the client's weaknesses.

Empathy is a philosophical stance that therapists take toward life. It is therapists' willingness to feel, to accept others as they are, to know their own limitations as helpers, and to stop fixing and help their clients find the strength and courage to continue. Empathic therapists are honest with their clients and with themselves. To be truly empathic is to be alone: I cannot fix my clients; that is their decision. Empathy comes from the acceptance that we can never live life for another.

Corrective emotional experience.   In the past few years there has been a resurgence of literature on a second aspect of the supportive relationship, the corrective emotional experience (Safran, 1993).

The term was coined in 1946 by Alexander and French, who abandoned the tenets of classic psychoanalysis and adopted a briefer, more direct form of intervention. Specifically, they believed that all the other techniques that a therapist utilizes are subordinate to the emotional relationship between a therapist and a client.

> The principal curative powers . . . lie in the fact that he can express his aggressiveness toward the therapist without being punished, and can assert himself without being censured. This actual experience is needed before the patient gains the emotional perception that he is no longer a child facing an omnipotent father. This type of emotional experience as it occurs during treatment, we call "corrective emotional experience" and we consider it the most important factor in all uncovering therapy. (Alexander & French, 1946, p. 22)

Alexander and French believed that the therapist must provide an environment that contrasts with the extreme position taken by the client's parents. If the client had harsh critical parents, then the therapist would provide a corrective emotional experience by tending to be less judgmental and more accepting of the client.

Alexander and French recited the story of Jean Valjean in Victor Hugo's (1862/1961) *Les Misérables*. Valjean had stolen candlesticks and other artifacts from a bishop. When the bishop discovered Valjean, instead of punishing him, the bishop offered Valjean kindness and food. This simple act of acceptance transformed Valjean's life.

Many people who seek therapy come from harsh environments. In such cases, the therapist provides a corrective emotional experience in which clients do not have to fear that they are going to be judged by the therapist. Winnicott (1965), who gained fame for humanizing the therapeutic relationship, coined the term *good enough mothering* and wrote of the therapist providing a *holding environment*. The strength of this type of environment is that the client feels accepted. Finding a sense of security, the client may be able to experiment with new thoughts, feelings, and behaviors.

Some clients have good reason to be angry, but they could not express their frustrations as a child, for fear of punishment or abandonment, and they learned over the years to keep their feelings hidden. It may be appropriate for them to express their anger in the therapy session.

Some people, however, come from overly permissive environments and require discipline and structure. Such clients are sometimes verbally abusive toward their therapists. Dunkelbau (1987) parodies this attitude by imagining a client who says, "Doc, you have to help me make more friends, you fat slob!" (p. 311). If a client had overly lenient parents, the therapist would provide structure as a corrective. As an example, consider Alexander's first use of corrective emotional experience:

> An unusually untidy patient complained for the umpteenth time
> how few people liked him and how he was avoided by many,
> even being accused of being untidy. This while the patient was
> lying on the couch soiling it with his dirty shoes. At this point
> Alexander remarked that he was not surprised at people's reac-
> tions to the patient since at this very moment he was dirtying
> the analyst's couch. The patient, whose excessively tolerant par-
> ents never corrected his attitudes or behavior, was startled to hear
> his analyst confront him with this different attitude. (Eisenstein,
> 1992, p. 1)

Therapists should not assume that the corrective emotional experience means providing clients with passive, nonconfrontive responses. Some clients need to be directly confronted on their maladaptive thoughts and behaviors. Clients who were raised in a permissive environment may have a sense of absolute entitlement, even at the expense of other's rights.

No matter what their orientation, effective therapists are probably providing a corrective emotional experience for the client. Thompson (1987) suggests that different orientations use different words for this practice:

> Terms such as "extinction of a generalized response," "role play-
> ing," "risk taking," "behavioral rehearsal," "reparenting," "home-

work," "directed behavior" may all be examples of procedures that could result in "corrective emotional experiences." (p. 335)

The corrective emotional experience is an integral component of the supportive relationship.

The Collaborative Relationship

The collaborative relationship consists of the belief by the therapist and the client that they are working together as a team; they have a sense of *weness*. The development of a collaborative relationship is one of the most difficult tasks for the client and therapist.

Note that the collaborative relationship depends on the attitudes of both therapist and client. "Psychotherapy above all else is a form of psychological influence, a collaborative endeavor in which the patient, from the beginning, is expected to play an active part" (Strupp, 1990, p. 65).

Beck and Haaga (1992) point out that collaboration is a new and important concept for cognitive therapists, who have tended to be dogmatically directive.

> Conceptualizing the therapeutic relationship as one of *collaborative empiricism*, in which the therapist works together with the patient to devise personally meaningful evaluations of negative assumptions, as opposed to directively suggesting particular substitute cognitions, seems a useful innovation. (p. 36)

It is difficult to develop a collaborative relationship if clients believe that the therapist will do all of the work. Many clients, no matter what their socioeconomic status, still believe that going to a therapist is like going to the doctor: they will describe how terrible they feel; the doctor will then ask the appropriate questions, make a diagnosis, and give them a prescription.

For their part, therapists can hinder the development of a collaborative relationship if they believe that they are responsible for fixing their clients. Many therapists believe that they should have all the answers for their clients. However, when we think that we have the answers, clients frequently don't follow our insights. Therapists continue to struggle with this issue of how responsible they are for their clients' improvement.

Ultimately, therapists must accept that they can never be responsible for another's life. But this sounds like a double-bind. If therapists can never be responsible for another, then why are clients coming in to see them?

Clients frequently seek the help of therapists because they have lost the knowledge that they are responsible for what happens in their life. While people cannot control whether a spouse is going to emotionally or physically abuse them, for example, they can be responsible for the decision to stay in an abusive relationship.

People in abusive relationships tend to assume that they have done something wrong to deserve the abuse. They assume too much responsibility for the abuse. They go to extremes to avoid upsetting their spouse; they try to read their spouse's mind, in an attempt to determine what to say and when; and they are overly supportive of the spouse.

Therapists get caught in a similar dilemma. By assuming too much responsibility for another's life, therapists can prevent the maturation of a collaborative relationship. We are not responsible for whether another person decides to change. We are responsible for providing a setting in which change can occur; we can only set the stage.

Bordin (1979) has achieved wide recognition in psychotherapy for his work on the therapeutic relationship and particularly the collaborative relationship.

> Bordin's concepts of bond, goal, and tasks involve collaboration and hinge on the degree of concordance and joint purpose between the counselor and client. This stance may be contrasted with the alternative hypotheses that rely either on the client's perception of the counselor's qualities or on the attitude and behavior of the counselor without taking into account the degree of agreement, willingness to collaborate, or mutuality that is present between the counselor and client. (Horvath & Greenberg, 1989, p. 224)

Developing a collaborative relationship is a team effort from the beginning. Client and therapist share the responsibility. Of course, some clients are better players than others; some even refuse to participate. What can the therapist do to facilitate a collaborative relationship? We consider that question in the next section.

THE THERAPIST AND THE THERAPEUTIC RELATIONSHIP

Rogers (1961) has described his evolution as a therapist in this way:

> In my early professional years I was asking the question, How can I treat, or cure, or change this person? Now I would phrase the question in this way: How can I provide a relationship which this person may use for his own personal growth? (p. 32)

What does a therapist actually do to provide a therapeutic relationship? In the remainder of this chapter, I outline suggestions made by therapists of the three major orientations in regards to what they do to create and enhance a therapeutic relationship.

Numerous psychodynamic therapists have written on "therapeutic misalliances," which they describe as therapeutic relationships that have failed to develop. A more realistic viewpoint is that such misalliances are usually not failures of the therapeutic relationship but phases in the evolution of a therapeutic relationship. Many resistant behaviors may be viewed as aspects of clients' struggle to develop a relationship: clients are learning to be honest with others, with the therapist, and with themselves.

Hartley and Strupp (1983) give representative examples of clients' resistant behaviors that may be warnings of a failed therapeutic relationship.

> Specific signals of something amiss in the alliance are absences and cancellations, tardiness, threats of termination, or "forgetting" agreed-upon tasks. Others may take the form of attacks, criticism, mistrust, persistent disagreement, or abstinant (sic) silence directed at the therapist. At the opposite pole are seductiveness, dependency, sexualization of the relationship, and blind submission. More subtle cues, often missed by the therapist, include undue regression, rumination, distancing, denial of problems, denial of feelings for the therapist, and maneuvers aimed at abdicating the usual therapeutic roles. (pp. 5–6)

Even though they might be reflective of the client's pervasive personality, these resistant behaviors often reflect the client's attempts to adapt to a relationship that suggests change.

Langs (1975) not only lists problematic client behaviors but also notes thoughts and feelings of the therapist that may signal a relationship in need of attention.

> Subjectively, therapeutic misalliances should be considered when the therapist senses a lack of progress . . . Beyond such cognitive awareness, the therapist may experience a range of thoughts, feelings, and fantasies: things are not right; he dislikes the patient, or has other unusual attitudes or feelings toward him; he feels used or manipulated, or that he is ineffectual as a therapist; he is aware of notably seductive or aggressive feelings toward the patient that he is unable to resolve; he cannot understand a stalemate or a regression in the patient. (p. 91)

When therapists notice warning signs in themselves or in the client, they need to address the therapeutic relationship. Once again, the therapist need feel no sense of failure; often, this is a signal that a new stage in the development of the therapeutic relationship is about to begin.

Addressing the Therapeutic Relationship

What exactly can a therapist do to foster a therapeutic relationship? A hallmark answer to this question is for the therapist to address the relationship directly with the client when resistance occurs.

Freud (1912/1990b) wrote on the failure of an analysand to free associate as representative of a failure in the attainment of a therapeutic relationship. The method by which Freud dealt with these "failures" is also an effective method for therapists of other orientations to adopt:

> If a patient's free associations fail, the stoppage can invariably be removed by an assurance that he [the patient] is being dominated at the moment by an association which is concerned with the doctor himself or with something connected with him [the doctor]. As soon as this explanation is given, the stoppage is removed, or the situation is changed from one in which the associations fail into one in which they are being kept back. (p. 5)

In their book *Direct Social Work Practice*, Hepworth and Larsen (1993) pick up where Freud left off, and they apply this approach to general therapeutic practice.

> The first step in managing resistance is to bring it into the light of discussion by focusing on here-and-now feelings that underlie the resistance. Sensitive and skillful handling is essential because personal feelings toward the practitioner are commonly associated with resistance and clients find it difficult to risk sharing these feelings. (Otherwise, they would have shared them already.) . . . Discussing here-and-now feelings is often all that is needed to surmount barriers to change, and clients thereafter resume productive work on their difficulties. Some clients, in fact, may grow as a result of such discussions, learning that they can express negative feelings without retaliation from the practitioner [which is a corrective emotional experience]. Further, by observing practitioners model mature and effective ways of dealing with interpersonal strain, clients may vicariously learn skills in dealing with interpersonal conflict. (p. 617)

Addressing the therapeutic relationship is important not so much as a technique to deal with resistance, but because it can provide a corrective emotional experience and promote the maturation of the therapeutic relationship as the two people work together.

A rather simple method that I use to enhance the therapeutic relationship is to be honest with my clients, to discuss what is happening in the relationship. It is very common for me to ask clients, "How did it feel to come in today?" I ask this question particularly if they were late, or the session began at a slow pace, or the previous session was overly emotional or overly intellectual. This simple question frequently spawns new information about our relationship and prevents a stalemate in its development.

I have noticed other similar patterns in my work that promote the maturation of the therapeutic relationship. If a client has previously seen another therapist, I will definitely look into what went sour with that relationship and pursue how this could happen in our relationship. I openly discuss this with my clients during the first session.

Women who are in a miserable relationship with a man will sometimes make global derogatory statements about men in general. I don't let this opportunity by; I will ask, "What about me? I'm a man." From my supervision of female therapists, I know that male clients make similar derogatory remarks about women.

Many clients have difficulty in expressing their anger. When clients are angry with me, I try to provide them an opportunity to express that anger directly. Not to do so is to risk that the client will continue a maladaptive relationship pattern with me. Along with the anger, many clients have dependency traits and fear abandonment. They usually welcome the opportunity to talk when I address these fears as they arise in the therapeutic relationship: "Could it be that you were angry with me last week for what I said but you must not tell me of your anger because you must protect me, as you have protected other people in your life?"

Nonverbal communications frequently give a strong indication of a client's immediate thoughts and feelings, particularly in reference to the therapeutic relationship. The tone and quality of a client's voice provide valuable information. I particularly pay attention if the client's voice gets tight. I might comment, "Your voice became tight, as if to keep you from saying something." Likewise, I pay attention when the client's voice is strong and alive; when it is, I tell the client so. Clients frequently direct such nonverbal communications toward the therapist. Therapists who actively listen are attuned to such nonverbal cues.

Research on Addressing the Therapeutic Relationship

Research has supported the contention that, by addressing the therapeutic relationship, the therapist can assist its development and, ultimately, foster a positive outcome.

In one investigation, six clients initially had a poor therapeutic relationship with their therapists. Three of the six clients went on to have improved therapeutic relationships and outcomes, and three of the clients went on to have unimproved therapeutic relationships and poor outcomes.

The following synopsis highlights a factor that differentiated the high and low therapeutic relationship groups (and corresponding positive and negative outcomes).

> In all six cases in this study, there was substantial interpretive work done. We found that a highly specific set of interpretations which were relevant to the [therapeutic relationship] made the difference. Interpretive work that avoided rather than addressed a poor alliance was not ultimately successful in attaining an improved alliance or good outcome. (Foreman & Marmar, 1985, p. 925)

Thus, when the therapist addressed the relationship directly, it was strengthened.

In reviewing interpersonal processes in cognitive therapy, Safran and Segal (1990) noted that the therapeutic relationship can deteriorate on account of an *alliance rupture*, which occurs when the client has negative feelings about the relationship, has negative feelings about the therapy, and/or does not follow the therapist's suggestions. They recommended that therapists in such ruptures focus on the misalliance—that is, that cognitive therapists assist clients in discussing their thoughts and feelings about their therapy and their thoughts and feelings toward their therapist.

A study with psychodynamic therapists found that to explore negative transference (by encouraging the expression of negative feelings and making past-present linkages) was beneficial only for highly motivated clients (Horowitz, Marmar, Weiss, DeWitt, & Rosenbaum, 1984). The therapist's failure to explore the negative feelings of highly motivated clients yielded a weaker therapeutic relationship and also a poorer outcome. However, less motivated clients required a more positive and supportive atmosphere; exploration of negative feelings with these clients undermined the therapeutic relationship. This finding indicates that therapists must be flexible with this technique.

The Therapeutic Relationship and Responsibility

Responsibility is perhaps the most neglected aspect of a therapist's training. Therapists who have addressed the issue of responsibility are more likely to be able to develop a collaborative relationship. Therapists who have not developed a sense of responsibility in their own lives tend to assume too much of the client's responsibility for change—either by blaming themselves when working with an extremely difficult client, or by praising themselves when working with someone who is bound to change. As in many aspects of life, we look for the balance—not to take on too much or too little responsibility for a given situation at a particular time.

How responsible is the therapist for the therapeutic outcome? The therapist is responsible at least to some degree. Clients seek help. They seek the help of an expert; they pay the expert. "The responsibility of all therapists is to foster in their patients that *inner* freedom which leads to maturity, acceptance of reality, and independence" (Mann, 1973, p. 60). Therapists are responsible for their actions during the therapy hour; they have a responsibility to help clients find their sense of independence and responsibility.

If, as therapists, we are too directive in an untimely manner, we may achieve only superficial change, because we rob the client of the knowledge that we cannot do the changing for them. If, as therapists, we are too passive, we may instill a sense of helplessness in the client. The client must decide whether to accept our interventions. The therapist must decide how active to be with a particular client at a particular time.

A major goal of all the three major styles of therapy is to enable clients to become more responsible. If therapists have not adequately dealt with their own responsibility issues, they will probably get in the way of their clients. Effective therapists have the gut knowledge that nobody can live their lives for them and that they cannot live the lives of their clients.

The Neophyte Therapist and Responsibility

Many people who enter graduate programs believe that they fully accept responsibility for themselves. How else could they have reached graduate school? Nobody else obtained for them the grades, the GRE scores, or letters of recommendations that they needed to get into graduate school. That's true. However, therapists require a particular sense of responsibility.

For therapists to be effective in helping clients, they must have a sense of the scope and limitations of their responsibilities to help others and to be helped by others. Yalom (1980) provided a succinct outline of how people tend to avoid responsibility in their lives; therapists use similar defenses to evade responsibility for their education and training. I now review these five common defenses.

Compulsivity.   For students, compulsivity expresses itself as a hurried, unceasing search for answers. This can be a healthy attitude, within limits. It can imply students' acceptance that they do not have answers right now. They may be in a developmental stage of moratorium.

Compulsivity gets students and practicing therapists into problems if they spend endless hours searching outside of themselves for the answers. The structure of many graduate programs fosters this obsessive and compulsive ritual. I remember instructors who would assign an enormous amount of reading and provide only a limited amount of time to digest the material.

To overcome this compulsive defense, therapists must recall why they originally entered the field. They must continuously and critically question the materials in books, lectures, and supervision, to see how this material applies to them and what they want from their education.

Displacement of responsibility.   A student who has adopted this defensive strategy might say, "I cannot learn what I really want to do because I have to take so many classes that are irrelevant to the practice of therapy." As with all these defenses, there is a grain of truth in this statement. It is when these attitudes interfere with students' ability to learn a craft that students need to examine them.

Many students get a sense of responsibility during their training when they gain a sense of groundlessness. They ask themselves, "The therapeutic approaches are so different; how am I to know if I am doing the right thing?" When that question arises, they may be on the right track. At least they are struggling with the issue of responsibility in their professional careers.

Innocent victim.   In this defensive strategy, students set themselves up for failure and then play dumb. This defense often plays out during supervision: the supervisee requests information from the supervisor; they work together on the topic and develop an agreed-upon intervention; but then the supervisee fails to follow through with the intervention during therapy. This situation is frustrating for all parties involved.

Losing control.   The student who has lost control might say, "I know I forgot to bring my tape to supervision for the third time. I didn't have any time to study for the exam. Professor, I am overwhelmed with everything at home and at school. Can I get an extension?" The payoff for losing control is that students can find caretakers—supervisors and professors who have not resolved their own responsibility issues and will give the students what they request.

Avoidance of autonomous behavior.   The ultimate defense against responsibility is this: "I was waiting for you to tell me what I need to do." Many students look outside of themselves for the ultimate rescuer. If we lose the myth that such a rescuer exists, we are face to face with our aloneness, with the realization that we alone are responsible for our own lives. Students who want to know how to develop a therapeutic relationship might begin by finding out how they are dealing with their own issues of responsibility in learning therapy.

In his book on Viktor Frankl, Gould (1993) explains that responsibility cannot be taught; it is a commitment to life.

> Education to responsibility cannot be superimposed on a person
> by society, parents, friends, or therapists. It is a commitment to
> life that each individual freely accepts for himself or herself . . .

Frankl (1978) adds, "I think that the danger is not so much inherent in shock treatment or drug treatment . . . as it is in the extremely technological attitude which dominates so many therapists." (p. 128)

This technological attitude, the endless search for the answer and the techniques to fix people, only strips clients—and, of course, therapists—of responsibility for their own lives. No matter how many books and seminars on the therapeutic relationship students complete, they can only provide a relationship that is superficial or even detrimental unless they understand the limits of their responsibility.

Irresponsibility and the Therapeutic Relationship

In order to discover how not to develop a therapeutic relationship, all we need do is to think of a colleague, friend, or relative who has not accepted responsibility for his or her own life. Such individuals create relationships that are empty and frustrating. A major contention of this book is that people who are not able to develop a therapeutic relationship are themselves frequently lacking in autonomy.

The following statements were rated by therapists as the least characteristic of an ideal therapeutic relationship (Fiedler, 1950b). As you read this list, imagine how such scenarios could be created by a therapist who, not knowing the limits of his or her responsibility, adopts a rescuing role, by being too active or passive.

- A punitive therapist.
- Therapist makes the patient feel rejected.
- The therapist seems to have no respect of the patient.
- An impersonal, cold relationship.
- The therapist often puts the patient "in his place."
- The therapist curries favor with the patient.
- The therapist tries to impress the patient with his skill or knowledge.
- The therapist treats the patient like a child. (p. 241)

When therapists adhere dogmatically to an approach, they are apt to be neglectful. Therapists of all persuasions can get lost in their techniques. Blind adherence to the techniques of a specific school of therapy—whether transference, the disputation of irrational thoughts, or the clarification of feelings—can be destructive to the therapeutic relationship.

To sum up, if therapists want to develop a therapeutic relationship, they need to take a long look at how they deal with their issues of responsibility. It is a lifelong struggle. With honesty, the struggle gets less severe, and crises are less frequent. Only when therapists have a respectful acceptance of their own autonomy can they set appropriate boundaries and actively listen to their clients.

SUMMARY

Unfortunately, therapists in training are subjected to so many obsessive-compulsive rituals that the human factor can easily be lost. The exams demand rote memory; theory courses sometimes do not relate to actual practice; students must learn a potpourri of techniques from seemingly contradictory approaches; the atmosphere is needlessly competitive; some of the professors may not have done therapy with a client in years; and some courses seem so far removed from the actual practice of therapy that students may wonder why they even entered this field. Even the criteria used to evaluate students' competency fit this pattern:

> Generally, the criteria for successful completion of the different training programs are not based primarily on competence in psychotherapy . . . Many of these are academic or intellectual criteria that do not necessarily bear a direct relationship to skills in psychotherapeutic activities. (Garfield & Bergin, 1986b, p. 11)

However, therapists cannot use these factors as an excuse for flaws in their practice of therapy. Therapists are ultimately responsible for what they learn—whether in graduate school or in life. Therapists must be honest with themselves; then they can be honest with their clients. If therapists have listened to themselves during their training, they are more likely to be able to hear what their clients are saying and requesting.

I propose that one reason that comparative research has not found differences in the efficacy between the varying approaches to therapy is that all the approaches rest on the most important process variable—the therapeutic relationship. There is no consistent evidence that any particular form of training (for example, social work, psychology, or psychiatry) is most likely to produce effective therapists (Beutler, Crago, & Arizmendi, 1986). Frank (1973) also found no evidence that one type of training was more, or less, effective than another; and he suggested that this was because all the training programs were equally good at teaching therapists how to develop a therapeutic relationship.

My opinion of the formal education process is less favorable than Frank's. I content that Frank could find no difference between the various training programs because the students who enter these programs include similar proportions of people who already provide the supportive aspect of the therapeutic relationship.

To help clients attain a sense of autonomy, the therapist should provide an opportunity for them to discuss their thoughts and feelings about their therapy and about their therapist. Then, instead of silently attempting to discover what appeases their therapists, clients realize that in their therapy it is safe and productive to be honest. If clients respond to the therapist's questioning by opting to disclose threatening information, the supportive relationship and then the collaborative relationship move forward, as clients regain a sense of autonomy.

When people come to see a therapist, they are not looking for a technician (even though they may say so), nor are they looking for a wet nurse (even though they may hint at that). People want to get on with their lives. Therapists need to give their clients the opportunity that they deserve.

> Whether they openly acknowledge it or not, individuals approaching a psychotherapist are seeking a "good" human relationship and a satisfying relatedness. If their history, which is embodied in their current functioning, allows them to enter such a relationship, and if the psychotherapist can provide the kind of relationship that allows them to form a satisfying relatedness, the basic conditions for a successful therapeutic result are met. If serious deficiencies are encountered from one or both sides, the relationship reaches an impasse, becomes stalemated, and aborts. (Strupp, 1980a, p. 603)

Note that the therapeutic relationship will develop *if* the client can do it and *if* the therapist can do it. People who come to therapists usually have some interpersonal problems; there is no reason to believe that these problems will not carry over into the therapy hour. If they have been honest with themselves, therapists have the ability to provide their clients with the needed empathy and a corrective emotional experience. From this supportive stance, a collaborative relationship can develop.

The remaining chapters of this book center on the therapeutic relationship. A purpose of this book is to provide a balance between the techniques and the phenomenological aspects of therapy—to bridge science and art. The next chapter focuses on the initial assessment. The first meeting with the client is crucial. During the first session, many things can go wrong and many things can go right, with a profound impact on the course of the therapeutic relationship.

CHAPTER EIGHT
THE INITIAL SESSION

Once a journey is designed, equipped, and put in process, a new factor enters and takes over . . . and all plans, safeguards, policing, and coercion are fruitless. We find after years of struggle that we do not take a trip; a trip takes us . . . Only then do the frustrations fall away. In this a journey is like marriage. The certain way to be wrong is to think you control it. I feel better now, having said this, although only those who have experienced it will understand it.

(Steinbeck, 1962/1986e, p. 4)

In this passage, Steinbeck is referring to a trip that he was preparing to take across the United States in a truck camper. He warns that we can never be fully prepared for a journey. Any journey—through the United States, through psychotherapy, or through life—is bound to go awry if the travelers believe that they have absolute control. However, without planning, they may find themselves in the middle of a thunderstorm without a tent.

I am reminded of a canoe trip that my wife and I took in the Boundary Waters between Minnesota and Canada. When we arrived at the outfitter's to rent our canoe, they had a checklist of the necessities for a trip. As my wife and I waited in the store for maps of the terrain, trying to deal with our anxiety as best we could, a young couple was checking out their canoe. As the man behind the counter was going over the checklist of necessities, I heard the neophyte adventurer ask, "Tent? Do you think we'll need one?" Lack of experience does not entitle us to be foolish.

I fully concur with Steinbeck that a person can never be fully prepared for the future. However, to not prepare for the future is flirting with unwanted mishaps. Therapists need to do what they can to make sure that their clients and they themselves are ready for the journey of therapy.

The initial session provides the foundation for the ensuing work with clients. In *Psychotherapy: A Basic Text*, Langs (1990b) devotes 206 pages to setting the ground rules and boundaries of psychotherapy with the client. If the therapist is unclear about what to expect from the journey of therapy, the client will also be unclear.

> In considering the most important aspect of brief therapy, it is clear that in some way the entire process of brief psychotherapy, or perhaps any therapy, is shaped by the first visit. The first encounter sets the tone, tenor, structure, direction, and foundation of the therapy. (Budman, Hoyt, & Friedman, 1992, p. 4)

Empirical research has also found that the first sessions have the greatest impact on positive change (Howard, Kopta, Krause, & Orlinsky, 1986).

When they begin counseling and psychotherapy, most clients are confused. A major task of the therapist is to aid the client in making some sense of their symptoms. However, I have worked as a supervisor with therapists differing in orientation and years of formal education who, through their lack of appreciation for the first session, intensified the client's confusion. The psychological literature abounds with information on the importance of using a formal initial assessment (Beck, Rush, Shaw, & Emery, 1979; Bellak & Small, 1978; Malan, 1979; Sifneos, 1987). These texts identify other important tasks of the first session: clarifying the client's misconceptions of therapy; familiarizing the client with the therapist's style of therapy; gathering pertinent information; and developing workable hypotheses. All of these tasks serve to enhance the therapeutic relationship. In the following sections I address these goals for conducting a formal initial assessment.

GOALS OF THE INITIAL SESSION

Beginning therapists sometimes feel overwhelmed in considering what questions to ask a new client and how to proceed with the initial session. Some opt not to do a formal initial assessment, in the belief that this may interfere with the human aspects of the therapeutic process. However, a neophyte therapist without a formal initial assessment is like the fellow who thought he did not need a tent because he wanted to sleep under the stars. The stars are not out during a thunderstorm.

> It is an aphorism in medicine that if you don't know what you are looking for, you won't see it, the diagnosis will be missed, the inappropriate treatment administered, and the patient will suffer—and inevitably the doctor will suffer as well. Rigorous application of principles, professional responsibility, and therapeutic readiness will do much to prevent unpleasant surprises. (Bellak & Faithorn, 1981, p. 11)

If you don't look, you won't see.

A sound initial assessment provides therapists with important information about their clients: the severity and duration of the presenting problem, recent and past stressors, traumatic events, support systems, weaknesses, and strengths.

Of course, the initial session will not provide all of the necessary information. Once a therapeutic relationship has developed and the client gains a sense of what therapy entails and comes to trust the therapist, other relevant information unfolds.

However, the initial assessment can help the therapist develop hypotheses about clients' suffering; address clients' tendency to withhold information; persuade clients that change is possible; and instill hope in clients. For all these reasons, which I now consider in turn, psychotherapists in training need to develop a formal initial assessment procedure.

Hypothesis Development

One goal of the initial assessment is to gather information that will allow the therapist to develop hypotheses about why this individual is suffering. Cognitive therapists Robins and Hayes (1993) suggest that the initial session is important because the "fire in the valley," the maladaptive behaviors, can be seen so clearly at this time in therapy.

> Dysfunctional beliefs are particularly likely to be accessible early in treatment when the patient is most distressed, so this phase of therapy can be critical for the eliciting of core dysfunctional beliefs, even if they may not be addressed until later in the therapy. (p. 211)

At the conclusion of the first session, and sometimes at the close of the second or even third session, the therapist should have at least one hypothesis about why the client is seeking therapy.

These hypotheses are crucial to the remaining sessions. People who seek counseling and psychotherapy need help; they want solutions. Clients' need for fresh cognitive insight into their condition is supported by research.

> Clients rated as most helpful those therapist interventions in which they indicated that they had learned something new about themselves, their problems, or the world. Those interventions that got the clients in touch with their feelings or that made them feel understood were perceived as less helpful. (Hill, Helms, Spiegel, & Tichenor, 1988, p. 33)

Without a hypothesis, the beginning therapist is likely to be caught in the web of the client's maladaptive patterns. Since hypothesis development (that is, cognitive insight) is so crucial to therapy, I have devoted Chapter 10 to this process variable.

An appropriately conducted initial assessment provides the information that the therapist needs to develop hypotheses.

Client Withholding

What seasoned psychotherapist cannot tell an anecdote of discovering, well into therapy, that the client was withholding information: "Well, that's how I deal with my problems. I've always drunk a case of beer a night."

Surreptitious withholding is not always so dramatic, but it is relatively common. Administering a format assessment minimizes the likelihood of such denial by the client. By asking questions, the therapist is also conveying that she or he will not be complicit in the withholding of information.

Expectations of Change

Many people go to see a counselor or psychotherapist because they have tried changing, to no avail. It is too difficult to change their ways. It is too difficult to face the truths—thoughts, feelings, and unforgivable behaviors. A well-conducted initial assessment is the first step in perceiving these unwanted truths. More importantly, it conveys to the client that therapy is going to be the arena in which to examine and live out these suppressed or repressed memories, whether recent or remote.

By asking for personal information, therapists are conveying to their clients that, in therapy, people discuss personal matters. During the socialization of clients, I always say that the information is confidential. The reason that this information is confidential is that it concerns people's intimate lives. Clients discuss with their therapist thoughts and feelings that they could not talk about with other people; that is one of the major curative factors of therapy.

For example, I always ask clients if they have been emotionally, physically, or sexually abused. If the client has been abused, it would be neglectful to not pursue this matter. If clients have no history of abuse, I am in effect telling them that, in therapy, we discuss thoughts and events no matter how painful or awful. The initial session promotes further self-disclosure by the client as a result of an unspoken communication: "In here, we can discuss the unthinkable." If all goes well in the first session, clients leave with the thought that, if they continue therapy, they will change.

The idea of changing can be frightening. Clients frequently fail to appear for their second appointment—not out of the belief that therapy will do them no good, but out of the fear that they will actually have to change. They will actually have to confront things that they would rather leave hidden. At the close of the first session, to help address those fears, I socialize clients on what to expect from therapy.

Instilling Hope

Not all clients benefit from therapy; to protect yourself, you need to evaluate the client's motivation for therapy. "Every effort should be made to assess motivation during the first interview" (Sifneos, 1992a, p. 96).

If a client is not motivated to your style, or to therapy, or to change, then you need to consider other forms of intervention. Even in 1938, Fuerst knew this primary rule of therapy: "The patient's desire to be treated and to be cured is one of the most necessary prerequisites; if this is not present or cannot be aroused after a few preliminary interviews, the case should not be accepted for psychotherapy" (Fuerst, 1938, p. 262).

Williams (1984), a cognitive therapist, reiterated that the client's expectations of change are crucial and pointed out that an initial assessment can help instill hope.

> A thorough assessment, especially in the context of a structured interview, may communicate hope to the patient that their symptoms are frequent and understandable correlates of the emotional disorder, and that they are not "dumb," "lazy," or "mad," but show discrete behaviors at specific times, at certain frequencies and at certain intensities. (p. 53)

A well-orchestrated initial assessment can communicate to clients that they may change if they continue in therapy. To some, as we have seen, the thought of changing may be so frightening that they prematurely stop their treatment. For others, the belief that therapy may be effective is a source of hope.

Yalom (1975) commented that the instillation of hope is a major factor that helps people to change in a group setting. Other authors have documented the importance of instilling hope in the client (Frank, 1968; French & Wheeler, 1963). If the client leaves the initial session with the belief that the therapist will be able to help, then a strong foundation has been laid.

STRUCTURING THE FIRST SESSION

Some therapists find the initial assessment requirements of an agency distasteful. They complain that an initial assessment can be too rigid. It may strip the emotional aspects from the therapeutic exchange. A stifled cognitive exercise does not promote change; it does not meet the needs of clients in profound emotional pain.

These concerns are valid. A therapist may conduct the initial session in a stifling, mechanistic manner. People who are suffering do not want to participate in an intellectual exercise: "This piece fits with this piece, and that is why you hurt."

However, the therapist determines how structured an initial assessment will be. Even if a therapist is a member of an agency or hospital that requires a concrete behavioral listing of problems and goals, this does not mean that the therapist must elicit this information in an impersonal manner. The art of therapy partially resides in the therapist's skill in obtaining information.

Three decades ago, well before managed health care, Bellak and Small made this point very clearly in their groundbreaking 1965 book, *Emergency Psychotherapy and Brief Psychotherapy.*

> History taking is not and certainly need not be traumatic. To the contrary, if accomplished tactfully, persistent and detailed questioning will afford the patient a degree of narcissistic gratification (indicating, as it were, the interest taken in him) and will increase his rapport with the therapist rather than upset him. For many an individual the history taking becomes a cathartic experience, in the sense that it may be a first opportunity to tell someone what is really troubling him, information which he may have concealed from family and friends. In such a case, the opportunity to share with a professional person provides a lessening of burdens, with concomitant improvement of symptomatology and certainly with an improvement in optimism concerning the situation. (Bellack & Small, 1978, p. 65)

When there is a lack of structure in the initial session, it is likely to be a result of the therapist's lack of empathy for the client's needs at that particular point in therapy.

Many therapists fail to gain the information they need because they are too supportive: it is as if they do not want to add further discomfort to a person who is already hurting. However, Sifneos (1987), a short-term psychoanalytic therapist, states that, in the initial assessment, "the patient should not be permitted to globalize in an effort to generalize and avoid anxiety" (p. 19). Cognitive therapists are particularly effective in keeping the patient on track during the assessment and therapy (Ellis, 1990). As with all interventions, the amount of anxiety a person can handle is dependent on a number of variables and varies over time. However, a therapist who is overly supportive may well be judged by the client as not having the skills to initiate change.

Some therapists in training I have supervised have wanted to play cognitive detective; they liked to intellectually put the pieces of a puzzle together. Such a stance may at first glance appear to come from the beginning therapist's desire to help; however, this intellectual pursuit is often a reflection of the therapist's need for control. For this reason, as we saw in Part One, therapists must have an honest understanding of why they entered the field. Clients whose therapist is an aloof puzzle solver are likely to do themselves a favor and stop therapy.

I compare therapy to a canvas on which the therapist makes light brush strokes.

> When someone understands how it feels and seems to be *me*, without wanting to analyze me or judge me, then I can blossom

and grow in that climate. And research bears out this common observation. When the therapist can grasp the moment-to-moment experiencing which occurs in the inner world of the client as the client sees it and feels it, without losing the separateness of his own identity in this empathic process, then change is likely to occur. (Rogers, 1961, pp. 62–63)

If, during the initial assessment, the client speaks of a trauma, that is not the time to make a blunt confrontation or interpretation. An untimely confrontation can only serve to heighten the client's defenses; besides, the therapist does not yet have enough information. Especially during the beginning sessions, while still developing a trusting supportive relationship, the therapist must tread lightly; it is helpful to utilize clarifications.

There is some concern that the active gathering of information during the first session may rob clients of their own responsibility for change (Kaiser, 1955). However, therapists must remember that the purpose of the initial session is to provide the client with hope, the prospect of a future with less suffering. The therapeutic value of the content of the information elicited is less important than the hope that arises from the therapist's thoughtful questions.

Therapy is founded on an emotional relationship. Part of the art of therapy is for the therapist to know how much anxiety a client can effectively handle. Rarely is a client prepared for an unstructured session from the beginning. Therapy tends to be directive at first, with extensive information gathering, and to become less directive as it progresses. All the time, therapists must consider the degree of responsibility—and the degree of structure—that is appropriate for the client. "The process of therapy is not designed to impose change on patients but to create conditions that allow internal changes to occur" (Strupp, 1990, p. 65).

Summarizing, completing a formal initial assessment can be an autocratic exercise. It is up to the therapist to determine how impersonal the formal assessment will be. Part of the art of psychotherapy is to gather information in a manner that ultimately helps clients to change and to assume more responsibility for their lives. When clients leave the therapist's office after the first session, they should feel hope that change is possible.

AN OUTLINE OF AN INITIAL SESSION

When therapists first meet a client, they often feel overwhelmed by information and unsure how to proceed. As an example of the abundance of information that therapists must sift through, consider the hypothetical example of a person who is depressed. Miraculously, we know that the depression is solely due to their work situation. Even in this artificially circumscribed example, there can be a host of reasons for the depression: the individual could be in a poor work environment; the boss may be dictatorial; co-workers might be overly competitive; maybe there is not enough time to do the work well; expectations could be too high or too low; the pay could be too little; the job might simply be boring; the boss may make too many changes in the client's prescribed duties; the employee may not be allowed to make input into decisions; he or she may lack skills or could be overqualified; the job might not be challenging; the physical stress could be too much; and so on.

In reality, of course, the situation is much more complex. Clients frequently come into the therapist's office saying that they have been depressed and they don't know why. An effective initial assessment can begin the process of narrowing down the alternatives.

If the therapist begins asking pertinent questions, the client may think, "This therapist is going to help me; this therapist asks the right questions and has a basic understanding of who I am."

Simply asking about a client's history in chronological order can provide much-needed structure for the client.

> One of the commonest mistakes trainees make is not to follow the patients' history sequentially; instead they jump around from points in the past to episodes in the present. It may be that patients provide information that they want to emphasize or they feel is important to them; they may want to avoid areas of their childhood that make them anxious. It should be remembered, however, that history taking is the evaluator's, not the patient's, task. Like the physician, who takes a medical history that includes questions about chief complaints and systems reviews in order to arrive at a diagnosis, the mental health evaluator must take the lead in obtaining a cohesive picture of the presenting complaints and of the patient's life. Part of the task is to get the story straight. (Sifneos, 1992b, p. 13)

With the rise of managed health care and other third-party payors, there has been an increased emphasis on short-term therapy; in this context, a structured initial assessment is of particular importance (Budman & Gurman, 1988).

The first session is so critical for the development of the process variables of change that I usually schedule an appointment of 1½ hours. Even with this extra 30 minutes, I cannot always finish the information-gathering process; it then extends into the second session.

In what follows, I outline an initial assessment, divided sequentially into six main categories: (a) the presenting problems, (b) social history, (c) mental status exam, (d) diagnosis, (e) hypothesis development, and (f) socialization. This outline is only a guide; therapists need to develop their own form of initial assessment, which reflects their therapeutic style.

Presenting Problems

Incredible as it seems, therapists frequently do not know what presenting problem brought their client into therapy. One function of the supervisor is to help the supervisee in treatment planning.

> Almost always, when my supervisees' patients are not making progress the root cause is the failure [of treatment planning]. Either the therapist and patient are not agreed on how they will work together, or having begun with what seemed like a workable plan, they are unable to carry it out. Although therapies may fail for many other reasons, difficulty with treatment planning pre-dominates in my own supervisory work. (Makover, 1992, p. 338)

How can people work with a problem if they do not know what the problem is? I had this all-important question posed to me during my training.

I had seen a man in therapy for three months. The client regularly made his appointments and I enjoyed his coming to the sessions, but there was no change, positive or negative. Looking back, part of the reason I liked this man was that he kept returning for his sessions; that alone made me feel good, even though there was no change. I now recall how boring and tedious were those sessions in which I would sit and passively listen.

After the three months, I changed supervisors, as is the custom during internships. When I met with the new supervisor and recited the client's history, he abruptly asked me, "Why is the client coming in for therapy?" A rather simple question. Although this man had a number of problems—marital difficulties, impulsive behaviors, and anxiety attacks—I was un-able to state explicitly what my goals or the client's goals were. When I met with the client again and posed this question, the client himself was unclear why he was coming in for therapy. I felt stupid that day, because I had seen the client for three months and yet had no idea why he was coming in for therapy. On the basis of my supervision of other therapists and of my own experience with clients, I have since realized that it is common for thera-pists not to know why clients have sought therapy.

There are a number of questions therapists may ask: "Where/how is the patient stuck? What is needed to help the patient get unstuck? and How can the therapist facilitate or provide what is needed?" (Hoyt, Budman, & Friedman, 1992, pp. 9–10). On a more concrete basis, Lazarus (1989) recommends that therapists ask their clients the following sequence of questions.

> If you were allowed only one single word to describe your prob-lems, what would that word be? . . . Next, one asks the client to use the selected word in a sentence. . . . The single word followed by the single sentence then leads into meaningful elaborations. (p. 49)

Finally, Beutler (1986) recommends the following sequence of opening questions: "*Why* are you here? Why are you *here*? and Why are you here *now*?" (p. 109).

A client's difficulty in stating a presenting problem may partially be a result of resistance to change. This resistance is usually not conscious. However, an effective way to not have to change is for clients to keep the therapist from knowing the presenting problem and to keep themselves from knowing. In that way, clients can continue to come into a therapist's office on a regular basis and get their emotional strokes, without having to change. With time, clients tire of this charade and stop their therapy, all the while being very gracious to their therapist—not for the therapist's help, but for being allowed not to change.

When I meet with a client for the first time, and after we both take our seats, I begin by asking, "What brings you here today?" I like this question because it is open-ended. Often, clients unwittingly provide the focus of therapy with their response (Sifneos, 1987). Some people begin with their symptoms, some with relationship problems, and some with tears. This is the time of clarifications and reflections. The therapist begins to apply light brush strokes to the canvas.

I am not quick to provide sympathy or reassurance. To do so might suggest that the therapist is judgmental without knowing all the information. Rather, the first session begins with expressed empathy: "It sounds as if you have been a fighter all your life and you are now tired . . . You sound as if you are in a bag, punching and punching to no avail . . . You'd like to curl up and make all of this go away . . . Nobody seems to understand . . . You've been hurting a long time."

The first minutes of the initial assessment are frequently emotional.

> That the counselor is able, often within the first few minutes, to relieve a client's apprehensions is a testimony to the consummate skill of the professional who is experienced at relationship building . . . Rapport is developed not by accident, nor by magic, but by the deliberate efforts of the well-trained counselor who understands the core conditions of nurturance in human relationships and can create them at will. (Kottler & Brown, 1992, p. 82)

Therapy is the last resort for many clients. It has taken much misguided suffering and enduring courage to make it to the office. Many people are afraid that they really may be crazy or may be locked up. The last thing someone needs in the first minutes of entering the office is a therapist adorned in the white smock of intellectual pretension.

Duration of presenting problem.   The length of time that the client has been aware of the presenting problem provides much information about the individual. When clients tell me that they have been depressed or angry all of their lives, I immediately begin to wonder whether they have a personality disorder. I will then say, for example, "That's a long time. How long has your problem been this severe?" It amazes me that many people respond that it has been a year or more and do not volunteer a precipitating event. Therefore, I then ask, "Were there any changes in your life at that time?"

If there was a precipitating event, which there usually is, this may provide information useful in the development of hypotheses. For example, if someone has no history of depression but becomes depressed after a divorce, a simple hypothesis begins to emerge.

The precipitating event may be a symbol of any number of problems in this individual's life. For example, a divorce may imply an ex-spouse who will not leave the client alone, abandonment issues, financial problems, problems with children, chronic relationship problems, or all the above. Further information is required: How has this divorce impacted this individual? What changes have occurred? During this opening phase of the first session, therapists need to let their client lead.

Factors maintaining the presenting problem.   I always ask my clients what appears to be maintaining their problem. This may sound like a rather obtuse question. A person suffering from depression might be expected to reply, "Well, if you'd been through what I've been through, you'd be depressed, too!" However, I have rarely received such a response, directly or indirectly. Rather, depressed clients respond with answers that highlight their maladaptive pattern of coping with stress: "I don't go out anymore. I stay in my house. I have a short fuse. I don't clean the house anymore. I've lost faith in God and no longer go to church." Clients' responses to this question highlight how they have been trapped in a maladaptive cycle—for example, "When I'm depressed, I withdraw; when I withdraw, I become more depressed; when I'm depressed, I withdraw." A confrontation of this cycle could be beneficial; it might indicate how the client is going to respond to further interventions. However, I usually opt to wait, because I have just met this individual and I do not want to get drawn into the game of problem-solving.

By asking clients what appears to maintain their symptoms, the therapist facilitates a crucial change in the relationship. Already, because of the therapist's empathic usage of clarification in the first minutes of the session, clients feel understood—in the sense that the therapist recognizes the client's suffering, not in the sense that the therapist has the answers. When therapists ask what maintains the presenting problem, they are actively helping clients to distance themselves from the emotional pain. The seed of a collaborative relationship has been sown.

Attempts to change.   Next, I ask the client, "What have you done to change?" This simple question alters the tone of the initial assessment. I am providing the client with an opportunity to express his or her strengths.

This question continues to help clients to gain some distance from their problems, to get a sense of perspective.

Reasons for seeking treatment. The two final questions in exploring the presenting problem are extremely important: "Why did you come in today? Why didn't you come in two weeks ago, two months ago, or one year ago instead?" Budman and Gurman (1988) stressed these questions in their book on brief therapy. I was more interested in the immediate events that affected the person's life than in personality problems that would not be amenable to short-term therapy. Research confirms that most clients have experienced one or more major life events within a period of three weeks to six months preceding therapy (Barrett, 1979; Brown, 1978; Thoits, 1985).

Even long-term psychoanalytic therapists recognize the need for the therapist to determine why clients made the decision to make their first appointment. As Langs (1981) comments, "Most pertinent usually is the determination of what prompted the present onset of the patient's symptoms and why he is seeking treatment now" (p. 224).

The client's response aids the therapist in forming hypotheses about the presenting problem. Sometimes the symptoms gradually became overwhelming; the client may be responding to pressure from an employer, friend, or relative. Usually, there is some precipitating event. The client's response may also reflect his or her resistance to therapy.

To sum up, the first few minutes of the initial session are a time of reflection; the therapist gives clients ample time to express their pain and confusion, and expresses respect for their strength in making it to the therapist's office. If the first few minutes of the initial assessment go smoothly, clients should feel that it is all right to hurt in this office; it is all right to be confused; this therapist is going to help. The supportive relationship has begun.

At the beginning of the initial assessment, therapists ask four main questions: "What brings you here today? What appears to maintain the problem? What have you done to change your problem? Why did you come in today?" The clients' responses foster further clarifications. Already, a collaborative relationship is beginning to develop.

This sequence—empathy followed by the work of therapy—is essential to all forms of therapy.

> The therapist must first listen empathetically and reflectively to the initial story line of the patient and then collaboratively help the client to transform his or her story. A nurturant, compassionate, nonjudgemental set of conditions is required for distressed clients to tell their story at their own pace. A number of clinical techniques, including reflective listening, Socratic dialogue, sensitive probes, imagery reconstruction of stressful experiences, and client

self-monitoring, are used to help clients relate what happened and why. Thus, the role of relationship variables is critical, as is the role of affect in the therapeutic process. (Meichenbaum, 1993, p. 203)

In the first five or ten minutes, the therapist has set a foundation for the supportive relationship by clarifying and reflecting the emotions that brought the client to therapy. Then, by asking thoughtful questions about the presenting problem, the therapist provides the opportunity for the collaborative relationship to take root.

Social History

After clarifying the emotional suffering that prompted the client to telephone, and after gaining a perfunctory understanding of the presenting problem, it is time to gather the background information. The following is a lengthy set of useful questions; I do not necessarily use all of them with all of my adult clients. Therapists must decide what questions they will ask for each particular client; this decision will be partially based on their therapeutic orientation.

Present relationships.   We are social creatures. To learn more about a person's phenomenological world, irrational thoughts, or intrapsychic dynamics, it is necessary for the therapist to gain an understanding of the client's present relationships.

Marital status. The therapist needs to know if the client is married or is involved in a long-term relationship. This information is usually volunteered, but asking whether a client is married paves the way for other questions.

"How long have you been married?" People who have been married for one or two years do not present with the same stressors as do those who have been married for ten to twenty years. The first year of marriage can be extremely stressful, as the partners attempt to adjust to each other's lifestyle.

"Have you or your spouse been married before?" This is an important question, because the divorce rate in the United States is high. An affirmative answer begs further questions: "How many previous marriages? When were you married and for how long? Why did you divorce?" If clients or their spouses have been through numerous marriages, they most likely have endured numerous major stressors in their lives. Clients' answers also supply valuable information about their decision-making abilities and interpersonal skills. Such questioning aids in ruling out a possible chronic personality disorder, which could be more amenable to long-term psychotherapy.

"When you disagree, what do you disagree about?" More often than not, people reply that they do not have arguments. In that case, the therapist says, "Everyone disagrees about something." Again, clients' responses to this question can provide much information about their current circumstances.

By asking questions about the client's closest personal relationship, therapists convey to the client that they want to know the client, and that they are able to provide the direction that the client needs in the confusing first session. The client feels understood and safe in the therapeutic relationship.

"Are there any sexual problems on anyone's part?" This may seem a very obtrusive question to be asking in the initial session. However, the metacommunication is that therapy is a personal venture and that such personal information will be discussed. Frequently, I have seen depressed clients who described their marriage as solid but then admitted that they had not been sexually active and that their marriage had been distant. The client's reply conveys information on how this individual's private life is progressing. If sexual dysfunctions are mentioned, sexual therapy may be an appropriate mode of intervention.

With gay and lesbian clients, the therapist needs to provide an opportunity for them to disclose their sexual preference. Note that the previous questions do not provide this opportunity. At one point in my initial assessment, I usually ask, "Is there anyone else in the home?" This at least provides the opportunity to disclose sexual preference; it may also reveal the presence of parents, grandparents, adult siblings, or others in the household.

Children. In regard to children, the therapist should ask, "Do you have any children? What are their ages?" These questions provide the therapist with more information about the client's home life. The therapist needs to know if the children are babies or infants, who demand more of the client's time and energy. A teenager could be going through a tumultuous and rebellious time. A child in late adolescence may be preparing to leave the home.

"Do you have any concerns about the welfare of your children?" A child may be acting out, having difficulty at school, or taking drugs. These other stressors need to be ruled out.

In this age of blended families, it is important for the therapist to ask specifically about stepchildren and how all of the children are relating to one another and to the parents. The therapist may also ask about visitations with the ex-spouse and the frequency and quality of the visitations.

Employment. Frequently, work-related problems are the precipitating event for those seeking therapy. At this point in the interview the therapist is attempting to obtain a well-rounded assessment of the client's current life situation.

"Do you work outside of the home?" I am careful to phrase the question in this manner with female clients. To ask female clients if they are a housewife is derogatory and condescending. Brief questions regarding the type of work, length of employment, and quality of work relationships provide a more balanced picture of the client's current life.

Family of origin.   Therapists of any theoretical orientation should get at least a brief history of the client's family of origin. The major goal is to highlight any relationships that may be related to the individual's presenting problem.

"Were you raised by your biological parents?" Many people have lost a parent during their childhood through divorce or death. In that case, further questioning is required.

"How was your relationship with your parents?" At this point in the therapy, it is common for the client to give a superficial answer, even though their relationship may have been tenuous. The purpose here is simply to offer the client the opportunity to express any concerns about their past relationship with their parents.

"How many siblings were there in the family, and where did you come in terms of birth order?" Here, the therapist simply wants more background information. However, a client who was the first born in a family of eight children may have had to assume many parental duties in the house, as a caretaker of the other children.

"How were your relationships with your brothers and/or sisters?" Once again, clients may provide superficial responses.

History of abuse.   All initial assessments should provide an opportunity for clients to disclose a history of abuse. I usually ask the following question: "Have you ever been emotionally, physically, or sexually abused?" An alarming number of people have been abused. As Langs (1981) noted: "Neurotic symptoms and most ego dysfunctions will not develop out of conscious and unconscious fantasies alone, but out of real traumas and their intrapsychic meanings to the patient" (p. 513). As I have found in my practice, clients who have been abused often develop maladaptive patterns of relating that are linked to their presenting symptoms.

Clients are initially hesitant about talking of past traumas. Asked if they have been abused, many clients hesitate and then say no. In that case, I tap: "You hesitated." If they give no further information, I do not pursue the matter any further at that time.

In a survey of 188 psychiatric patients, Carmen, Rieker, and Mills (1984) found that 43% had been physically or sexually abused as a child or as an adult. That result is astonishing. Readers may believe that the figure is so high because the studies were done only on people who sought therapy—people in emotional pain. What do studies of the general population show? A recent review reported:

> The best estimates for memories of childhood sexual abuse we now have for the United States are 40 percent for girls and 30 percent for boys, almost half directly incestuous for girls and about a quarter directly incestuous for boys. (Demause, 1991, p. 135)

Even this estimate may be conservative. In a review of another study, Kahr (1991) suggested that "the majority of women in America today were sexually abused as girls" (p. 424). The fact that many studies on sexual abuse are based on what people recall—or are willing to admit—implies that these results may be underestimates.

> Until someone is courageous enough to directly question the children themselves whether they have been molested—a simple procedure that has never been done in any published study to date—60 and 45 percent [for girls and boys, respectively] should be considered as the most reliable national incidence rates we now have available for the U.S. (Demause, 1991, p. 136)

In the light of these numbers, therapists must be sure to ask if clients have been emotionally, physically, or sexually abused; and, to be ready to add, "You hesitated."

Psychiatric history.   It is important to get a brief psychiatric history. Has the client been seen by other mental health professionals? Was the client ever hospitalized? The therapist needs to ask what medication clients are presently taking (medical and psychotropics) and whether they have previously taken psychiatric medication. I also ask, "Does anyone in your family have nerve problems? Have they ever had nerve problems?" Non-professionals seem more familiar with the term "nerve problems" than with "psychological problems." The psychiatric history helps the therapist determine whether a medical intervention would be beneficial.

Drug/alcohol history.   Therapists frequently overlook clients' drug usage. People with an alcohol problem who seek therapy generally fail to admit that they are drinking excessively.

The following questions should be included in all initial assessments: "What type of alcohol do you prefer to drink? How often do you drink? How much do you drink when you drink?" An old rule of thumb that I have picked up from chemical-dependency counselors is to take the amount people say they drink and multiply by 2. If a person says he or she drinks 4 to 6 beers on weekend nights, make a tentative assumption that the person may be drinking 12 beers a night.

Two questions have proved helpful in ruling out alcoholism. The first addresses whether the person drinks so much that they suffer blackouts: "When is the last time that you drank a pretty good amount and someone said the next day, 'Don't you remember doing that or saying that?'"

The second question is: "Do you find that you used to drink two to three beers to get a buzz, and now it takes four to six to get the same effect?" People with alcohol-related problems frequently respond to these two questions by remarking, in one way or another, "Doesn't everyone?"

If a client admits to drinking alcohol on a regular basis, has consumed enough alcohol to have had a blackout in the past year, and acknowledges increased tolerance to alcohol, I will question the client further and confront his or her drinking pattern. I refuse to see clients with an alcohol problem unless they also meet regularly with a chemical-dependency counselor. There is no reason to try to treat people for depression if they are consuming a depressant beverage.

It is also important to ask the client about any present usage of street drugs and about any drugs they have experimented with in the past. Many clients do not currently use street or prescription drugs but have a history of abuse that will give the therapist a fuller picture of their experiences.

Finally, it is important to ask the individual about caffeine consumption. This may seem like a trivial question. However, many people go to see a therapist for anxiety-related problems, and their anxiety may be produced or enhanced by excessive caffeine usage. Brody (1987) noted the term *caffeinism* sometimes used to describe patients who drink excessive amounts of caffeine and exhibit symptoms including headaches, jitteriness, upset stomach, and sleep disruption. Therapy would be a waste of the client's and the therapist's time if the best form of treatment would be for this individual to cut back on caffeine intake. I usually rule out caffeinism by asking, "How much coffee, tea, or soda do you drink daily?"

Mental Status Exam

The mental status exam has been a standard procedure of psychiatrists, to determine whether a patient may benefit from psychotropic medication. It is somewhat surprising that other professionals do not employ a mental status examination to explore whether a patient may benefit from medication. The mental status exam also serves as a useful behavioral measure for change and may be welcomed by the client as a sign that finally someone understands and can ask the right questions.

Sometimes I do the mental status exam in the first minutes of the initial session, when the client's opening remarks suggest it might be appropriate. For example, some clients who are depressed state that they can't sleep and they don't have the energy that they once did. In order to stay with them, to build a supportive relationship, I ask the mental status exam questions at the beginning of the session.

The mental status exam evaluates overt behaviors or symptoms that the person presently manifests. I usually make a note about the client's behavior during the initial assessment: Was the client cooperative? Did he or she become more animated as the session progressed? I also note whether the client's speech was logical, sequential, circumstantial, tangential, or pressured. Finally, I note briefly whether the client's affect during the interview was broad, restricted, blunt, or flat. The reader is referred to the glossary in the latest edition of the *Diagnostic and Statistical Manual of Mental Disorders* (DSM-IV) (American Psychiatric Association, 1994) for definitions of these useful terms.

I ask the client, "How would you describe your mood in the past week?" Then I ask, "How has your sleep been?" If the client does not understand this question, I elaborate: "Do you have problems falling asleep? Do you wake up in the middle of the night and have difficulty going back to sleep? Do you wake up earlier than you want to and then find that you can't get back to sleep?" Those three questions correspond, respectively, to initial, middle, and terminal insomnia. I then follow with, "How has your energy level been?" (to rule out anergia). To identify anhedonia, I ask, "Do you find things that used to be enjoyable are no longer enjoyable?" Another important question is: "Has there been any weight change?" If so, the therapist should find out whether the weight change was consciously made or was due to a change in appetite associated with an emotional problem. If the client is sleeping more, the client could be suffering from an atypical depression and might respond better to an MAO inhibitor rather than a tricyclic antidepressant, if medication is warranted.

To rule out suicidal ideation, I ask, "Do you have thoughts of hurting yourself?" This question may seem vague. However, I believe that, by avoiding the word *suicide*, with all its connotations, I encourage clients to reply in the affirmative. Out of the hundreds of people I have seen, only two did not understand this question. Both were individuals with a borderline personality disorder who had a history of self-mutilation; they thought I was referring to their self-mutilative behavior.

Beginning therapists are sometimes reluctant to ask depressed people about suicidal ideation, out of fear that they may give their clients the idea of killing themselves. However, if asked about suicidal ideation, a depressed client will most likely feel a sense of relief; the question sends the message that the therapist is willing to talk about anything.

When clients admit to suicidal thoughts, the therapist should follow up by asking whether they have a plan regarding how they might kill themselves. At this point, many clients state that they have at times fleetingly wished they were dead. However, some clients have an active suicide plan, such as taking an overdose of pills from their medicine cabinet at home. If the client has a plan, the therapist must ask further questions to establish the lethality of the plan and the possible need for hospitalization.

It is also necessary to rule out hallucinations and delusions. To rule out auditory and visual hallucinations, I ask, "Do you ever hear voices or see things that are not there?" Again, this question may seem vague, but I have repeatedly been able to diagnose active hallucinations in clients who had not revealed this symptom to other mental health professionals. Frequently, these clients are young adults in a premorbid phase of schizophrenia or people with borderline personality disorders who decompensate under stress (Kernberg, Selzer, Koenigsberg, Carr, & Appelbaum, 1989). Further psychological testing may be required to diagnose a thought disorder. Some patients hesitate when I ask this question and then deny. I then tap: "You hesitated." At that point, the individual will sometimes admit to hearing voices.

Diagnosis

Having clarified the presenting problem that brought the client to therapy, solicited a social history, and conducted a mental status examination, therapists should be prepared to make a diagnosis and formulate tentative hypotheses regarding the client's symptoms. Some therapists, especially those within the humanistic camp, question the value of diagnoses and active hypothesis development (Szasz, 1974).

Diagnoses and hypotheses can be an asset or a liability. Any tool can be maliciously or benignly applied; it depends on the user.

> Even if practitioners are required to diagnose someone for administrative or insurance reasons, they are not bound rigidly to the view of their client. The diagnostic category is merely a framework for viewing and understanding a pattern of symptoms and for making treatment plans. It is not necessary to restrict clients to a label or to treat them in stereotypical ways. It is essential that practitioners be aware of the dangers of labeling and adopt a tentative stance toward diagnosis. As therapy progresses, additional data are bound to emerge, which may call for a modification of an original diagnosis. (Corey, 1991, p. 13)

A diagnosis is a descriptive aid, as is clearly stated in the introduction to DSM-IV:

> Making a DSM-IV diagnosis is only the first step in a comprehensive evaluation. To formulate an adequate treatment plan, the clinician will invariably require considerable additional information about the person being evaluated beyond that required to make a DSM-IV diagnosis. (American Psychiatric Association, 1994, p. xxv)

Simply knowing that someone's symptoms meet the criteria of major depression provides no information about how or why the person is depressed or how to proceed with therapy.

A person's problems can never be fully summarized by a verbal label. This is where I believe many opponents of nosology get confused: diagnosis is simply a short-hand form of communication that, in its current usage, is not intended to dictate treatment. Diagnoses can be used to convey basic information about an individual.

However, if the therapist neglects to make a differential diagnosis, immediate therapeutic failure can result. A study by Malan and Osimo (1992) found that psychotherapeutic failures could be directly attributed to the therapist's inability or unwillingness to diagnose a long-standing personality disorder. This result "emphasizes the paramount importance of a psychiatric diagnosis before therapy is undertaken, and it also suggests that there are dangers in having initial assessment interviews carried out by relatively inexperienced trainees" (Malan & Osimo, 1992, p. 210). Therapists need to develop diagnostic skills.

Hypothesis Development and Socialization

Because the development of hypotheses (that is, cognitive insight) and the socialization of a client (that is, client expectations) are key process variables of change, I discuss them at length in the next two chapters. I include them briefly here because it is usually at the close of the first session that I present clients with a tentative hypothesis as to why they have been suffering. Based on the limited information I have gained from the client in the initial assessment, this hypothesis is presented in broad terms, on the understanding that further information about the client will emerge as therapy progresses.

> In the [session] summary, the therapist attempts to clarify cooperatively with the patient what has transpired over the course of the session examining the focus of the patient's presentation and perhaps the focus of the therapy. There is also planning for future sessions (if needed). We consider it to be unacceptable to end a session, especially an initial session, by merely saying, "Time to stop" or "See you next week." The session summary helps give form and structure to a meeting and helps the patient have some ideas (and hope) about the future course and direction of treatment. (Budman, Hoyt, & Friedman, 1992, p. 123)

I usually conclude the initial session by socializing the client to my style of therapy. Socializing the client—educating the client about the therapist's approach and what to expect from counseling and psychotherapy—is frequently mentioned in the literature but is rarely a formal part of training. New clients frequently believe a number of myths about therapy. Socialization is an effective means of promoting a positive outcome. At the end of the first session, I also invite the client to socialize the therapist—to tell me what he or she expects from therapy.

SUMMARY

One goal of the initial session is to gain information about the client. Some therapists are hesitant about conducting a formal initial assessment in the belief that it interferes with the naturally evolving exchange within the therapeutic relationship. However, the therapist determines how rigid the gathering of this information will be; the initial assessment can be an empathic appreciation of the evolving therapeutic relationship.

Therapy entails finding an ever-changing balance between structure and experiencing; the balance depends on the particular client, the particular situation, and the particular time. When clients enter therapy, they want to feel understood and they seek guidance. The initial session is crucial to the establishment of the supportive and collaborative aspects of the therapeutic relationship.

> Inappropriate activity and questioning on the part of the interviewer can only heighten the patient's anxiety and prevent the communication of important data. At the same time, inappropriate silence or passivity on the part of the interviewer will also frighten the patient. (Console, Simons, & Rubinstein, 1993, p. 14)

The gains of doing an initial assessment far outweigh the losses. A well-orchestrated initial assessment fosters hypothesis development, prevents the neglect of important information (such as a history of sexual abuse), and helps instill hope in the client. Therapists who do not do a formal assessment may become overwhelmed by information, fall prey to the client's resistances toward therapy, neglect important background information, and misdiagnose.

A formal initial assessment is not a fact-finding mission. At the onset of the first session, counselors and psychotherapists heavily utilize the technique of clarification: they reflect back to their client in an attempt to gain a clearer understanding of the presenting problem. The first few minutes are usually primarily emotional. As the client begins to feel emotionally understood, or at least accepted in a nonjudgmental way, the therapist proceeds to gain information about the client's social history. In this phase of the initial assessment, the therapist is more directive and asks specific questions about the person's present and past relationships. The client then begins to believe that the therapist at least knows his or her background and that in therapy difficult topics can be, and are, discussed. The therapist may then opt to pull the client back to the present with a mental status exam, which, if effectively conducted, promotes further trust in the therapist because the client believes that this person at least asks the right questions.

At the end of the initial session, the therapist presents a global hypothesis about the client's suffering and socializes the client to her or his style of therapy. To many therapists, the initial assessment outlined in this chapter may appear extremely demanding. Even though I schedule one and one-half hours for the first session, I usually do not have time to ask all the questions outlined in this chapter. Each therapist must adopt a form of initial assessment that meets his or her own style of therapy.

The four process variables outlined in this book begin to be established in the first session: emotional experiencing, hypothesis development, and the alignment of appropriate expectations together help to establish a therapeutic relationship—a supportive and collaborative endeavor for change.

Chapter Nine

Socializing the Client to Therapy

"Trouble is, a guy tries to shove it out of his head. That don't work. What you got to do is kind of welcome it.

"Take it's something kind of long—you start at the beginning and remember everything you can, right to the end. Every time it comes back you do that, from the first right through the finish. Pretty soon it'll get tired and . . . before long the whole thing will go."

I tried it and it worked. I don't know whether the headshrinkers know this but they should.

(Steinbeck, 1961/1986d, p. 114)

In this passage from a John Steinbeck novel, the speaker suffers from "shell shock" or, as it is known today, posttraumatic stress syndrome. He has tried to forget the horrors of combat, but without success; the nightmares continued. He advises his friend not to avoid the horrors but to welcome them—to face them head-on. In the last paragraph, the friend reports that he took the advice: he began to confront his fears and memories, and "it worked."

Counselors and psychotherapists, no matter what their orientation, are all too aware that clients adopt debilitating patterns in order to avoid the original horror. However, therapists are usually not as fortunate as Steinbeck's character; they rarely are able to simply tell the client to recall what is being avoided. Clients' symptoms are often vague, and the original horror is far from clear. A goal of therapy is to develop a relationship with clients so that they can find the strength to clarify and face their original horrors. Therapists can help clients to face the unthinkable, the emotional pain, if they prepare their clients for therapy, by explaining what to expect.

PREPARING CLIENTS FOR THERAPY

Therapists have used various terms for the process by which clients are prepared for therapy: systematic preparation and role induction interview (Hoehn-Saric et al., 1964), anticipatory socialization (Orne & Wender, 1968), vicarious therapy pretraining (Truax & Wargo, 1969), and role preparation (Sloane, Cristol, Pepernik, & Staples, 1970).

In this book, I use the term *socialization*, which was originally adopted from sociology by Orne and Wender (1968).

The term "socialization" refers to the process by which the individual who grows up in a particular culture learns what is expected of him in a variety of situations, and what he may legitimately expect of the individuals with whom he is interacting in these situations. (p. 1204)

Socialization allows clients to anticipate what is expected in the culture of therapy. It ensures that the client will not be needlessly surprised, frustrated, and/or fearful of the unexpected.

Socializing a client to therapy helps to dispel some of the myths that clients bring to therapy, and prepares clients to expect future resistance to change. With a sound socialization, clients are prepared to take on more responsibility for their lives. Socializing clients to therapy is a simple technique, but its benefits are momentous.

In addition, Strupp (1975) noted that clients have a *right* to know what the services entail and therapists have an *obligation* to inform their clients of what to expect. Therapists are obligated to inform their clients what orientation of therapy (or lack of orientation) they practice, without going into great detail.

Freud (1905/1953) was keenly aware of the role of clients' expectations in psychoanalysis: "Expectation colored by hope and faith is an effective force with which we have to reckon . . . in *all* our attempts at treatment and cure" (p. 289). Freud warned his patients how long psychoanalysis would take (Gay, 1988). He would explicitly tell his patients what to expect from psychoanalysis, and he coined the term *analytic pact* to describe his process of socializing clients to psychoanalysis.

Hoehn-Saric et al. (1964) are credited with being the first to research the role of socializing clients to therapy. The following is the information they conveyed to their clients in their classic study.

1. A rationale for psychotherapy was given to the patient. He was told in terms that he could comprehend what to expect from his therapist and what would be expected of him. These instructions led, at least initially, to a more desirable in-therapy behavior which gave the patient and the therapist a better opportunity to explore and work through the patient's problems.

2. The possibility of negative feelings about therapy was anticipated and explained. The patient was thereby led to view these feelings not as an indication that he was getting worse but rather as a positive sign that he was progressing since the feelings were evidence that he was becoming involved. In this context the importance of regular attendance, especially at times when one is inclined not to come was emphasized. (pp. 276–277)

Even this brief account makes intuitive and practical sense.

THE THREE MAJOR
ORIENTATIONS AND SOCIALIZATION

Leaders of all three major styles of counseling and psychotherapy have commented on socializing the client to therapy.

Luborsky (1984), a leading psychodynamic therapist, notes the necessity of socializing the client to a style of therapy in order to encourage a client's appropriate expectations about therapy. "In the course of this form of preparatory interview [socialization] the patient is told how the psychotherapy is conducted, what the patient is to do, and what the therapist is to do" (pp. 50–51).

The cognitive therapists Dryden and Ellis (1988) use the term *induction* to describe their socialization procedure. "Induction procedures generally involve showing clients that RET is an active-directive structured therapy oriented to discussion about clients' present and future problems, and one that requires clients to play an active role in the change process" (p. 237). They tell their clients that the past is not important in their style of therapy and that the therapist will not be passively sitting back.

Yalom (1989), an existential therapist, prepares his clients for the length of treatment and addresses the resistance that may emerge from therapy on account of increased emotional pain.

> But be forewarned, individual treatment will most likely require many months, even a year or longer, and it will not be a rose garden. Painful thoughts or memories may emerge which will temporarily make you more uncomfortable than you are right now. (p. 244)

Therapists have the responsibility to give their clients a realistic expectation of how long therapy may take. Warning clients that their symptoms may become more pronounced decreases the probability of premature termination.

As we saw in Chapter 6, research has overwhelmingly supported the efficacy of socializing clients to therapy. In one review of 34 studies, 22 of them found a significantly higher number of positive outcomes (client-rated, therapist-rated, observer-rated, or objective measures) for an experimental group that had been socialized to their therapy, in comparison to a control group that had not been socialized (Orlinsky & Howard, 1986).

In the remainder of this chapter, I outline the myths and misconceptions that clients frequently bring to therapy and highlight some of the techniques used in socialization to decrease resistance to therapy. I explain how socialization can help address a major paradox of counseling and psychotherapy—that clients come to a therapist's office to be more responsible for their lives and yet they depend on someone else (the therapist) to become more autonomous. Finally, I present a sample format for client socialization based on the four fundamental process variables of change.

CLIENTS' MYTHS ABOUT THERAPY

Clients rarely volunteer their expectations of therapy. Therefore, the therapist must specifically ask clients what they hope to attain from therapy and must also briefly explain his or her style of therapy. One error that many therapists make is to assume that they and their clients have the same goals and expectations of therapy.

I know that my goals in therapy have changed over the years, along with my methods and general approach of working with clients. How are my clients supposed to know that I have changed my approach? How are my clients supposed to know what my original approach was? As therapists, we can get caught in a mind-reading game: "You should have known what I was thinking."

Clients' perceptions of what therapy entails are often extremely distorted; they are based on movies, radio and television talk shows, reports of friends and relatives, and newspaper advice columns. Socializing clients to therapy helps to dismiss erroneous assumptions about therapy and to foster a collaborative relationship.

Let's look at six common misconceptions—usually unspoken—that clients have when they first meet with a therapist.

People in Therapy Are Crazy or Go Crazy

I don't know how this unfortunate myth got started. It is reflected in the jokes made about counseling and psychotherapy.

Many jokes and anecdotes characterize what I call the incredible client: a person unlike the "normal" individual, a person who has very unusual concerns that only a therapist can understand. A sampling of these jokes follows:

> *Patient:* Doc, my wife thinks she's a refrigerator.
> *Doctor:* Well, how is that a problem?
> *Patient:* See, she sleeps with her mouth open, and the light keeps me awake.
>
> *Doctor:* So you think you are a dog, eh? How long has this been going on?
> *Patient:* Since I was a puppy. (Dunkelblau, 1987, p. 310)

The message from such jokes is: "You've got to be pretty weird to see a therapist."

When I was working on this chapter, I met with a 24-year-old client who exclaimed at the first session, before I could utter a word, "I am not crazy!" When I hear such a statement, I simply respond, "I don't see people who are crazy; I only see people who are emotionally hurting and feel stuck."

Some clients believe they will go crazy *because* they are in therapy. If a client should even glancingly suggest such a fear, the therapist must address this issue directly; failure to do so guarantees premature termination of therapy. Who wants to do something that makes people crazy? In this situation, the therapist may tell the client:

> Yes, you may go through times in therapy that will be painful. You will look at painful memories, events, or thoughts that you might rather just cover up or put on a shelf. However, honesty does not turn you into someone who is crazy or turn you into some kind of monster. Therapy is a rare opportunity in our society to be fully honest with someone else and with yourself, without being judged. By being honest about your thoughts, feelings, and behaviors, you will grow and become stronger. We will take our time; you have been hurting for a long time and it takes time to get on the right track again.

It is important for the therapist to find out what clients mean by the term *crazy*. It's possible that the client has a borderline personality disorder and fears a psychotic episode. Individuals with this disorder are emotionally labile and do sometimes go through times of a transient psychotic thought disturbance (Hartocollis, 1977). The therapist should be prepared to undertake a complete psychosocial history and psychological testing in order to rule out a borderline personality disorder and other disorders.

However, most clients who express a fear that therapy will make them crazy are referring to confusion and emotional pain rather than a psychotic break. Determine what people mean by the term *crazy*; do not allow them to use such global derogatory words in reference to their situation. Usually, it is enough to tell the client that you do not see crazy people and that therapy does not make people crazy.

People Become Completely Different after Therapy

Some individuals have an intense fear of change and the future and believe that therapy may make them a totally different person. They seem to regard therapy as a machine that punches out perfect people. Clients simply need to be reminded that they will always be themselves; nobody can ever take that away. The changes they make in therapy will only be the changes that they desire.

Clients who express such a myth may have pronounced dependency needs. These may be individuals who try to make few changes in their life out of their fear of losing themselves. If so, they are likely to attempt to get the therapist to do all of the work in therapy. When working with such clients, therapists need to be aware of their own countertransference issues—particularly their need to care for others.

Therapists Can Read People's Minds

This fairly common myth can be very detrimental to the development of a working relationship. Therapists can foster this myth by making supposedly intuitive comments without letting their clients know how they developed these insights. This can lead clients toward too much dependency on the therapist and rob them of their autonomous functioning.

Therapists will rarely hear a client articulate this myth; they must be alert for signs of its presence. A client who makes the therapist do all the work may harbor this misconception: "You should have known what I needed without me telling you!"

The therapist needs to attend to the relationship. If there are any behaviors suggesting that the client is giving the therapist too much power, the therapist must address this issue and clarify the roles of client and therapist. This myth can be superficially gratifying to the therapist, but will ultimately interfere with the establishment of a collaborative relationship and with the client's growth.

People in Therapy Become
Dependent on the Therapist

The movies are particularly good at promoting this myth of therapy. I think of the Woody Allen movies in which he needs to talk with his psychoanalyst before he can make the most mundane decisions. Some clients still do not realize that psychoanalysis is only one type of therapy.

If a client should express such a concern, explicitly or implicitly, the therapist has an opportunity to explain the necessity of working together, to highlight the basic features of the therapeutic relationship, and to acknowledge that the client may at times become dependent on the therapist. Finally, the therapist might say, "Should either one of us believe you are becoming too dependent on me or your therapy, we will discuss it. The goal of your therapy is to help you become more independent."

Therapists Just Say "Uh-Huh" and Do Nothing

Clients who voice such a concern are bringing to therapy a strong resistance. The therapist must clarify and confront this myth, not in a harsh manner but in order to develop a collaborative relationship. If this concern is expressed during the initial session, the client is probably angry to be in therapy.

However, should this concern arise later in therapy, it may mean that the client wants the therapist to do all of the work. The client may hope that the therapist will not explore painful areas. This may be an individual who hurts in the session but cannot voice his or her emotional pain. Such a client may be well on the way to abandoning therapy.

Another possibility is that this concern reflects the client's dependent stance in life. In that case, the therapist can use this experience to the client's advantage. Confronting the therapist on being overly passive took some courage on the part of the client. The therapist can look to see where that courage came from.

Finally, the client may be right: perhaps the therapist is being overly passive out of personal needs and motives.

To sum up, clients who voice a concern about the therapist's passivity may be revealing their need for dependency—their need for people to tell them what to do. Alternatively, this concern may be an accurate depiction of a therapist. How the therapist decides to intervene can have a major impact on the therapeutic relationship and the client's struggles toward increased autonomy.

Therapists Give a Prescription

This myth is fostered, in part, by the client's encounters with the other helping professions—most likely their clergy or family physician. Psychodynamic therapists Bauer and Kobos (1987) capture the essence of these experiences:

> In other situations, patients expect to (1) present symptoms, (2) be told what to do, and (3) receive a cure in return for doing what s/he is told to do. Psychotherapy patients must be taught to play a more active, responsible, and collaborative role in treatment. (p. 179)

Lesse (1973) concurs:

> One of the most important and often one of the most difficult tasks that the psychotherapist has to perform with this type of patient is the modification of his more traditional, dependent, medical role expectancy. The earlier this conceptualization is altered, the smoother will be the course of psychotherapy. (p. 607)

To some degree, all of the myths and misconceptions are linked to this core myth of therapy. All of the people seeking therapy are suffering and have tried to change, but to no avail; many want their therapist to provide the blueprint for change.

Because this myth is so prevalent, and so destructive to the therapeutic process, I devote an entire section later in this chapter to a means of encouraging clients to become more autonomous.

Some clients exhibit what cognitive therapists Kanfer and Schefft (1987) call the "drive-in syndrome": they want advice and fast, easy cures.

> Clients who expect therapists to solve their problems without a need for the clients to change their behaviors present another common difficulty for therapists. We have called this the "drive-in syndrome." Clients with this perception of therapy act as if they could bring in their problems at 8:00 A.M., drop them off, and come back at 5:00 P.M., expecting to have everything cleaned up. (p. 21)

Clients who expect the therapist to give them advice need to be made aware that they hold the answers themselves; the therapist is a guide on the journey of discovery. The therapist might say, "Advice is cheap. I'm sure you have had family and friends give you advice but it doesn't seem to help. Let's look at what's getting in your way."

Summary on Myths

Clients entering therapy frequently bring a number of misconceptions with them. These myths arise from the mass media, friends, relatives, and other professionals and also from their resistance to change. If therapists are not actively listening for signs of these misconceptions, therapy is bound to start off on the wrong foot and premature termination is likely.

Socializing a client to therapy takes away some of the mystery of therapy and fosters the development of a collaborative relationship.

> The most effective format for psychotherapy involves therapist and patient in a collaborative venture. By regarding the patient as a collaborator, the therapist conveys respect and gains valuable assistance. On the other hand, the presentation of therapy in a mysterious light induces dependency by implying that the patient lacks the ability to completely understand and participate in therapy. Demystifying the treatment process helps to define the patient as a more competent person, who is fully capable of initiating and maintaining the steps necessary for self-improvement. (Bedrosian & Beck, 1980, p. 135)

Therapists must be prepared to address and correct clients' misconceptions. Because they are so prevalent, the clinic with which I am associated has produced a brochure that lists common myths, with a brief comment on each one. We display these brochures in our waiting room and distribute them in the community. When I give talks to civic organizations and industry groups, I usually discuss these myths. If time permits, I comment on some of these myths in my first session with clients.

When the myth appears to reflect the client's core problem, the therapist must be ready to address it, as the same issues will recur throughout therapy. Do not regard a myth as necessarily a liability: it can readily be turned into an asset in fostering the client's growth within the therapeutic relationship and, ultimately, in relationships outside of therapy. The socialization format presented at the end of this chapter helps to rid clients of these common myths. With a sound socialization to therapy, a collaborative relationship is more likely to develop.

SOCIALIZATION AND RESISTANCE TO CHANGE

Socializing the client to therapy can also be useful in decreasing the client's resistance to change. Many defenses, distortions, illogical processes, and acting-out behaviors prevent people from changing. Psychodynamic therapist Strupp (1962) accentuates the pervasiveness and tenacity of resistance.

> Every neurotic patient is unconsciously committed to maintaining the status quo; thus psychotherapy—particularly if aimed at confronting the patient with his inner conflicts—proceeds against powerful unconscious resistances. Unless there is a strong conscious desire to be helped and to collaborate with the therapist, the odds against a favorable outcome may be insuperable. (p. 602)

The effective therapist appreciates the multitude of ways in which clients resist change. Therapists need to honor their clients' resistance to change and gain an understanding of what clients want from therapy.

Clients may say they want to change, yet take little initiative to that end. Until the soil is prepared, don't waste your time planting a garden. Nichols and Paolino (1986) cite Laing's comment that people need not only to deny, but to deny that they are denying, and deny that they are denying that they are denying, and so on.

Mahoney (1988), a cognitive therapist, asserts that what therapists refer to as resistance may actually be a productive aspect of the client's life, and therapists need to respect that these same behaviors may have served the client well.

> From a developmental perspective, however, resistance reflects natural and healthy self-protective processes that guard against

changing too much, too quickly. In this view, resistance to core structural change is fundamentally adaptive and should therefore be worked "with" rather than "against" . . . Respect for these processes is more likely to facilitate progressive psychological development than their denial or attempted domination. (p. 377)

Socializing a client to therapy is not a first-encounter attempt to strip clients of their resistance. Rather, an effective socialization softens the change process so that it may not seem so abrupt, unexpected, and frightening. As therapists, we don't fight the resistance; we highlight the patterns.

Socializing clients to therapy is one step in mitigating the resistance to change; therapists forewarn clients of some common behavioral resistances. Two common patterns of resistance (besides the dependency associated with the myths of therapy) are: (a) an increase in the presenting problem; and (b) feelings of anger directed toward the therapy and/or the therapist.

Increased Symptoms during Therapy

A crucial element of socialization is to tell clients that they will go through frustrating phases: "You may go through times when you are bored with therapy, or you may feel there has been no change, or you may even feel worse than when you initially began." At these times, clients may stop therapy prematurely.

Orne and Wender (1968) communicate to their clients that therapy is not always a positive stepwise progression.

It is emphasized that almost all patients go through a period where they feel hopeless and negativistic, that apparently good, cogent reasons will appear which make it "impossible to come to a particular session" but that at these times it is particularly vital to continue . . . In this context, it is explained that progress is not in a steady fashion but that there will be ups and downs. (p. 1208)

The psychoanalytic writers Kernberg, Selzer, Koenigsberg, Carr, and Appelbaum (1989) make a similar disclosure in their work with people suffering from personality disorders.

In establishing the initial contract, the therapist should forewarn the patient of the wish to quit: "As you continue to experience the suffering that brought you into therapy, you are likely to become discouraged. You may well begin to feel you have gotten the wrong therapist or the wrong treatment, and will be tempted to leave. In this way you could prevent us from understanding what your painful experience is all about." Having warned the patient of this eventuality, the therapist can refer to the prediction later. (p. 162)

Thompson (1987) notes, "I frequently tell patients to expect a return of some of their original symptoms and I explain their purpose" (p. 361). Thompson tells his clients that the original symptoms return because the client, having grown emotionally stronger, is more capable of facing the original horrors.

On the basis of their work with people suffering from depression, cognitive therapists Beck et al. (1979) conclude, "It is important for the therapist to inform the patient that, although there is a reasonable expectation for improvement, they both must be prepared for the exacerbation of symptoms and intensification of problems" (p. 75).

I usually continue to tell the client, "On those days that you do not want to come into therapy, tell me. For some reason, it is during those times that people are frequently preparing to make a change in their lives. It may be difficult, but come in anyway, and let me know how difficult it was to come in." Such warnings make clients more able to deal with the heightened resistance when it does emerge. Frequently, clients remember this disclosure more than any other made in the initial session: "I didn't want to come in today, but you told me to come in anyway and tell you. That's what I'm doing." Usually, strong affective sessions grow out of such honest statements made by clients.

It is easy to say that change is difficult: change *is* difficult!

If one considers the feelings of being confronted and coming up with new insights, it is not surprising that clients feel worse and want to run away and avoid the pain. There is probably a balance needed between a certain level of painful feelings and feeling understood, so that the client can tolerate the pain. (Hill et al., 1988, pp. 33–34)

Warning clients that their presenting problems may intensify during therapy reduces the likelihood of premature termination or superficial change, a flight into health.

Anger toward the Therapist

Even more threatening to the therapist than clients' reluctance to come to a session is the form of resistance in which clients have negative feelings toward their therapist: "You aren't helping me. You just sit there. You don't understand how I hurt. You sit there being smug while I'm the one who's hurting." When clients openly disclose their negative feelings toward their therapist, positive change is frequently just around the corner.

Unless therapists tell their clients that it is all right to voice negative emotions about their therapy, clients' frustration and anger may express itself covertly.

> When progress halts or falters, one factor worth questioning is whether issues or feelings vis-à-vis client and therapist may account for this lack of improvement. Sometimes misunderstandings arise that are readily corrected when straightforward communications and metacommunications are examined. (Lazarus, 1989, p. 134)

Therapists need to actively listen to their clients and provide them with an opportunity to openly express their frustrations.

When a client does express frustration or anger toward the therapist, the therapist should not be defensive. The therapist has probably worked very hard to get to that point. Inability to express their anger to others is often what brings people to therapy.

Allowing the client's anger to emerge is one of the most difficult and frustrating experiences for the neophyte therapist. This is where good supervision enters the picture. "Perhaps the problem is that counselors are generally not comfortable with and have not been trained to deal with negative emotions. Specific training in dealing with negative emotions might prepare counselors to cope during the sessions" (Regan & Hill, 1992, p. 173). A supervisor who has a thorough understanding of the vicissitudes of counseling and psychotherapy can be of great help and support during these intimidating times. Forewarned by the therapist, the client is more likely to be emotionally prepared for these thoughts when they do emerge and is more likely to express them. Resistance to therapy is not something to be avoided, but is a natural phenomenon that should be welcomed by the therapist (Strupp & Binder, 1984).

SOCIALIZATION AND CLIENT AUTONOMY

One goal of therapy is for the client to become more independent and autonomous. However, there is a paradox inherent in this goal: clients depend on someone to become more autonomous. Socializing clients to therapy can be a tremendous benefit in fostering their increased autonomous functioning.

The Paradox of Therapy

Clients frequently enter therapy because they feel stuck; they are not willing to make a move—ultimately, to take a risk. Underlying this is a pervasive need for someone to do something for them. However, therapists cannot live the life of another. What we do is to help people find the strength to change through the therapeutic relationship and, ultimately, to find the strength within themselves.

Rarely is therapy as clean as that description makes it sound. Clients sometimes rebel—not so much against the therapist, though it may take this form, but against the change process. One goal of therapy is to provide an environment in which the client can muster the strength to rebel. Letting clients know that they may rebel in therapy can ease the process of change.

Preparing clients for change is one of the more difficult tasks of therapy that beginning therapists face. To provide an environment in which clients are more likely to change is to take the risk that clients may get angry at their therapist, may get angry at their lack of progress, and/or may act out in self-defeating ways. The ideal client is not a suggestible person. Clients who are prepared for the vicissitudes of therapy may be willing to take the risks that they have so desperately tried to avoid.

Clients enter therapy with the imprudent notion that they are unable to change and prefer to obstinately hold onto their problems and patterns rather than change. Commonly, they do not want the therapist to disturb their charade of irresponsibility and helplessness. Therapists who are not prepared frequently get drawn into the client's game. The client's stance is: "Don't you understand? I can't change."

The therapist's persistent, gentle questioning—the soft brush strokes described in the previous chapter—may at least persuade the client that someone understands the pain. By developing and disclosing hypotheses, the therapist engages the client in the change process. Socializing the client to therapy serves the same goal.

In describing clients' resistance to change, Perls and Baumgardner (1975) list three tasks of the therapist: "to recognize how the patient tries to get support from others rather than to provide his own, to avoid getting sucked in and taking care of the patient and to know what to do with patient's manipulative behavior" (p. 44). This is sound advice for therapists of any orientation. The beginning therapist must be aware that the client's inexhaustible need for support arises from feeling stuck, from not having viable alternatives, and from fear of the future. Socializing a client to therapy helps the therapist not to get stuck with the client. It nourishes movement; it offers the client the gift of a future.

Preparing the Client to Assume More Responsibility

At the risk of belaboring the notion that the client is resistant to change, some theorists view that abnormal behavior is a fruitless endeavor to get someone to assume the client's responsibility for life. In his best-selling book *If You Meet the Buddha on the Road, Kill Him!* Kopp (1972) depicted clients' pilgrimage through therapy.

> Patients in therapy all begin by protesting, "I want to be good." . . . Being neurotic is being able to act badly without feeling responsible for what you do.
> The therapist must try to help the patient to see that he is exactly wrong, that is, that he is lying when he says he wants to be good. He really wants to be bad. Morality is an empirical issue. Worse yet, he wants to be bad but to have an excuse for his irresponsibility, to be able to say, "But I can't help it." (p. 108)

The task of the therapist is to not get stuck with the client. The therapist's goal is to set up conditions conducive to change.

Szasz (1974) boldly accuses the medical and psychiatric establishments of treating clients as infants, in order to meet their own narcissistic power needs:

> I submit that . . . most of what now passes for "medical ethics" is nothing but a set of paternalistic rules whose aim is to diminish the patient while aggrandizing the physician. Genuine improvement in medical, and especially psychiatric, care requires the liberation and full enfranchisement of the patient—*a change that can be accomplished only at the cost of full commitment to the ethic of autonomy and reciprocity.* This means that all persons—whether sick or wicked, bad or mad—must be treated with dignity and respect—and that they must also be responsible for their conduct. If such a change in medical perspective were instituted, what patients would gain in dignity and control over the medical situation, they would lose in no longer being able to use illness as an excuse. [emphasis added] (pp. 176–177)

Therapists must treat clients with dignity and respect, thereby depriving clients of the excuse that illness prevents them from taking responsibility for their lives: this is much easier said than done.

Socializing clients to therapy demystifies the process. Most therapists respect the idea that clients are ultimately responsible for their lives. Cognitive therapists Kanfer and Schefft (1987) note this fundamental existential premise of therapy. "The therapist operates on the implicit assumption that every client can assume at least some degree of responsibility for his or her own actions or thoughts" (p. 47). By assuming the position that clients are capable of making their own decisions about their therapy, the therapist is already helping clients to becoming more autonomous.

The therapist who educates clients about what to expect from the process places them in the position of having to make a decision about whether to continue their therapy. Clients discover that the therapist takes his or her role seriously. They discover that the therapist is not going to just sit idly by and allow them to continue in their self-defeating ways. This can be a mixed blessing for clients: it promises a future, but also the frightening prospect of change and risk.

Whether cognitive, humanistic, or psychodynamic, the therapist is likely to be more directive when clients first enter therapy, and to become less directive as the therapy progresses. The therapist appreciates the confusion within the client's phenomenological world and provides time for a collaborative relationship to develop.

By being directive initially and informing the client what to expect from therapy, the therapist is treating the client as a rational human being who is responsible for his or her own life and needs to make informed decisions. A therapist who fails to socialize a client to therapy risks getting caught in the client's manipulations and becoming a caretaker, with negative consequences for the outcome.

ADMINISTRATIVE REASONS FOR SOCIALIZING CLIENTS

Therapists need to set the administrative and financial parameters with their clients. This includes the handling of payments, missed appointments, and confidentiality. By willingly discussing these issues with clients, instead of assigning this chore to a secretary, therapists help their clients to set up appropriate boundaries in regard to the therapy. That is, therapists are informing clients that this is a contractual relationship between two adults. The therapist is not going to be the magical white knight who rides into clients' lives and rescues them.

KEEPING THE THERAPIST ON TASK

A point that is often forgotten is that socializing a client to therapy also keeps the therapist on task. Therapists who neglect to socialize their clients to therapy may themselves be manifesting resistance; many therapists refuse the responsibilities of their role.

Even some experienced therapists prefer to keep the process of therapy a mystery in order to meet their narcissistic needs. As Welt and Herron (1990) noted, "the needs of the therapist, such as those for personal satisfaction, prestige, and companionship in the relationship with the patient, can be eliminated through the contracting process [socialization]" (p. 116). Socializing a client to therapy not only helps the client to have appropriate expectations but also helps to keep the therapist's expectations in line. Therapists who deny their client's right to be socialized to therapy, on the pretext that therapy is too flexible a process to structure, need to examine their countertransference issues.

A SAMPLE SOCIALIZATION FORMAT

I present here a sample socialization format that is applicable to any style of therapy. Therapists need to develop their own version. You may want to leave time for socialization at the conclusion of the initial session and/or you may want to have a written socialization statement that you can give to clients. At our clinic, we are experimenting with a one-page socialization that we give to clients at the conclusion of the first session. We also schedule initial appointments lasting one and one-half hours so that we have enough time to find out what clients expect from therapy and how they expect therapy works and also enough time to tell our clients how we usually work in therapy. Allowing time for such an exchange promotes the development of a therapeutic relationship.

Since therapy is a collaborative effort, the therapist does not dictate how the client should behave and react in therapy. Rather, the therapist begins the socialization phase of the first session with questions about the client's expectations of therapy.

> What did you expect to happen before you came in today? Now that we've met, how do you see what you will do and what I will do in our future sessions? Do you think this will help?
>
> Now let me tell you about some of the common patterns that happen when people come in to see me.
>
> I usually do much of the talking when I first meet with people in therapy, because I am getting information—particularly information about your past and present relationships that may be related to your present situation. In our future sessions, I will tend to do less of the talking. We will work together in finding out what is preventing you from getting on with your life.
>
> Many people who come to therapy are hurting emotionally and expect their therapist to give them some type of advice that will immediately make the pain go away. Unfortunately, I don't have a magic wand that can make people's pain subside. Yes, there are different things I can say or do to help people with immediate problems, but I've found that, with most people whom I see, the hurt has been there some time, and it takes time to discover the right track to pursue.
>
> Advice is cheap. You may already have received well-intended advice from numerous people in your life. These people may know

you well and may have encountered similar problems. However, the advice doesn't seem to help.

The most important person to help you get back on your feet is you. Something right now is preventing you from getting on with your life. We will work together to find out what this something is that is keeping you from living a more balanced life.

What do we do in therapy? The first thing is for you to decide what you want to get out of your therapy. That is, when will we know that we no longer need to continue to meet on a regular basis? Finding out what you want from therapy can be frustrating, because often everything seems confusing and overwhelming. We need to work together to decide exactly what you want from therapy, so that we will be working toward the same goal.

Most people feel, at times in their therapy, that they are not getting better; many times, they feel they are getting worse. That is often an indication that the person has the strength to begin the process of changing, but the changes can seem puzzling, if not frightening. Also, prior to a major change in life, people tend to retreat to old ways of dealing with problems that make them feel worse. You may also feel that you do not want to go to a particular session, for no apparent reason. When you feel you do not want to come in for a session—no matter if you think you are getting worse or because you have made drastic improvement—always keep your scheduled appointment. When you come in, tell me how you were feeling. Those particular sessions can be turning points. The only way to protect yourself is to not allow yourself to judge how important any given session will be, but instead to decide beforehand that you are going to be here no matter what.

The goal of therapy is not to make you the healthiest, the most lovable, the most perfect person. You will still encounter problems, but your therapy will help you to get more satisfaction and fulfillment from your life.

Many people are scared when they develop strong feelings toward their therapist. You may go through a time in which you believe I'm a total idiot or a time in which you believe that I can do no wrong. This is another aspect of therapy. Should such thoughts and feelings arise, you need to be honest and communicate them. Otherwise, they tend to get in the way of your therapy.

One of the main things that makes therapy different from other relationships is that you can be totally honest. It's not wise to tell a boss that he or she is a total idiot. However, it's not only appropriate to tell your therapist, it may also be an important part of your therapy. To be honest can be embarrassing, frightening, and terribly difficult, but it's the most important thing that you do in therapy. The road to a full and rich life is to know ourselves, to be honest with our thoughts and feelings.

Because you have insurance, you need to make your copayment at every session. If you will be unable to make a payment, bring it up and we can discuss a payment plan if necessary.

Missing an appointment in therapy is different from missing an appointment with a family physician. If you are aware that you are going to have to miss an appointment, please inform me at least 24 hours in advance. This time is set aside for your therapy only, and I am unable to fill appointment times as readily as a family doctor.

Everything you say in a session is confidential. I have to obtain a signed authorization of release from you before I communicate with anyone about your coming in for therapy. The only exception to this rule is if I believe that you may harm someone else or yourself. I am bound not only legally, but ethically, to report these incidences.

When I first meet with people, I think it's important for both of us to know if we can work together. Therefore, I ask all people that I meet with to make a commitment to come in for two more sessions. At the end of our third session, we will have had an opportunity to determine whether there is a need to continue, whether we are on the right track, or whether we can even work together. If either one of us does not think that we can work together, I will help you find another therapist who may be of some help.

I know it was hard for you to come here today. I admire your strength and courage that allowed you to do so. The most important thing you need to do in your therapy is to be as honest as possible with yourself and with me.

SUMMARY

As we saw in Chapter 6, the majority of clients stop therapy prematurely, after only a few sessions (Garfield, 1986b). We do not need research to tell us this. I have been surprised, after sessions in which the client and I seemed to be working well together, to find that the client stopped coming in for therapy before we had reached our goals. In retrospect, I realize that, in many of these cases of premature termination, the client was simply being compliant during the sessions where I thought that I was doing great work. In other words, the client was taking care of my needs.

Because [clients] are in awe of the therapist, they politely answer all his questions and he thinks everything is going well; but all the

time the patients are wondering what it is all about, until suddenly
they quit without warning. (Frank, 1973, p. 163)

Socializing a client to therapy can at least give clients an idea of what it is
all about.

A well-prepared socialization of clients does more than simply spell
out what to expect from therapy. Psychodynamic therapists Strupp and
Bloxom (1973) summarize the benefits of their form of socialization.

> The primary contribution of a role-induction [socialization] pro-
> cedure is (a) to provide accurate information concerning the
> process of therapy; (b) to dispel misconceptions and prejudice that
> are abundant in all strata of the population, particularly among
> unsophisticated persons; (c) to enhance the prospective patient's
> motivation for psychotherapeutic change; and perhaps most im-
> portant, (d) to pave the way for a more realistic view concerning
> emotional problems in living and their resolution. The latter en-
> tails an acceptance of the position that the individual must take a
> more active role in mastering his problems, assume greater re-
> sponsibility for himself, and oppose the tendency for dependency
> and passivity. (p. 383)

Many therapists refuse to socialize their clients to therapy on the grounds
that it interferes with the process. However, there can be no interference
with the process if there is no process.

As I have stated throughout this book, a goal of therapy is to help the
client to become more autonomous. When they enter therapy, many clients
feel overwhelmed and want someone to fix them. Socialization of clients
can aid them in the process of therapy and in assuming responsibility for
their lives.

The socialization must be appropriate to the particular client. It is
definitely not a time for therapists to befuddle their clients with a display
of esoteric terms or theories. Butler, Strupp, and Binder's (1992) recommendations on socialization to time-limited dynamic psychotherapy
(TLDP) are applicable to all counselors and psychotherapists.

> It is important to socialize patients to the tasks of psychotherapy
> by explaining in simple language its *modus operandi*, the roles to
> be played by patient and therapist, and the kinds of changes that
> may be expected from TLDP. Such explanations should be realistic
> and down-to-earth. The therapist should maintain a cautiously
> optimistic attitude, but the future cannot be predicted. (p. 105)

Keep it simple. Therapists need to use language that clients can readily
comprehend. Some people need metaphors; some need concrete terms.
Therapists need to listen to their clients, to refer back to examples from

the first session, and to present their style of therapy in a manner that clients can hear.

In socializing clients to therapy, the therapist must remain flexible; that's why, at our clinic, we not only have a written form of socialization that we give to clients after the first session but also allot time at the end of the session to talk with the client about the process of therapy and get the client's feedback. There is no question that socializing is an exchange.

Research on socialization began in the 1960s. The emphasis at that time was on people of lower socioeconomic classes, who were believed to be the only people with misconceptions about therapy. This prejudiced attitude did not escape criticism:

> We believe that educative efforts [socializations] alone do not constitute a balanced approach to treatment innovation for two reasons: they are directed almost exclusively toward lower-class patients, and they begin and end with therapists', not patients', notions about what is "desirable" and "helpful." [We are not] advocating a treatment approach in which patients are, without question, given what they want. As we have suggested in the past, what patients want should be integrated with what their therapist believes they need. (Frank, Eisenthal, & Lazare, 1978, pp. 68–69)

While socialization must take account of the client's particular characteristics—a particular social and economic history, a particular set of present relationships, a particular style of dealing with stress, and so on—it is applicable to *all* people seeking therapy.

Socializing clients to therapy does not connote that we have all of the answers. Indeed, just the opposite is true. Clients also need an opportunity to express what they hope to gain from their therapy and how they expect it to happen.

As we have seen throughout this chapter, the importance of socialization has been recognized by leading therapists in the three major styles of therapy. More than 30 years ago, Heine and Trosman (1960) wrote:

> Therapists may sometimes not take patients' initial expectations sufficiently into account in the crucial early hours of therapy, and thereby may "lose" the patient before a pattern of mutual collaboration can be firmly established. Thus, in training therapists, it is perhaps more useful initially to direct attention to the variety of possible conceptions and expectations of therapy which patients may bring to initial hours. (p. 278)

It is time that we paid heed to these practical words.

CHAPTER TEN
ADVICE-GIVING AND HYPOTHESIS DEVELOPMENT

*You know how advice is. You only want it if it
agrees with what you wanted to do anyway.*

(STEINBECK, 1961/1986D, P. 165)

ADVICE-GIVING

As Steinbeck wrote, people only accept advice that agrees with what they want to hear. Who has not experienced painful events and had a friend provide unwanted advice? Such unsolicited advice can be upsetting for all parties involved. The recipient of the advice often feels angry toward the advice giver for not understanding the unique nature of his or her problems. The advice giver, on the other hand, feels angry because of the recipient's failure to change or to express gratitude. Because of such pitfalls, the rule of thumb for the counselor and psychotherapist has historically been: "Don't give advice!" As used in this book, the term *advice* means giving a client concrete directives on what to do to remedy his or her situation.

Pitfalls of Giving Advice

Historically, the psychodynamic school of therapy has cultivated the myth that giving advice is always damaging. In the following two sections, I quote exclusively from the psychodynamic literature, in which the terms *advice* and *suggestion* are interchangeable. As psychoanalyst Kernberg (1982) notes, "Suggestion, comprising a broad spectrum of psychotherapeutic techniques, includes rational counseling, advice, and emotional suggestions (e.g., hypnosis)" (p. 23).

The attitudes expressed in the psychodynamic literature are not surprising, given the opinions expressed by Sigmund Freud, the founder of psychoanalysis. Freud (1921/1955a) assaulted the use of advice in therapy, describing it as, "an evident injustice and an act of violence" (p. 89). This implies that a therapist—at least, a psychoanalytic therapist—who gave advice would have to be sadistic.

Abraham (1925/1955) stated that advice "spares the patient a laborious adjustment to reality" (p. 326). He believed that to give advice was to risk continuing a dependent relationship, with the ultimate result that clients would be ignorant of their own desires, wants, and needs and ignorant also of the options that might change their life. Thus, according to Abraham, advice-giving is worse than ineffective as an intervention because, on those few occasions that the client accepts the advice, it promotes ignorance.

Malan (1979) listed other reasons why the therapist should not give advice:

> One of the reasons is that no one can be omniscient and foresee all the consequences of a given line of action; another is that it is far better for a patient to take responsibility for his own decisions. But the two most important reasons are simply that the advice is likely to be ineffective, and that clarification of the feelings may make advice unnecessary. (p. 26)

Because therapists are human, they cannot be expected to always know the best path for the client. Therefore, Malan believes that clients should be responsible for their own choices and that therapists should not try to rob their clients of this responsibility by giving them advice.

Nichols and Paolino (1986) see advice-giving as even more malicious: "Suggestion is designed more to flatter the suggestionist and bolster his or her sense of power than to cure the patient" (p. 42). They believe that some counselors and psychotherapists adopt a very structured and directive intervention out of their own narcissistic needs—for example, the need to be admired—and, in so doing, paralyze the development of a collaborative relationship.

As we saw in Chapter 1, therapists need to be aware of their own issues, as revealed in the reasons that they elected to enter the mental health field. Therapists must decide whether a directive intervention such as advice-giving is founded on the eventual growth of the client or on the therapist's narcissistic needs.

Nichols and Paolino (1986) also highlight therapists' tendency to develop an unequal and dependent therapeutic relationship by encouraging clients to believe that the therapist has all the answers. They remind us that

> the patient is the one with the answers. Even if we are convinced that he or she cannot see what needs to be seen, and we from our favored vantage point have a much clearer view of the terrain, that view will not help the patient until the patient can connect it with his or her own experience. (p. 76)

In other words, Nichols and Paolino believe that advice from the therapist is neither desirable nor necessary, because clients can eventually draw the same conclusions themselves.

Note that Nichols and Paolino's argument could be interpreted to mean not that advice-giving is always wrong, but that advice must be well timed. Therapists should not try to convince a client of errors in thinking or behavior until the client is prepared for such confrontations. Metaphorically, we may say that therapists should not waste their time sowing an unplowed field; the ground must first be prepared.

On the basis of my training experiences and conversations with colleagues, I conclude that therapists of a wide variety of orientations agree with the psychodynamic school's lesson: never give advice! For a therapist to give advice is to risk (a) taking on an omniscient and omnipotent position; (b) playing out narcissistic needs; and (c) having the client adopt the advice without a deeper understanding of its meaning.

One would fervently hope that individuals in training and experienced therapists would be aware of these pitfalls of advice-giving. Indeed, empirical research finds that therapists in training tend to be less directive in their interventions in comparison to people with no psychiatric training (Bohn, 1965; D'Augelli, Danish, & Brock, 1976; Parsons & Parker, 1968). One explanation for these findings is that therapists develop a keen understanding of the futility of giving advice.

The Reality of Giving Advice

As we have seen, many therapists and supervisors believe that it is always wrong to provide direct advice, because it deprives the client of the suffering necessary in attaining autonomy. However, such dogmatic thinking is potentially dangerous: some clients, at times, need direct advice to help them break free of their maladaptive behaviors.

Failure to provide direct advice can even impair the therapeutic relationship. Sometimes people are aware of their self-defeating behaviors and are waiting for someone whom they admire, trust, and respect to confront them. If the client believes the therapist is taking a passive position—is merely watching the client suffer—the therapeutic relationship suffers and little change ensues. To provide advice can reflect a genuine concern for the client—a concern that the client perceives and appreciates. It is the trusting relationship that results, rather than the client's suffering, that helps the client to become more autonomous. As such, the content of the advice is not as important as its timing.

In the early sessions, when clients are feeling overwhelmed, they often benefit from a more directive stance. Advice-giving may be appropriate whenever clients need to be reminded of their self-defeating behaviors and of alternatives that might allow them to break free from a maladaptive spiral (Basch, 1988).

It is interesting that the same psychodynamic therapists who so belittle the use of advice have also noted its benefits when used in a timely manner. In fact, Nichols and Paolino (1986), who warned therapists about the untimely use of suggestion, also chide psychodynamic therapists for not utilizing advice: "Since indirect suggestion is ubiquitous in all psycho-therapies, and indeed in all interpersonal relationships, psychodynamic psychotherapists ignore this powerful technique at their patients' expense, and at their own peril" (p. 49).

Malan (1979), who listed pitfalls of advice, picks up where Nichols and Paolino leave off: "Advice is something that it is absolutely correct to give in its proper place, particularly when one has expert knowledge not possessed by the other person" (p. 26). Why would a therapist withhold his or her expert knowledge? Reasons may include blind adherence to a theoretical school; lack of experience; or disregard for the client as a suffering human being. Therapists must not neglect the use of advice out of a narrow-minded interpretation of a theoretical position. Instead, therapists need to listen to their clients and to their clients' needs at a particular time.

Finally, even Freud (1912/1990b), who characterized suggestion as a violent act, also proclaimed that "the results of psychoanalysis rest upon suggestions" (p. 7).

Cognitive therapists actively use directives (Beck et al., 1979; Taylor & Arnow, 1988; Williams, 1984). In the early days of cognitive therapy, clients were openly confronted on their maladaptive thoughts and were directly told by their therapist what alternatives were available to change their behaviors—for example, thought stopping, homework assignments, or systematic desensitization. However, with the rise of the constructivist perspective, cognitive therapists have become less directive in their approach. (See Chapter 2 for a more comprehensive review of this change in the cognitive approach.)

When advice is appropriate, it may take various forms: perhaps a simple question or perhaps strong and repeated confrontations. Neverthe-less, Steinbeck's (1961/1986d) foreboding words about advice remain largely true: "You only want it if it agrees with what you wanted to do anyway" (p. 165).

Summarizing, advice-giving is an integral part of the therapist's arma-ment in helping the client to change. Often, in supervision, therapists will move from being extremely directive to a more balanced approach based on the particular client's needs.

If advice is to be effective, it must be given in a timely manner, and therapists must be sure that the advice arises from the goal of fostering the client's autonomy and not from their own need to be in a powerful position or from a narrow application of a style of therapy.

HYPOTHESIS DEVELOPMENT AND DISCLOSURE

In counseling and psychotherapy, a hypothesis is an educated hunch that is grounded in theory. Hypotheses also emerge from the interaction between the client and therapist. In the insightful words of Elvin Semrad, "Think about the purpose of the symptoms: what does the symptom do for the person?" (cited in Rako & Mazer, 1983, p. 163). Ultimately, hypotheses develop between a particular therapist and a particular client at a particular time; they do not originate solely from an inert theoretical orientation.

The development and disclosure of hypotheses are critical components of any mode of psychotherapy. Cognitive insight is a major process variable. No matter what their orientation, therapists must have a hunch about why the client is suffering. Cognitive therapists insist on the role of cognitive distortions (Beck, 1976); behaviorists insist that the client suffers from faulty learning conditions (Skinner, 1953); psychodynamic therapists focus on symptoms emerging from unconscious conflict (Malan, 1979).

It is clear that hypothesis development plays a key role in cognitive-behavioral and psychodynamic therapies. However, the role of hypothesis development within the humanistic school is confusing. Therefore, I now review Carl Rogers's writings on this subject.

Rogers (1951a) comments, "Only when the counselor, through one means or another, has settled within himself the hypothesis upon which he will act, can he be of maximum aid to the individual" (p. 48). At first glance, it appears that hypothesis development plays a key role in Rogers's form of nondirective counseling.

However, the astute student of Rogers's nondirective approach is aware that it gives the client the freedom to discover his or her own impediments to growth. The therapist is not responsible for hypothesis development: clients are to develop their own idiosyncratic hypotheses.

This contradiction arises out of Rogers's differing uses of the term *hypothesis*. Within the same book, he speaks of a hypothesis both when he means a theoretical orientation and when he means an idiosyncratic notion about the etiology of a specific client's presenting problem.

Rogers advocates hypothesis development in the sense that the therapist should take on a theoretical orientation. He abhors hypothesis development of the second type, because he believes that it relieves clients of responsibility for their own lives. Like many therapists in training, Rogers is reluctant to develop hypotheses about a client's particular situation for fear of inflicting his own values and interpretations on the client.

However, therapists cannot avoid the fact that their values—and the hypotheses that they base on them—have an impact on therapy. If therapists deny their life experiences and values, they risk isolation in an intellectual ivory tower.

In any case, it is extremely naive to pretend that therapists' experiences and values do not matter and have no effect on the therapy process. Simply by attending to some of the clients' reports and neglecting others, therapists are expressing their values. For example, Bergin (1980) reviewed verbatim transcripts of therapy conducted by Carl Rogers and concluded that Rogers "systematically rewarded and punished expression that he liked and did not like in the verbal behavior of clients" (p. 37). Of course Rogers and other humanistic therapists express hypotheses. Hypothesis development must not be confused with being directive.

Summarizing, hypothesis development plays a key role in the interventions of all major schools of psychotherapy. Therapists need to be aware of where they are taking the client and, to do so, they must be aware of their hypotheses.

The Necessity of Hypothesis Development

Without hypothesis development to provide a focus, therapists risk having vague, amorphous sessions. As the humanistic therapist Bugental (1987) comments, "Experienced therapists come to recognize how important it is to stay with a theme or experiential dimension rather than allowing the conversation and its process dimensions to wander" (p. 59). Therapists are apt to become passive, rather than active, listeners when they are not working toward the elaboration of hypotheses. They run the risk of aiding and abetting the client's resistance to change. Sessions are focused when client and therapist work together, in a collaborative relationship, on discovering hypotheses and underlying themes.

Keeping the sessions focused.   Cognitive and short-term psychodynamic therapists are particularly aware of the need to keep sessions focused. Many of these therapists have become disillusioned by more nondirective forms of intervention. Ellis (1990) recalled the frustration he had experienced in his work as a psychoanalyst.

> Why, when I seemed to know perfectly well what was troubling a patient, did I have to wait passively, perhaps for a few weeks, perhaps for months, until he, by his own interpretive initiative, showed that he was fully "ready" to accept my own insight? Why, when patients bitterly struggled to continue to associate freely, and ended up by saying only a few words in an entire session, was it improper for me to help them with several pointed questions or remarks? (p. 7)

Many clients who enter counseling and psychotherapy need structure in their lives; they feel confused and do not know which way to turn. In the initial session, I sometimes describe the client's confusion graphically by intertwining the fingers of my hands in a convoluted manner and saying to the client, "It sounds as if everything is a mess and you're wanting to make some sense of all of this." This seemingly minor move can help in the process of beginning a supportive relationship. It is fundamental for clients to find the form that is missing in their life (Luborsky, 1984). Simply labeling the confusion can be a major therapeutic gesture. "I would regard labeling primarily as a means of reducing anxiety by dispelling ambiguity" (Frank, 1980, p. 335).

A key element of hypothesis formation is that the therapist and the client need to determine what the presenting problems are. As we saw in Chapter 8, this is one of the major tasks of the first session. Many beginning therapists have the misconception that clients will come into their office and tell them what the therapeutic focus will be. It rarely works that way.

No hypotheses can be made about the client's suffering unless client and therapist are aware of the presenting problems. A client's inability to work with the therapist on identifying a presenting problem or related symptoms discloses much about the client's strengths and weaknesses (Sifneos, 1987): it may indicate that the client's life is characterized by lack of focus and definition. Thus, the inability to identify and define the problem may be part of the problem. This, in itself, is important information for the therapist. The therapist must also realize that, without a circumscribed presenting problem, sessions may be characterized by short-term interventions, by putting out fires, rather than by work toward enduring change.

When clients have vague complaints, I try to enlist their aid in clarifying symptoms, by offering them the following metaphor:

> It sounds as if you're imprisoned in a bag and keep punching and punching. You've been a fighter, but you're getting nowhere and now you're tired. No matter where you punch the bag, it just bends. Our job is for you to have more control over getting out of this bag when you choose to do so.

Such metaphors facilitate the movement toward a collaborative relationship by providing the client with an opportunity to feel emotionally understood (Hammer, 1990).

In hypothesis formation, therapist and client work together to clarify what the person hopes to obtain from therapy. This helps keep sessions focused, and can help to give much-needed direction to the client's life.

Preventing inappropriate expectations for change.   A second reason to develop hypotheses is that it helps prevent therapists from developing inappropriate expectations. Particularly in many training programs, clients often present a host of chronic problems and stressors: single-parent families, unemployment, history of child abuse, lack of finances, and so on. If therapists do not actively work on hypotheses with their clients, both the client and the therapist may become overwhelmed and have disparate expectations.

An early experience of mine illustrates this problem. My first job as a therapist involved working with families with a pattern of child abuse. Most of these families lived in welfare housing, and the parents often came from abusive backgrounds themselves. The families lived in constant emotional and physical danger. Overall, their dreams of a better future were long gone. With the energy of a young crusader intent on saving these people from their horrendous lives, I pushed my middle-class values on them.

Before I began this job, I had been concerned about my own employment. As a result of these concerns, my first thought was to help the unemployed financial caretakers in these families to find jobs. I was oblivious to other aspects of the clients' lives, and I failed to actively listen. Once I started to listen more deeply to their pain, however, I realized my error. There were days that I drove home with tears streaming down my cheeks. I was learning to accept the pain that surrounded these families, rather than trying to play savior. It was a hard lesson to learn, but, as a result, I began to realign my expectations and my hypotheses. With time, I could really hear their pain, and only then did I begin to admire their strengths.

Many therapists I have supervised have fallen into the same trap at one time or another. They failed because they could not hear or accept their client's life. They pushed their values and issues onto their client.

In order to keep from giving up on these families, I had to endure the pain of my limitations; I had to adjust my expectations and goals to meet the client's reality.

Hypothesis development helps to keep the therapist's expectations in line with reality. If the hypothesis is wrong, the therapist will find out. Since hypothesis development is dependent on the therapist's expectations, an error in one may reflect an error in the other. By paying careful attention to hypothesis development, the therapist can judge whether or not the therapist and the client are on the right track.

Challenging the client's interpretation of the problem. Active attention to hypothesis development also helps the therapist avoid getting caught in the trap of keeping sessions safe. When clients who enter therapy already have a hunch about the cause of their suffering, this hypothesis most likely has a defensive purpose. If clients were able to tolerate the original source of their emotional pain, they would not have had to come to a therapist. In other words, clients' initial hunches often help to conceal their core pain.

For example, Dessie, the depressed woman I described in Chapter 1, said she knew why she was depressed: it was because she needed to emotionally let go of her adult daughter. However, it quickly became apparent that Dessie was depressed because she could not tolerate the thought of getting older. By worrying obsessively about her daughter's life, she did not have to examine her own life. A goal of hypothesis development and disclosure is to remind clients of what they are attempting to avoid.

Therapists need to be wary of the client's initial hypothesis about the presenting problem. This does not mean that therapists should ignore or discount the client's initial hypotheses; rather, therapists should not accept them at face value.

Fostering a collaborative relationship.   During a case conference in a graduate program, a student was asked by a supervisor why she thought the client's symptoms had subsided. The therapist replied, "I just listened." On further discussion, it was apparent that this therapist was not a passive listener. She was very active in her interventions, in a nondirective manner.

Hypothesis development helps the therapist avoid becoming a passive listener. Passive listening only accentuates the lack of structure in a client's life; it is the nodding response of a therapist who lacks the courage to take risks. Active listening, on the other hand, is being able to say things that others cannot, or will not, say.

By being passive, a therapist may become an empty friend. As Semrad poignantly reminds therapists, "A therapist who is not oriented to going after what the patient avoids could sit with [the client] for five years and get nowhere" (cited in Rako & Mazer, 1983, p. 143). If you want to be remembered for being nice, stay passive. If you want to be remembered for helping people to change and grow, be an active listener.

I was fortunate enough to attend a workshop in which Jeffrey Zeig of the Eriksonian school was a presenter. He reminded the participants that clients enter therapy with a gift to the therapist, their pain. As in any growth-enriching relationship, there is an exchange: as therapists, we can in return give clients a gift. By listening with an active ear, by hearing clients' pain, we give them something in return—frequently, a hypothesis. Even if incorrect, a hypothesis is an important gift. Psychodynamic therapists Kernberg, Selzer, Koenigsberg, Carr, and Appelbaum (1989) capture the essence of this gift.

> The patient may respond with relief if an inexact characterization [hypothesis] organizes a previously chaotic experience—even the incorrect formulation may be taken by the patient as a gift from the therapist, as a token of the therapist's belief that understanding is possible; on the other hand, the patient may react with dismay, realizing that the therapist cannot always understand, is not om-niscient, and is separate. (p. 106)

The development of a hypothesis, even an incorrect one, can be viewed as a reciprocal gift to the client.

Yalom (1980) has noted the importance of hypothesis formation, or cognitive insight, in his humanistic style of therapy.

> The patient is gratified by having his or her inner world scrutinized with such thoroughness; the therapist is charmed by the intellectual challenge, and all the while the real agent of change, the therapeutic relationship, is silently germinating. (p. 340)

The value of hypothesis formation—of cognitive insight, of interpretation—is perhaps not its direct influence on the outcome, but rather its indirect influence on the outcome by enhancing the collaborative relationship.

Summary. We have considered four experiential reasons for utilizing hypotheses in counseling and psychotherapy. The first is that hypothesis development acts as an aid in keeping the sessions focused. When there is no focus, the therapist risks boredom. Boredom is keeping everything on safe ground; boredom is the same thing over and over again; boredom is lack of affect; boredom is lack of change. Most likely, if therapists are bored, it is because they are not working with the client toward developing hypotheses. When therapists become bored with a particular client, they are usually helping the client avoid changing; the sessions become stale. Having a focus, working toward hypotheses, brings the sessions to life.

The second reason for active hypothesis development is that it keeps the therapist's expectations appropriate to a particular client at a particular time in a particular situation. The therapist's expectations are often inappropriate—too low or too high. Hypotheses help keep the expectations aligned with the client's present reality.

A third reason for hypothesis development is that it keeps the sessions from being safe. Therapists and clients are more apt to take risks when actively working toward hunches that offer an explanation for the clients' suffering.

A fourth reason for hypothesis development is that it fosters the development of a collaborative relationship. The client's pain is exchanged for the therapist's understanding, as expressed in the hypothesis. Even an incorrect hypothesis is a gift. The active development of a hypothesis helps to create an enriching, beneficial, and collaborative relationship.

Why Therapists Do Not Use Hypotheses

Many counselors and psychotherapists refuse to actively speculate on the etiology of a person's symptoms because of (1) the notion that one person can never fully know another, (2) poor training, and (3) the interference of countertransference issues. I now address these three issues in more detail.

Therapists' ideology.   Some therapists fear that, by actively developing hypotheses, they will, in effect, be pushing their worldview onto the client. If someone is suffering and you say, "I understand," the recipient of this comment, as you probably know, generally replies, "No, you don't understand, unless you've gone through this yourself." To attempt to explain the origins of the individual's suffering would definitely be presumptuous, the imposition of one person's values on another.

Greben (1979) describes therapists' fear of exhibiting

> an attitude which is all too prevalent in some psychiatric and psychoanalytic circles, one which has been ironically labelled as the view that "in psychiatry the customer is always wrong." Such a view, when it occurs in therapists, would be amusing if it were not so damaging. (p. 507)

Some therapists have opted not to develop hypotheses out of a reluctance to be judgmental. As we noted earlier, humanistic therapists are the most likely to feel this reluctance.

However, therapists must realize that we all develop some hypotheses. We differ in how we communicate the hypothesis to the client. For example, therapists who believe a particular topic is worthy of further exploration will follow the client's verbalization by saying "uh-hu," leaning forward, opening the eyelids, adopting a richer tone of voice, and/or uttering a direct question or statement. Therapists need to be aware of these responses and of where they lead the client.

We all have hypotheses about why an individual suffers. A major task of therapists is to make hypotheses explicit, at least to themselves. They then have more control over how hypotheses are conveyed to clients. Many therapists claim to refute hypothesis formulation on ideological grounds. However, many of these same therapists fail to develop and disclose their hypotheses as a result of inadequate training rather than ideology.

Poor training.   A second major reason therapists do not actively make hypotheses is their poor training. Learning the art of developing hypotheses is an integral part of any counselor's training. The core of a therapist's course work involves the accumulation of knowledge that aids the development of plausible hypotheses. If properly taught, courses in personality, theory, abnormal psychology, counseling and psychotherapy, and sociology make an important contribution to the therapist's ability to develop hypotheses.

Unfortunately, the link between course work and the practice of therapy is very weak in some programs. The situation is most alarming in the supervision, practicum, and internship programs. At one agency, I was involved in supervising other therapists, some of whom had 20 years of experience or more. I quickly realized that, in at least 80% of the cases in which change was nonexistent or negative, the therapist did not have a focus or hypothesis. In effect, the therapists were saying they had no idea why the person was exhibiting the presenting problems.

I find this quite remarkable. Frequently it was only after active questioning that the supervisee realized that he or she did not have a hypothesis.

In my supervision of beginning therapists, I repeatedly ask, "What is your hypothesis? What is your hunch about the person's pain?" I do this because I believe that the formulation of hypotheses is one of the most difficult tasks in counseling and psychotherapy.

As Persons (1991) noted, "The most demanding clinical task of any therapist is to choose a problem and an attack on that problem that will be helpful to that particular patient for that particular problem at that particular moment" (p. 101). As therapists gain more experience and their style of therapy evolves, this task becomes less overwhelming.

If students do not prematurely give up out of frustration, they will be rewarded in time with more enriching and accurate hypotheses, which, whether explicitly disclosed or not, will help the client to change.

Countertransference.   A third major reason that counselors and psychotherapists avoid hypothesis development is that of countertransference issues. Therapy can be viewed as a means to help people make a decision— to make a commitment to themselves and to others, and to assume more responsibility for their lives. It is tough to make decisions, to take a stand and put oneself on the line; there is always the risk of being wrong. Clients may prefer the pain and confusion they feel to the risk of making a decision and being wrong. One task of counseling and psychotherapy is to help clients see the futility of such behavior and to help them find the strength and courage to meet the challenge of change.

Therapists are human, too. It is tough to develop hypotheses; there is always the risk of being wrong. I propose that countertransference issues are the major reason therapists do not engage in hypothesis formation. If the therapist develops a hypothesis and is wrong, will the client rebel?

Earlier, I described an incident during my training, in which a supervisor confronted me on not knowing the presenting problem of a client whom I had been seeing for three months. Not only did I not know what the hypotheses were, but I did not know what problems the client wanted to work on!

Looking back, I realize that this client's way of avoiding change was to keep things vague. However, my own countertransference issues were largely responsible for my predicament. This client came in for every appointment, was congenial, and made me feel good. He was a respected leader in the community. Why should I rock the boat? If I did, he might abandon therapy. He might abandon me, and I would feel incompetent. With further supervision, I worked with the client on delineating what he wanted from therapy, and then our work began.

I have also been fortunate enough to supervise students who have openly expressed the same fears. To make a hypothesis is to make a decision. To make a decision is to take a risk—the risk that the client may resist and prematurely terminate therapy. It is much safer to passively listen. Early in his career, Ellis was trained in classic psychoanalysis and was passive in his approach. His clients liked him, but many failed to get better.

> I discovered many years ago, when experimenting with Ferenczi's (1952) technique of being nice and warm to my clients, that they loved their therapy session and me. However, many of them . . . became more dependent and sicker. That was one important reason why I abandoned psychoanalysis and created RET [rational emotive therapy]. (Marmor, Ellis, Frances, & Kline, 1990, p. 32)

Therapists are wrong to believe that they help their client by passively listening. Instead, they are falling prey to the client's fear of change. Eventually, the client will tire of this pretense and leave therapy anyway.

With the cultivation of hypotheses, there is a risk of premature termination—not so much because the hypothesis may be incorrect or unpalatable, but because it prompts the client's terrifying realization that the therapist really does expect him or her to change. When the therapist actively develops and discloses hypotheses, the message to the client is that the therapist is taking therapy seriously. This can frighten the client.

The client's reaction will depend, in part, on how the hypothesis is elicited and presented; this is an important part of the art of therapy. In the early stages of therapy, the therapist will be doing much of the hypothesis development and disclosure.

> The therapist's usual position, particularly in the initial stage of therapy, is of necessity that of external observer. From this more abstract and less emotionally evocative position, one is able to consider the relationship between the many elements in the patient's narrative. One can study its general flow just as playgoers occasionally step back from the scenes that have captured their attention to consider the drama as a whole. The major function is that of pattern matching, looking for themes that bring stories together. (Berger, 1987)

The goal is for the client to also become an active participant in this process and to be inspired by the therapist's curiosity and enthusiasm. With appropriate development and disclosure of hypotheses, the client feels a welcome anticipation of change, even though this awareness may sometimes be painful and somewhat frightening.

When to Develop and Disclose Hypotheses

Hypothesis development is an ongoing process; it evolves from the first time the therapist hears the client's name until the last session, when the client is leaving therapy. If the therapist has sufficient skill and experience, hypotheses develop around a core theme that helps clients in their growth. Developing and disclosing hypotheses are two distinct, yet related, processes. I discuss them separately in the next two sections.

When to develop hypotheses. When should a therapist begin to develop hypotheses? In practice, it happens automatically. For example, therapists are frequently well on their way to developing hunches about their clients even before they meet them. For example, in an agency or hospital setting where a secretary or paraprofessional does the telephone intakes, the therapist may be forewarned that a particular client was upset about coming in because he or she could not have a specific appointment time. Even with that little bit of information, the therapist may unwittingly begin to expect a client with resistance and little desire to change. Before even meeting with the individual, the therapist may unintentionally give up on trying to help this client.

On some telephone intake sheets, the presenting problem, age, and employment status are noted. Solely on the basis of the telephone intake sheet, therapists have begun developing hypotheses. As an example, consider the therapist's enthusiasm at seeing a 39-year-old administrator for recent onset of "anxiety attacks" as against seeing a 26-year-old unemployed court-referred person for violent behaviors. Of course hypotheses are developed early in treatment.

A classic study in social psychology warns therapists to be aware of their initial impressions of clients. Luchins's (1957) experiment on the primacy effect found that first impressions of people have a lasting impact on relationships: if your first impression of someone is positive, you are likely to continue to have a favorable impression, and vice versa. This implies that many therapists who do not actively work on developing hypotheses may be relating to their clients mainly on the basis of their initial impression, even though later information should have countered that initial impression. Luchins (1957) stated that people can counter first impressions by avoiding snap judgments and by consciously weighing all the evidence. This is excellent advice for therapists.

We all develop impressions and hypotheses about other people's pain, no matter how limited our information may be. However, many therapists have difficulty verbalizing their hypotheses, even after meeting with a client for a number of sessions. This lack of awareness is alarming. It leaves the therapist at the mercy of countertransference issues (Epstein & Feiner, 1983; Gorkin, 1987).

The therapist needs to be an active, aware participant in hypothesis development. Hypothesis formulation is at the center of the therapeutic process, as Stricker notes:

> My approach in psychotherapy is one of continuous hypothesis formation, confirmation, and rejection. Much like the process involved in construct validity, a nomological net is constructed, elaborated, and revised. My framework is psychodynamic, but this same process can be used with any orientation. (Mahrer, Stricker, Powell, & Rice, 1990, p. 48)

With experience and the development of a therapeutic orientation, the therapist increasingly is able to filter out irrelevant information and to construct hypotheses that promote positive changes in the client.

When to disclose hypotheses. In the vast majority of cases, the verbal disclosure of the therapist's hypothesis is a necessary but not sufficient condition for effective therapy. The form this disclosure takes will depend on the strength of the therapeutic relationship and the stage of therapy.

With the increased usage of short-term forms of therapy, emphasis on the early disclosure of hypotheses has been growing. Usually, if the therapist is actively working on developing hypotheses, a focus of intervention—a hypothesis—materializes in the first few sessions. Alexander and French (1946), two of the initial proponents of short-term psychoanalytic therapy, believed it was useful to develop a hypothesis early in treatment.

> Alexander compared the therapist during the initial interview to a traveler standing on top of a hill overlooking the country through which she/he is about to journey. At this time it was possible to see the whole anticipated journey in perspective. Once the traveler descends into the valley, one may examine small parts of the landscape in much greater detail than is possible when viewing them from a distance, but the broad relationship will no longer be so clear. (Bauer & Kobos, 1987, p. 36)

Since this is such a rich metaphor of hypothesis development, I will elaborate further.

The role of the therapist during the initial session is to let the client know that the therapist is looking at the correct valley. This is done by asking appropriate questions to ascertain the presenting problem, social history, and so on. During the initial session, the therapist gains a general sense of the person's life.

To develop the metaphor further, the therapist in the initial interview smells smoke in the valley and tells the client that there is a fire—a problem of which the therapist is aware. Then, to elicit the collaborative relationship, the therapist asks the client to descend into the valley and examine the extent and source of the fire—to help identify and define the presenting problems. This is when the client's resistance begins to emerge, and the art of therapy comes to the forefront.

At this point in the therapy, there is only the smell of smoke. The therapist still doesn't know the source and intensity of the smoke. However, by letting the client know that there is danger from a possible fire, the therapist may be providing helpful knowledge; previously, the client has been aware of danger, but hasn't known why; at least now the client can begin to take some type of action.

Malan (1979) refers to these initial hypotheses as trial interpretations. Briefly, the purpose of these trial interpretations is to (a) strengthen the collaborative relationship; (b) decrease the resistance to change by highlighting the problem and mobilizing the defense; (c) test the appropriateness of hypotheses; and (d) assess the client's ability to work in a particular style of therapy.

Davanloo (1992b) also comments on the role of trial interpretations in short-term dynamic psychotherapy.

> I have come to the conclusion that no one can really tell anything about the patient's likely response without exposing him to some of the important ingredients of the therapy that he will receive. Therefore a specific kind of psychotherapeutic session—amounting in fact to trial therapy—is an essential part of the initial evaluation process. (p. 99)

Not all therapists, however, are open to such trial interpretations. Langs (1981), a psychoanalytically oriented therapist, openly criticizes the use of interpretations so early in treatment: "I object in principle to such interventions and to any concept which suggests that the patient is on trial and being tested" (p. 83). However, every therapist must determine whether the particular client can work within the therapist's therapeutic style. To accept a client that is ill-suited for the therapist's orientation is a tragic disservice to the client; it is also unethical.

It appears that Langs's primary concern is with the judgmental connotations of the term *trial*. He continues, "In the final minutes or so of the session, inform the patient, very briefly and in simple language, as to your impression of his problems" (Langs, 1973, p. 224). Thus, he does recommend the disclosure of hypotheses. By making global disclosures early in therapy, therapists can demonstrate to the client that they will be playing an active role in the process.

Cognitive therapists present their hypotheses as early in therapy as possible and administer directives even in the first session (Beck et al., 1979). The cognitive behaviorists perceive themselves as fire fighters: when they smell smoke, they go to work. Again, clients are on trial initially to determine whether they can work within a directive approach. If not, there is no reason to promise the client a more nondirective approach; that would be false advertising.

Even the humanistic therapist Rollo May (1975) realized the role of hypothesis formation in the beginning phase of therapy.

> The communication with me in the first session may be seen as the preliminary step in this creative process [therapy]. Then came the "aha" experience as the needed insight, preferable as an image, is born in the individual's consciousness. The third step is the making of the decisions, which the young man did between the second and third sessions, as a result of the newly achieved form. (p. 168)

When starting therapy, the client is often confused and does not know what to do. The therapist can provide structure and form to this chaotic situation by developing hypotheses. May (1975) continues: "The creative process is the expression of this passion for form. It is the struggle against disintegration, the struggle to bring into existence new kinds of being that give harmony and integration" (p. 168).

The process by which hypotheses are developed and disclosed is more important than the content of any particular hypothesis. The words that are said to the client in hypothesis disclosure are not as necessary to the therapeutic process as are the timing, significance, and relevance of the communication. Effective hypothesis disclosure sends the client the message that, finally, someone understands. In Dollard and Miller's (1950) celebrated attempt to integrate learning theory and psychoanalysis, they discussed hypothesis development and disclosure at length. They argued that the therapist

> should be constantly refining his hypotheses to get as good a fit to the facts as possible . . . The skillful therapist . . . does not make interpretations on mere hunches. He waits until he has strong evidence for his hypothesis before he supplies a label, points out a transferred response, or teaches a discrimination. If the patient is to be convinced, the evidence must be convincing. The fewer ill-founded notions the therapist utters, the greater his authority when he does speak. (p. 284)

The hypothesis is disclosed when the therapist feels confident that it is relevant to the particular client.

The humanistic therapist Yalom (1989) once told a client that the client and Yalom's wife had had a similar upsetting experience. This disclosure turned out to be a major part of the client's therapeutic change, not because of its content, but because it was a gift.

> Going "beyond words," that was what counted. It was what I did, not what I said. It was actually doing something for the patient. Sharing something about my wife was doing something for

Marge, giving her a gift. The therapeutic act, not the therapeutic word! (p. 220)

In exchange for the client's honesty and courage, therapists make a gift of their consideration, appreciation, and understanding presented in the form of a hypothesis.

Hypothesis development and disclosure is an ongoing process throughout therapy. The therapist should at least be able to smell smoke during the initial assessment and should so inform the client. Hypothesis disclosure begins during the initial session. However, it is an ongoing process, as Bauer and Kobos (1987) note: "Establishment of a workable focus often takes more than one session. In fact, the entire course of treatment could be conceptualized as a continual formulation and deepening of the treatment focus" (p. 161).

The active development of hypotheses tends to move from vague, soft hunches to hypotheses that are more specific and are grounded in theoretical, historical, and experiential data. That is, as the therapy progresses, the relationship between the various hypotheses becomes more apparent to the therapist and the client; a theme emerges. Luborsky (1984) extrapolates the kernel of hypothesis development in the following quote.

> While engaged in each session, the process of listening and understanding, as experienced by the therapist, is like tracking a "red thread" across a field (to use Dr. Ellen Berman's analogy). The thread comes into view only from time to time . . . The red thread corresponds to the clinical formulation of the main problem. (p. 121)

To elaborate on this analogy, beginning therapists who are struggling to develop hypotheses may feel that they are in a room with many strands of rope, only one of which contains the red thread. With the continued experience of active listening, therapists begin to rule out some of the ropes and to be more effective in teasing out that red thread.

How to Present Hypotheses

The three major schools of counseling and psychotherapy place a different emphasis on how to present the working hypothesis to the client. These range from the nondirective approach of the humanistic school to the directive approach of the cognitive school.

Within the humanistic camp, reflection is the major technique for hypothesis disclosure. At first glance, reflection may not seem to be a viable method of presenting hypotheses. However, as we saw earlier in this chapter, reflection directs attention to a particular statement by the client, which is a form of hypothesis disclosure. It says to the client, "This appears to be important; tell me more."

Explicit disclosure of the therapist's hypothesis is a fundamental premise of the cognitive camp. The hypothesis focuses on the client's faulty cognitions. The cognitive therapist highlights the client's distortions and offers active means to alter these maladaptive thoughts.

The manner in which inferences are drawn from a client's comments and behaviors has long been neglected in the psychodynamic literature (Ramzy & Sherrin, 1976). However, Bibring (1954), in a classic paper, clearly outlined five basic techniques of psychodynamic psychotherapy that are means of presenting hypotheses: suggestion, catharsis, manipulation, clarification, and interpretation. The goal within psychoanalysis is to move from "the copper of direct suggestion" and alloy it eventually with the "pure gold of analysis, interpretation" (Freud, 1919/1955b). Before a therapist can make a psychogenic interpretation, the stage must be set with the less ego-dystonic techniques of suggestion, catharsis, manipulation, and clarification.

Even though the three orientations vary in their styles of hypothesis disclosure, they all appreciate that clients resist the therapist's disclosure of a hypothesis. In all three schools, the hypothesis must be presented in a timely manner and expressed in a way that can be heard by the client. Sometimes, strong confrontation of a client's behavior may be required to get the client's attention and to make clear that the therapist will not participate in the client's current denial or self-defeating behaviors.

Resistance to hypothesis disclosure.   It takes a great deal of courage on the part of a client to make it to a therapist's office. To go to a therapist explicitly connotes change and implicitly connotes loss—loss of old patterns. The client has an underlying fear of losing cherished behaviors, even though they may be self-defeating. I often tell therapists, "One of the tasks of clients is to not change." This is my working definition of resistance. It reflects a major paradox of therapy: clients come to therapy asking for help in changing their lives, but they simultaneously behave in ways that are not conducive to change.

People do not want to give up their habits. They fear change. To change is to face the unknown. Clients prefer the security of their maladaptive thoughts and behaviors to the risks of change.

Psychodynamic therapists have long known that the underlying hypotheses cannot be presented until the client's resistance to change has been addressed (Wolberg, 1954). Cognitive therapists also appreciate clients' courage and resistance. They often begin the initial session by asking, "How do you feel about seeing a therapist?" or, "How did you feel about coming here today?" (Beck et al., 1979, p. 87). To distinguish their view of resistance from the traditional psychoanalytic stance, Beck et al. (1990) prefer the term *patient noncollaboration.*

Beginning therapists are particularly aware of the resistance that often follows hypothesis disclosure and, as a result, hold back on developing and disclosing hypotheses. However, with experience and the development of a coherent therapeutic orientation, therapists realize that resistance is not something to be avoided. It is a component of change to be expected and respected.

This resistance to change has served the client well; therapists do not need to take away what Winnicott (1965) calls the client's *transitional objects* unless they have begun to give the client something else in their place. That something is the therapeutic relationship. Hypothesis development is part of the growth of the therapeutic relationship, which is the foundation of successful therapy.

Hypothesis development and the collaborative relationship are interdependent: hypothesis development evolves throughout therapy, as client and therapist learn to work together as a team. Hypothesis development is definitely not a cold, sterile, one-sided relationship in which the therapist intones, "You are depressed because . . . " If hypothesis disclosure is timely and empathic, the client gains further trust and respect for the therapist.

As clients gain more trust in the therapist, they disclose more relevant information about themselves. Ultimately, clients' heightened self-disclosure is not directed so much toward their therapist as toward themselves. Clients' resistance to therapy begins to wane as they learn to trust the therapist and themselves.

The ability to disclose hypotheses while also respecting the client's resistance to change forms a large part of the art of therapy. I now consider hypothesis disclosure in more detail.

The Process of hypothesis disclosure.   Clients seek out counselors and psychotherapists because they do not feel strong enough to engage their troubling thoughts, feelings, and behaviors on their own. They cannot face their own truths. I am reminded of a sign that is in the foyer at a local YMCA: "People want to know how much you care before they care how much you know." Clients are not seeking therapists for our great pearls of wisdom. Clients are human beings in this changing, frenzied, and sometimes terrifying world; they feel confusion, fear, hurt, anger, disappointment, and aloneness. The therapist helps clients to gain strength, whether by providing emotional support, reality testing, or by behavioral assignments. To demand too much from clients may prompt them to run away—emotionally, by withdrawing during the sessions; cognitively, by demanding that the therapist fix them but then not following through; or physically, by not showing up for the next appointment.

Having a focus, or a hypothesis, keeps the therapist and the client on task. But the timing of hypothesis disclosure is all-important. First the client needs to feel understood.

> If disconfirming data are presented too early . . . the patient may
> dismiss or distort these data. The therapist will find himself in an
> adversary role rather than a collaborator or guide. It seems that
> only after patients feel they have had a chance to "present their
> case" and be understood, will they be ready to consider disconfirm-
> ing data. (Beck et al., 1979, p. 63)

How does one go about developing and disclosing a hypothesis? The
hypothesis evolves from the therapist's orientation and from the interaction with a particular client; it is a never-ending process. The goal is for a
coherent, underlying theme to develop from the therapist's theoretical
orientation, from the client's verbal and nonverbal information, and from
the therapist's interactions with the client.

In the early stages of therapy, as I mentioned in Chapter 8, hypothesis
development and disclosure proceed with a series of light brush strokes—
soft, unobtrusive interventions. The therapist tries to clarify what the
problem is, by using reflection and being with the client in the here and
now. The brush strokes set the emotional tone of therapy: "You've been
alone." "You're a fighter, and you're growing tired." "It sounds confusing."
"That must have hurt." "Nobody was there." "It sounds frustrating." If the
therapist is skillful and empathic, the client becomes less guarded and
begins to feel understood.

The second major intervention in the development and disclosure of
hypotheses is to use a technique that I call tapping. As in obtaining the
client's social history, the therapist asks direct and relevant questions. The
client's verbal and nonverbal responses may show the therapist a soft spot,
a possible link to the individual's maladaptive behaviors. Tapping continues around that soft spot. The therapist, always aware of the client's
defenses and pain, is guided by experience, theoretical orientation, and the
client's responses. Tapping is a powerful technique. What therapist has not
had clients admit a history of sexual abuse that they had no intention of
disclosing? Therapists who use tapping as a major source of intervention
become more astute with experience.

Adopting Berman's analogy, we have described hypothesis development as a search for the red thread. Tapping helps the therapist to tease
out that red thread, as psychodynamic therapist Mann (1973) outlines:

> The most effective means for involving the patient in the treatment
> process lies in selecting a central issue that is both genetically and
> adaptively relevant, hence one that has been recurrent over time.
> A close study of the patient's history will disclose some thin red
> line that began in the past and remains active in the present, one
> that denotes both genesis and adaptive effort dictated by the
> genesis. (p. 17)

For example, consider the following taps: "Since your father died, nobody in the family has discussed him . . . You were a child without a father and left with confusing feelings . . . Even today your family doesn't mention his death . . . Your present relationship appears to mirror your confusing memories of your father . . . At times you idealized him and, at other times, you wished he was gone." Of course, tapping does not only involve making past-present links. For a cognitive therapist, it may mean making links between a person's feelings and irrational thoughts.

Throughout therapy, therapists consistently brush and tap, brush and tap. The brush-tap technique provides an indirect means by which the therapist can present the working hypothesis. At times, it is appropriate to disclose a hypothesis directly, but the use of the brush-tap technique is more frequent. This technique allows the client's resistance to decrease, because the client does not feel judged by the therapist.

Skillfully used, the brush-tap technique allows clients to come as close as possible to making their own hypotheses and identifying the underlying theme of therapy. Thompson (1987) notes:

> In my experience, we therapists generally only have hypotheses: and the patient's interpretations always take precedence over those hypotheses. For, it is only they who harbor the full truth about themselves. (p. 283)

By utilizing the brush-tap method, the therapist fosters the development of a collaborative relationship, in which clients learn to trust the therapist. From this emerging relationship, clients gather strength to face issues that they have elected to avoid. By direct and indirect disclosure of hypotheses, the therapist provides the client with new information to consider—more fuel for the fire of change. The client must choose whether to use or discard that information, on the basis of their more complete knowledge of themselves.

Direct expression of hypotheses. Both cognitive and psychodynamic orientations recommend eventual direct disclosure of hypotheses. For cognitive therapists, hypothesis disclosure means pointing out maladaptive cognitions and replacing these cognitions with more adaptive beliefs. Psychodynamic therapists express hypotheses in the form of interpretations. However, if therapy mainly consisted of statements of the therapist's hypotheses, it would be a stale and nonproductive relationship. The brush-tap technique is much more extensively used.

Nevertheless, some situations demand a more urgent intervention. For example, I once worked with a single man, 28 years old, who was evidently suffering from a characterological disorder and was harboring a great deal of rage. This man, whom I shall call Lennie, had sought therapy because he was feeling overwhelmed and depressed. His voice was loud, and he was of a strong build. He seemed dangerous and I felt threatened by his rage. When I was obtaining his biographical data, he stated that, as a child, and throughout adolescence, he had a compulsion to put objects in sevens or to count to seven repeatedly for hours. His prior therapist had interpreted this compulsive behavior as his need to be assured that all seven of the family members were still in the home.

On the basis of his history and his chronic rage, I confronted him, in a soft, yet affirmative voice: "It wasn't the fear that a member of your family would abandon you. It was the fear of your own rage—the fear that you would kill one of them. You had to be sure that all seven would be safe from your anger." At that point his eyes grew wide, and he made fierce, terrifying eye contact with me. Then his body began to violently shake. Those years of rage were emerging. After a few moments, still emotionally distraught, he exclaimed, "That's it! Nobody has ever said that. That's it!" We then began our work.

Such dramatic times of intuitive statements are few, although I would like to believe that intuition guides all of my interventions to some degree; I would hate to think that therapy is solely an intellectual exercise.

A willingness to get at clients' level and to feel their pain and hurt allows therapists to hear what their clients are so desperately attempting to say.

Judging Whether a Hypothesis Is Correct

As we have seen, the content of a hypothesis is not as important as the process of hypothesis development and disclosure. Garfield (1990) makes the intriguing observation that, in research on cognitive insight, a correct hypothesis is not judged on the basis of the client's reactions, but instead

> is determined by some authority or a group of judges in terms of a specific theoretical orientation. Thus, a correct Freudian interpretation is unlikely to be the correct Adlerian, Jungian, or Sullivanian interpretation . . . In my view, the interpretation or explanation that is accepted by the patient is the one that may have some positive therapeutic impact, not necessarily the one that is dictated by a particular theory. (p. 276)

That viewpoint is adopted in the following remarks on the correctness of a hypothesis. The emphasis is not on the content of the hypothesis, but rather on the impact that the hypothesis has on the therapeutic relationship and, ultimately, on positive change.

If the therapist adopts the brush-tap method of hypothesis development, ideally, the client's resistance gradually decreases, more information becomes available, and a strong collaborative relationship develops. With time, the theme naturally emerges. However, the therapist is frequently the first to become aware of the emerging theme. The therapist then must decide when and how to confront the client with the theme and must be prepared for an increase of resistance. As Freud (1913/1958a) noted, "the truer the guess, the more violent the resistance" (p. 140). That insight can be used to judge how correct the hypothesis was.

Peter Sifneos (1987) suggests that a therapist can judge whether the hypothesis disclosed was on target by paying close attention to the client's reaction.

> The evidence that the therapist's intervention has had an effect should be gauged not only by the words that are being spoken, but also by observation of sudden shifts in the patient's associations, slips of tongue, uncomfortable silences, blushing, inappropriate facial expressions, or finally, postural changes. (p. 133)

Does the client change the subject? Does the quality of the client's voice change? Changes in the client's behavior during the therapy hour can be evidence of heightened resistance.

It may help to draw attention to this behavior. A light brush may be all that is needed: "Did you notice your voice became tighter when I said that?" or, "What are you feeling right now?" With major confrontations of a theme, be prepared for the accompanying resistance and make a brush comment on the observable change in the client's behavior.

Malan (1979) suggested that the therapist can judge the correctness of a hypothesis on the following basis.

1. That events in the patient's life, and particularly precipitating factors, suggest the nature of the conflict [hypothesis] underlying the symptom.

2. That a detailed mechanism can be clearly formulated whereby the symptom represents or expresses the conflict.

3. That interpretation of this mechanism to the patient brings the conflict clearly into consciousness.

4. That this results in the disappearance of the symptom. (p. 107)

The disclosure of a hypothesis should ultimately result in the disappearance of the symptom.

When a hypothesis is on target, the client will frequently begin to spill forth information in a guilt-free manner, as if to say, "Look at what I've done. Look at how I've wasted my life. I knew it all along." This is a powerful time in therapy and one that keeps therapists in the field. Moments when a client comes into contact with what they had been so tragically attempting to deny are magical. However, it still takes time for the client to integrate this insight into his or her life and move forward. Therapists need to be ready for the door to close, and must be prepared to refer back to the initial disclosure.

SUMMARY

Torrey (1986) offers a humorous exposition of a fundamental point:

> There is an old Spanish recipe for making horse-and-canary pie: Take one horse, add one canary, mix thoroughly, and bake. This also turns out to be the recipe for successful psychotherapy, with the horse represented by the basic components of psychotherapy [the process variables] and the canary represented by specific techniques of the various schools or brands [the styles of therapy]. It is not to say that the canary adds nothing to the pie—to a highly discerning palate it may make the difference between a mediocre and a really tasty pie. Rather what this recipe implies is that for most clients it is fatuous to spend long hours arguing about what specific type of canary would go best in the pie. (p. 197)

If you are going to bake horse-and-canary pie, you must have a canary, a style of therapy. However, the bulk of the pie is the horse—the common process variables, one of which is hypothesis development. All orientations rely on hypotheses, on the client obtaining cognitive insight. The content of the hypotheses may be different—a client's depression may be attributed to unresolved oedipal problems, illogical thoughts, ontological anxiety, or a host of transient problems—but every therapist must develop hypotheses of some kind.

In the absence of a shaping hypothesis, therapy is unfocused, sessions may become boring and stale, and the client is not challenged to change. It has been my experience that therapists neglect to develop hypotheses because of their personal issues rather than their ideology.

Every client a therapist encounters is going to have different needs in terms of hypothesis development and disclosure. This is part of the richness of therapy; therapy is different with each and every client. With submissive and dependent clients, a directive stance may be more effective (Beutler, Pollack, & Jobe, 1978). With clients experiencing complex symptoms, a nondirective approach may be more effective (Sloane, Staples, Cristol, Yorkston, & Whipple, 1975). Therapists must be flexible.

When people come to the therapist's office, they are emotionally hurting. The last thing they want is to hurt more. It is no wonder that one of the client's major tasks is to not change, to avoid the risk of greater anxiety and emotional pain. Knowing this, the therapist must take care in selecting an appropriate style of hypothesis development and disclosure. Therapists need to be prepared for resistance, but they need not fight it. The client's defenses have at least gotten the client this far. Resistance melts with time and understanding, as the therapeutic relationship matures. Therapists usually need to let the client do the work.

CHAPTER ELEVEN

EMOTIONS AND THERAPY

For man has to have feelings and then words before he can come close to thought and, in the past at least, that has taken a long time.

(STEINBECK, 1962/1986E, P. 33)

EMOTIONS AND COGNITIONS

In the preceding passage, Steinbeck might be speaking directly to counselors and psychotherapists about the importance of emotions in the change process. When psychoanalysis was the major form of therapy, it took many months or even years for the linking of emotions and cognitions.

Sometimes, students, instructors, supervisors, and experienced therapists forget that listening and attending to a client's experiential world requires the inclusion of emotional experience. Advice, interpretations, or confrontations are perceived as empty directives unless the therapist also attends to the client's emotional world.

Therapy is not a linear process, in which the therapist first listens to the emotions and then attends to the cognitive aspects of the client. The association of cognitions and emotions in therapy is more aptly described as circular; the therapist can intervene at either one of these levels (and at the behavioral level).

When therapists deny any aspect of their client's psychological world (behaviors, cognitions, or emotions), the result is likely to be superficial change. More than half a century ago, Fuerst (1938) wrote on the limitations of working solely at a cognitive level: "Experience shows that a single intellectual interpretation has frequently no influence upon the patient's emotional reactions which continue to follow the old patterns" (p. 261). Effective therapists strive to find a balance between the affective and cognitive needs of each client. Therapists of any orientation must gauge how much emotional and supportive work a client requires and how much cognitive work a client requires at a particular time in their therapy. This balance between the emotional and cognitive levels varies across clients, across therapists, and across stages of therapy.

Alexander (1935), one of the authors who first described the corrective emotional experience of therapy, also wrote on the role of cognition and emotions in therapy.

> Abreaction without insight and insight without abreaction are two extremes, between which in practice there are all degrees of combination and analyses [therapies] do in fact consist of such differently graded mixtures of insight and emotional experience. (p. 595)

Students of therapy are sometimes so involved in trying to learn the intellectual teachings of their particular school of therapy that they forget the crucial role of emotions in the change process.

Therapists strive for a level of awareness that is both cognitive and emotional: the client can state the hypotheses for their suffering, and they can feel it in their bones. "Ideally, change in analytic treatment [or any style of therapy] has been considered most likely to occur with a combination of cognitive awareness and release of affect, or so-called 'emotional insight'" (Marmor, 1982, p. 61).

I have heard my experiential colleagues ask, "If cognitive insight is so important to the change process, then why did Sigmund Freud continue to keep smoking cigars until his death, even though he had known for years that he had jaw cancer? He knew that he had cancer; why didn't he stop smoking cigars?" A key distinction must be made here. People may fully recognize self-destructive behaviors or thoughts; however, they may lack the corresponding emotional insight. To recognize a defeatist pattern intellectually is a soulless experience; it is not personal. However, with emotional insight, the recognition becomes personal. The individual senses his or her responsibility and understands the futility of the self-defeating patterns. As therapists, we strive for these emotional insights. Freud fully recognized the self-destructive behavior of smoking cigars: however, he lacked the emotional insight (Becker, 1973).

EMOTIONS AS A NECESSARY CONDITION FOR CHANGE

As we saw in Chapter 6, there is some research—albeit not very robust—to support the idea that the expression of emotions and the experiential aspects of therapy are necessary for change in counseling and psychotherapy; they constitute a process variable. Our life experiences help us to appreciate this process variable.

In *The Art of the Psychotherapist*, Bugental (1987) captures one essential role of emotions, particularly painful emotions.

> Pain cannot be taken for granted, nor can we let it govern our work. Simply to reduce pain is not therapy. Pain is a natural signal that something has gone wrong with the human system and needs attention. Simply quieting pain is as unwise as pasting cardboard over a persistently flashing red light on the car's instrument panel. (p. 203)

Painful emotions tell the therapist and the client that something is not right.

Some counselors and psychotherapists wait for a supportive relationship to develop before they work with the client on the expression of painful emotions. However, this is a mistake: the expression of emotions early in therapy is vital to the development of a supportive relationship.

> The overall conclusion about affects is that *almost any affect is better than no affect, and that anxiety and depression are probably the two "best" initial affects.* The presence of these strong affects may indicate the patient is in pain and asking for help. The absence of affect very likely goes along with a state in which the patient is not reaching out for help, or has given up. (Luborsky, Chandler, Auerbach, Cohen, & Bachrach, 1971, p. 150)

Therapists need to help their clients express emotions. They can use soft brush strokes, particularly in the beginning phase and during crucial stages of change.

Hart (1986), an eclectic therapist, also recognized the role of emotions, and even emotional upheaval, in therapy. "The real work of therapy is to sustain, and sometimes even to provoke, crises in order to undo old, bad habits and foster new, good habits" (p. 207). These times of emotional upheaval—violent tears, rage, anxiety, or hysterical laughter—are not always to be minimized or blocked. Alexander and French (1946) referred to them as "benign traumata" (p. 164). They noted that such emotional crises are frequently followed by a sense of relief and positive behavioral change.

Because so much of the psychological literature focuses on the role of techniques, therapists need to be reminded that people have emotions. In the candid words of Semrad, "The most important part of a person's life is his affect" (cited in Rako & Mazer, 1983).

EMOTIONS AND THE THREE THERAPEUTIC APPROACHES

As they have matured, the three major approaches to counseling and psychotherapy have come to acknowledge the role of emotions as a key process variable. "Several theorists have suggested that it is when particular thoughts and attitudes are tested in the context of appropriate affective arousal that fundamental change can occur" (Robins & Hayes, 1993, p. 211). This finding alone is not that remarkable.

What is interesting is that each major school of therapy passed through a stage in its early days when work in the affective domain was discouraged. As a result of this history, each approach has been stereotyped in a particular way.

The Humanistic Approach

Emotions have played a key role in the development and stability of the humanistic approach. However, a stereotype of the humanistic therapist persists. Humanistic therapists are seen as attempting to be good, as denying the dark side of our emotions—particularly the negative emotions of frustration, anger, and hostility. Because of their own need for a secure environment, this stereotype continues; humanistic therapists do not truly allow clients to experience their world in the full richness of their emotions. Humanistic therapists stifle clients' growth by not allowing them to express their anger within the therapy hour, event though it could help them to become more autonomous and independent.

Cognitive and psychodynamic therapists mainly perpetuate this stereotype of the humanistic school. However, two leading humanistic writers, Carl Rogers and Rollo May, have openly admitted this pattern of neglect toward negative emotions, at least during the infancy of nondirective, client-centered therapy.

May (1982/1989) began this dialogue by writing to Rogers about his participation in a landmark three-year study conducted by Rogers during the 1960s. May was one of 12 judges selected to rate the therapy audiotapes of numerous client-centered therapists. Along with other judges, he noted a "glaring omission" by the client-centered therapists: they failed to deal with clients' feelings of anger and hostility. May even quoted one of the conclusions reached by Rogers and his colleagues:

> Particularly striking was the observation by all the theorists that the client-centered process of therapy somehow avoids the expected and usual patient expressions of negative, hostile, or aggressive feelings. The clear implication is that the client-centered therapist for some reason seems less open to receiving negative, hostile, or aggressive feelings. Is it that the therapists have little respect for, or understanding of their own negative, hostile, or aggressive feelings, and are thus unable to receive these feelings from the patient? Do they simply "not believe in" the importance of negative feelings? (Rogers, Gendlin, Kiesler, & Truax, 1967, p. 503)

In his response to May, Rogers did not deny this pattern. How could he deny it? May had quoted Rogers's own words. Rogers further admitted that, in the past, he himself had denied the importance of the negative emotions.

> You [Rollo May] speak at length of the failure of people like myself
> and client-centered therapy to recognize, accept, and respond to
> feelings of anger, hostility, and negative feelings in general, per-
> haps especially those directed toward the therapist. I think that to
> some extent this was definitely true of me in the distant past,
> although I have also published examples of the way in which I dealt
> with bitter hostility toward me in therapy. (Rogers, 1982/1989)

Rogers's development in working with negative feelings mirrors the experience of most therapists in all styles of therapy.

Initially, therapists earnestly want clients to like them. They want
clients to get better. They fear that, if clients get angry with them, they
must be inadequate as therapists. With experience, therapists learn how
important these negative emotions are in therapy and in our lives.

In his response to May, Rogers conceded that, even in 1982, "there may
be truth in what you say, that client-centered therapists have a tendency
not to accept or respond to such feelings. If so, I regret this as much as
you" (Rogers, 1982/1989, p. 253).

The Psychodynamic Approach

In the same year that Rogers admitted to May that client-centered therapists
may neglect the role of negative emotions, a therapist described how the
psychodynamic approach views negative feelings as a keystone of change.

> In many ways, dynamic therapists are the allies of aggression. With
> the proviso that aggression should be expressed but not acted out,
> they look on it as a potentially constructive force that reestablishes
> contact following extreme withdrawal, that fortifies boundaries,
> that promotes individuation, and that supplies energy, provided
> the aggression is worked through and processed. In dynamic
> psychotherapy, the patient is helped to become aware of his
> aggression. Inklings of aggressive thoughts, feelings, and impulses
> ready to break through defensive barriers are heeded and wel-
> comed. The direct expression of aggression is encouraged in the
> therapeutic setting. (Fried, 1982, p. 256)

That sounds good, but how does it play out in practice?

The stereotype of psychodynamic therapists is that they aspire to be
omnipotent, narcissistic detectives. The stereotype goes like this: "Psychodynamic therapists keep such an impersonal distance it is no wonder
that they speak of hostility directed to the therapist. If clients get bold
enough to express their negative feelings, they are going to be confronted
with a torrent of transference interpretations. Clients who come late to a
session because of a flat tire on the highway during rush hour or because

they were mugged outside the therapist's office lay themselves open to an interpretation of latent hostility directed toward the therapist because their mother weaned them too early."

There is at least a grain of truth in this.

> Understandably, we analysts might be tempted to consider as transference manifestations all hurtful remarks made by the patient. In that way, we defend ourselves against recognizing our painful traits or behavior and our faulty interpretations. (Greenson, 1972/1990a, p. 91)

Greenson, a psychoanalyst, gained fame because he argued that analysts adopt an overly objective approach to analysis, at the expense of the therapeutic relationship between two living people. He accused analysts of using transference interpretations as a defense against the personal aspects of the therapeutic relationship.

> I believe that the whole school of analysts which believes that psychoanalytic treatment consists of "only interpreting" is guilty of using transference interpretations as a defense. Some of them seem to interpret the transference so frequently in the course of an hour because they are afraid of the painful affects that they or their patients might otherwise develop. (Greenson, 1971/1990b, p. 92)

Humanistic and psychodynamic therapists have been accused of fostering undue dependency in their clients—that is, of setting up conditions that hinder autonomous functioning. Greenacre (1954/1990), a leading psychoanalyst, noted "that those analysts who talk most about the dangers of dependence seem rarely to consider the reciprocal relationship between tenacious dependency and unanalyzed negative transference [negative emotions]" (p. 20).

Therapists should avoid negative emotions if they want their clients to like them and to become dependent on them. However, if therapists are looking for respect and an honest relationship, they need to allow, and help, clients to express their negative emotions. Then clients will have a full repertoire of emotions, they will become more independent and responsible, and they will change.

The Cognitive Approach

Cognitive therapists have long been mocked for neglecting the role of emotions as a key process variable of change. Even the name of their approach seems to exclude the expression of affect.

However, two leading cognitive therapists, Aaron Beck and Albert Ellis, clearly recognize the role of emotional expression and experience in their respective approaches. Beck has written, "A rule of thumb is that cognitive change depends on a certain level of affective experience" (Beck et al., 1990, p. 80). Ellis has gone even further, by defining his style of cognitive therapy as rational emotive therapy (RET).

Ellis is eloquent in presenting his approach:

> RET holds that cognitions, emotions, and behavior are practically never pure or disparate but integrally and holistically interact with and include each other. Although it is highly philosophical, RET fully recognizes that feelings and behaviors have an important influence on beliefs, and that feelings affect beliefs and behaviors. (Ellis, 1962, 1988, 1991b)

Elsewhere, Ellis (1993) adds, "RET is always multimodal and uses a good number of cognitive, emotive, and behavioral methods with most clients" (p. 199). Writing with Dryden, Ellis insists on the uniqueness of their approach:

> RET is unique among the cognitive-behavioral therapies in emphasizing the employment of such interventions that fully involve clients' emotions. Thus, RET therapists suggest that clients can help themselves go from intellectual to emotional insight by vigorously disputing their irrational beliefs. (Dryden & Ellis, 1988, p. 248)

In the following passage, Ellis (1990) is even more explicit:

> Most rational-emotive sessions start with the patient's current *feelings*: with his describing exactly how badly or well he felt when this event or that relationship occurred in his life. The patient is not asked to talk about his thoughts or deeds, but largely about how he *feels* about these ideas and actions. Then, when his feelings prove to be negative and self-defeating, he is shown their cognitive and ideational sources. (p. 332)

I have opted to quote from Ellis because he writes so clearly about the role of emotions in therapy, just as the proponents of the humanistic and psychodynamic camps have done.

Despite these strong statements by Beck and Ellis, cognitive therapists are stereotyped as lacking appreciation of the role of emotional expression and experience in the therapy hour. They are seen as obsessive-compulsives, as people who have never suffered themselves, or even as robots. Critics argue that, unable to feel themselves, cognitive therapists simply feed on clients' masochistic suffering or wrongdoings and cannot provide the necessary supportive foundation of change.

Some of the writings of the cognitive school appear to confirm these changes. For example, consider this declaration by Ellis (1973):

> I am deliberately not very warm or personal with most of my clients, even those who crave and ask for such warmth, since, as I quickly explain to them, their main problem is usually that they

think they need to be loved, when they actually do not; and I am there to teach them that they can get along very well in this world without necessarily being approved or loved by others. I therefore refuse to cater to their sick love demands. (p. 155)

It seems safe to say that, in regard to the emotional and experiential aspects of the therapeutic relationship, the client-centered and the rational emotive styles of therapy are like oil and water.

In the preface of his *Handbook of Cognitive-Behavioural Therapies*, Dobson (1988), another leading cognitive therapist, expressed concern about the cognitive perspective:

One disturbing aspect of this book, at least for me, is the manner in which the treatment models discussed in this text deal with the topic of emotion. The mediational model assumes emotional responses follow cognitive appraisal, which is a theoretically and empirically defensible position. What is much less completely described in cognitive-behavioral terms, however, is the reciprocal relationship between emotion and cognitive processes. (p. xi)

On a more practical level, Mahoney, also a leading cognitive therapist, compared two trends within cognitive therapy: the traditional rationalist approach, which views emotions as an unwanted interference in the therapy hour, to be controlled or eliminated; and the developmental cognitive therapies, which view emotions as natural elements of development and change.

Feelings somehow integrate past, present, and anticipated experiences, and—much more consistently than their neocortical counterparts—they covary with pituitary, endocrine, and lymphatic activities. It is not surprising, therefore, that developmental cognitive therapists tend to encourage emotional experience, expression, and exploration. (Mahoney, 1988, p. 377)

In a later article, Mahoney (1993) concluded that the cognitive approach to therapy is becoming more like the humanistic and psychodynamic schools in its appreciation of the role of experiential and emotional factors.

Rather than simply reason their way from feeling bad to feeling good, an increasing number of clients in cognitive treatment are being encouraged to actively experience, explore, and express a much broader range and more complex mixture of affect. In the process, they are also more likely to be offered exercises and techniques that have been traditionally associated with experiential therapies. (p. 191)

The cognitive therapists are becoming more experiential as their approach is developing.

In Chapter 7, we noted that the corrective emotional experience, originally described by Alexander and French in 1946, is increasingly being recognized as a key aspect of the therapeutic relationship. Mahoney (1993) comments that cognitive and behavioral therapists

> are also discovering that the terrain of affectively lived experience has long been a haunt of their psychodynamic counterparts. The "corrective emotional experiences" afforded by well-coordinated psychoanalysis turn out to be strikingly similar to those reported to be important in behavioral, cognitive, and humanistic approaches. (p. 191)

Although, in the past, cognitive therapists have tended to neglect the role of emotions, today most cognitive therapists appreciate the importance of this factor in effective therapy. A recent comparative study "found no differences between the C-B [cognitive-behavioral] and P-I [psychodynamic-interpersonal] orientations in the degree of emotional experiencing achieved by clients" (Wiser & Goldfried, 1993, p. 894).

Summary

At least during its early stages, each of the three major styles of therapy neglected the powerful role of emotions—particularly negative emotions—in the change process. However, as it has matured, each approach has developed a deeper understanding of the role of emotions as a process variable of change in counseling and psychotherapy.

EMOTIONS AS A PROCESS VARIABLE

A number of hypotheses have been offered to explain how and why emotions are a key process variable of counseling and psychotherapy. It is well beyond the scope of this chapter to review all the various theories of emotion. For example, I do not discuss the physiological aspects of emotional expression. Readers seeking a more intensive analysis of emotions could start with the books *Emotion in Psychotherapy* (Greenberg & Safran, 1987) and *Catharsis in Psychotherapy* (Nichols & Zax, 1977).

In the following sections, I review four reasons why it is important to address emotions in therapy: (a) emotions foster motivation; (b) focusing on emotions helps clients to untangle their confused feelings; (c) experiencing our pain and anger can help us develop a sense of autonomy; and (d) a full emotional repertoire enriches our lives.

Emotions and Motivation

On an experiential level, it seems all too clear that emotions are an important facet of the change process. Think of a significant loss you have had—perhaps a separation, a divorce, or the death of a loved one. How did your friends and relatives respond to your loss? Some people who had been through a similar experience may have given advice; this advice did not seem to help. Particularly at holidays, other friends and relatives may have never even brought the subject up. When they were gone, you were left feeling empty, as if nobody cared or understood.

However, if you were fortunate, you may have had a friend or relative who seemed to listen. They did not try to fix or cure you; they did not avoid the hurtful emotions that came with your loss. Essentially, they were there with you and gave you the opportunity to feel hurt, frustrated, angry, or alone. And then, just because of who that person was, you somehow got strength through their listening; what you needed to do became clearer. You were then able to move ahead with your life.

This example clearly illustrates the supportive and emotional aspects of therapy; I use it in my talks to civic organizations. Unfortunately, our teachings and writings on therapy frequently distance therapists from emotions.

Fiction writers particularly can bring therapists back to their emotions. DeCourcell (1988) described Tolstoy's and Dostoyevsky's novels as a "continuous, unending struggle with their feelings" (p. 349). This struggle can be seen in a passage from Dostoyevsky's (1866/1968) *Crime and Punishment*.

> Suffering is also a good thing. Go and suffer . . . I know it's hard
> to believe, but give yourself up to life directly, without sophistry;
> don't puzzle over it. Don't worry. It will carry you straight to shore
> and set you on your feet. (p. 443)

There is something about suffering—about our emotions—that can free us from maladaptive patterns.

People who do not express emotional pain are among the most difficult to work with in therapy. Many people who seek therapy have become emotionally numb. Overwhelmed by their emotions, they have, in effect, quit feeling; it has become too painful. Part of the role of the therapist, particularly during the initial sessions, is to help clients feel their emotional hurt.

To many beginning therapists, these comments may seem sadistic. I am sure that some therapists do act on their own sadistic needs in therapy, but these therapists are few and far between. Rather, to me, it is sadistic not to help clients feel the hurt. Most people who come to our offices have been emotionally (and often physically) hurt by others and have developed maladaptive patterns of thinking and behaving that only serve to heighten their pain. As therapists, we do not want to be like your relatives at the holidays who seemed not to care because they did not ask about your loss.

Therapists who do not actively listen to clients' emotional pain risk a breakdown of the therapeutic relationship. Mohr et al. (1990) note that the therapist must help activate clients' emotions in effective therapy.

> Apparently an awareness of disturbed functioning, even if one is unable to specify its source or nature, is important for motivating change in psychotherapy. The absence of such self-acknowledged dysfunction may even portend treatment-related deterioration . . . This lack of acknowledgment of one's own contribution to levels of distress may predispose anger, projection, and other destabilizing forces in the psychotherapy relationship, resulting in negative change. (p. 627)

If the therapist does not recognize and attend to clients' emotional suffering, clients may act out toward the therapist, because they do not feel understood.

Emotions are powerful agents of change; they provide us with the motivation we need. The humanistic therapist Frankl (1965) provides a metaphor: "Only under the hammer blows of fate, in the white heat of suffering, does life gain shape and form" (p. 111). Psychodynamic therapists Bauer and Kobos (1987) elaborate on this metaphor: "Unless the fire is hot (i.e., emotions are high), the metal (attitudes, ways of viewing the world) is not receptive to change in shape. Getting at the patient's feelings is a way of stoking the fire" (p. 191).

Clarification of Emotions

A second reason that focusing on clients' emotions makes it a necessary process variable is that it helps clients clarify what they feel. When they enter therapy, many people feel confused and overwhelmed. They are experiencing a mass of contradictory and conflicting feelings—love, hate, sadness, joy, anxiety, rage.

The therapist can help explore this confusion by applying brush strokes of empathic comments and gestures.

> If [the client] will let himself get deeply into the experience of being stuck, only then will he reclaim that part of himself that is holding him. Only if he will give up trying to control his thinking, and let himself sink into his confusion, only then will things become clear. (Kopp, 1972, p. 64)

Empathy is essential. If clients are confused when they enter therapy, stay with their confusion. For example, as I noted in Chapter 10, I sometimes intertwine my fingers in a convoluted manner and tell the client, "It sounds as if everything is confused." Even such a simple gesture prompts clients to list what has been happening in their lives. As clients proceed, then therapists can follow with more specific comments; for example, "That must be frustrating."

This idea that clients frequently cannot say how they feel when they first enter therapy is not new. Frankl (1965) coined the term *melancholia anaesthetica*, the emotional numbing of clients.

> There is a type of melancholia in which sadness is conspicuous by its absence. Instead, the patients complain that they cannot feel sad enough, that they cannot cry out their melancholy, that they are emotionally cold and inwardly dead. Such patients are suffering from what we call *melancholia anaesthetica*. (p. 111)

The psychodynamic therapist Sifneos (1987) coined the term *alexithymia* (based on Greek roots meaning "no words for feelings") to describe this phenomenon.

> Although the alexithymic patient is able to be aware of emotions and to think, he seems unable to connect any thoughts with his emotions. Thus he has an inability to experience feelings—a *feeling* being defined as "a biological emotion *plus* the thoughts which accompany it." (p. 38)

By focusing on the affective domain of the therapeutic relationship, the therapist can help the client to experience emotions that were previously unacceptable.

Again, the therapist does not need years of experience to realize that being involved in an emotional relationship can be a powerful catalyst for acceptance, insight, and change. Just having a good cry can be therapeutic.

Change means mourning a loss and the accompanying anxiety of an unknown future. A major loss is the death of a loved one. How we experience our emotions at funerals can reflect how we work with emotions in therapy. Frankl (1965) comments that many people effectively deal with death and do not attempt to escape the negative painful emotions.

> Mourners, in fact, ordinarily rebel against, say, taking a sedative instead of weeping all through the night. To the trite suggestion that he take a sleeping-powder the grief-stricken person commonly retorts that his sleeping better will not awaken the lost one who he mourns. Death—that paradigm of the irreversible event—is not wiped off the slate by being pushed out of consciousness, any more than when the mourner himself takes refuge in absolute non-

consciousness—the non-consciousness and the non-responsibility of his own death. (p. 110)

Taking a sedative—by means of medication or psychological numbing—does not make good the loss. We feel stuck when we don't feel.

Often, we are unable to express our emotions at funerals because we are ambivalent. We may feel thankful that the person no longer has to suffer, but sad that we will never see the person again. We may even harbor feelings of guilt that we were not there when the person died, and also anger that he or she did not wait for us to get there. As ridiculous as it may sound, we may even be joyous that we were not there.

Likewise, clients typically enter therapy with a number of conflicting emotions. Just a good cry can get them on the right track again. One of the therapist's tasks is to help them get unstuck. As well as the physiological factors that explain why we feel better after an emotional expression, a catharsis, there are psychological reasons: expressing and experiencing painful emotions helps the client to focus, to feel less confused.

> Experience is no longer colored gray, with vague uneasiness or dissatisfaction . . . The relief inherent in really knowing that "here it hurts" is that knowing carries the implication that only that hurts, not everything. (Nichols & Paolino, 1986, p. 121)

If the therapist stays with a client's initial confusion, then the client will be more apt to express specific emotions within the session. The therapist could say, "Did you notice how your voice got stronger and louder when you talked about how you have felt betrayed by your spouse?" A major goal of working with emotions is to help the client express emotions that they thought were not permissible.

One of the difficulties inherent in counseling and psychotherapy is that, in our society, it is not always acceptable to be depressed or angry. Therefore, I avoid these words in my therapy. Instead of *depression*, I may talk of feeling blue, sad, or tired. Instead of *anger*, I may speak of feeling frustrated, irritated, annoyed, or stepped on. The key is to use words that the client can hear. The best words to use are those of the client.

Emotions and Autonomy

A third reason for helping clients to express and experience their emotions is that it fosters autonomy.

Liebowitz, Stone, and Turkat (1986) report that, in treating clients with personality disorders, they base their work with emotional expression on

> guidelines once given a medical school class about the treatment of a dermatologic disorder: "if it's wet, dry it; if it's dry, wet it." We encourage the histrionic patient . . . to "cool it," with respect to

> emotional display . . . With the compulsive, we adapt in an oppo-
> site way, often expressing in a rather dramatic way ("You mean to
> say your father died last Saturday, and you didn't even mention it
> till now!") what the patient may characteristically report in a
> perfunctory and affectless manner. (p. 358)

When I first read this witty analogy, "If it's wet, dry it; if it's dry, wet it," I
was struck with how it applies to my work with the emotions of depression
and anger. My clients who are depressed often have difficulty being
assertive. They tend to set themselves up for abuse; people constantly use
them. At some point in that process, they became irritated. I've learned to
actively look for feelings of anger in clients who are depressed.

I've also noticed that my clients who are bitter and angry when they
come in tend, over time, to become sad about past, present, and future
events and relationships. Now I actively pursue the depression in my
clients who are, as they say in the helping professions, "agitated." My rule
of thumb goes like this: "When the client is depressed, look for the anger;
when the client is angry, look for the depression." Other therapists have
reached a similar conclusion.

> An important aspect of the human experience of anger is the
> awareness of "emotional hurt." Indeed, anger and hurt may be
> considered to represent two sides of the same emotional coin.
> Anger, however, is an externally directed feeling, whereas hurt is
> internally directed. Because of their dialectic relationship, when
> anger is denied direct expression, it is often expressed as hurt, and
> vice versa. (Daldrup, Beutler, Engle, & Greenberg, 1988, p. 6)

As with all rules of thumb, there are numerous exceptions.

At this point, the reader may be feeling that there is too much emphasis
on the negative emotions in this book. The same charge has been leveled
at the existential school of the humanistic camp. Frankl (1961/1967a)
responded to this accusation.

> It has become fashionable to blame existential philosophy for
> overemphasizing the tragic aspects of human existence . . . This
> however, must not be interpreted as evidence of a pessimistic slant
> and bias. What we rather have to deal with is an optimistic
> position; namely, the conviction that even dying and suffering are
> potentially meaningful . . . One should not approach them as if, in
> a given case, he just had to deal with bad luck. Pain, death, and
> guilt are inescapable; the more the neurotic tries to deny them, the
> more he entangles himself in additional suffering. (pp. 87–88)

Most people could get someone who is hurting to forget their hurt for at
least 50 minutes by using a Dale Carnegie (1936) approach, but then what
happens when the individual gets home?

People who meet with a therapist are in emotional pain. To work with negative emotions is usually a requirement for effective therapy. In the blunt words of Fritz Perls (1969):

> *The awareness of, and the ability to endure, unwanted emotions are the sine qua non for a successful cure;* these emotions will be discharged once they have become Ego-functions. This process, and not the process of remembering, forms the *via regia* to health. (p. 179; cited from Patterson, 1986, p. 363)

When I first began doing therapy, I thought that, if my client was depressed, it was my job to get rid of this feeling. For the client to be depressed in my office—or, even worse, to get more depressed—was a fatal blow. I was not doing my job. With time, I learned to actively listen to my clients. I found out that it was a fruitless task for me to deny these feelings, and that clients seemed to get better when I helped their depressed feelings to emerge. As a result, I became more effective as a therapist.

My next hurdle was working with clients who were angry. I simply did not want people to tell me that they were getting worse, that I was not helping them, that they were mad at me. I did not accept that their anger toward me could be therapeutic; I did not realize that they were taking a risk, the risk of change.

> Angry, self-assertive feelings are perhaps the most difficult ones to learn to express because they are inherently separating in nature. And yet it is the expression of these very feelings which allows the individual to develop a sense of agency [autonomy]. The process of expressing their dissatisfaction with the therapist when an alliance rupture takes place, can thus play an important role in helping clients to develop a sense of themselves as responsible and creative agents who can influence their own destinies. (Safran, 1993, p. 20)

Yes, the expression of dissatisfaction with the therapist is frequently a signal of the client becoming more autonomous. Therapists need to appreciate that, when a client expresses anger, they have provided the conditions that allowed the client to be assertive.

Habib Davanloo (1992a), a practitioner of dynamic psychotherapy with a very confrontive approach, considers the client's expression of anger in therapy to be so essential to the client's growth that he actively pursues such disclosures.

> The therapist must watch for the subtle indications of the emergence of anger, however minor, in the transference [relationship]. Those who have watched me in action have seen that I often suddenly break into what I am doing and ask the patient, "What

do you feel right now?" What emerges is the same old process, "Well . . . I don't feel anything." [alexithymia] And I continue to focus on "What do you feel right now? How do you feel inside?" Then the patient says, "Well . . . I was a little upset." I say, "Upset?" The patient says, "Well . . . I was a little irritated." Finally he admits he was angry. (p. 67)

Davanloo argues that such interventions enhance the therapeutic relationship and that the relationship may deteriorate if therapists do not provide their clients with an opportunity to express their anger in the therapeutic hour.

Summarizing, the expression of negative emotions—particularly anger—provides the client with an opportunity to appreciate his or her separateness in life. This can further foster a sense of isolation and accompanying depression. The person can gain a sense of responsibility and autonomy from these negative emotions. Once we can live alone, we can live together. A need to be with others becomes a desire to be with others, and each of us assumes sole authorship for our own life.

Emotions and a Full Life

A fourth reason that therapists work with clients' emotions is to help people to live a full and rich emotional life. Many, if not most, of the people who come into our offices have been going through times of turmoil and frustrations. They have a right to be depressed and angry. However, many clients feel they need permission to be upset. Our job is to let them stop pretending that everything is all right. It's their therapy. If they get depressed, they have a right; if they get angry, they have a right.

Beginning therapists, particularly those who have not fully scrutinized their reasons for entering the profession, often believe that the client should agree with everything the therapist says. These therapists leave sessions feeling that they did a good job; the client leaves unchanged.

Many clients, men and women, come into therapy because they have been caretakers: they have learned not to rock the boat, to sacrifice themselves for others, to make others feel good. All the while, they don't know what they are feeling.

Therapists are in this field to help people to live a full life, not to help them continue a masquerade. "One does not become free from feelings in the course of maturation or in the course of becoming well during psychoanalysis [or any form of therapy]; one becomes, instead, increasingly free to experience feeling of all sorts" (Searles, 1966/1979, p. 35). It is only human to feel depressed and angry at times.

Summary on Negative Emotions

Emotions—especially unwanted, negative emotions—are an effective tool in the therapy process. Many clients enter their therapy feeling emotionally numb; at some level of awareness, they have decided to stop feeling. This is not a good sign. Particularly at the beginning of therapy, negative emotions provide the fuel for change.

Working on the expression of emotions helps the client to feel less confused and overwhelmed. As therapists work on empathizing with their clients' confusion, they generally take the opportunity to use a light brush stroke, where appropriate. "Did you notice how your voice just tightened?" The expression of emotions helps clients to clarify for themselves that not *everything* is messed up.

Anger is a powerful emotion for fostering autonomy. If clients direct their anger at the therapist, the therapist does not need to run away. Clients are seeking a full life; so often, when they enter therapy, they describe their life as empty. Effective therapists give their clients the present of negative emotions, independence, and autonomy.

Without emotions, therapy would be a stale, nonproductive enterprise. Therapy is an experience shared by two people; it is not an intellectual exercise.

> One thing seems incontrovertibly clear. Whatever may bring about therapeutic change, it is not a class of communications, such as interpretations per se, but rather the conjunction of a particular communication by the therapist . . . with a state of "readiness" existing in the patient . . . The critical, mutative communication is the decisive intervention that may occur when the time is right—when the patient is in a particular frame of mind, *usually aroused emotionally*, and ready to apprehend something he has never apprehended before in quite the same way. [emphasis added] (Strupp, 1980a, p. 601)

The emotional arousal of clients is a key factor that keeps our interventions from falling on deaf ears.

HUMOR AND THERAPY

Laughter can be a powerful expression of emotion. In rational emotive therapy, "a number of humorous methods are employed to encourage clients to think rationally by not taking themselves too seriously" (Dryden & Ellis, 1988, p. 248). Sometimes, as therapists, we cannot help clients because we are too stoic and humorless. Using humor in therapy offers a number of benefits.

> Humor in psychotherapy can be used to alleviate anxiety and tension, encourage insight, increase motivation, create an atmosphere of closeness and equality between therapist and client, expose absurd beliefs, develop a sense of proportion to one's importance in life situations, and facilitate emotional catharsis. (Dimmer, Carroll, & Wyatt, 1990, pp. 795–796)

It just seems to make practical sense that a balanced therapist would be able to tap into both the negative and positive emotions.

During my first years in learning therapy, I was troubled to see how little humor was discussed. Like a good cry, a good laugh can help us over a hurdle. Being able to laugh is being able to feel. However, in many training programs, and even in the way the literature is written, it is as if humor has no place in therapy.

The Controversy about Humor

Some instructors and supervisors believe that therapists use humor to prevent the client from feeling negative emotions and, in so doing, hinder the client's process of change. Kubie (1971) wrote a paper called "The Destructive Potential of Humor in Psychotherapy."

> Kubie's chief objections centered around therapist humor . . . causing patient confusion as to whether the therapist is serious, mocking, joking, or masking his or her own hostilities. Further, Kubie stated that humor can be a form of self-display or exhibitionism, or a defense against dealing with psychological pain, and can blunt self-observing and correcting mechanisms in the therapist. (Killinger, 1987, p. 22)

Trying to help people to change is serious business. However, it is not serious in the sense that we have to be unfeeling or to focus only on negative emotions. By working with a person's positive emotions and introducing humor into the sessions, the therapist can help make the change process effective.

> It is time for humor to take its legitimate place as an important therapeutic tool. It is time to change the traditional image of the therapist as a neutral screen or as an unresponsive figure. The therapist's transparency and his or her appropriate expression of patient-related emotional reactions, including humor, can bring a sense of realism and warmth to the therapeutic process. Solemnity is not synonymous with either effectiveness or seriousness about one's work. Humor helps us do our work more seriously, more energetically, and more effectively. (Salameh, 1987, p. 238)

I fully agree. I also agree with Kubie's concerns about the abuse of humor.

Some therapists readily use humor in their approach; some completely neglect the use of humor. In the following section I review two authors who adamantly believe in the use of humor as a powerful technique of therapy.

Are Clients Fragile or Robust?

Just as many therapists decline to work with the client's negative emotions because they view the client as too fragile, many therapists believe it is unwise to use humor, for the same reason. Farrelly strongly dissents from that view. He uses humor in an extremely confrontive style of therapy known as Provocative Therapy, which is very similar to Fritz Perls's approach.

> The psychological fragility of clients is vastly overrated both by themselves and others. Provocative Therapy maintains that it is ultimately nontherapeutic to offer large amounts of positive regard while withholding genuine feelings of occasional doubt, irritation, or anger so as not to "harm" the client. The provocative therapist believes in the adaptability and resiliency of humankind. (Farrelly & Lynch, 1987, pp. 83–84)

In Provocative Therapy, the therapist openly confronts clients on their maladaptive patterns. This approach can definitely be threatening to the client.

Ellis (1987) likewise uses humor in an extremely confrontive approach with his clients.

> When my clients insisted that they automatically or unconsciously kept overeating or smoking against their own will, and when they denied that they used any Beliefs . . . to make themselves act self-defeatingly, I would say something like, "What do you keep telling yourself immediately before you cram that stuff down your gullet and into your craw? 'I hate food? I just eat to keep up my strength? I'll fix my dead mother by showing her that I can eat all I want without getting fat?' Or do you mean to tell me that the food automatically jumps out of the refrigerator, onto your plate, into your mouth and forces you to swallow it?" (Ellis, 1987, p. 269)

To attempt such a confrontive intervention, particularly during the initial phase of therapy, would require a sound and stable therapeutic stance and good supervision.

Every therapist decides how confrontive she or he will be. For me, a confrontive approach such as Farrelly and Ellis advocate is simply not my style. Humor is part of my therapeutic style but, once again, this is a personal decision for each therapist to make.

When to Use Humor in Therapy

The question is not whether humor is effective in therapy, but rather when it is effective. My general pattern is to use humor with my clients once a supportive relationship has been established and we are working in a collaborative manner. If the therapist begins therapy with jokes and humorous anecdotes, clients may feel that the therapist does not care, is not willing to help them, or is making a mockery of their pain.

> Use of humor in the initial phases of treatment could be interpreted as a sign that the therapist is not taking their problems seriously. Humor cannot be introduced in these situations until symptom relief results from the patient's appreciation of the therapist's confidence in his or her ability to improve. Once it becomes clear that the patient has gained some trust in himself or herself and in the therapist, then one can use humor. (Greenwald, 1987, p. 44)

For a time, I met with a client of the Mormon faith. We had an ongoing joke that, when she became overly perfectionistic and demanding of herself, she had adopted a "Molly Mormon" mentality. That allowed her to laugh at herself and to get some distance. If I had made such a joke at the beginning of her therapy, she might have thought that I was attacking not only her maladaptive patterns but also her religion.

What makes humor such an effective intervention is that, when applied in a timely manner, it helps us to gain distance from our problems. Roth (1987) cites an example from psychoanalysis.

> Once, as a patient lay down on the couch to begin an analysis, he said: "psychoanalysis is like marriage. It's something you hope you have to do only once." . . . The humor revealed his observing ego, which took some distance from experience of himself, and suggested his capacity for reflective self-observation. It helped make the unbearable bearable, which, after all, is much of what the psychotherapeutic process is all about. (pp. 104–105)

When client and therapist begin to use humor, the therapy is going through a change. The client is no longer feeling stuck. A similar change occurs when, after several sessions, the client asks, "Has that picture on the wall always been there?" The client is seeing things differently.

Those sessions when I laugh with my clients are usually exciting. The relationship is evolving to a new level. The client is feeling more autonomous; the therapist has moved from a respectful acceptance of the client's predicament to a healthy fondness for the person. Each is getting closer to terminating, to saying good-bye.

The therapist's use of humor will be different for each client. With some clients, the first session is punctuated by laughter. With other clients, laughter never appears. The rule of thumb, to which there are always exceptions, is to avoid using humor too early. Used prematurely, humor may be perceived as sarcasm and the development of the therapeutic relationship may be impaired.

SUMMARY

Effective therapy is usually an emotional experience. In Chapter 10, we saw that the development of hypotheses with the client can foster a collaborative relationship. However, cognitive insight alone leaves the client feeling empty.

We all are aware that we will be in better physical shape if we eat well and exercise. Do we act on this knowledge? Probably not. An important ingredient is missing. Intellectual knowledge is not enough.

> The problem in therapy is always how to move from an ineffectual intellectual appreciation of a truth about oneself to some emotional *experience* of it. It is only when therapists enlist deep emotions that it becomes a powerful force for change. (Yalom, 1989, p. 35)

When we decide to change our lives, we need to feel it in our bones. We need to feel, "This is not what I want." That feeling comes from an intense emotional experience or from a long series of frustrations.

Therapy is painful. It connotes change and anxiety—anxiety about an unknown future. The saving grace is that the client is apt to gain strength from the therapeutic relationship in order to face the pain. As Semrad noted, "No therapy is comfortable, because it involves dealing with pain. But there's one comfortable thought: that two people sharing pain can bear it easier than one" (cited in Rako & Mazer, 1983, p. 106).

CHAPTER TWELVE
ACTIVE LISTENING AND TERMINATION

She said, "Joe Saul knows one trick, one ingredient. You haven't heard about it. Maybe you never will. Without that trick you'll one day go screaming silently in loss. Without it there are no good methods or techniques."

"What is this ingredient?"

"Affection," she said softly. "You have never learned it. Very many people never do."

(STEINBECK, 1950/1979, PP. 19–20)

ACTIVE LISTENING

Without affection, there are no good methods or techniques. Effective therapists must have a bond with their clients; that bond, a brotherly or sisterly concern, comes from an appreciation of the human predicament.

This emotional bond allows therapists to be flexible with their clients, to hear what clients need to change. When therapists actively listen to their clients, everything else—the four process variables and the therapist's specific techniques—falls into place.

Defining Active Listening

Active listening does not mean waiting for clients to become involved in their therapy. It is not the chit-chat that occurs with the neighbor over the fence. It is not the fortitude to sit, and sit, and sit, and sit as someone pours forth his or her problems.

The psychoanalyst Fromm-Reichmann understood the importance of active listening.

> What, then, are the basic requirements as to the personality and the professional abilities of a psychotherapist? If I were asked to answer this question in one sentence, I would reply: "The psychotherapist must be able to listen." This does not appear to be a startling statement, but it is intended to be just that. To be able to listen and to gather information from another person, in this other person's own right, without reacting along the lines of one's own problems or experiences . . . is an art of interpersonal exchange which few people are able to practice without special training. (cited from Greben, 1979, p. 508)

Unobtrusive active listening.   To actively listen is to be unobtrusive. In her novel *Jane Eyre*, Charlotte Bronte (1847/1960) instructed the protagonist on the role that listening would play in her life.

> Know, that in the course of your future life you will often find yourself elected the involuntary confidant of your acquaintance's secrets: people will instinctively find out, as I have done, that it is not your forte to tell of yourself, but to listen while others talk of themselves; they will feel, too, that you listen with no malevolent scorn of their indiscretion, but with a kind of innate sympathy; not the less comforting and encouraging because it is very unobtrusive in its manifestations. (p. 139)

Unobtrusive active listening has to be learned; it doesn't just happen. To use an analogy with tennis, it may seem that returning the ball over the net is a simple procedure. However, beginning players become aware that this procedure involves many maneuvers, all of which require practice.

Beginners tend to think hard about their craft in all its aspects; it's an important developmental stage in the learning process. To return to our tennis analogy, the beginner has so many things to think about when serving: how high to toss the ball; how far from the body to toss the ball; focusing visually on the ball; having a mental image of the ball's placement; following through with the stroke; and so on.

Eventually, through practice and deliberate work on the serve, tennis players have those moments when they are focused not on some aspect of the serve, but on the game as a whole. Everything seems to be clicking; they get into a rhythm.

Likewise, in learning therapy, beginning therapists go through stages when they are mainly conscious of the cognitive aspects, phases when they are more aware of the emotional aspects, and other times when they are largely concerned with behavioral goals. Then, after this deliberate study, there are times when therapists focus not on one aspect of the client's life, but on the process as a whole. Everything seems to click, they get into the rhythm of therapy. The therapist is fully engrossed in helping the person change.

This is one reason that I suggest that beginning therapists adopt an orientation. As we have seen, becoming an active listener is a struggle. In order to struggle, you have to have something to struggle with. If you have committed to an orientation, your struggle can focus on implementing the techniques favored by that orientation.

With discipline and continued engagement, you will experience those times when things just seem to click, when you can let go and actively listen to the client, yourself, and the relationship.

Flexibility and active listening.   Many therapists mistakenly believe that to be unobtrusive means to listen passively, to sit there and say "uh-huh," to deepen their voice, and, if they can, to raise one eyebrow in a timely manner.

What it means to be unobtrusive depends on the particular client. Sometimes to be more direct and even challenging can be unobtrusive for that individual's experiential world. For example, I recently saw a client whom I shall call Sharon. Sharon has an excellent work history but, when she came in to see me, she had not been at work for the past three weeks. This absence put her job in jeopardy. When she was going to work, Sharon had experienced intense crying spells, even though she reported no work-related problems. Several significant changes in Sharon's life appeared to be related to her inability to return to work, but my attempts to highlight these stressors and Sharon's ineffectual attempts to cope with them met with considerable resistance. Sharon adamantly stated that she wanted to return to work, "but I can't." The client is overly perfectionistic and demanding of herself, and she felt that she had little control over her life.

I requested that Sharon's husband come in for the second session, so that I could gain further information and observe how they interacted in the office. The husband did not report any major problems in his life, and there were no significant marital problems. At my request, Sharon signed a release so that I could talk with her supervisor at work. Sharon's supervisor also noted no significant problems at work and said that Sharon had always been a good worker. The supervisor had no idea why this had come about.

In Sharon's case, making contact with her husband and supervisor was a form of active listening. Sharon was caught up in a whirlwind and needed someone from the outside to make an active intervention. I decided to put her on a behavioral desensitization program in which I controlled how much time she was to spend at work. At first, she went to work for two hours per day and then went home. It was a graduated program: when she was able to go to work for two hours with no major problems, she was allowed to work for four hours. Even if Sharon felt that she could stay longer than the agreed-upon time, she was not permitted to do so until we discussed it at our next session. Her supervisor agreed to this arrangement.

It may seem that my approach with Sharon does not reflect my conviction that therapy must help clients to assume more responsibility for their lives: I asked to meet her husband, I talked with her work supervisor, and then I set up an extremely directive intervention. However, I believe that my actions reflect unobtrusive active listening.

Sharon's life had been chaotic and unmanageable. To have taken a less directive approach would have been failing to listen to what was happening to her. She was on the verge of being fired from her job. She said she wanted to return to work, but she would not do so. The immediacy of her situation called for a directive intervention.

After several weeks of the behavioral desensitization program, Sharon returned to work full time; she and her supervisor are happy that the therapy worked out.

A therapist's expression of active listening is dependent upon the needs of a particular client. When we hear what our client's predicament is, we can then respond on the basis of their calling, not of our calling to help.

It is by actively listening to their clients that pioneering therapists have moved away from their original leanings and developed new modes of counseling and psychotherapy. Active listening guides therapists in developing their own style of therapy and in developing appropriate interventions with each individual client.

Even if therapists opt to adopt a rather directive style of intervention, they still depend on active listening to be effective. Clients need to be heard. Once they feel safe with the therapist, they will usually disclose their own hypotheses; the therapist will hear if he or she listens.

> The technique . . . is a very simple one . . . It consists simply in not directing one's notice to anything in particular and in maintaining the same "evenly-suspended attention" (as I have called it) in the face of all that one hears. In this way we spare ourselves a strain on our attention which could not in any case be kept up for several hours daily, and we avoid a danger which is inseparable from the exercise of deliberate attention. (Freud, 1912/1990a, p. 392)

It is important to emphasize that active listening takes different forms in different phases. Whether the beginning therapist is struggling with discrete facets of the process or is able to let go and be engaged, it is all active listening; one is not more pure than the other. Days when it all comes together depend on those days when the therapist was focused on one particular aspect. Effective therapists work on active listening with their clients until their office door closes for the last time. And, some days, everything clicks.

The therapist's presence.   As we have seen, active listening requires an unobtrusive stance. This does not mean that therapists must give up their theoretical orientation nor their life and therapeutic experiences. Rather, if therapists are to take an unobtrusive stance, they must place their need for structure in the background.

Bugental (1987) coined the term *presence* to describe the therapist's active listening stance. "It calls our attention to how genuinely and completely a person is in a situation rather than standing apart from it as observer, commentator, critic, or judge" (p. 26). This is in many ways similar to Carl Rogers's (1957) conditions of unconditional positive regard, congruence, and empathy.

Beginning therapists, in particular, attempt to push the client into a structure with which they feel comfortable. They want to help the client get unstuck; sometimes their sense of urgency leads them to resort to what they know best. These therapists would do well to recall an old saying: "Some learn the tricks of the trade; the masters learn the trade." In counseling and psychotherapy, what's of primary importance is not the techniques of the various approaches but the supportive and collaborative relationship with the client. On the basis of interviews with 50 seasoned therapists (with an average of 30.35 years of therapeutic experience), Goldberg (1992) concluded, "There are emotional ingredients to wisdom that technological knowledge does not have" (p. 147). And Greenson (1971/1990b) adds, "By and large, technical errors may cause pain, but they are usually repairable: human errors are much harder to remedy" (p. 95).

Respect for the client.   It may seem unnecessary to even mention that therapists must respect their clients. A therapist cannot actively listen when their clients become things. Kohut (1977), the originator of self psychology, which is a psychodynamic approach akin to humanistic therapy, notes the importance of a warm therapeutic environment.

> Man can no more survive psychologically in a psychological milieu that does not respond empathetically to him, than he can survive physically in an atmosphere that contains no oxygen. Lack of emotional responsiveness, silence, the pretense of being an inhuman computer-like machine which gathers data and emits interpretations, do no more supply the psychological milieu for the most undistorted delineation of the normal and abnormal features of a person's psychological makeup than do an oxygen-free atmosphere and a temperature close to the zero-point supply the physical milieu for the most accurate measurement of his physiological responses. (p. 253)

Greenson has chastised psychoanalytic therapists for being too analytical and stresses the human aspects of the therapeutic relationship.

> Civility towards the patient, compassion for his plight, respect for him as a human being, recognition of his achievements, and the acknowledgment of our own lapses when they become visible to the patient, are vital ingredients for a productive psychoanalytic atmosphere. These elements are beyond transference and interpretation, and are more difficult if not impossible to teach. They should not need to be taught. They should, however, be recognized as essential components of therapeutic psychoanalysis. (Greenson, 1972/1990a, p. 101)

Respect for clients cuts across the differences between the three schools of therapy.

> In what way it was wondered, are therapists of almost opposite styles the same? How is the persuasive, probing, controlling thera-

pist similar to the accepting, reflecting, unobtrusive one? It was concluded that what is common among the various forms of therapy and therapists is a striving to communicate to clients their understanding of them and their problems, their respect, and their wish to be of help. (Reisman, 1971, pp. 123–124)

Therapists' respect for their clients is not to be taken lightly. Without respect, without a basic love for people, therapists cannot actively listen. Without active listening, the therapeutic relationship cannot thrive.

The Novice Therapist and Active Listening

Active listening is often difficult for beginning therapists, for three main reasons: they tend to become theory-bound; they try too hard; and they want to prove to the client that they know what they are doing. Let's consider each of these in turn.

Within each of the three major approaches, there is much room for therapists to be flexible. Cognitive therapists are often stereotyped as overly structured in their approach and as forcing the client to adopt their view of the world. However, Beck, a leading figure in the cognitive school, issues a clear warning about

the therapist [who] is so theory-bound that he actually misses the patient's problem. In addition to having to grapple with his own crazy view of the world, the patient is forced to incorporate the therapist's theories. This not only weakens the patient's structure of reality, but the various interpretations by the therapist often undermine his customary coping strategies and adaptive mechanisms. (cited in Strupp, Hadley, & Gomes-Schwartz, 1977, pp. 235–236)

Therapists must decide how flexible they will be with their own approach. Therapists who are theory-bound cannot actively listen to their clients.

Lazarus (1987), the founder of multimodal therapy, describes another error that can prevent beginning therapists from actively listening to clients.

Among my trainees, perhaps the most common error is that of trying too hard to effect change. The students are often eager to prove to their supervisors (and to themselves) what effective change agents they are, so that they tend to rush their clients to take action—very prematurely at times. (p. 314)

To actively listen is to use unobtrusive brush strokes followed by light tapping. However, beginning therapists tend to be in too much of a hurry. Rather than using a light brush-tap intervention, they pick up a two-by-four. For example, they may disburse homework assignments before the client is ready to follow through, or they may use a progressive muscle relaxation technique for all of their clients. The end result of an ill-timed intervention is that the therapist says, "I guess they weren't ready to change."

Finally, beginning therapists may fail to actively listen because they are trying to prove to the client that they know what they are doing. In the practicum or internship, the beginning therapist discovers that many of the clients are older in years. Why would an older person seek the help of some young pup—especially some pup of the opposite sex? If they attempt to prove how smart they are through the recitation of statistics, research studies, or clinical jargon, these young pups may sabotage the development of a therapeutic relationship.

> Psychotherapy can be a personally threatening and ambiguous situation, especially for an unskilled practitioner, making it tempting to clutch at "the pretense of knowledge" rather than confess ignorance. Certainly the most difficult task in working with graduate students is to persuade them to discard glib clinical jargon, to face the client as a unique, unpredictable, and basically unknown fellow human being, and to resolutely resist the temptation to try to show the client that they are smarter and better adjusted than he or she. (Maxwell & Maxwell, 1980, p. 396)

Indeed, doing therapy usually is threatening for the beginning therapist. Many beginning therapists, and experienced therapists, clutch at the pretense of knowledge rather than confess ignorance of a client's needs in therapy.

The Therapist's Struggles toward Active Listening

In becoming an active listener, therapists frequently pass between developmental phases in which they are first passive listeners and then overly directive. Like many of my colleagues, I can testify to this pattern.

When I was a passive listener, I knew what I needed to do: say "uh-huh," nod my head, use some of the same words that my clients used, and be silent at times. Then I went through an overly directive phase. I would confront my clients forcefully on their self-defeating patterns; I had no sense of timing.

Therapists feel relatively secure during these phases: they finally know what to do; they have the answers. However, they pay little attention to who the person is that is sitting across from them.

When therapists take a very passive or very directive stance, some clients will respond to that therapeutic climate and will change. However, when therapists are flexible, they can create a range of conditions to suit particular clients' needs, and more of their clients will change.

It is natural for therapists to take some false routes as they learn to be active listeners. They test the waters; they attempt to find the balance. If we truly are involved as therapists, all of us can expect to get stuck in occasional phases of being overly passive or overly directive.

To actively listen is to take risks. Yalom (1980) suggests:

> The major task of the maturing therapist is to learn to tolerate uncertainty. What is required is a major shift in perspective: rather than strive to order the interview "material" into an intellectually coherent framework, the therapist must strive toward authentic engagement. (pp. 410–411)

According to Yalom, the therapist should not try to order material in an intellectually coherent framework. Yet we know that cognitive insight—developing hypotheses—is an important process variable. Isn't there a contradiction here?

Cognitive Insight versus Authentic Engagement

Actually, working toward hypotheses and authentic engagement are not mutually exclusive. Dogmatic adherence to an orientation runs counter to being authentic, but each of the three major approaches offers enough latitude for the therapist to be flexible. The therapist establishes a fluid balance between being engaged in the therapeutic relationship and maintaining the distance required to develop hypotheses.

> A psychiatrist [or a therapist] needs to be attentive, absorbed, and spontaneous [authentically engaged] while at the same time observing, evaluating, and modifying his behavior "from a distance" [hypothesis development]. When he is working well he is, at one and the same time, both intensely involved and yet also detached. (Hobson, 1985, p. 167)

When authentic engagement and hypothesis development are balanced, they become a single process. Musicians, dancers, and athletes exhibit this balance when at their peak performance.

The brush-tap technique allows the therapist to reach this balance, at least briefly. In this technique, client and therapist are exploring together; they are engaged in an authentic relationship. The therapist is not passively waiting for the client, nor dragging the client along. The collaborative development of hypotheses feeds the therapeutic relationship; the therapeutic relationship feeds the development of hypotheses; and so on. It is a circular relationship, not a one-way, linear relationship.

As usual, therapists are searching for a balance with a particular client at a particular point in therapy. Sometimes, being more directive is appropriate; sometimes, being more passive is appropriate (whether a therapist leans toward a cognitive, humanistic, or psychodynamic approach). This balance between being passive (or supportive) and directive (or distant) is described in an introductory social work text.

> To be most helpful to the client, the worker must not be carried away by sympathy, but must be able to stand off and look at the client and the client's problem dispassionately, to find a balance between involvement and distance. (Piccard, 1988, p. 56)

Listening to a particular client's needs at a particular point in therapy in a manner that fosters growth—that is authentic engagement.

Though it sounds simple, to actively listen is very difficult to do. To take just one example, we saw in Chapter 11 that therapists need to attend to the client's negative emotions. Therapists must

> listen carefully to what clients say, grasp the underlying accompanying feelings, and find a way to let clients know that the therapist understands and is touched by their experience. However, it is not easy for most beginning therapists to do this with clients. Most of us have been strongly socialized to "hear" in a limited, superficial way that denies the painful, conflicted aspects of people's communications. (Teyber, 1992, p. 39)

Active listening is more than a technique to help the client express and experience negative emotions. Timing is critical. To hound the client to experience or express these emotions can be countertherapeutic in certain situations. There are no hard and fast rules. In making a commitment to active listening, the therapist has to accept some degree of uncertainty. Experience and a therapeutic orientation can serve as guides, but the uncertainty always exists.

We must respect the client as a unique, unpredictable, and basically unknown fellow human being. And, in the words of Frankl (1965), "To experience one human being as unique means to love him" (p. xiii).

Loving Our Clients

Particularly in graduate-level textbooks, there are few comments by leading therapists on the role of therapists' love for their clients. In his best-selling book *The Road Less Traveled*, Scott Peck (1978) comments, "It is remarkable, almost incredible, that the voluminous professional literature in the West on the subject of psychotherapy ignores the issue of love" (p. 173).

Peck even accuses the humanistic school of hiding behind a veil of jargon in an attempt to deny the critical role of therapists' love for their clients. He argues that the essential ingredient of effective therapy is not "unconditional positive regard," nor is it magical words, techniques or postures; it is human involvement and struggle. It is the willingness of the therapist to extend himself or herself for the purpose of nurturing the patient's growth—willingness to go out on a limb, to truly involve oneself at an emotional level in the relationship, to actually struggle with the patient and with oneself. In short, the essential ingredient of successful deep and meaningful psychotherapy is love. (Peck, 1978, p. 173)

Other authors' comments on this subject need not detain us for long. In a letter to Jung, Freud wrote, "Psychoanalysis is in essence a cure through love" (cited in Thompson, 1987, p. 157). Burton (1967) wrote, "After all research in psychotherapy is accounted for, psychotherapy still resolves itself into a relationship best subsumed by the word 'love'" (pp. 102–103). And Thompson (1987) wrote, "Loving is really hearing that other person!" (p. 154).

Does this mean that effective therapists must be in love with all of their clients? In the English language we have a very limited number of words for snow conditions (e.g., blizzard, hardpack); whereas the Eskimos have over 50 words for snow because it is such an important aspect of their lives. Perhaps our limitations of the word *love* is reflective of our society. I suggest that at least two types of love are involved in the therapeutic relationship.

The first is expressed as a concern for the welfare of others. May (1969) used the Greek word *agape* to describe this brotherly or sisterly love for clients. This love encompasses a respect for the client as a person and an appreciation of his or her suffering. As therapists, we accept this other person who can awaken unwanted thoughts, feelings, and behaviors in us, and we feel a love for the person's strengths and fortitude. We accept the person sitting across from us as a separate human being with his or her own past, present, and future. This brotherly or sisterly love we can offer to all of our clients. This type of love I refer to as *acceptance*, in the fullest meaning of the term.

The second type of love that can flourish within the therapeutic hour is a *fondness* for some of our clients. This love develops from the struggles of two people: the times of confusion, the mixed feelings, the frustrations, the joys, the bonding. These emotions are similar to those we feel for close friends. Therapists cannot actively command this second type of love to evolve; it develops as part of the process. To expect this type of love to be available to *all* clients is foolhardy and iatrogenic; instead of fostering an environment conducive to growth, therapists who expect a deep love and caring with all clients are likely to be involved in an "enmeshed" (Minuchin, 1974) relationship, in an attempt to get their own needs met.

Most therapists have entered the field to help others; they have a concern for the welfare of others; they have a basic *acceptance* of the human race. With some clients, this acceptance matures into a deep relationship of mutual respect and admiration—*fondness*. Where this second type of love exists, saying our good-byes—terminating, in the cold professional terminology—can be a painful process for the client and the therapist but can also have a therapeutic value. In the remainder of this chapter, I discuss some of the major aspects of termination.

TERMINATION

Is the termination of a client something welcomed by the client and the therapist? Or is termination an integral part of the therapeutic process that is met with new struggles? The answer is that it can be both; it just depends. For the majority of clients in brief therapy, termination is welcomed. For other clients, termination is a significant loss, accompanied by feelings of sadness and resentment.

With many clients the termination process goes very smoothly. If the therapist and client have been working in a collaborative manner on the creation of tenable hypotheses and the expression and experiencing of emotions, the client may welcome the time to say good-bye as a sign of new-found strength. Davanloo (1992a), a short-term psychodynamic therapist, notes, "Dependence on the therapist is rarely an issue, and the patient usually leaves with the feeling that with the help of the therapist he has done hard work and has achieved many of the results by his own efforts" (p. 68). Especially with the rise of short-term therapy, the number of overly dependent clients has begun to wane.

Sometimes it is grandiose of therapists to expect termination to be a traumatic or crucial phase of therapy. Most clients spend one hour per week with their therapist; that's 0.5% of their time each week. And, with the rise of short-term therapy, the median number of visits is now less than ten (Sue, McKinney, & Allen, 1976; Taube, Burns, & Kessler, 1984). Clearly, the dependency needs of the client (and of the therapist) are not as pronounced as in long-term therapy.

Beutler (1986) has suggested that "termination may best be seen as a *phase of treatment*, rather than the *end of treatment*" (p. 114). There is not necessarily a clear-cut end of therapy. Many clients return for a few sessions months after termination. Yalom has also noted that many clients' issues are never resolved, and some clients return to reinforce what they had learned from their therapy. For this reason, Yalom (1989) comments that psychotherapy is frequently referred to as "cyclotherapy" (p. 115).

If therapists align their expectations with their clients', they do not expect to have cured all of their clients' problems. The therapist's major task in brief therapy is to help people to get back on the right track.

However, for some clients the termination phase is a critical part of their therapy, and certain important questions must be addressed: When is it time to terminate? How do clients deal with the loss of their therapy and the loss of their therapist? What can the therapist do to make termination a productive phase in the client's therapy? These questions are addressed in the following sections. If the therapist is not aware of the vicissitudes of termination, the therapist and the client may never reach this stage.

When to Terminate?

At first glance, the answer may seem obvious: when the client's original problems have been addressed and are no longer obstacles in the client's life. In practice, however, this question is not so simple. Just as many clients enter their therapy without a clear statement of their problems (Chapter 8), the termination phase can also be plagued by amorphous problems.

Sifneos (1987), a psychodynamic therapist, believes that, in determining when to terminate, "evidence of problem solving as well as differences in attitudes, behavioral patterns, and overall change in the patient are what the therapist should be looking for" (pp. 175–176).

For example, if a withdrawn client realizes and accepts his or her pattern of withdrawing when feeling overwhelmed and, instead, finds new ways to reach out and become involved with other people, that would be evidence of new-found problem-solving abilities.

Another of Sifneos's criteria for termination is that the client can explain his or her own "psychodynamics"; that is, the client has gained a new understanding of his or her presenting problem, has accepted this cognitive insight, and can verbalize this understanding.

Sifneos also noted that some form of behavioral change is expected. On my initial assessment I usually write down three behavioral goals that I expect to be met by termination. For the person suffering from depression, these behavioral goals usually involve a positive change in the vegetative symptoms—for example, a positive change in sleep, appetite, concentration, energy level, affect, and so on. These goals do not dictate what I should do; rather, they serve to indicate when we are approaching termination.

In addition to clients' demonstrating a new awareness and understanding of the presenting problems, new problem-solving abilities, and behavioral change, the final, and perhaps most important, indication that termination is appropriate is that clients raise the subject themselves. In the majority of cases, when clients say that they are ready to stop their therapy, it is time to stop. They have received and experienced what they needed.

Most clients welcome the new-found independence of the termination phase; for others, even though therapy may have been brief, termination only serves to heighten their anxieties and fears of independence. I now turn to these latter clients, who have difficulties with separation.

Termination as a Loss

Life may be regarded as a series of decisions, and with each decision there is a loss: life is a series of losses. The loss of a humane relationship with someone who understands and has helped to bring renewed vitality is significant, even if it was only a brief encounter.

Therapy and termination. For some people, the termination phase is going to be a significant part of their therapy, because it focuses attention on how they have dealt with losses in the past and how they are dealing with losses in the present.

It is naive for therapists to believe that all clients will have a smooth, nonemotional termination phase. Some therapists may downplay the significance of termination because they have not adequately dealt with their own separation issues. As a result, they may not be able to utilize this powerful phase of therapy to foster their clients' growth.

Clients come to therapists' offices and disclose thoughts and feelings they have never told anyone before, or even admitted to themselves. Clients sometimes reveal intimate sexual information. They may express strong emotions, only to recover and say, "That is not like me." They have found a place of acceptance to explore. Why should they be in such a hurry to leave?

Some clients are like the newborn foal, and their legs are still wobbly. They need the termination phase to test out their autonomy.

Termination and autonomy. Therapy can be viewed as helping people to find more appropriate, growth-inducing ways to react to losses. Cognitive therapists Kohlenberg and Tsai (1987) are fully aware of the association between termination and losses.

> Terminations can bring up concerns about self-reliance and independence . . . It is a chance for the client to learn to say good-bye properly by expressing the range of feelings engendered by the ending of a special but transitional relationship. How the client reacts to termination is likely to be an indication of how she or he reacts to endings and beginnings in other areas of life. (p. 421)

The therapist has the opportunity to reflect back to the client how she or he is reverting to old, maladaptive patterns during the termination phase. The therapist gives the client an opportunity within the therapy hour to say that he or she is feeling sad about this separation, is anxious about stopping therapy, and/or is angry at the therapist. What a wonderful gift to someone who has had difficulty in self-assertion and self-expression!

Termination can be a very powerful time in therapy. The therapist returns to the brush-stroke technique and encourages the client to describe and experience his or her emotions and thoughts. "Since anger, rage, guilt, and their accompaniments of frustration and fear are the potent factors that prevent positive . . . mature separation, it is these that must not be over-looked in [the termination] phase of the time-limited therapy" (Mann, 1973, p. 36).

Therapists are in this field to help people accept and experience life to its fullest—the positive and the negative emotions. The acceptance of negative emotions is critical on the path toward separation and autonomy. In this respect, the termination phase not only helps reassure the client that everything will be okay, but also helps the client with one of the fundamental struggles of human existence.

The termination phase can be the most important phase of therapy for some clients, who gain from it an increased sense of responsibility and autonomy. Provide the opportunity for the client to separate: "How do you feel about our pending termination date?" "You were late today. This is unlike you. Do you believe it has to do with our pending termination?" "Your voice got soft when you mentioned that next week will be our last session." "I know that you said you are looking forward to our final session. Sometimes people have ambivalent feelings and even feel betrayed when they stop their therapy, even though in their head they believe this is right. Are you experiencing any feelings of doubt or betrayal with me?"

This is not the time to start confining people within some theoretical straightjacket. By utilizing the brush-tap technique, therapists provide the arena for the clients to experience their feelings. A client who says no to the therapist at this stage of therapy—in other words, who experiences and expresses negative emotions—is separating from the therapist.

Relapse of presenting problems and premature termination. Many people who enter therapy, especially those with repeated and/or extremely stressful life crises, bring with them maladaptive coping patterns: denial, withdrawal, social isolation, obsessive rumination, emotional numbing, rage, extreme dependency, and so on. With a pending termination date, some clients return to these old ways of relating with others and with themselves.

However, this return of maladaptive patterns is not necessarily unwanted. Volkan (1987), a psychodynamic psychotherapist who specializes in people with a diagnosis of borderline personality disorder, notes that the return of the presenting problems during the termination phase may represent the client's dependency on the therapist, but may also imply that the client is mourning the loss of old ways of relating.

> It is usual for my adult patients to exhibit some symptom revival, and I do not consider this an indication of failure; it is accompanied by an observing ego [by the clients distancing themselves from their problems] and does not lead to disorganization . . . I see this as part of a last effort to take stock and, more importantly, part of the mourning process. Patients revive their symptoms in order to part with them. (p. 102)

The client is in the process of saying good-bye to these old patterns. When a client's presenting problems return, the therapist's task is not to get defensive and to scurry around trying to find out what went wrong with the therapy. There can be a host of reasons for the reappearance of the presenting problems. Therapists need to be careful not to close this powerful therapeutic window.

Another pattern with which clients react to the termination phase, besides a reactivation of their presenting problems, is that clients terminate their therapy before they are prepared. In the majority of cases, when clients state that they are ready to terminate, the therapist is also prepared to terminate. However, some clients terminate prematurely so that they do not have to deal with the separation and the accompanying losses and anxiety.

Clients' desire to stop their therapy early is often a sign of resistance. Clients may prematurely stop their therapy if they have a history of overtly running from their problems, if they have been in therapy for a long time, or if they have a pattern of being overly dependent in relationships. Therapists who believe that the client is attempting to run from therapy must at least point out these patterns to the client.

Under pressure from third-party payors, administrators, supervisors, and colleagues, the therapist may not notice that termination is premature. However, in cases of premature termination, one of the major reasons the therapist allows the client to miss this opportunity for growth is that the therapist is not ready for the loss.

The therapist and termination. To be effective therapists, we must accept and appreciate our clients. With some clients, a deeper feeling of fondness develops. In those cases, in particular, therapists experience a significant loss at termination.

> If the therapist is not in touch with this sense of loss, he is almost certain to intrude on the patient's termination process. For instance, in order to escape his own sense of loss, the therapist might be inclined to go along with or encourage a certain watering down of the termination phase; he may, for example, not allow a long enough termination phase [that is, prematurely terminate] . . . Alternatively, in his unwillingness to face the loss of the patient, the therapist might hold onto him, continually looking for and

discovering lacunae that require further exploration. (Gorkin, 1987, p. 267)

Having grown fond of a client, therapists may try to evade their feelings of loss by supporting a premature termination or by unnecessarily continuing therapy.

Therapists must be careful that, out of their own needs, they do not deny their clients the benefits of an important phase of therapy, termination. Therapists' exploration of their own motivations is never complete.

Methods to Support the Termination Process

As we have seen, for many, if not most, clients, termination is a rather smooth process; the client has achieved what he or she sought from therapy. However, termination may be the most critical phase of therapy for some clients, particularly clients with a history of dependent relationships, clients who have not developed a social support network, and/or clients seen over a prolonged time, as well as in situations where fondness has developed between client and therapist. In those cases, there are tools that the therapist can use to support a beneficial termination. The therapist must determine when and how to apply these tools with a particular client.

Setting a date and reducing session frequency. Two key methods of ensuring an effective termination are to set a termination date and to decrease the frequency of sessions. In setting a termination date, some therapists prefer to agree on a fixed number of final sessions, while others prefer to set a specific calendar date. There are pros and cons to both approaches.

In situations where I believe only one or two more sessions are needed for a successful termination, I talk with the client about setting a specific number of sessions. With other clients for whom termination is a critical phase of therapy, I may prolong the termination and set a calendar date. The benefits of the latter approach are that I do not have to keep a count of the number of sessions and that clients' rescheduling of appointments becomes even more significant, in that the fixed date prevents them from prolonging their therapy and avoiding their salient issues.

According to psychodynamic therapist Marmor (1982), setting a termination date

> implicitly says to the patient: "I, the analyst, now have sufficient confidence in your strength and capacity to function autonomously that I can cut you loose." Although the initial reaction of patients is one of separation anxiety and even feelings of rejection, once these feelings have been worked through, patients usually take a giant step forward in self-confidence and autonomy. Thus, letting

the patient go is the final and quintessential therapeutic maneuver in the production of change in analytic treatment. (p. 69)

Setting a termination date can be a crucial aspect of some clients' therapy.

Cognitive therapists Bedrosian and Beck (1980) suggest that a pattern of termination in which the frequency of sessions is reduced and, finally, three booster sessions are scheduled at intervals of two, three, and six months can help clients continue to deal successfully with their problems.

Cognitive therapists Kanfer and Schefft (1987) advise against abrupt termination.

> Although a variety of different strategies are used to approach the termination process, the general rule is to avoid abrupt termination. Increased interview focus on future events, a reduction in the frequency of meetings, and a gradual reduction of the therapist's activity level mark the phasing-out process. (p. 45)

However, therapists should also guard against undue prolongation of therapy, which, like premature termination, can result from clients' and therapists' separation issues.

Besides setting a termination date and changing the frequency of sessions, there are other methods therapists may use to ease the termination process.

Socializing the client to termination.   Socializing clients on what to expect during the termination phase can make them feel more comfortable with the process.

The therapist can stress to clients that they need to disclose their thoughts and feelings about the pending termination date. In some cases, the therapist can remind clients that their presenting problems reflected patterns of behavior by which they dealt with loss and warn them that similar maladaptive patterns may return during the loss of their therapy.

During the termination phase, Luborsky (1984) makes remarks such as the following to his clients:

> You believe that the gains you have made are not part of you but depend on my presence. You fear that you will lose the gains when we stop our regular schedule of sessions and your initial symptoms will come back, as they have recently begun to in anticipation of termination. (p. 28)

If therapists suspect that termination may be a particularly important part of a client's therapy, they may socialize the client to termination by openly discussing the pending termination date and its likely impact.

Self-disclosure of the therapist.   Many therapists have been trained never to self-disclose. In some circumstances, however, self-disclosure can be therapeutic.

Of course, self-disclosure of the therapist's thoughts and feelings is integral to any form of therapy. Awareness and disclosure of what I am feeling and thinking toward a client is at the heart of my style of therapy. This pattern continues during the termination phase. As Gorkin (1987) notes, "I would view it as a useful part of termination for the therapist to disclose some of his feelings of loss" (p. 268).

More controversial is therapists' self-disclosure of personal information: whether they are married or have children, where they live, and so on. Often, when I say that therapists need to check their motivations when they self-disclose personal information, beginning therapists in my classes or under my supervision protest that self-disclosure expresses the human aspect of the therapeutic relationship; they do not want to be viewed as different from the client. Does the disclosure of the therapist's personal past, present, and future actually make the relationship more humane and therapeutic? In my experience, a therapist's self-disclosure of personal information usually does not enhance the therapeutic relationship.

Sometimes when therapists opt to self-disclose personal information, they want to befriend the client; they are working too hard at being equal. A more empathic awareness of the client's phenomenological world might reveal that the client needs a strong person to depend on, not a buddy.

Woody, Hansen, and Rossberg (1989) differentiate between therapists' self-disclosing and self-involving statements.

> It appears that self-involving disclosures keep the focus on the client and that self-disclosing statements may provide a conversational shift to the counselor. Reynolds and Fischer (1983) confirm these findings. McCarthy (1982) reports such results across all possible counselor/client gender pairings. We can conclude that it is more effective for the counselor to use self-involving statements than self-disclosing statements in keeping the client focused on self-exploration and understanding. (p. 64)

Research and experience support the contention that the therapist's untimely disclosure of personal information can be detrimental to the client's growth. However, during the termination phase, such self-disclosure can be a powerful tool to help the client gain a sense of autonomy.

Psychoanalyst Greenson (1971/1990b) states, "My clinical experience leads me to believe that the final resolution of the transference neurosis depends to a great extent on the transference neurosis being replaced by a real relationship" (p. 95). Generalizing to counseling and psychotherapy, we can say that the final resolution of the client's maladaptive behaviors depends to a great extent on the client's dependency on the therapist being replaced by an egalitarian relationship.

During the termination phase of therapy, the client rightly seeks an equal relationship with the therapist. Even psychoanalytic therapists, though opposed to therapists' self-disclosure, acknowledge the need for greater equality in termination. Langs, a psychoanalyst, asks his patients to no longer lie on the psychoanalytic couch during the termination phase, but to sit in a chair (Langs & Searles, 1980). The symbolism is obvious: he is moving toward what Greenson called a real relationship.

The therapist's self-disclosure of personal information during termination helps the client to move from dependency on the therapist to a more equal relationship. I vividly recall the first time that I disclosed personal information about myself to a client during the termination phase. In the session, the client and I began to talk about the future. I had already discovered that talking with clients about their future plans—whether later in the day, in a year, in five years, or in the rest of their lives—is a natural part of termination. The session had a flavor of two long-term friends talking. I had grown fond of him and was proud of the progress he had made in his therapy, as was he.

He told me that he was going skiing over the weekend. I disclosed that I lived only two miles from the ski slopes he mentioned and that I skied there regularly. We talked lightly about how terrible the snow conditions were. From there, I disclosed information about my two sons. He hadn't known that I had children.

That termination session was an important step in this client's search for autonomy. I firmly believe that my timely personal self-disclosure contributed to its importance. At the end of that session, we parted like two old friends. We were now on an equal footing; he had found his strength. My self-disclosure had helped him to say good-bye.

At that time, my personal self-disclosure was intuitive. Since then, I have adopted a technique of regularly disclosing personal information about myself during the termination phase. This practice can have a powerful impact on the relationship, especially when therapists tend to disclose little or no personal information during the initial and middle stages of therapy.

SUMMARY

Therapists must be flexible during all stages of therapy. People who are too rigid make terrible therapists. Likewise, people who are too conciliatory make terrible therapists. The search for a balance with a particular client, at a particular phase of therapy, is part of what makes counseling and psychotherapy so difficult. For therapists, flexibility implies actively listening to their clients.

Active listening rests on a love of life—a love that can be extended to others. The therapist appreciates the other person's suffering and strengths. In some cases, as client and therapist struggle through the process of therapy, they develop a deeper bond, a fondness.

In termination, the therapist must continue to actively listen to clients. Many, if not most, clients go through the termination phase with an acceptance of their new-found freedom, strength, and independence. For others, the termination phase is critical to their therapy.

There are no set rules for termination—or for therapy itself. "The most fundamental skill of the psychotherapist is productive listening" (Bugental, 1987, p. 71). To be an active listener, the therapist must first love people.

EPILOGUE:
THE SCIENCE AND ART
OF THERAPY

Few people outside this field are even aware of Professor Rumorgue's Separate entitled Tendencies and Symptoms of Hysteria in Red Clover . . . *M. Rumorgue himself emerged with honor and was able to work quietly on his forthcoming book on "Inherited Schizophrenia in Legumes"—a group of Mendelian by-laws.*

(STEINBECK, 1957/1986c, P. 20)

Hysteria in red clover? Schizophrenia in legumes? Why would anybody be interested in such nonsensical trivia?

Steinbeck's lines serve as a satire of the research on counseling and psychotherapy. Some therapists claim that the empirical literature has little to do with the practice of therapy. They are likely to add that therapy is an art, not a science. Are they correct?

THE SCIENCE OF THERAPY

In the following sections, I review the debate on the role of science in counseling and psychotherapy.

Science as the Study of Trivia

Irvin Yalom, the distinguished author of *The Theory and Practice of Group Psychotherapy* (1975), has commented, accurately, "Again and again one encounters a basic fact of life in psychotherapy research: the precision of the result is directly proportional to the triviality of the variables studied. A strange type of science!" (Yalom, 1980, p. 24).

Therapists have been accused of ignoring the current trends in empirical research. However, if the results of the studies are not relevant to the actual practice of therapy, then why should therapists waste their limited time on such trivia?

> The contemporary approach to outcome research contributes to this gap [between the research and the practice of therapy] because it focuses on assessment and treatment strategies that are different from those described by current models of psychotherapy. If researchers produced studies that represented the model of case

conceptualization and treatment described by theories of psychotherapy, practitioners might be more receptive to research findings. (Persons, 1991, p. 104)

Practicing therapists contend that the design and methodology of empirical studies lead to research findings that are irrelevant to the actual
practice of therapy.

However, the empirical literature has become vastly more sophisticated during the 1980s and 1990s. Outcome studies have given way to
comparative studies. The field is now actively examining the role of the
process variables of change.

> Unfortunately, one might argue that improved research sophisti-
> cation is the most detectable outcome of past decades of counsel-
> ing research; that is, relatively few counselors pay attention to
> research beyond their training years, partially because research
> results often appear to add little to current practice. However,
> research, theory, and practice must be increasingly integrated if
> counseling is to progress as a science. (Meier & Davis, 1993, p. 80)

But do we want the field to progress as a science?

Even though most practicing therapists pay little attention to the
scientific literature after graduation, it seems as though the field has fared
well enough. Can the increased sophistication of the research actually
benefit the field? Hill and Corbett (1993) are optimistic:

> As research methods become more sophisticated . . . enabling
> counseling psychologists to better answer the essential questions
> of how therapy operates, we hope that research will begin to take
> a more leading role in informing practitioners about therapy
> process and outcome. (p. 16)

Research has traditionally taken a back seat in regards to the training and
practice of therapy. Is it time to change?

With the increased sophistication of the scientific study of therapy,
therapists are now being called to be accountable by third-party payors,
educators are teaching the process variables of change which has partially
grown from the comparative studies of therapy, and there is an overall
recognition of the increased role of science in the practice of therapy.

The Call for Relevant Research

Increasingly, therapists are being asked for evidence of their effectiveness,
particularly by the third-party payors of managed health care systems.
Relevant scientific research can provide that evidence. Spending $5.00 for
a refill of medication, or paying 50% of a therapist's charge for each visit,

where is our society heading in regards to mental health care? If therapy is to remain a viable form of intervention, we must be able to account for change and the variables of change.

Almost 60 years ago, Fuerst (1938) suggested that, despite the

> social, economic and technical changes which have occurred and will continue to make our outside life even more different from that of preceding generations, the basic emotional problems of man are much more alike and much less different through the ages than we might expect. Science has entered a field which was closed before. Science has changed the outer world—science must teach us how to master our inner world. (p. 264)

Science can provide information on which paths to pursue further and which paths to discard. As the previous quote notes, science has changed the outer world, it is time to see if it can help us to also change our inner worlds. The statement quoted earlier was made by Fuerst in 1938. Now with the increased role of accountability in our society, this cry for the need for science to help us in examining our inner world is much louder.

Since 1938, there has been some application of science in the various styles of therapy. Carl Rogers's client-centered therapy was founded on research that supported the three variables of change. Though that research has been questioned, it provided therapists with a new direction to pursue. This research also lent legitimacy to the practices of Carl Rogers and his colleagues, and thereby hastened their acceptance in the profession.

Truax and Carkhuff (1964), two of the leading researchers in the client-centered approach, suggested an important role for science in therapy.

> Psychotherapy research can converge on this goal of practice [that is, making unhappy people happy or allowing malfunctioning people to function] by focusing its effort upon discovering and isolating the effective elements in the psychotherapeutic process which lead to constructive change in the patient. That is, we can attempt to discover what elements, among all that occur during psychotherapy, contribute to the patient's constructive change. (p. 126)

It is time to heed their words. We are now in a revolution that is going to have a major impact on how we teach and practice counseling and psychotherapy. The growing acceptance of the process variables of change is substantially due to the results of research in this area.

Humanistic therapists are not alone in their embrace of science. Cognitive therapists have cited numerous empirical studies on the efficacy of their approach in treating depression (Beck et al., 1979).

Finally, the psychodynamic approach, which historically was founded on theoretical concerns, is increasingly aware of the role of science in therapy, as a recent review makes clear:

What emerges from this overview of the six [review] articles on dynamic psychotherapy research may be a surprise to some: Rather than decreasing in recent decades, research on dynamic psychotherapy has increased. The increased quantity of dynamic psychotherapy research is confirmed as well by Beutler and Crago's (1991) survey of all psychotherapy research programs—18 of the 40 programs worldwide are now devoted to dynamically oriented psychotherapy research. Current studies on dynamic psychotherapy have been conducted with more innovative approaches than ever before and they have been distilling the essence of the curative factors in dynamic psychotherapy. (Luborsky, Barber, & Beutler, 1993, p. 540)

The call for research relevant to the practicing therapist is now being met. Science is going to alter the practice of counseling and psychotherapy, for better or for worse.

The Role of Science in Therapy

To meet the demands of government agencies, third-party payors, health plan administrators, and professors in training programs, scientific research, as it becomes more sophisticated, is playing a more active role in determining how therapy is taught and practiced; this trend will continue. Administrators, educators, and practitioners of the new generation are going to be listening more to the results of research. Many fear that this will be the downfall of our profession. Certainly, it promises profound change for the profession.

Throughout this book, I have referred to the empirical literature on therapy. For example, surveys conducted with therapists have identified common themes in therapists' motives for entering the helping professions. Surveys have shown us what other therapists throughout the world are practicing: even though there is a trend toward eclectic therapy, the vast majority of therapists practice from a specific orientation or an integration of approaches. Research has supported the common belief that therapists go through developmental stages.

As we saw in Chapter 4, the outcome literature overwhelmingly supports the contention that counseling and psychotherapy are effective means of helping people with emotional or psychological problems. Therapists do not have to rely solely on their personal convictions in this matter.

The screech of the dodo bird, which fostered an investigation of the process variables of change, resulted from the null findings of comparative studies. Theorists had been talking about this dodo bird since Rosenzweig introduced it in 1936. It was not until the review of the comparative literature by Luborsky, Singer, and Luborsky in 1975 that we finally began to take seriously these process variables of change.

The results of studies on process variables lent legitimacy to what many have silently believed for many years: that the techniques of a specific approach may be important, but the aspects of therapy are the fundamental agents of change that operate across all therapeutic styles.

We can see from this brief review that science has already given much to the profession. As research continues and becomes more sophisticated, therapists will gain a deeper understanding of the fundamentals and subtleties of change. Schaffer (1982) suggested that "when therapist behavior is studied with more adequate methodology, it may be possible to reach more definitive conclusions about the way specific and nonspecific factors interact to determine outcome" (p. 670). A few of those conclusions have already been established in the years since Schaffer wrote. Nye (1992) contends:

> Perhaps the best way for science to progress is to have dedicated researchers pursue different avenues of thought with vigor and determination. In the future, when various dead ends have been reached and alternative paths have been relatively successful, there may be a weeding out, a slimming down, a tying in, and so on, so that as a result facets of every theory will become integrated into a thorough understanding of human behavior. (pp. 147–148)

The impact that science has had on the practice of therapy thus far is nothing compared to what is to come. It is a time of change for the profession; we are undergoing a revolution.

Defining Science

Thus far in this chapter, I have been interpreting science in a narrow sense, as empirical research. Actually, most effective therapists are practicing a science. "To the extent that psychotherapy attempts a systematic and self-conscious manipulation of variables in a human relationship and notes its effects, it has the makings of a scientific discipline" (Strupp, 1962, p. 577). All therapists look for patterns that result in the desired outcome. "In one sense, every therapist is, or ought to be, engaged in research all the time—research as the word itself states, as a 'search' for the sources" (May, 1969, p. 18).

As we have seen, some therapists decline to adopt a structured approach to therapy because they prefer to remain passive, while hoping and working to keep the power in their hands. Helping people to change is not their primary goal.

> If psychotherapy is at the stage that we can allow students or supervisees to do whatever they feel like doing, then it is not even

an art, much less a science, and there would be no justification for attempting to teach it. (Patterson, 1983, p. 25)

The pendulum is swinging. The days when therapists could do whatever they pleased behind closed doors have ended. Increasingly, therapists are being asked to justify their actions, as are educators and supervisors.

THE ART OF THERAPY

Although it's good that therapists are being asked to be more accountable, science alone is not the answer. Therapy is, and always will be, an art. "There is no pretense that reason and reason alone, or that science and science alone, can prevail by themselves in any kind of human relationship, personal or therapeutic" (Mann, 1973, p. 48).

Science Alone Is Not the Answer

Therapy can never be a pure science, in the sense that its practitioners discover hard and fast patterns. There is simply too much room for variability. Whether therapy is a science or an art is

> comparable to the question posed to a chess champion, "Tell me, Master, what is the best move in the world?" There simply is no such thing as the best or even a good move apart from a particular situation in a game and the particular personality of one's opponent. (Frankl, 1963, pp. 171–172)

With continued research, we are going to become more appreciative of the common process variables, the subtle effects of the various styles of therapy, and the art of therapy as a whole.

Therapy will always remain an art because people are different. We can generate statistical data about interventions, but in the end the therapist will have to rely on active listening to the particular client.

> Because a truly individualized treatment approach means that every treated case is unique or different, it is difficult for me to see how an investigator . . . can secure meaningful generalizations in terms of theory or approach. (Garfield, 1991, p. 1350)

However, an individualized treatment approach does not dictate that the therapist must go in and simply wing it. The therapist already has ideas about why people behave as they do and how to help people make positive change. Science, the systematic study of how people change, can strengthen, and add new knowledge to, the understanding that we already have.

When clients enter therapy, they are looking for a relationship with another person who will help the pain to subside. They are not looking for a scientist; they want to feel understood. Empathy is at the core of therapy.

> In his essay, "What is Art?" Leo Tolstoy wrote, "It is on the capacity of man to receive another man's expression of feeling and experience those feelings himself that the activity of art is based." The word *therapist* could as validly be substituted for *art*, for Tolstoy's observation catches the very essence of empathy. (Hammer, 1990, p. 189)

Therapists do not develop empathy by reading texts or learning techniques or process variables. Empathy comes from the therapist who is willing to risk the uncertainty of not having the answers. Counseling and psychotherapy are based on a human relationship between two people. The therapist must provide a relationship that is conducive to change—a relationship that is both supportive and collaborative. The ability to develop such a relationship with widely different people is the essence of therapy.

Therapy is a healing art. Therapists are artists. Some paint by numbers; many create works worth pondering; and a few create therapeutic relationships that are masterpieces.

The Rise of Science in the Art of Therapy

As we have seen, the therapist must reconcile art and science.

> Truly excellent therapists, a relatively rare breed, share important elements with the artist; that is, the practice of psychotherapy involves a fair amount of creativity and intuition. At the same time, I continue to believe that psychotherapy has the potential to become a scientific discipline. (Strupp, 1991, p. 318)

Will the infusion of scientific rigor benefit counseling and psychotherapy? For an answer, we might look to medicine. Technological advances during the past century have been accompanied by enormous progress in the field of medicine. However, despite these drastic changes, the practice of medicine has remained an art. Effective physicians realize that knowing how to take a blood pressure reading and knowing what tests to run is not enough. They know that they must pace their questions differently for different patients; they must empathize with their patients. Their personality, their bedside manner, has a direct impact on their patients' compliance.

The practice of psychotherapy, like the practice of medicine, remains an art, only certain aspects of which are susceptible to specification and measurement. In particular, the therapist's personality is a critical component of the therapeutic equation [that is, of the therapeutic relationship]. (Strupp, 1992, p. 25)

At this stage of its evolution, therapy remains an art profoundly dependent on the personality of the therapist. "The challenge for the psychotherapist is to be able to use his or her own personality in the therapeutic process in a manner that facilitates competence and growth in the patient" (Kroll, 1988, p. 219).

The increased emphasis on science in the practice of therapy certainly means change. However, it need not mean that the art of therapy will be lost. Indeed, science can be used to strengthen our understanding that therapy is an art: an empirical study found that clients were most likely to cite qualities of the therapist as the major factor responsible for their improvement, rather than any specific techniques used by the therapist (Sloane, Staples, Cristol, Yorkston, & Whipple, 1975). The broader introduction of empirical research in the training and practice of therapists does not necessarily mean that we will become technicians. Science is a tool. As in the practice of medicine, science can be used to foster growth, while maintaining the art.

The increased usage of manuals to guide therapists, the growing prestige of empirical studies, and the rise of managed health care all pose the risk that we could produce a generation of technicians. Therapists must decide whether the manuals and the empirical data are to be used as tools to enhance their work or are to be allowed to dictate their future. By being politically active, therapists can make a difference.

THE SCIENCE AND ART OF THERAPY

The practice of therapy is, was, and always will be a science and an art. Therapists must know what they are doing in therapy, yet at the same time be with the client. It is a dynamic and precarious balance. In the words of Kroll (1988), "Therapy entails ongoing judgements as to the optimal balance of supportive and exploratory interventions with the patient. This is the heart of therapy" (p. 100). The therapist balances emotions and knowledge, art and science.

Like all great art, the art of psychotherapy is the skillful and creative application of scientific knowledge to human problems. Ruskin wrote, "Fine art is that in which the hand, the head and the heart of man go together." (Braceland, 1973, p. 603)

When therapists can blend the knowledge and the relationship, they are on their way in developing a masterpiece.

Although empathy is at the core of therapy, it is not solely responsible for the change that occurs. "Therapists have learned that knowing a method is not effective without having the personal qualities necessary to apply it. At the same time, empathy is not a substitute for knowledge or knowing what to do" (Welt & Herron, 1990, p. 160).

Therapists who can conceptualize but cannot experientially be with their clients risk becoming no-change technicians; those who cannot conceptualize risk becoming nebulous no-change therapists. Cognitive therapists Beck et al. (1990) fully recognize the need to blend the science and art of therapy.

> The most effective application of techniques depends not only on a clear conceptualization of the case . . . and the formation of a friendly working relationship, but also on the artistry of the therapist. The *art of therapy* involves the judicious use of humor, anecdotes, metaphors, and self-disclosure of the therapist's experiences, as well as the standard cognitive and behavioral techniques. (p. 79)

If a technique is to be effective, the therapist must actively listen to the client. The objective realm of techniques is not enough; the therapist as a person must be present with his or her feelings of vulnerability and confusion. As Gutsch (1990) puts it, "Psychotherapy . . . is a process based primarily on the art of relating and the science of understanding behavior change" (p. 151).

In a memorable image, Hammer (1990) compares therapy to a ladder between the poles of science (on the ground) and art (in the sky). The therapist who takes a midway position "encompasses a capacity for both tough-minded and tender-minded approaches, for oscillating between obsessive-compulsive and hysteroid potentials in oneself, without getting stuck at either polarity" (Hammer, 1990, p. 29).

For the past century, therapists have been too close to what Hammer called the hysteroid pole. At that pole, therapists lack an appreciation of the process variables of change; they follow the winds of those who yell the loudest. Their reliance on intuition without structure results in chaotic sessions. Hammer (1990) characterized the hysteroid pole as akin to "a painting done by a chimpanzee—all random impulse, undirected by a guiding intelligence" (p. 29).

Now, with the increased emphasis on science, on empirical data, the profession risks falling to the ground and becoming inflexible and obsessed with detail. The practice of counseling and psychotherapy is undergoing a change.

Therapists are attempting to find a balance between the two extremes described by Charlotte Bronte (1847/1960) in her novel *Jane Eyre*.

> True, generous feeling is made small account of by some; but here were two natures rendered, the one intolerably acrid [science], the

other despicably savourless for the want of it [art]. Feeling without judgment is a washy draught indeed; but judgment untempered by feeling is too bitter and husky a morsel for human deglutition. (p. 239)

The practice of therapy is attempting to find this balance between the art and the science.

SUMMARY

In the Midst of a Revolution

The profession is entering a new phase in its development. A struggle is underway between two fundamental philosophies. The basic issue is, as a recent journal article asked, whether therapists are to be "robots or revolutionaries" (Simmermon & Simmermon, 1994). Are therapists to mechanically apply the cherished techniques of a particular orientation or, instead, are they to embrace our new understanding of the process variables that promote change across all styles of therapy?

It has been estimated that there are now over 400 different styles of therapy (Kazdin, 1986). The practice of eclectic therapy is on the rise (Zook & Walton, 1989). Although proponents of the three major styles of therapy insist that their specific techniques are the major change agents, comparative research does not show that one style of therapy is more effective than another (Elkin et al., 1989). Research supports the significant role of process variables in therapy (Bergin & Garfield, 1994).

The helping professions—counseling, psychotherapy, and social work—are changing. There is a growing acceptance that the specific techniques of any particular therapeutic approach are not as potent as the nonspecific process variables of change. In my view, this acceptance of process variables constitutes what Kuhn (1970) calls a scientific revolution, one of "the tradition-shattering complements to the tradition-bound activity of normal science" (p. 6). Not surprisingly, many proponents of the three major styles are resisting this trend.

The revolution is just beginning. What will emerge is still uncertain; however, as has been emphasized throughout this book, it is too soon to discard the various theories of change and adopt a common-factors eclecticism (Daldrup, Beutler, Engle, & Greenberg, 1988). As we saw in Chapter 2, it is still important for a therapist to have an orientation to work from.

As it grows more sophisticated and applicable, research will continue to have a profound impact on this revolution, as will outside forces—specifically, managed health care. Therapists who are not flexible, and who do not stay current with trends, risk being left behind. The next decades promise to be an exciting time of change.

Timshel

As we have seen throughout this book, the fundamental goal of all therapies is to help people to become more autonomous, to accept that they are ultimately responsible for their lives. Existential therapists have written extensively on this theme.

> We are interrogated by life, and we have to answer. *Life*, I would say, *is a life-long question-and-answer period.* As to the answers, I do not weary of saying that we can only answer to life by answering for our lives. *Responding* to life means *being responsible* for our lives. (Frankl, 1978, p. 110)

Just as we work with our clients to become more autonomous, we must continue to accept that, as therapists, we are ultimately responsible for our own education and practice of therapy.

It seems fitting to end with another passage from John Steinbeck. When he was working on his novel *East of Eden*, he made the following comment in a personal journal.

> I began to realize that without this story [*East of Eden*]—or rather a sense of it—psychiatrists would have nothing to do. In other words this one story is the basis of all human neurosis—and if you take the fall along with it, you have the total of the psychic troubles that can happen to a human (7/11/51). (cited in Benson, 1984, p. 685)

In Genesis 4:7, Steinbeck found what he regarded as the answer to all human emotional suffering. In the book of Genesis, God commanded Cain to be responsible for his life, lest sin overpower him. God said, "Thou mayest rule over it." In therapeutic terms, when people recognize and accept that they are responsible for their lives, they are less likely to suffer needlessly.

In Hebrew, "thou mayest" is *Timshel*. Steinbeck incorporated this word, which connotes free will, into *East of Eden*.

> "*Timshel*—and you said—"
> "I said that word carried a man's greatness if he wanted to take advantage of it."
> "I remember Sam Hamilton felt good about it."
> "It set him free," said Lee. "It gave him the right to be a man, separate from every other man."
> "That's lonely."
> "All great and precious things are lonely."
> "What is the word again?"
> "*Timshel*—thou mayest." (Steinbeck, 1952/1988a, p. 675)

Appendix
Citation Letter and Therapist Questionnaire

The letter and questionnaire used for the citations in Part One are reproduced in the following pages. The survey was not conducted for an empirical analysis; 15 questionnaires were completed by 8 graduate students and 7 experienced therapists.

I have used their citations throughout the first three chapters to highlight the common empirical and theoretical trends of learning and doing therapy. The small number of subjects (15) proved satisfactory for this purpose.

CITATIONS FROM STUDENTS AND PROFESSIONALS

I am gathering information for a graduate level textbook on counseling and psychotherapy to be published by Brooks/Cole. One major goal of the book is to provide the reader direct quotes from fellow students and experienced therapists on what their learning experience has been, or was, like. The beginning student is frequently overly anxious. For the beginning therapist to know that others are, or were, in a similar boat with similar experiences and fears, may make their anxiety more manageable.

I expect the book to be published by the Fall of 1995. The working title of the book is *Learning and Understanding Counseling and Psychotherapy: The Process Variables of Change*. I cannot promise, at this time, whether I will be using people's names with the quotes. However, if I do then please write a check mark below that you would like your name included with your quote. Also, if you complete the information below on your address, I will mail you a card letting you know that your quote was used in the book.

Thank you for your time and assistance,

Fred Walborn, Ph.D.

_____ YES, I would like my name included in the quotation.

If my quote is included in the book, please mail a card to my address below to let me know.

_____

Name

_____

Address

_____

City   State   Zip

THERAPIST QUESTIONNAIRE

This questionnaire is designed for therapists, of varying orientations and years of training, to provide beginning therapists an opportunity to realize that many of the fears that they have about doing therapy are common. This is not a bonafide research project. It is an opportunity for you to simply help others in the process of this field of learning therapy. *Please* attempt to limit your statements to three to six sentences. However, if necessary, complete your statements on the back of the first page.

I. Professional Background

Type of degree program presently enrolled or graduated from:

M.A.   M.S.   M.S.W.   Ed.D.   M.D.   Ph.D.   Psy.D.   Other _____

If presently enrolled in graduate school circle the present graduate year:

1   2   3   4   other _____

Type of graduate program enrolled in or graduated from:

counseling   psychology   psychiatry   social work   other _____

If already graduated, number of years post-grad.

1–5   6–10   11–15   16–20   21–25   26–30   30 plus

II. Why Entered Field

A. Many therapists decided to enter the "helping professions" during their childhood or adolescence, but not specifically in the field of counseling, psychology, or social work. When you first decided to enter the general field of the helping professions (nursing, medicine, etc.), (1) what specific field were you going to enter, (2) how old were you, and (3) describe the reason(s) *at that time in your life* that you thought you wanted to pursue a career in the helping professions.

1. Specific field(s)

2. Age

3. Reason(s)

B. When you first entered graduate school, describe the reason(s) *at that time* that you thought you entered the field.

C. Now, with some experience and the ability of hindsight, why do you think that you *originally* entered the helping professions?

D. Now, with some experience, why do you stay in the field?

E. Numerous authors have stated that therapists enter the field due to being in a caretaker role in their youth, power, intimacy, isolation, or other personal issues. Do any of these, or other reasons, seem applicable to you and explain.

F. Based on your relationships with others in the field, what do you believe are the major reasons that other therapists and therapists-in-training got into the field?

III. Selection of an Orientation

A. Realizing that all of the three major approaches to doing therapy (psychodynamic-psychoanalytic, humanistic-existential, cognitive-behavioral) appreciate the necessity of being flexible within their approach, which of the three approaches (or being eclectic or integrative) would be most apt to describe your approach?

B. Do you believe selection of an orientation, in order to provide structure for the therapist and the therapy, to be a beneficial aspect during the learning of therapy? Why or why not?

IV. Supervision

A. Briefly recall thoughts and feelings during your first experience in supervision as a supervisee that other students just beginning their own supervision would like to read about.

B. What words of wisdom would you give to students entering supervision for the first time?

C. If you provide supervision, as the supervisor briefly describe a rewarding *and* a difficult aspect of being a supervisor.

V. Learning Experience

A. Briefly describe a humorous (perhaps even comic tragedy) experience of learning therapy that other students beginning their training may welcome hearing.

B. Briefly describe one of the major joys of your education.

C. What was, or has been, the most frustrating aspect of your education of being a therapist?

D. In general, in a brief quote, describe what you would like to tell beginning therapists of varying orientations and schools about learning therapy so that they might feel that they are not so alone.

YOU MUST SIGN BELOW TO BE CONSIDERED FOR A QUOTE

I fully understand that the purpose of this questionnaire is to aid other therapists-in-training to realize that others in the field have had similar or even more difficult experiences in the learning of therapy. I authorize Dr. Walborn to include my quotes in this survey in his book. If required, editing decisions may be made for clarity and space requirements.

_____

YOUR SIGNATURE

REFERENCES

Abraham, K. (1955). Psychoanalytic notes on Cove's system of self-mastery. In H. Abraham (Ed.), *Clinical papers and essays on psycho-analysis* (H. Abraham & D. R. Ellison, Trans.) (pp. 306–327). New York: Basic Books. (Original work published 1925)

Abramowitz, S. I., & Abramowitz, C. U. (1976). Sex role psychodynamics in psychotherapy supervision. *American Journal of Psychotherapy, 30,* 583–592.

Alexander, F. (1935). The problem of psychoanalytic technique. *Psychoanalytic Quarterly, 4,* 588–611.

Alexander, F., & French, T. M. (1946). *Psychoanalytic therapy: Principles and application.* New York: Ronald Press.

Alexander, L. B., & Luborsky, L. (1986). The Penn Helping Alliance Scales. In L. S. Greenberg & W. M. Pinsof (Eds.), *The psychotherapeutic process: A research handbook* (pp. 325–366). New York: Guilford Press.

Allport, G. W. (1937). *Personality: A psychological interpretation.* New York: Henry Holt and Company.

Altucher, N. (1967). Constructive use of the supervisory relationship. *Journal of Counseling Psychotherapy, 14*(2), 165–170.

American Psychiatric Association. (1994). *Diagnostic and statistical manual of mental disorders* (4th ed.). Washington, DC: Author.

Andrews, G., & Harvey, R. (1981). Does psychotherapy benefit neurotic patients? A reanalysis of the Smith, Glass, and Miller data. *Archives of General Psychiatry, 38,* 1203–1208.

Applebaum, S. A. (1978). Pathways to change in psychoanalytic therapy. *Bulletin of the Menninger Clinic, 42,* 239–251.

Ard, B. N. (1973). Providing clinical supervision for marriage counselors: A model for supervisor and supervisee. *The Family Coordinator, 22,* 91–97.

Arlow, J., & Brenner, C. (1964). *Psychoanalytic concepts and the structural theory.* New York: International Universities Press.

Aronson, H., & Weintraub, W. (1978). Patient changes during classical psychoanalysis as a function of initial status and duration of treatment. In S. Fisher & R. P. Greenberg (Eds.), *The scientific evaluation of Freud's theories and therapy* (pp. 375–389). New York: Basic Books.

Atthowe, J. (1973). Behavior innovation and persistence. *American Psychologist, 28,* 34–41.

Auerswald, M. C. (1974). Differential reinforcing power of restatement and inter-pretation on client production of affect. *Journal of Counseling Psychology,* *21*(1), 9–14.

Austin, B., & Altekruse, M. K. (1972). The effects of group supervisor roles on practicum students' interview behavior. *Counselor Education and Supervision, 12,* 63–68.

Aveline, M. (1992). The use of audio and videotape recordings of therapy sessions in the supervision and practice of dynamic psychotherapy. *British Journal of Psychotherapy, 8*(4), 347–358.

Bandura, A., Jeffrey, R. W., & Wright, C. L. (1974). Efficacy of participant modeling as a function of response induction aids. *Journal of Abnormal Psychology,* *83*(1), 56–64.

Barnat, M. (1977). Spontaneous supervisory metaphor in the resolution of trainee anxiety. *Professional Psychology, 8,* 307–315.

Barrett, J. E. (1979). The relationship of life events to the onset of neurotic disorders. In J. E. Barrett (Ed.), *Stress and mental disorder* (pp. 87–109). New York: Raven Press.

Barrett-Lennard, G. T. (1962). Dimensions of therapist response as causal factors in therapeutic change. *Psychological Monographs: General and Applied, 76*(43, Whole No. 562), 1–36.

Barrett-Lennard, G. T. (1981). The empathy cycle: Refinement of a nuclear con-cept. *Journal of Counseling Psychology, 28,* 91–100.

Bartlett, W. E. (1983). A multidimensional framework for the analysis of supervi-sion of counseling. *The Counseling Psychologist, 11,* 9–17.

Basch, M. F. (1988). *Understanding psychotherapy.* New York: Basic Books.

Bascue, L. O., & Yalof, J. A. (1991). Descriptive dimensions of psychotherapy supervision. *Clinical Supervisor, 9*(2), 19–30.

Bauer, B. P., & Kobos, J. C. (1987). *Brief therapy: Short-term psychodynamic intervention.* Northvale, NJ: Aronson.

Beck, A. T. (1963). Thinking and depression: I. Idiosyncratic content and cognitive distortions. *Archives of General Psychiatry, 9,* 36–46.

Beck, A. T. (1976). *Cognitive therapy and the emotional disorders.* New York: International Universities Press.

Beck, A. T. (1989). Foreword. In J. Scott, J. M. G. Williams, & A. T. Beck (Eds.), *Cognitive therapy in clinical practice: An illustrative casebook* (pp. vii–xv). New York: Routledge.

Beck, A. T. (1993). Cognitive therapy: Past, present, and future. *Journal of Consult-ing and Clinical Psychology, 61,* 194–198.

Beck, A. T., Freeman, A., Pretzer, J., Davis, D. D., Fleming, B., Ottaviani, R., Beck, J., Simon, K. M., Padesky, C., Meyer, J., & Trexler, L. (1990). *Cognitive therapy of personality disorders.* New York: Guilford Press.

Beck, A. T., & Haaga, D. A. (1992). The future of cognitive therapy. *Psychotherapy,* *29,* 34–38.

Beck, A. T., Rush, A. J., Shaw, B. F., & Emery, G. (1979). *Cognitive therapy of depression.* New York: Guilford Press.

Becker, E. (1973). *The denial of death.* New York: Free Press.

Beckham, E. E. (1992). Predicting patient dropout in psychotherapy. *Psychother-apy, 29*(2), 177–182.

Bedrosian, R. C., & Beck, A. T. (1980). Principles of cognitive therapy. In M. J. Mahoney (Ed.), *Psychotherapy process: Current issues and future directions* (pp. 127–152). New York: Plenum Press.

Bellak, L., & Faithorn, P. (1981). *Crises and special problems in psychoanalysis and psychotherapy.* New York: Brunner/Mazel.

Bellak, L., & Small, L. (1978). *Emergency psychotherapy and brief psychotherapy* (2nd ed.). New York: Grune & Stratton.

Benson, J. J. (1984). *The true adventures of John Steinbeck, writer.* New York: Penguin Books.

Berger, D. M. (1987). *Clinical empathy.* Northvale, NJ: Aronson.

Berger, S. S., & Buchholz, E. S. (1993). On becoming a supervisee: Preparation for learning in a supervisory relationship. *Psychotherapy, 30,* 86–92.

Bergin, A. E. (1971). The evaluation of therapeutic outcomes. In A. E. Bergin & S. L. Garfield (Eds.), *Handbook of psychotherapy and behavior change* (pp. 217–270). New York: Wiley.

Bergin, A. E. (1980). Psychotherapy and religious values. *Journal of Consulting and Clinical Psychology, 48,* 95–105.

Bergin, A. E., & Garfield, S. L. (Eds.). (1994). *Handbook of psychotherapy and behavior change* (4th ed.). New York: Wiley.

Bergin, A. E., & Lambert, M. J. (1978). The evaluation of therapeutic outcomes. In S. L. Garfield & A. E. Bergin (Eds.), *Handbook of psychotherapy and behavior change: An empirical analysis* (pp. 139–189). New York: Wiley.

Bergin, A. E., & Suinn, R. M. (1975). Individual psychotherapy and behavior therapy. *Annual Review of Psychology, 26,* 509–556.

Bergman, D. V. (1951). Counseling method and client responses. *Journal of Consulting Psychology, 15,* 216–224.

Berman, J. S., Miller, R. C., & Massman, P. J. (1985). Cognitive therapy versus systematic desensitization: Is one treatment superior? *Psychological Bulletin, 97,* 451–461.

Berman, J. S., & Norton, N. C. (1985). Does professional training make a therapist more effective? *Psychological Bulletin, 98,* 401–407.

Bettelheim, B. (1982). *Freud and man's soul.* New York: Vintage Books.

Beutler, L. E. (1983). *Eclectic psychotherapy: A systematic approach.* New York: Pergamon Press.

Beutler, L. E. (1986). Systematic eclectic psychotherapy. In J. C. Norcross (Ed.), *Handbook of eclectic psychotherapy* (pp. 94–131). New York: Brunner/Mazel.

Beutler, L. E., & Crago, M. (Eds.). (1991). *Psychotherapy research—An international review of programmatic studies.* Washington, DC: American Psychological Association.

Beutler, L. E., Crago, M., & Arizmendi, T. G. (1986). Therapist variables in psychotherapy process and outcome. In S. L. Garfield & A. E. Bergin (Eds.), *Handbook of psychotherapy and behavior change* (3rd ed., pp. 257–310). New York: Wiley.

Beutler, L. E., Johnson, P. T., Neville, C. W., & Worman, S. N. (1972). "Accurate empathy" and the A-B dichotomy. *Journal of Consulting and Clinical Psychology, 38,* 372–375.

Beutler, L. E., Pollack, S., & Jobe, A. M. (1978). "Acceptance," values and therapeutic change. *Journal of Consulting and Clinical Psychology, 46,* 198–199.

Bibring, E. (1954). Psychoanalysis and the dynamic psychotherapies. *Journal of the American Psychoanalytic Association, 2,* 745–770.

Blanck, G., & Blanck, R. (1974). *Ego psychology: Theory and practice.* New York: Columbia University Press.

Bloch, S., & Lambert, M. J. (1985). What price psychotherapy? A rejoinder. *British Journal of Psychiatry, 146,* 96–98.

Blocher, D. H. (1983). Toward a cognitive developmental approach to counseling supervision. *The Counseling Psychologist, 11*(1), 27–34.

Bohn, M. J., Jr. (1965). Counselor behavior as a function of counselor dominance, counselor experience, and client type. *Journal of Counseling Psychology, 12,* 346–352.

Book, H. E. (1973). On maybe becoming a psychotherapist, perhaps. *Canadian Psychiatric Association Journal, 18,* 487–493.

Borders, L. D., & Fong, M. L. (1991). Evaluation of supervisees: Brief commentary and research report. *Clinical Supervisor, 9*(2), 43–51.

Bordin, E. S. (1979). The generalizability of the psychoanalytic concept of the working alliance. *Psychotherapy: Theory, Research and Practice, 16,* 252–260.

Bordin, E. S. (1983). A working alliance based model of supervision. *The Counseling Psychologist, 11,* 35–42.

Braaten, L. J. (1961). The movement from non-self to self in client-centered psychotherapy. *Journal of Counseling Psychology, 8,* 20–24.

Braceland, F. J. (1973). The art of psychotherapy. In J. H. Masserman (Ed.), *Handbook of psychiatric therapies* (pp. 597–603). Northvale, NJ: Aronson.

Brody, J. (1987). *Jane Brody's nutrition book.* New York: Bantam Books.

Brody, N. (1983). Author's response: Where are the emperor's clothes? *The Behavioral and Brain Sciences, 6,* 303–308.

Bronte, C. (1960). *Jane Eyre.* New York: Signet. (Original work published 1847)

Brown, B. B. (1978). Social and psychological correlates of help-seeking behavior among urban adults. *American Journal of Community Psychology, 6,* 425–439.

Bruce, W. E., & Sims, J. H. (1974). Birthorder among psychotherapists: A see-saw phenomenon. *Psychological Reports, 34,* 215–220.

Budman, S. H., & Gurman, A. S. (1988). *Theory and practice of brief therapy.* New York: Guilford Press.

Budman, S. H., Hoyt, M. F., & Friedman, S. (1992). First words on first sessions. In S. H. Budman, M. F. Hoyt, & S. Friedman (Eds.), *The first session in brief therapy* (pp. 3–6). New York: Guilford Press.

Bugental, J. F. (1987). *The art of the psychotherapist.* New York: Norton.

Bugental, J. F., & Bracke, P. E. (1992). The future of existential-humanistic psychotherapy. *Psychotherapy, 29,* 28–33.

Burton, A. (1967). *Modern humanistic psychotherapy.* San Francisco: Jossey-Bass.

Bush, C. (1969). Transference, countertransference and identification in supervision. *Contemporary Psychoanalysis, 5,* 158–162.

Butler, S. F., Strupp, H. H., & Binder, J. L. (1992). Time-limited dynamic psychotherapy. In S. H. Budman, M. F. Hoyt, & S. Friedman (Eds.), *The first session in brief therapy* (pp. 87–110). New York: Guilford Press.

Carkhuff, R. R., & Truax, C. B. (1965). Lay mental health counseling. *Journal of Consulting Psychology, 29,* 426–431.

Carmen, E., Rieker, P., & Mills, T. (1984). Victims of violence and psychiatric illness. *American Journal of Psychiatry, 141,* 378–383.

Carnegie, D. (1936). *How to win friends and influence people.* New York: Simon & Schuster.

Carroll, L. (1981). *Alice's adventures in wonderland and through the looking glass.* New York: Bantam Books. (Original works published 1865 and 1871, respectively)

Chessick, R. D. (1971). How the resident and the supervisor disappoint each other. *American Journal of Psychotherapy, 25,* 272–283.

Chickering, A. W. (1969). *Education and identity.* San Francisco: Jossey-Bass.

Chinsky, J. M., & Rappaport, J. (1970). Brief critique of meaning and stability of "accurate empathy" ratings. *Psychological Bulletin, 73,* 379–382.

Claiborn, C. D. (1982). Interpretation and change in counseling. *Journal of Counseling Psychology, 29,* 439–453.

Cohen, L. (1980). The new supervisee views supervision. In A. K. Hess (Ed.), *Psychotherapy supervision* (pp. 78–84). New York: Wiley.

Cohen, R. J., & DeBetz, B. (1977). Responsive supervision of the psychiatric resident. *American Journal of Psychoanalysis, 37,* 51–64.

Colby, K. M. (1964). Psychotherapeutic processes. In P. R. Farnsworth, O. McNemar, & Q. McNemar (Eds.), *Annual review of psychology* (pp. 347–370). Palo Alto: Annual Review.

Console, W. A., Simons, R. C., & Rubinstein, M. (1993). *The first encounter: The beginning in psychotherapy.* New York: Aronson.

Corey, G. (1991). *Case approach to counseling and psychotherapy* (3rd ed.). Pacific Grove, CA: Brooks/Cole.

Corey, G., Corey, M. S., & Callanan, P. (1988). *Issues and ethics in the helping professions* (3rd ed.). Pacific Grove, CA: Brooks/Cole.

Corey, M. S., & Corey, G. (1989). *Becoming a helper.* Pacific Grove, CA: Brooks/Cole.

Corsini, R. J. (Ed.). (1981). *Handbook of innovative psychotherapies.* New York: Wiley.

Cross, D. G., & Brown, D. (1983). Counselor supervision as a function of trainee experience: Analysis of specific behaviors. *Counselor Education and Supervision, 22,* 333–341.

Cross, D. G., & Sheehan, P. W. (1982). Secondary therapist variables operating in short-term insight-oriented and behavior therapy. *British Journal of Medical Psychology, 55,* 275–284.

Daldrup, R. J., Beutler, L. E., Engle, D., & Greenberg, L. S. (1988). *Focused expressive psychotherapy: Freeing the overcontrolled patient.* New York: Guilford Press.

D'Augelli, A. R., Danish, S. J., & Brock, G. W. (1976). Untrained paraprofessionals' verbal helping behavior: Description and implications for training. *American Journal of Community Psychology, 4,* 275–282.

Davanloo, H. (1992a). A method of short-term dynamic psychotherapy. In H. Davanloo (Ed.), *Short-term dynamic psychotherapy* (pp. 43–71). Northvale, NJ: Aronson.

Davanloo, H. (1992b). Trial therapy. In H. Davanloo (Ed.), *Short-term dynamic psychotherapy* (pp. 99–128). Northvale, NJ: Aronson.

DeCourcel, M. (1988). *Tolstoy: Man and work.* New York: Viking.

Delaney, D. J., & Moore, J. C. (1966). Students' expectations of the role of the practicum supervisor. *Counselor Education and Supervision, 6,* 11–17.

Demause, L. (1991). The universality of incest. *The Journal of Psychohistory, 19,* 123–164.

Deutsch, C. J. (1985). A survey of therapists' personal problems and treatment. *Professional Psychology: Research and Practice, 16,* 305–315.

Dimmer, S. A., Carroll, J. L., & Wyatt, G. K. (1990). Uses of humor in psychotherapy. *Psychological Reports, 66,* 795–801.

Dittes, S. J. (1957). Extinction during psychotherapy of GSR accompanying "embarrassing" statements. *Journal of Abnormal and Social Psychology, 54,* 187–191.

Dobson, K. S. (Ed.). (1988). *Handbook of cognitive-behavioural therapies.* London: Hutchinson.

Dollard, J., & Miller, N. E. (1950). *Personality and psychotherapy: An analysis in terms of learning, thinking, and culture.* New York: McGraw-Hill.

Dostoyevsky, F. (1968). *Crime and punishment* (S. Monas, Trans.). New York: Signet Classic. (Original work published 1866)

Dryden, W., & Ellis, A. (1988). Rational-emotive therapy. In K. S. Dobson (Ed.), *Handbook of cognitive-behavioural therapies* (pp. 214–272). London: Hutchinson.

Dryden, W., & Spurling, L. (Eds.). (1989). *On becoming a psychotherapist.* New York: Tavistock/Routledge.

Dunkelblau, E. (1987). "That'll be five cents, please!": Perceptions of psychotherapy in jokes and humor. In W. F. Fry & W. A. Salameh (Eds.), *Handbook of humor and psychotherapy: Advances in the clinical use of humor* (pp. 307–314). Sarasota, FL: Professional Resource Exchange.

Durlak, J. A. (1979). Comparative effectiveness of paraprofessional and professional helpers. *Psychological Bulletin, 86,* 80–92.

Egan, G. (1990). *The skilled helper: A systematic approach to effective helping* (4th ed.). Pacific Grove, CA: Brooks/Cole.

Eisenberg, G. M. (1981). Midtherapy training: Extending the present system of pretherapy training (Doctoral dissertation, University of South Florida, 1980). *Dissertation Abstracts International, 41,* 2754B.

Eisenstein, S. (1992). The contributions of Franz Alexander. In H. Davanloo (Ed.), *Short-term dynamic psychotherapy* (pp. 25–42). Northvale, NJ: Aronson.

Ekstein, R., & Wallerstein, R. (1972). *The teaching and learning of psychotherapy.* New York: Basic Books.

Elkin, I. E., Parloff, M. B., Hadley, S. W., & Autry, J. H. (1985). NIMH treatment of depression collaborative research program. *Archives of General Psychiatry, 42,* 305–316.

Elkin, I. E., Shea, T., Watkins, J. T., Imber, S. D., Sotsky, S. M., Collins, J. F., Glass, D. R., Pilkonis, P. A., Leber, W. R., Docherty, J. P., Feister, S. J., & Parloff, M. B. (1989). National Institute of Mental Health treatment of depression collaborative research program. *Archives of General Psychiatry, 46,* 971–982.

Elliott, R. (1985). Helpful and nonhelpful events in brief counseling interviews: An empirical taxonomy. *Journal of Counseling Psychology, 32*(3), 307–322.

Elliott, R., Barker, C. B., Caskey, N., & Pistrang, N. (1982). Differential helpfulness of counselor verbal response modes. *Journal of Counseling Psychology, 42*(4), 354–361.

Ellis, A. (1962). *Reason and emotion in psychotherapy.* Secaucus, NJ: Citadel.

Ellis, A. (1973). *Humanistic psychotherapy: The rational-emotive approach.* New York: Julian Press.

Ellis, A. (1987). The use of rational humorous songs in psychotherapy. In W. F. Fry & W. A. Salameh (Eds.), *Handbook of humor and psychotherapy: Advances in the clinical use of humor* (pp. 265–286). Sarasota, FL: Professional Resource Exchange.

Ellis, A. (1988). *How to stubbornly refuse to make yourself miserable about anything—Yes, anthing!* Secaucus, NJ: Lyle Stuart.

Ellis, A. (1990). *Reason and emotion in psychotherapy.* Secaucus, NJ: Carol Publishing Group.

Ellis, A. (1991a). My life in clinical psychology. In C. E. Walker (Ed.), *The history of clinical psychology in autobiography: Vol. 1* (pp. 1–37). Pacific Grove, CA: Brooks/Cole.

Ellis, A. (1991b). The revised ABCs of rational-emotive therapy. *Journal of Rational-Emotive and Cognitive-Behavior Therapy, 9,* 139–192.

Ellis, A. (1993). Reflections on rational-emotive therapy. *Journal of Consulting and Clinical Psychology, 61,* 199–201.

Ellis, A., & Harper, R. A. (1961). *A guide to rational living* (6th ed.). Hollywood, CA: Wilshire.

Epstein, L., & Feiner, A. H. (1983). *Countertransference: The therapist contribution to the therapeutic situation.* Northvale, NJ: Aronson.

Erikson, E. H. (1968). *Identity: Youth and crisis.* New York: Norton.

Eysenck, H. J. (1952). The effects of psychotherapy: An evaluation. *Journal of Consulting Psychology, 16,* 319–324.

Eysenck, H. J. (1983). The effectiveness of psychotherapy: The specter at the feast. *The Behavioral and Brain Sciences, 6,* 290.

Fairbairn, W. R. D. (1952). *Psychoanalytic studies of the personality.* London: Tavistock/Routledge.

Farrelly, F., & Lynch, M. (1987). Humor in provocative therapy. In W. F. Fry & W. A. Salameh (Eds.), *Handbook of humor and psychotherapy: Advances in the clinical use of humor* (pp. 81–106). Sarasota, FL: Professional Resource Exchange.

Feldman-Summers, S., & Pope, K. S. (1994). The experience of "forgetting" childhood abuse: A national survey of psychologists. *Journal of Consulting and Clinical Psychology, 62,* 636–639.

Fenichel, O. (1941). *Problems of psychoanalytic technique.* New York: The Psychoanalytic Quarterly.

Ferenczi, S. (1952). *Further contributions to the theory and technique of psychoanalysis.* New York: Basic Books.

Fiedler, F. E. (1950a). A comparison of therapeutic relationships in psychoanalytic, nondirective, and Adlerian therapy. *Journal of Consulting Psychology, 14,* 436–445.

Fiedler, F. E. (1950b). The concept of an ideal therapeutic relationship. *Journal of Consulting Psychology, 14,* 239–245.

Fiedler, F. E. (1951). Factor analysis of psychoanalytic, nondirective, and Adlerian therapeutic relationships. *Journal of Consulting Psychology, 15,* 32–38.

Fisher, B. L. (1989). Differences between supervision of beginning and advanced therapists: Hogan's hypothesis emperically revisited. *The Clinical Supervisor, 7,* 57–74.

Fleming, J. (1953). The role of supervision in psychiatric training. *Bulletin of the Menninger Clinic, 17,* 157–169.

Foreman, S. A., & Marmar, C. R. (1985). Therapist actions that address initially poor therapeutic alliances in psychotherapy. *American Journal of Psychiatry, 142*(8), 922–926.

Foulds, G. (1958). Clinical research in psychiatry. *Journal of Mental Science, 104,* 259–265.

Frank, A., Eisenthal, S., & Lazare, A. (1978). Are there social class differences in patients' treatment conceptions? *Archives of General Psychiatry, 35,* 61–69.

Frank, G. H., & Sweetland, A. A. (1962). A study of the process of psychotherapy: The verbal interaction. *Journal of Consulting Psychology, 26*(2), 135–138.

Frank, J. D. (1959). The dynamics of the psychotherapeutic relationship. *Psychiatry, 22,* 17–39.

Frank, J. D. (1968). The role of hope in psychotherapy. *International Journal of Psychiatry, 5,* 383–395.

Frank, J. D. (1973). *Persuasion and healing.* Baltimore: Johns Hopkins University Press.

Frank, J. D. (1980). Aristotle as psychotherapist. In M. J. Mahoney (Ed.), *Psychotherapy process: Current issues and future directions* (pp. 335–337). New York: Plenum Press.

Frank, J. D., Gliedman, L. H., Imber, S. D., Nash, E. H., Jr., & Stone, A. R. (1957). Why patients leave psychotherapy. *Archives of Neurology and Psychiatry, 77,* 283–299.

Frankl, V. E. (1963). *Man's search for meaning: An introduction to logotherapy* (Part 1) (I. Lasch, Trans.) New York: Pocket Books. (Original work published 1959)

Frankl, V. E. (1965). *The doctor and the soul* (2nd ed.) (R. Winston & C. Winston, Trans.). New York: Random House. (Original work published 1955)

Frankl, V. E. (1967a). Logotherapy and the challenge of suffering. In V. E. Frankl, *Psychotherapy and existentialism: Selected papers on logotherapy* (pp. 87–94). New York: Washington Square Press. (Reprinted in abridged form from *Review of Existential Psychology and Psychiatry,* 1961, *1,* 3–7.)

Frankl, V. E. (1967b). Paradoxical intention: A logotherapeutic technique. In V. E. Frankl, *Psychotherapy and existentialism: Selected papers on logotherapy* (pp. 143–163). New York: Washington Square Press. (Reprinted from *American Journal of Psychotherapy,* 1960, *14,* 520–535.)

Frankl, V. E. (1978). *The unheard cry for meaning: Psychotherapy and humanism.* New York: Simon & Schuster.

Frantz, T. G. (1992). Learning from anxiety: A transtheoretical dimension of supervision and its administration. *Clinical Supervisor, 10*(2), 29–55.

French, T., & Wheeler, D. (1963). The role of hope in psychotherapy. *International Journal of Psychiatry, 5,* 383–395.

Freud, S. (1953). Psychical (or mental) treatment. In J. Strachey (Ed. and Trans.), *The standard edition of the complete psychological works of Sigmund Freud* (Vol. 7, pp. 283–302). London: Hogarth Press. (Original work published 1905).

Freud, S. (1955a). Group psychology and the analysis of the ego. In J. Strachey (Ed. and Trans.), *The standard edition of the complete psychological works of Sigmund Freud* (Vol. 18, pp. 69–143). London: Hogarth Press. (Original work published 1921)

Freud, S. (1955b). Lines of advance in psycho-analytic therapy. In J. Strachey (Ed. and Trans.), *The standard edition of the complete psychological works of Sigmund Freud* (Vol. 17, pp. 159–168). London: Hogarth Press. (Original work published 1919)

Freud, S. (1958a). On beginning the treatment (further recommendations on the technique of psychoanalysis). In J. Strachey (Ed. and Trans.), *The standard edition of the complete psychological work of Sigmund Freud* (Vol. 12, pp. 121–144). London: Hogarth Press. (Original work published 1913)

Freud, S. (1958b). The psychotherapy of hysteria. In J. Strachey (Ed. and Trans.), *The standard edition of the complete psychological works of Sigmund Freud* (Vol. 2, pp. 253–305). London: Hogarth Press. (Original work published 1895)

Freud, S. (1961, 1963). Introductory lectures on psychoanalysis. In J. Strachey (Ed. and Trans.), *The standard edition of the complete psychological works of Sigmund Freud* (Vols. 15 & 16). London: Hogarth Press. (Original work published 1923)

Freud, S. (1964). New introductory lectures. In J. Strachey (Ed. and Trans.), *The standard edition of the complete psychological works of Sigmund Freud* (Vol. 22, pp. 3–182). London: Hogarth Press. (Original work published 1933)

Freud, S. (1990a). Recommendations to physicians practising psycho-analysis. In R. Langs (Ed.), *Classics in psychoanalytic technique* (rev. ed., pp. 391–396). Northvale, NJ: Aronson. (Reprinted from *The standard edition of the complete psychological works of Sigmund Freud*, 1958, Vol. 12, pp. 111–120. London: Hogarth Press.) (Original work published 1912)

Freud, S. (1990b). The dynamics of transference. In R. Langs (Ed.), *Classics in psychoanalytic technique* (rev. ed., pp. 3–8). Northvale, NJ: Aronson. (Reprinted from *The standard edition of the complete psychological works of Sigmund Freud*, 1958, Vol. 12, pp. 97–108. London: Hogarth Press.) (Original work published 1912)

Fried, E. (1982). On "working through" as a form of self-innovation. In S. Slipp (Ed.), *Curative factors in dynamic psychotherapy* (pp. 243–258). New York: McGraw-Hill.

Friedlander, M. L. (1981). The effects of delayed role induction on counseling process and outcome (Doctoral dissertation, Ohio State University, 1980). *Dissertation Abstracts International, 41*, 3887B–3888B.

Friedlander, S. R., Dye, N. W., Costello, R. M., & Kobos, J. C. (1984). A developmental model for teaching and learning in psychotherapy supervision. *Psychotherapy, 21*, 189–196.

Friedman, H. J. (1963). Patient-expectancy and symptom reduction. *Archives of General Psychiatry, 8*, 61–67.

Fromm, E. (1955). *The sane society.* New York: Holt, Rinehart & Winston.

Fuerst, R. A. (1938). Problems of short time psychotherapy. *American Journal of Orthopsychiatry, 8*, 260–264.

Gallagher-Thompson, D., Hanley-Peterson, P., Thompson, L. W. (1990). Maintenance of gains versus relapse following brief psychotherapy for depression. *Journal of Consulting and Clinical Psychology, 58*, 371–374.

Gaoni, B., & Neumann, M. (1974). Supervision from the point of view of the supervisee. *American Journal of Psychotherapy, 24*, 108–114.

Garfield, S. L. (1957). *Introductory clinical psychology.* New York: Macmillan.

Garfield, S. L. (1974). *Clinical psychology. The study of personality and behavior.* Chicago: Aldine.

Garfield, S. L. (1982). Eclecticism and integration in psychotherapy. *Behavior therapy, 13*, 610–623.

Garfield, S. L. (1983). Does psychotherapy work? Yes, no, maybe. *The Behavioral and Brain Sciences, 6*, 292–293.

Garfield, S. L. (1986a). An eclectic psychotherapy. In J. C. Norcross (Ed.), *Handbook of eclectic psychotherapy* (pp. 132–162). New York: Brunner/Mazel.

Garfield, S. L. (1986b). Research on client variables in psychotherapy. In S. L. Garfield & A. E. Bergin (Eds.), *Handbook of psychotherapy and behavior change* (3rd ed., pp. 257–310). New York: Wiley.

Garfield, S. L. (1990). Issues and methods in psychotherapy process research. *Journal of Consulting and Clinical Psychology, 58,* 273–280.

Garfield, S. L. (1991). Psychotherapy models and outcome research. *American Psychologist, 46,* 1350–1351.

Garfield, S. L. (1992). Comments on "Retrospect: Psychology as a profession" by J. McKeen Cattell (1937). *Journal of Consulting and Clinical Psychology, 60,* 9–15.

Garfield, S. L., & Bergin, A. E. (1971). Therapeutic conditions and outcome. *Journal of Abnormal Psychology, 77,* 108–114.

Garfield, S. L., & Bergin, A. E. (Eds.). (1986a). *Handbook of psychotherapy and behavior change* (3rd ed.). New York: Wiley.

Garfield, S. L., & Bergin, A. E. (1986b). Introduction and historical overview. In S. L. Garfield & A. E. Bergin (Eds.), *Handbook of psychotherapy and behavior change* (3rd ed., pp. 3–22). New York: Wiley.

Garfield, S. L., & Kurtz, R. M. (1974). A survey of clinical psychologists: Characteristics, activities and orientation. *The Clinical Psychologist, 28,* 7–10.

Gaston, L. (1990). The concept of the alliance and its role in psychotherapy: Theoretical and empirical considerations. *Psychotherapy, 27,* 143–153.

Gay, P. (1988). *Freud: A life for our time.* New York: Norton.

Gillan, P., & Rachman, S. (1974). An experimental investigation of desensitization and phobic patients. *British Journal of Psychology, 124,* 392–401.

Glass, G. V., Smith, M. L., & Miller, T. I. (1983). Placebo effects in psychotherapy outcome research. *The Behavioral and Brain Sciences, 6,* 293–294.

Glover, E. (1931). The therapeutic effect of inexact interpretation: A contribution to the theory of suggestion. *The Interpersonal Journal of Psycho-Analysis, 12*(4), 397–411.

Goldberg, C. (1992). *The seasoned psychotherapist: Triumph over adversity.* New York: Norton.

Goldberg, J. G. (1993). *The dark side of love: The positive role of our negative feelings—Anger, jealousy, and hate.* New York: Putnam.

Goldfried, M. R. (1980). Toward the delineation of therapeutic change principles. *American Psychologist, 35,* 991–999.

Goldman-Eisler, F. (1956). A contribution to the objective measurement of the cathartic process. *Journal of Mental Science, 102,* 78–95.

Goldsamt, L. A., Goldfried, M. R., Hayes, A. M., & Kerr, S. (1992). Beck, Meichenbaum, and Strupp: A comparison of three therapies on the dimension of therapist feedback. *Psychotherapy, 29*(2), 167–176.

Goldstein, A. P. (1960). Patients' expectancies and nonspecific therapy as a basis for (un)spontaneous remission. *Journal of Clinical Psychology, 16,* 399–403.

Goldstein, A. P. (1962). *Therapist-patient expectancies in psychotherapy.* New York: Macmillan.

Goldstein, A. P., & Shipman, W. G. (1961). Patient expectancies, symptom reduction and aspects of initial psychotherapeutic interview. *Journal of Clinical Psychology, 17,* 129–133.

Gomes-Schwartz, B. (1978). Effective ingredients in psychotherapy: Prediction of outcome from process variables. *Journal of Consulting and Clinical Psychology, 46,* 1023–1035.

Goodyear, R. K., & Bradley, F. O. (1983). Theories of counselor supervision: Points of convergence and divergence. *The Counseling Psychologist, 11*, 59–67.

Gordon, J. E. (1957). Leading and following psychotherapeutic techniques with hypnotically induced repression and hostility. *Journal of Abnormal and Social Psychology, 54*, 405–410.

Gorkin, M. (1987). *The uses of countertransference.* Northvale, NJ: Aronson.

Gormally, J., & Hill, C. E. (1974). Guidelines for research on Carkhuff's model. *Journal of Counseling Psychology, 21*, 539–547.

Gould, W. B. (1993). *Victor E. Frankl: Life with meaning.* Pacific Grove, CA: Brooks/Cole.

Grater, H. A. (1985). Stages in psychotherapy supervision: From therapy skills to skilled therapist. *Professional Psychology's Research and Practice, 16*, 605–610.

Greben, S. E. (1979). The influence of the supervision of psychotherapy upon being therapeutic: I. Introduction and background to the supervisory relationship: II. Modes of influence of the supervisory relationship. *Canadian Journal of Psychiatry, 24*, 499–513.

Greenacre, P. (1990). The role of transference. In R. Langs (Ed.), *Classics in psychoanalytic technique* (rev. ed., pp. 17–23). Northvale, NJ: Aronson. (Reprinted from *Journal of the American Psychoanalytic Association,* 1954, *2*, 671–684.)

Greenberg, L. S. (1980). Supervision from the perspective of the supervisee. In A. K. Hess (Ed.), *Psychotherapy supervision* (pp. 85–91). New York: Wiley.

Greenberg, L. S., & Safran, J. D. (1987). *Emotion in psychotherapy: Affect, cognition, and the process of change.* New York: Guilford Press.

Greenberg, L. S., & Safran, J. D. (1989). Emotion in psychotherapy. *American Psychologist, 44*, 19–29.

Greenberg, L. S., & Webster, M. C. (1982). Resolving decisional conflict by Gestalt two-chair dialogue: Relating process to outcome. *Journal of Counseling Psychology, 29*, 468–477.

Greenson, R. R. (1990a). Beyond transference and interpretation. In R. Langs (Ed.), *Classics in psychoanalytic technique* (rev. ed., pp. 97–101). Northvale, NJ: Aronson. (Reprinted from *International Journal of Psycho-Analysis,* 1972, *53*, 213–217.)

Greenson, R. R. (1990b). The "real" relationship between the patient and the psychoanalyst. In R. Langs (Ed.), *Classic in psychoanalytic technique* (rev. ed., pp. 87–96). Northvale, NJ: Aronson. (Reprinted from M. Kanzer (Ed.). *The unconscious today,* 1971, pp. 213–232. New York: International Universities Press.)

Greenson, R. R. (1990c). The working alliance and the transference neurosis. In R. Langs (Ed.), *Classics in psychoanalytic technique* (rev. ed., pp. 279–290). Northvale, NJ: Aronson. (Reprinted from *Psychoanalytic Quarterly,* 1965, *34*, 155–181.)

Greenwald, H. (1987). The humor decision. In W. F. Fry & W. A. Salameh (Eds.), *Handbook of humor and psychotherapy: Advances in the clinical use of humor* (pp. 41–54). Sarasota, FL: Professional Resource Exchange.

Gross, M. L. (1978). *The psychological society: A critical analysis of psychiatry, psychotherapy, psychoanalysis, and the psychological revolution.* New York: Random House.

Grossman, D. (1952). An experimental investigation of a psychotherapeutic technique. *Journal of Consulting Psychology, 16*, 325–331.

Guest, P. D., & Beutler, L. E. (1988). Impact of psychotherapy supervision on therapist orientation and values. *Journal of Consulting and Clinical Psychology, 56*(5), 653–658.

Guggenbuhl-Craig, A. (1979). *Power in the helping professions.* New York: Spring Publications.

Guidano, V. F., & Liotti, G. (1983). *Cognitive processes and emotional disorders: A structural approach to psychotherapy.* New York: Guilford Press.

Gurman, A. S. (1977). The patient's perception of the therapeutic relationship. In A. S. Gurman & A. M. Razin (Eds.), *Effective psychotherapy: A handbook of research* (pp. 503–543). New York: Pergamon Press.

Gurman, A. S., & Razin, A. M. (Eds.). (1977). *Effective psychotherapy: A handbook of research.* New York: Pergamon Press.

Gutsch, K. U. (1990). Cognitive psychotherapy. In J. K. Zeig & W. M. Munion (Eds.), *What is psychotherapy? Contemporary perspectives* (pp. 151–154). San Francisco: Jossey-Bass.

Hafner, J. L., & Fakouri, M. E. (1984). Early recollections and vocational choice. *Individual Psychology: Journal of Adlerian Theory, Research, and Practice, 40,* 54–60.

Haggard, E. A., & Murray, H. A. (1942). The relative effectiveness of three therapy procedures on the reduction of experimentally induced anxiety. *Psychological Bulletin, 39,* 439–441.

Hammer, E. (1990). *Reaching the affect: Style in psychodynamic therapies.* Northvale, NJ: Aronson.

Harper, R. A. (1959). *Psychoanalysis and psychotherapy: 36 systems.* Englewood Cliffs, NJ: Prentice-Hall.

Hart, J. T. (1986). Functional eclectic therapy. In J. C. Norcross (Ed.), *Handbook of eclectic psychotherapy* (pp. 201–225). New York: Brunner/Mazel.

Hartley, D. E., & Strupp, H. H. (1983). The therapeutic alliance: Its relationship to outcome in brief psychotherapy. In J. Masling (Ed.), *Empirical studies in analytic theories* (pp. 1–37), Hillsdale, NJ: Erlbaum.

Hartmann, H. (1958). *Ego psychology and the problem of adaptation.* New York: International Universities Press.

Hartocollis, P. (Ed.). (1977). *Borderline personality disorders: The concept, the syndrome, the patient.* Madison, CT: International Universities Press.

Hattie, J. A., Sharpley, C. F., & Rogers, H. J. (1984). Comparative effectiveness of professional and paraprofessional helpers. *Psychological Bulletin, 95,* 534–541.

Heine, R. W. (1962). *The student physician as psychotherapist.* Chicago: University of Chicago Press.

Heine, R. W., & Trosman, H. (1960). Initial expectations of the doctor-patient interaction as a factor in continuance in psychotherapy. *Psychiatry, 23,* 275–278.

Henry, W. E. (1966). Some observations on the lives of healers. *Human Development, 9,* 47–56.

Henry, W. E., Sims, J. H., & Spray, S. L. (1971). *The fifth profession: Becoming a psychotherapist.* San Francisco: Jossey-Bass.

Henry, W. E., Sims, J. H., & Spray, S. L. (1973). *Public and private lives of psychotherapists.* San Francisco: Jossey-Bass.

Heppner, P. P. (1989). Chance and choices in becoming a therapist. In W. Dryden & L. Spurling (Eds.), *On becoming a psychotherapist* (pp. 69–86). New York: Tavistock/Routledge.

Hepworth, D. H., & Larsen, J. (1993). *Direct social work practice: Theory and skills* (4th ed.). Pacific Grove, CA: Brooks/Cole.

Herink, R. (Ed.). (1980). *The psychotherapy handbook.* New York: Meridian.

Hess, A. K. (1986). Growth in supervision: Stages of supervisee and supervisor development. *The Clinical Supervisor, 4,* 51–67.

Hill, C. E., Carter, J. A., & O'Farrell, M. K. (1983). A case study of the process and outcome of the time-limited counseling. *Journal of Counseling Psychology, 30*(1), 3–18.

Hill, C. E., & Corbett, M. M. (1993). A perspective on the history of process and outcome research in counseling psychology. *Journal of Counseling Psychology, 40*(1), 3–24.

Hill, C. E., Helms, J. E., Spiegel, S. B., & Tichenor, V. (1988). Development of a system for categorizing client reactions to therapist interventions. *Journal of Counseling Psychology, 35*(1), 27–36.

Hobson, R. F. (1985). *Forms of feeling: The heart of psychotherapy.* New York: Tavistock.

Hoehn-Saric, R., Frank, J. D., & Gurland, B. S. (1968). Focused attitude change in neurotic patients. *Journal of Nervous and Mental Disease, 147,* 124–133.

Hoehn-Saric, R., Frank, J. D., Imber, S. D., Nash, E. H., Stone, A. R., & Battle, C. C. (1964). Systematic preparation of patients for psychotherapy: I. Effects on therapy behavior and outcome. *Journal of Psychiatric Research, 2,* 267–281.

Hoehn-Saric, R., Liberman, B., Imber, S. D., Nash, E. H., Stone, A. R., Pande, S. K., & Frank, J. D. (1972). Arousal and attitude change in neurotic patients. *Archives of General Psychiatry, 26,* 52–56.

Hogan, R. A. (1964). Issues and approaches in supervision. *Psychotherapy: Theory, Research and Practice, 1,* 139–141.

Hogan, R. A. (1968). The implosive technique. *Behavior Research and Therapy, 6,* 423–432.

Hogan, R. A., & Kirchner, J. H. (1967). A preliminary report of the extinction of learned fears via short term implosive therapy. *Journal of Abnormal Psychology, 72,* 106–111.

Horner, A. (1989). *The wish for power and the fear of having it.* Northvale, NJ: Aronson.

Horney, K. (1942). Self-analysis. In *The collected works of Karen Horney* (Vol. 2, pp. 5–309). New York: Norton.

Horowitz, M. J., Marmar, C., Weiss, D., DeWitt, K. N., & Rosenbaum, R. (1984). Brief psychotherapy of bereavement reactions: The relationship of process to outcome. *Archives of General Psychiatry, 41,* 438–448.

Horvath, A. O., & Greenberg, L. S. (1989). Development and validation of the Working Alliance Inventory. *Journal of Counseling Psychology, 36*(2), 223–233.

Horvath, A. O., & Symonds, B. D. (1991). Relation between working alliance and outcome in psychotherapy: A meta-analysis. *Journal of Counseling Psychology, 38*(2), 139–149.

Howard, K. I., Kopta, S. M., Krause, M. S., & Orlinsky, D. E. (1986). The dose-effect relationship in psychotherapy. *American Psychologist, 41,* 159–164.

Hoyt, M. F., Budman, S. H., & Friedman, S. (1992). Introduction to individual brief therapy approaches. In S. H. Budman, M. F. Hoyt, & S. Friedman (Eds.), *The first session in brief therapy* (pp. 9–13). New York: Guilford Press.

Hugo, V. (1961). *Les Miserables* (C. E. Wilbour, Trans.). New York: Fawcett Premier. (Original work published 1862)

Hurvitz, N. (1973). Psychotherapy as a means of social control. *Journal of Consulting and Clinical Psychology, 40*, 232–239.

Imber, S. D., Pilkonis, P. A., Sotsky, S. M., Elkin, I., Watkins, J. T., Collins, F. F., Shea, M. T., Leber, W. R., & Glass, D. R. (1990). Mode specific effects among three treatments for depression. *Journal of Consulting and Clinical Psychology, 58*, 352–359.

Jackel, M. M. (1982). Supervision in dynamic psychotherapy. In M. Blumenfield (Ed.), *Applied supervision in psychotherapy* (pp. 5–43). New York: Grune & Stratton.

Jacobs, D., Charles, E., Jacobs, T., Weinstein, H., & Mann, D. (1972). Preparation for treatment of the disadvantaged patient: Effects on disposition and outcome. *American Journal of Orthopsychiatry, 42*(4), 666–674.

Jarmon, D. D. (1972). Differential effectiveness of rational-emotive therapy, bibliotherapy, and attention-placebo in the treatment of speech anxiety. (Doctoral dissertation, Southern Illinois University, 1972). *Dissertation Abstracts International, 33B*, 4510B.

Jones, E. E., & Pulos, S. M. (1993). Comparing the process in psychodynamic and cognitive-behavioral therapies. *Journal of Consulting and Clinical Psychology, 61*, 306–316.

Kahr, B. (1991). The sexual molestation of children: Historical perspectives. *The Journal of Psychohistory, 19*, 191–214.

Kaiser, H. (1955). The problem of responsibility in psychotherapy. *Psychiatry, 18*, 205–211.

Kaiser, H. (1965). In L. Fierman (Ed.), *Effective psychotherapy: The contribution of Helmuth Kaiser* (pp. 1–202). New York: Free Press.

Kanfer, F. H., Phillips, J. S., Matarazzo, J. D., & Saslow, G. (1960). Experimental modification of interviewer content in standardized interviews. *Journal of Consulting Psychology, 24*, 528–536.

Kanfer, F. H., & Schefft, B. K. (1987). Self-management therapy in clinical practice. In N. S. Jacobson (Ed.), *Psychotherapists in clinical practice: Cognitive and behavioral perspectives* (pp. 10–77). New York: Guilford Press.

Karle, W., Corriere, R., & Hart, J. (1973). Psychophysiological changes in abreaction therapy. Study I: Primal therapy. *Psychotherapy: Theory, Research and Practice, 10*, 117–123.

Karle, W., Corriere, R., Hart, J., Gold, S., Maple, C., & Hopper, M. (1976). The maintenance of psychophysiological changes in feeling therapy. *Psychological Reports, 39*, 1143–1147.

Kazdin, A. E. (1986). Comparative outcome studies of psychotherapy: Methodological issues and strategies. *Journal of Consulting and Clinical Psychology, 54*, 95–105.

Kazdin, A. E., & Bass, D. (1989). Power to detect differences between alternative treatments in comparative psychotherapy outcome research. *Journal of Consulting and Clinical Psychology, 57*, 138–146.

Kazdin, A. E., & Wilcoxin, L. A. (1976). Systematic desensitization and nonspecific treatment effects: A methodological evaluation. *Psychological Bulletin, 83*, 729–758.

Keet, C. D. (1948). Two verbal techniques in a miniature counseling situation. *Psychological Monographs, 62* (Serial No. 294).

Kelly, E. L. (1961). Clinical psychology—1960: Report of survey findings. *American Psychological Association, Division of Clinical Psychology Newsletter, 14*, 1–11.

Kelly, E. L., Goldberg, L. R., Fiske, D. W., & Kikowski, J. M. (1978). Twenty-five years later: A follow-up study of the graduate students in clinical psychology assessed in the V.A. selection research project. *American Psychologist, 33,* 746–755.

Kernberg, O. F. (1980). *Internal world and external reality.* New York: Aronson.

Kernberg, O. F. (1982). The theory of psychoanalytic psychotherapy. In S. Slipp (Ed.), *Curative factors in dynamic psychotherapy* (pp. 21–43). New York: McGraw-Hill.

Kernberg, O. F., Selzer, M. A., Koenigsberg, H. W., Carr, A. C., & Appelbaum, A. H. (1989). *Psychodynamic psychotherapy of borderline patients.* New York: Basic Books.

Killinger, B. (1987). Humor in psychotherapy: A shift to a new perspective. In W. F. Fry & W. A. Salameh (Eds.), *Handbook of humor and psychotherapy: Advances in the clinical use of humor* (pp. 21–40). Sarasota, FL: Professional Resource Exchange.

Kivlighan, D. M., Angelone, E. O., & Swafford, K. G. (1991). Live supervision in individual psychotherapy: Effects on therapist's intention use and client's evaluation of session effect and working alliance. *Professional Psychology: Research and Practice, 22*(6), 489–495.

Klein, M. (1948). *Contributions to psychoanalysis (1921–1945).* London: Hogarth Press.

Klein, M. H., Mathieu-Coughlan, P., & Kiesler, D. (1986). The Experiencing Scales. In L. S. Greenberg & W. Pinsof (Eds.), *The psychotherapeutic process: A research handbook.* New York: Guilford Press.

Klein, M. H., Mathieu, P. L., Gendlin, E. T., & Kiesler, D. J. (1969). *The Experiencing Scale: A research and training manual* (Vol. 1). Madison: University of Wisconsin Extension Bureau of Audiovisual Instruction.

Klerman, G. L. (1986). Drugs and psychotherapy. In S. L. Garfield & A. E. Bergin (Eds.), *Handbook of psychotherapy and behavior change* (pp. 777–818). New York: Wiley.

Klerman, G. L., Weissman, M. M., Rounsaville, B. J., & Chevron, E. S. (1984). *Interpersonal psychotherapy of depression.* New York: Basic Books.

Kohlenberg, R. J., & Tsai, M. (1987). Functional analytic psychotherapy. In N. S. Jacobson (Ed.), *Psychotherapists in clinical practice: Cognitive and behavioral perspectives* (pp. 388–443). New York: Guilford Press.

Kohut, H. (1971). *The analysis of the self.* New York: International Universities Press.

Kohut, H. (1977). *The restoration of the self.* New York: International Universities Press.

Kohut, H. (1984). *How does analysis cure?* Chicago: University of Chicago Press.

Kohut, H. (1990). The role of empathy in psychoanalytic cure. In R. Langs (Ed.), *Classics in psychoanalytic technique* (rev. ed., pp. 463–473). Northvale, NJ: Aronson. (Reprinted from A. Goldberg & P. Stepansky (Eds.), *How does analysis cure? Heinz Kohut,* 1984, Chicago: University of Chicago Press.)

Kopp, S. B. (1972). *If you meet the Buddha on the road, kill him! The pilgrimage of psychotherapy patients.* New York: Bantam Books.

Kottler, J. A. (1993). *On being a therapist* (rev. ed.). San Francisco: Jossey-Bass.

Kottler, J. A., & Brown, R. W. (1992). *Introduction to therapeutic counseling* (2nd ed.). Pacific Grove, CA: Brooks/Cole.

Kovacs, M., Rush, A. J., Beck, A. T., & Hollon, S. D. (1981). Depressed outpatients treated with cognitive therapy or pharmacotherapy. *Archives of General Psychiatry, 38,* 33–39.

Kroll, J. (1988). *The challenge of the borderline patient: Competency in diagnosis and treatment.* New York: Norton.

Kubie, L. S. (1971). The destructive potential of humor in psychotherapy. *American Journal of Psychiatry, 127,* 861–866.

Kuhn, T. S. (1970). *The structure of scientific revolutions* (2nd ed.). Chicago: University of Chicago Press.

Laing, R. D. (1967). *The politics of experience.* New York: Ballantine.

Lambert, M. J. (1976). Spontaneous remission in adult neurotic disorders: A revision and summary. *Psychological Bulletin, 83,* 107–119.

Lambert, M. J. (1986). Implications of psychotherapy outcome research for eclectic psychotherapy. In J. C. Norcross (Ed.), *Handbook of eclectic psychotherapy* (pp. 436–462). New York: Brunner/Mazel.

Lambert, M. J., & DeJulio, S. S. (1978, March). *The relative importance of client, therapist and technique variables as predictors of psychotherapy outcomes: The place of "non-specific" factors.* Paper presented at the midwinter meeting of the Division of Psychotherapy, American Psychological Association, Scottsdale, AZ.

Lambert, M. J., DeJulio, S. S., & Stein, D. M. (1978). Therapist interpersonal skills: Process, outcome, methodological considerations and recommendations for future research. *Psychological Bulletin, 85,* 467–489.

Lambert, M J., Shapiro, D. A., & Bergin, A. E. (1986). The effectiveness of psychotherapy. In S. L. Garfield & A. E. Bergin (Eds.), *Handbook of psychotherapy and behavior change* (3rd ed., pp. 157–212). New York: Wiley.

Landis, C. (1938). Statistical evaluation of psychotherapeutic methods. In S. E. Hinsie (Ed.), *Concepts and problems of psychotherapy* (pp. 155–165). London: Heineman.

Landman, J. T., & Dawes, R. M. (1982). Psychotherapy outcome: Smith and Glass conclusions stand up under scrutiny. *American Psychologist, 37,* 504–516.

Langs, R. (1975). Therapeutic misalliances. *International Journal of Psychoanalytic Psychotherapy, 4,* 77–105.

Langs, R. (1981). *The technique of psychoanalytic psychotherapy* (Vol. 1). Northvale, NJ: Aronson.

Langs, R. (Ed.). (1990a). *Classics in psychoanalytic technique* (rev. ed.). Northvale, NJ: Aronson.

Langs, R. (1990b). *Psychotherapy: A basic text.* Northvale, NJ: Aronson.

Langs, R., & Searles, H. F. (1980). *Intrapsychic interpersonal dimensions of treatment.* New York: Aronson.

Lazarus, A. A. (1987). The multimodal approach with adult outpatients. In N. S. Jacobson (Ed.), *Psychotherapists in clinical practice: Cognitive and behavioral perspectives* (pp. 286–326). New York: Guilford Press.

Lazarus, A. A. (1989). *The practice of multimodal therapy: Systematic, comprehensive, and effective psychotherapy* (2nd ed.). Baltimore: Johns Hopkins University Press.

Lazarus, R. S. (1980). Cognitive therapy as psychodynamics revisited. In M. J. Mahoney (Ed.), *Psychotherapy process: Current issues and future directions* (pp. 121–126). New York: Plenum Press.

Lesse, S. (1973). Expectations in psychotherapy. In J. H. Masserman (Ed.), *Handbook of psychiatric therapies* (pp. 604–610). Northvale, NJ: Aronson.

Levison, P. K., Zax, M., & Cowen, E. L. (1961). An experimental analogue of psychotherapy for anxiety reduction. *Psychological Reports, 8,* 171–178.

Lewis, H. B. (1981). *Freud and modern psychology: The emotional basis of mental illness* (Vol. 1). New York: Plenum Press.

Lick, J., & Bootzin, R. (1975). Expectancy factors in the treatment of fear: Methodological and theoretical issues. *Psychological Bulletin, 82,* 917–931.

Liebowitz, M. R., Stone, M. H., & Turkat, I. D. (1986). Treatment of personality disorders. In A. J. Frances & R. E. Hales (Eds.), *Psychiatry update: American Psychiatric Association annual review* (Vol. 5, pp. 356–393). Washington, DC: American Psychiatric Association.

Little, K. B. (1972). Bazelon challenge requires soul searching. *APA Monitor, 3,* 2.

Littrell, J. M., Lee-Borden, N., & Lorenz, J. A. (1979). A developmental framework for counseling supervision. *Counselor Education and Supervision, 19,* 129–136.

Loganbill, C., Hardy, E., & Delworth, U. (1983). Supervision: A conceptual model. *The Counseling Psychologist, 10*(1), 3–42.

Lower, R. (1972). Countertransference resistances in the supervisory situation. *American Journal of Psychiatry, 129,* 156–160.

Luborsky, L. (1984). *Principles of psychoanalytic psychotherapy: A manual for supportive-expressive treatment.* New York: Basic Books.

Luborsky, L., Barber, J. P., & Beutler, L. (1993). Introduction to special section: A briefing on curative factors in dynamic psychotherapy. *Journal of Consulting and Clinical Psychology, 61,* 539–541.

Luborsky, L., Chandler, M., Auerbach, A. H., Cohen, J., & Bachrach, H. M. (1971). Factors influencing the outcome of psychotherapy: A review of quantitative research. *Psychological Bulletin, 75*(3), 145–185.

Luborsky, L., McLellan, A. T., Woody, G. E., O'Brien, C. P., & Auerbach, A. (1985). Therapist success and its determinants. *Archives of General Psychiatry, 42,* 602–611.

Luborsky, L., Singer, B., & Luborsky, L. (1975). Comparative studies of psychotherapies. Is it true that everyone has won and all must have prizes? *Archives of General Psychiatry, 32,* 995–1008.

Luchins, A. S. (1957). Primacy-recency in impression formation. In C. I. Horland (Ed.), *The order of presentation in persuasion.* New Haven, CT: Yale University Press.

Mahoney, M. J. (1988). The cognitive sciences and psychotherapy: Patterns in a developing relationship. In K. S. Dobson (Ed.), *Handbook of cognitive-behavioral therapies* (pp. 357–386). London: Hutchinson.

Mahoney, M. J. (1993). Introduction to special section: Theoretical developments in the cognitive psychotherapies. *Journal of Consulting and Clinical Psychology, 61,* 187–193.

Mahoney, M. J., & Arnkoff, D. B. (1978). Cognitive and self-control therapies. In S. L. Garfield & A. E. Bergin (Eds.), *Handbook of psychotherapy and behavior change: An empirical analysis* (pp. 689–722). New York: Wiley.

Mahoney, M. J., & Eiseman, S. C. (1989). The object of the dance. In W. Dryden & L. Spurling (Eds.), *On becoming a psychotherapist* (pp. 17–32). New York: Tavistock/Routledge.

Mahrer, A. R., Stricker, G., Powell, D. H., & Rice, L. N. (1990). The diplomat. In N. Saltzman & J. C. Norcross (Eds.), *Therapy wars: Contention and convergence in differing clinical approaches* (pp. 35–67). San Francisco: Jossey-Bass.

Makover, R. B. (1992). Training of psychotherapists in hierarchical treatment planning. *Journal of Psychotherapy Practice and Research, 1*(4), 337–350.

Malan, D. H. (1979). *Individual psychotherapy and the science of psychodynamics.* Boston: Butterworths.

Malan, D., & Osimo, F. (1992). *Psychodynamics, training, and outcome in brief psychotherapy.* Boston: Butterworth-Heinemann.

Mallinckrodt, B., & Nelson, M. L. (1991). Counselor training level and the formation of the psychotherapeutic working alliance. *Journal of Counseling Psychology, 38*(2), 133–138.

Mann, J. (1973). *Time-limited psychotherapy.* Cambridge, MA: Harvard University Press.

Marcia, J. E. (1966). Development and validation of ego identity status. *Journal of Personality and Social Psychology, 3,* 551–558.

Marcia, J. E. (1967). Ego identity status: Relationship to change in self-esteem, "General Maladjustment," and authoritarianism. *Journal of Personality, 35,* 118–133.

Marmar, C. R. (1990). Psychotherapy process research: Progress, dilemmas, and future directions. *Journal of Consulting and Clinical Psychology, 58,* 265–267.

Marmar, C. R., Horowitz, M. J., Weiss, D. S., & Marziali, E. (1986). The development of the Therapeutic Alliance Rating System. In L. S. Greenberg & W. M. Pinsof (Eds.), *The psychotherapeutic process: A research handbook* (pp. 367–390). New York: Guilford Press.

Marmor, J. (1982). Change in psychoanalytic treatment. In S. Slipp (Ed.), *Curative factors in dynamic psychotherapy* (pp. 60–70). New York: McGraw-Hill.

Marmor, J., Ellis, A., Frances, A., & Kline, M. V. (1990). The spaceman. In N. Saltzman & J. C. Norcross (Eds.), *Therapy wars: Contention and convergence in differing clinical approaches* (pp. 15–34). San Francisco: Jossey-Bass.

Marshall, W. R., & Confer, W. N. (1980). Psychotherapy supervision: Supervisees' perspective. In A. K. Hess (Ed.), *Psychotherapy supervision* (pp. 92–100). New York: Wiley.

Martin, B., Lundy, R., & Lewin, M. (1960). Verbal and G.S.R. responses in experimental interviews as a function of three degrees of "therapist" communication. *Journal of Abnormal and Social Psychology, 60,* 234–240.

Maslow, M. H. (1968). *Toward a psychology of being* (2nd ed.). New York: Van Nostrand.

Masters, J. C., Burish, T. G., Hollon, S. D., & Rimm, D. C. (1987). *Behavior therapy: Techniques and empirical findings* (3rd ed.). San Diego: Harcourt Brace Jovanovich.

Maultsby, M. C. (1984). *Rational behavior therapy.* Englewood Cliffs, NJ: Prentice-Hall.

Maxwell, M. L., & Maxwell, G. (1980). Psychotherapy and science: Impurely rhetorical. In M. J. Mahoney (Ed.), *Psychotherapy process: Current issues and future directions* (pp. 395–399). New York: Plenum Press.

May, R. (1969). *Love and will.* New York: Dell.

May, R. (1975). *The courage to create.* New York: Bantam Books.

May, R. (1989). The problem of evil: An open letter to Carl Rogers. In H. Kirschenbaum & V. L. Henderson (Eds.), *Carl Rogers: Dialogues* (pp. 239–251). Boston:

Houghton Mifflin. (Reprinted from *Journal of Humanistic Psychology*, 1982, *22*(3), 10–21)

May, R. (1992). Foreword. In D. K. Freedheim (Ed.), *History of psychotherapy: A century of change* (pp. xx–xxvii). Washington, DC: American Psychological Association.

McCarthy, P. (1982). Differential effects of counselor self-referent responses and counselor status. *Journal of Counseling Psychology, 29*, 125–131.

Meichenbaum, D. (1977). *Cognitive behavior modification.* New York: Plenum Press.

Meichenbaum, D. (1993). Changing conceptions of cognitive behavior modification: Retrospect and prospect. *Journal of Consulting and Clinical Psychology, 61*, 202–204.

Meier, S. T., & Davis, S. R. (1993). *The elements of counseling* (2nd ed.). Pacific Grove, CA: Brooks/Cole.

Miles, H. W., Barrabee, E. I., & Finesinger, J. E. (1951). Evaluation of psychotherapy. *Psychosomatic Medicine, 13*, 83–105.

Miller, R. C., & Berman, J. S. (1983). The efficacy of cognitive behavior therapies: A quantitative review of the research evidence. *Psychological Bulletin, 94*, 39–53.

Minuchin, S. (1974). *Families and family therapy.* Cambridge, MA: Harvard University Press.

Mitchell, K. M., Bozart, J. D., & Krauft, C. C. (1977). Reappraisal of the therapeutic effectiveness of accurate empathy, non-possessive warmth, and genuineness. In A. S. Gurman & A. M. Razin (Eds.), *Effective psychotherapy* (pp. 482–502). New York: Pergamon Press.

Mohr, D. C., Beutler, L. E., Engle, D., Shoham-Saloman, V., Bergan, J., Kaszniak, A. W., & Yost, E. B. (1990). Identification of patients at risk for nonresponse and negative outcome in psychotherapy. *Journal of Counseling and Clinical Psychology, 58*(5), 622–628.

Moldawsky, S. (1980). Psychoanalytic psychotherapy supervision. In A. K. Hess (Ed.), *Psychotherapy supervision* (pp. 126–135). New York: Wiley.

Moore, A. C. (1982). Well-being and the woman psychiatrist. *Journal of Psychiatric Treatment and Evaluation, 4*, 437–439.

Morgan, R., Luborsky, L., Crits-Christoph, P., Curtis, H., & Solomon, J. (1982). Predicting the outcomes of psychotherapy by the Penn Helping Alliance Rating Method. *Archives of General Psychiatry, 39*, 397–402.

Morgan, W. G. (1973). Nonecessary conditions or useful procedures in desensitization: A reply to Wilkins. *Psychological Bulletin, 79*, 373–375.

Morris, R. J., & Suckerman, K. R. (1974a). Therapist warmth as a factor in automated systematic desensitization. *Journal of Consulting and Clinical Psychology, 42*, 244–250.

Morris, R. J., & Suckerman, K. R. (1974b). The importance of therapeutic relationship in systematic desensitization. *Journal of Consulting and Clinical Psychology, 42*, 148.

Morris, R. J., & Suckerman, K. R. (1975). Morris and Suckerman reply. *Journal of Consulting and Clinical Psychology, 43*, 585–586.

Mueller, W., & Kell, B. (1972). *Coping with conflict: Supervising counselors and psychotherapists.* New York: Appleton-Century-Crofts.

Mullen, J., & Abeles, N. (1971). Relationship of liking, empathy, and therapist's experience to outcome of therapy. *Journal of Counseling Psychology, 18*, 39–43.

Newman, A. (1981). Ethical issues in the supervision of psychotherapy. *Professional Psychology, 12,* 690–695.

Nichols, M. P. (1974). Outcome of brief cathartic psychotherapy. *Journal of Consulting and Clinical Psychology, 42,* 403–410.

Nichols, M. P., & Bierenbaum, H. (1978). Success of cathartic therapy as a function of patient variables. *Journal of Clinical Psychology, 34,* 776–778.

Nichols, M. P., & Paolino, T. J. (1986). *Basic techniques of psychodynamic psychotherapy: Foundation of clinical practice.* New York: Gardner Press.

Nichols, M. P., & Zax, M. (1977). *Catharsis in psychotherapy.* New York: Gardner Press.

Nietzel, M. T., & Fisher, S. G. (1981). Effectiveness of professional and paraprofessional helpers: A comment on Durlak. *Psychological Bulletin, 89,* 555–565.

Nietzel, M. T., Russell, R. L., Hemmings, K. A., & Gretter, M. L. (1987). The clinical significance of psychotherapy for unipolar depression. A meta-analytic approach to social comparison. *Journal of Consulting and Clinical Psychology, 55,* 156–161.

Noonan, E., & Spurling, L. (Eds.). (1992). *The making of a counselor.* New York: Tavistock/Routledge.

Norcross, J. C. (1986). Eclectic psychotherapy: An introduction and overview. In J. C. Norcross (Ed.), *Handbook of eclectic psychotherapy* (pp. 3–24). New York: Brunner/Mazel.

Norcross, J. C., & Guy, J. D. (1989). Ten therapists: The process of becoming and being. In W. Dryden & L. Spurling (Eds.), *On becoming a psychotherapist* (pp. 215–239). New York: Routledge.

Norcross, J. C., & Prochaska, J. O. (1982). A national survey of clinical psychologists: Affiliations and orientations. *The Clinical Psychologist, 35,* 1–6.

Norcross, J. C., & Saltzman, N. (1990). The clinical exchange: Toward integrating the psychotherapies. In N. Saltzman & J. C. Norcross (Eds.), *Therapy wars: Contention and convergence in differing clinical approaches* (pp. 1–14). San Francisco: Jossey-Bass.

Norcross, J. C., Strausser, D. J., & Missar, C. D. (1988). The process and outcomes of psychotherapists' personal treatment experiences. *Psychotherapy, 25,* 36–43.

Nye, R. D. (1992). *Three psychologies: Perspectives from Freud, Skinner, and Rogers* (4th ed.). Pacific Grove, CA: Brooks/Cole.

O'Farrell, M. K., Hill, C. E., & Patton, S. M. (1986). A comparison of two cases of counseling with the same counselor. *Journal of Counseling and Development, 65,* 141–145.

Olivieri-Larsson, R. (1993). Superego conflicts in supervision. *Group Analysis, 46*(2), 169–176.

Olsson, G. (1991). The supervisory process reflected in dreams of supervisees. *American Journal of Psychotherapy, 45*(4), 511–526.

Orlinsky, D. E., & Howard, K. I. (1986). Process and outcome in psychotherapy. In S. L. Garfield & A. E. Bergin (Eds.), *Handbook of psychotherapy and behavior change* (3rd ed., pp. 311–384). New York: Wiley.

Orne, M. T., & Wender, P. H. (1968). Anticipatory socialization for psychotherapy: Method and rationale. *American Journal of Psychiatry, 124*(9), 1202–1212.

Overall, B., & Aronson, H. (1962). Expectations of psychotherapy in lower socioeconomic class patients. *American Journal of Orthopsychiatry, 32,* 271–272.

Parloff, M. B. (1976, February 21). Shopping for the right therapy. *Saturday Review,* pp. 135–142.

Parloff, M. B., & Elkin, I. (1992). The NIMH treatment of depression. In D. K. Freedheim (Ed.), *History of psychotherapy: A century of change* (pp. 442–449). Washington, DC: American Psychological Association.

Parsons, L. B., & Parker, G. V. (1968). Personal attitudes, clinical appraisals, and verbal behavior of trained and untrained therapists. *Journal of Consulting and Clinical Psychology, 32,* 64–71.

Patterson, C. H. (1974). *Relationship counseling and psychotherapy.* New York: Harper & Row.

Patterson, C. H. (1983). A client-centered approach to supervision. *The Counseling Psychologist, 11,* 21–25.

Patterson, C. H. (1985). *The therapeutic relationship: Foundations for an eclectic psychotherapy.* Pacific Grove, CA: Brooks/Cole.

Patterson, C. H. (1986). *Theories of counseling and psychotherapy* (4th ed.). New York: Harper & Row.

Payne, P. A., & Gralinski, D. M. (1969). Effects of supervisor style and empathy on counselor perceptions in simulated counseling. *Personnel and Guidance Journal, 47,* 557–563.

Payne, P. A., Winter, D. E., & Bell, G. E. (1972). Effects of supervisor style on the learning of empathy in a supervision analogue. *Counselor Education and Supervision, 11,* 262–269.

Peck, M. S. (1978). *The road less traveled: A new psychology of love, traditional values and spiritual growth.* New York: Simon & Schuster.

Perls, F. S. (1969). *Ego, hunger and aggression: The beginning of Gestalt therapy.* New York: Random House.

Perls, F. S. (1972). *In and out of the garbage pail.* New York: Bantam Books.

Perls, F. S., & Baumgardner, P. (1975). *Legacy from Fritz.* Palo Alto, CA: Science and Behavior Books.

Persons, J. B. (1991). Psychotherapy outcome studies do not accurately represent current models of psychotherapy: A proposed remedy. *American Psychologist, 46*(2), 99–106.

Piccard, B. J. (1988). *Introduction to social work: A primer* (4th ed.). Chicago: Dorsey Press.

Pierce, R. A., Nichols, M. P., & DuBrin, J. R. (1983). *Emotional expression in psychotherapy.* New York: Gardner Press.

Pine, F. (1990). *Drive, ego, object, and self.* New York: Basic Books.

Piper, W. E. (1988). Psychotherapy research in the 1980s: Areas of consensus and controversy. *Hospital and Community Psychiatry, 39,* 1055–1063.

Piper, W. E., Debbane, E. G., Bienvenu, J. P., & Garant, J. (1982). A study of group pretraining for group psychotherapy. *International Journal of Group Psychotherapy, 32*(3), 309–325.

Polster, E., & Polster, M. (1973). *Gestalt therapy integrated: Contours of therapy and practice.* New York: Brunner/Mazel.

Poser, E. G. (1966). The effect of therapists' training on group therapeutic outcome. *Journal of Consulting Psychology, 30,* 283–289.

Prioleau, L., Murdock, M., & Brody, N. (1983). An analysis of psychotherapy versus placebo studies. *The Behavioral and Brain Sciences, 6,* 275–310.

Prochaska, J. O. (1984). *Systems of psychotherapy: A transtheoretical analysis* (2nd ed.). Pacific Grove, CA: Brooks/Cole.

Prochaska, J. O., & Norcross, J. C. (1983). Contemporary psychotherapists: A national survey of characteristics, practices, orientations, and attitudes. *Psychotherapy: Theory, Research and Practice, 20,* 161–173.

Raimy, V. (1980). A manual for a cognitive therapy. In M. J. Mahoney (Ed.), *Psychotherapy process: Current issues and future directions* (pp. 153–156). New York: Plenum.

Rako, S., & Mazer, H. (Eds.). (1983). *Semrad: The heart of a therapist.* Northvale, NJ: Aronson.

Ramzy, I., & Sherrin, H. (1976). The nature of the inference process: A critical review of the literature. *International Journal of Psychoanalysis, 57,* 151–159.

Rapaport, D. (1967). *The collected papers of David Rapaport* (M. Gill, Ed.). New York: Basic Books.

Regan, A. M., & Hill, C. E. (1992). Investigation of what clients and counselors do not say in brief therapy. *Journal of Counseling Psychology, 39*(2), 168–174.

Reik, T. (1948). *Listening with the third ear.* New York: Farrar, Straus & Giroux.

Reising, G. N., & Daniels, M. H. (1983). A study of Hogan's model of counselor development and supervision. *Journal of Counseling Psychology, 30,* 235–244.

Reisman, J. M. (1971). *Toward the integration of psychotherapy.* New York: Wiley-Interscience.

Reynolds, C., & Fischer, C. (1983). Personal versus professional evaluations of self-disclosing and self-involving counselors. *Journal of Counseling Psychology, 30,* 451–454.

Rice, L. N. (1980). A client-centered approach to the supervision of psychotherapy. In A. K. Hess (Ed.), *Psychotherapy supervision* (pp. 136–147). New York: Wiley.

Rich, C. L., & Pitts, F. N. (1980). Suicide by psychiatrists: A study of medical specialists among 18,730 consecutive physician deaths during a 5-year period, 1967–72. *Journal of Clinical Psychiatry, 41,* 261–263.

Rioch, M. (1963). *United States public health services progress report.* Unpublished manuscript. Washington School of Psychiatry, Washington, DC.

Rioch, M. J. (1980). The dilemmas of supervision in dynamic psychotherapy. In A. K. Hess (Ed.), *Psychotherapy supervision* (pp. 68–77). New York: Wiley.

Roback, H. B. (1974). Insight: A bridging of the theoretical and research literatures. *The Canadian Psychologist, 15,* 61–88.

Robertson, M. (1979). Some observations from an eclectic therapist. *Psychotherapy: Theory, Research, and Practice, 16,* 18–21.

Robiner, W. (1982). Role diffusion in the supervisory relationship. *Professional Psychology, 13,* 258–267.

Robins, C. J., & Hayes, A. M. (1993). An appraisal of cognitive therapy. *Journal of Consulting and Clinical Psychology, 61,* 205–214.

Rogers, C. R. (1951a). *Client centered therapy.* Boston: Houghton Mifflin.

Rogers, C. R. (1951b). *Therapy: Implications and theory.* Boston: Houghton Mifflin.

Rogers, C. R. (1957). The necessary and sufficient conditions of therapeutic personality change. *Journal of Consulting Psychology, 21,* 95–103.

Rogers, C. R. (1958). A process conception of psychotherapy. *American Psychologist, 13,* 142–149.

Rogers, C. R. (1961). *On becoming a person.* Boston: Houghton Mifflin.

Rogers, C. R. (1975). Empathic: An unappreciated way of being. *Counseling Psychologist, 5*(2), 2–10.

Rogers, C. R. (1980). *A way of being.* Boston: Houghton Mifflin.

Rogers, C. R. (1989). Reply to Rollo May's letter. In H. Kirschenbaum & V. L. Henderson (Eds.), *Carl Rogers: Dialogues* (pp. 251–255). Boston: Houghton Mifflin. (Reprinted from *Journal of Humanistic Psychology*, 1982, *22*(4), 85–89.)

Rogers, C. R., Gendlin, E., Kiesler, D., & Truax, C. (1967). *The therapeutic relationship with schizophrenics*. Madison: University of Wisconsin Press.

Rogers, C. R., & Stevens, B. (1967). *Person to person: The problem of being human: A new trend in psychology*. Lafayette, CA: Real People Press.

Ronnestad, M. H., & Skovholt, T. M. (1993). Supervision of beginning and advanced graduate students of counseling and psychotherapy. *Journal of Counseling and Development, 71*(4), 396–405.

Rosenthal, D., & Frank, J. D. (1956). Psychotherapy and the placebo effect. *Psychological Bulletin, 53,* 294–302.

Rosenthal, T. L. (1983). Outcome research: Isn't sauce for the goose sauce for the gander? *The Behavioral and Brain Sciences, 6,* 299–300.

Rosenzweig, S. (1936). Some implicit common factors in diverse methods of psychotherapy. *American Journal of Orthopsychiatry, 6,* 412–415.

Roth, S. (1987). *Psychotherapy: The art of wooing nature*. Northvale, NJ: Aronson.

Rubinstein, G. (1992). Supervision and psychotherapy: Toward redefining the differences. *Clinical Supervisor, 10*(2), 97–116.

Ruesch, J., & Prestwood, A. R. (1949). Anxiety: Its initiation, communication and interpersonal management. *Archives of Neurology and Psychiatry, 62,* 527–550.

Rush, A. J., Beck, A. T., Kovacs, M., & Hollon, S. (1977). Comparative efficacy of cognitive therapy and pharmacotherapy in the treatment of depressed outpatients. *Cognitive Therapy Research, 1,* 17–37.

Safran, J. D. (1993). Breaches in the therapeutic alliance: An arena for negotiating authentic relatedness. *Psychotherapy, 30,* 11–24.

Safran, J. D., & Segal, Z. V. (1990). *Interpersonal processes in cognitive therapy*. New York: Basic Books.

Salameh, W. A. (1987). Humor in integrative short-term psychotherapy (ISTP). In W. F. Fry & W. A. Salameh (Eds.), *Handbook of humor and psychotherapy: Advances in the clinical use of humor* (pp. 195–240). Sarasota, FL: Professional Resource Exchange.

Salvendy, J. T. (1993). Control and power in supervision. *International Journal of Group Psychotherapy, 43*(3), 363–376.

Sansbury, D. L. (1982). Developmental supervision from a skills perspective. *The Counseling Psychologist, 10*(1), 53–57.

Schachtel, E. G. (1966). *Experiential foundations of Rorschach's test*. New York: Basic Books.

Schaffer, N. D. (1982). Multidimensional measures of therapist behavior as predictors of outcome. *Psychological Bulletin, 3,* 670–681.

Scissons, E. H. (1993). *Counseling for results: Principles and practices of helping*. Pacific Grove, CA: Brooks/Cole.

Searles, H. F. (1979). Feelings of guilt in the psychoanalyst. In H. F. Searles (Ed.), *Countertransference and related subjects* (pp. 28–35). New York: International Universities Press. (Original work published 1966)

Shadish, W. R., & Sweeney, R. B. (1991). Mediators and moderators in meta-analysis: There's a reason we don't let dodo birds tell us which psychotherapies should have prizes. *Journal of Consulting and Clinical Psychology, 59,* 883–893.

Shaffer, C. S., Shapiro, J., Sank, L. I., & Coghlan, D. J. (1981). Positive changes in depression, anxiety, and assertion following individual and group cognitive behavior therapy intervention. *Cognitive Therapy and Research, 5,* 149–157.

Shapiro, D. A. (1976). The effects of therapeutic conditions: Positive results revisited. *British Journal of Medical Psychology, 49,* 315–323.

Shapiro, D. A., & Shapiro, D. (1982). Meta-analysis of comparative therapy outcome studies: A replication and refinement. *Psychological Bulletin, 92,* 581–604.

Sharaf, M. R., & Levinson, D. J. (1964). The quest for omnipotence in professional training. *Psychiatry, 27,* 135–149.

Shaw, B. F. (1983, July). *Training therapists for the treatment of depression: Collaborative study.* Paper presented at the meeting of the Society for Psychotherapy Research, Sheffield, England.

Shoben, E. J. (1949). Psychotherapy as a problem in learning theory. *Psychological Bulletin, 46,* 366–392.

Sifneos, P. E. (1987). *Short-term dynamic psychotherapy.* New York: Plenum Medical Book Company.

Sifneos, P. E. (1992a). Motivation for change. In H. Davanloo (Ed.), *Short-term dynamic psychotherapy* (pp. 93–98). Northvale, NJ: Aronson.

Sifneos, P. E. (1992b). *Short-term anxiety-provoking psychotherapy: A treatment manual.* USA: Basic Books.

Silverman, M. S. (1972). Perceptions of counseling following differential practicum experiences. *Journal of Counseling Psychology, 19,* 11–15.

Simmermon, R. D., & Simmermon, J. (1994). Psychologists of generation X: Robots or revolutionaries? *Psychotherapy Bulletin, 29,* 43–46.

Skinner, B. F. (1953). *Science and human behavior.* New York: Free Press.

Skynner, R. (1990). Make sure to feed the goose that lays the golden eggs: A discussion on the myth of altruism. In J. R. Schlapobersky (Ed.), *Institutes and how to survive them: Mental health training and consultation* (pp. 155–169). New York: Routledge.

Sloane, R. B., Cristol, A. H., Pepernik, M. C., & Staples, F. R. (1970). Role preparation and expectation of improvement in psychotherapy. *The Journal of Nervous and Mental Disease, 150*(1), 18–26.

Sloane, R. B., Staples, F. R., Cristol, A. H., Yorkston, N. J., & Whipple, K. (1975). *Psychotherapy versus behavior therapy.* Cambridge, MA: Harvard University Press.

Smith, D. (1982). Trends in counseling and psychotherapy. *American Psychologist, 37,* 802–807.

Smith, M., Glass, G., & Miller, T. (1980). *The benefits of psychotherapy.* Baltimore: Johns Hopkins University Press.

Snyder, W. U. (1945). An investigation of the nature of nondirective psychotherapy. *Journal of General Psychology, 33,* 193–223.

Spiegel, S. B., & Hill, C. E. (1989). Guidelines for research on therapist interpretation: Toward greater methodological rigor and relevance to practice. *Journal of Counseling Psychology, 36*(1), 121–129.

Spurling, L., & Dryden, W. (1989). The self and the therapeutic domain. In W. Dryden & L. Spurling (Eds.), *On becoming a psychotherapist* (pp. 191–214). New York: Routledge.

Steinbeck, J. (1979). *Burning bright.* New York: Penguin Books. (Original work published 1950)

Steinbeck, J. (1986a). *Cup of gold.* New York: Penguin Books. (Original work published 1929)

Steinbeck, J. (1986b). *In dubious battle.* New York: Penguin Books. (Original work published 1936)

Steinbeck, J. (1986c). *The short reign of Pippin IV.* New York: Penguin Books. (Original work published 1957)

Steinbeck, J. (1986d). *The winter of our discontent.* New York: Penguin Books. (Original work published 1961)

Steinbeck, J. (1986e). *Travels with Charlie.* New York: Penguin Books. (Original work published 1962)

Steinbeck, J. (1987). *Sweet Thursday.* New York: Penguin Books. (Original work published 1954)

Steinbeck, J. (1988a). *East of Eden.* New York: Penguin Books. (Original work published 1952)

Steinbeck, J. (1988b). *The grapes of wrath.* New York: Penguin Books. (Original work published 1939)

Steinbrueck, S. M., Maxwell, S. E., & Howard, G. S. (1983). A meta-analysis of psychotherapy and drug therapy in the treatment of unipolar depression with adults. *Journal of Consulting and Clinical Psychology, 51,* 856–863.

Steppacher, R. C., & Mausner, J. S. (1973). Suicide in professionals: A study of male and female psychologists. *American Journal of Epidemiology, 98,* 436–445.

Sterba, R. (1934). The fate of the ego in analytic therapy. *International Journal of Psychoanalysis, 15,* 117–126.

Steuer, J. L., Mintz, J., Hammen, C. L., Hill, M. A., Jarvik, L. F., McCarley, T., Motoike, P., & Rosen, R. (1984). Cognitive-behavioral and psychodynamic group psychotherapy in treatment of geriatric depression. *Journal of Consulting and Clinical Psychology, 52,* 180–189.

Stiles, W. B., Shapiro, D. A., & Elliot, R. (1986). Are all psychotherapies equivalent? *American Psychologist, 41,* 165–180.

Stoltenberg, C. D. (1981). Approaching supervision from a developmental perspective: The counselor complexity model. *Journal of Counseling Psychology, 28,* 59–65.

Stoltenberg, C. D., & Delword, U. D. (1987). *Supervising counselors and therapists: A developmental approach.* San Francisco: Jossey-Bass.

Stone, L. (1961). *The psychoanalytic situation.* New York: International Universities Press.

Storr, A. (1980). *The art of psychotherapy* (2nd ed.). New York: Routledge.

Strupp, H. H. (1958). The performance of psychoanalytic and client centered therapists in an initial interview. *Journal of Consulting Psychology, 22,* 265–274.

Strupp, H. H. (1962). Patient-doctor relationships: The psychotherapist in the therapeutic process. In A. S. Bachrach (Ed.), *Experimental foundations of clinical psychology* (pp. 576–615). New York: Basic Books.

Strupp, H. H. (1973). On the basic ingredients of psychotherapy. *Journal of Consulting and Clinical Psychology, 41,* 1–8.

Strupp, H. H. (1975). On failing one's patient. *Psychotherapy: Theory, Research and Practice, 12,* 39–41.

Strupp, H. H. (1980a). Success and failure in time-limited psychotherapy: A systematic comparison of two cases: Comparison 1. *Archives of General Psychiatry, 37,* 595–603.

Strupp, H. H. (1980b). Success and failure in time-limited psychotherapy: A systematic comparison of two cases: Comparison 2. *Archives of General Psychiatry, 37,* 708–716.

Strupp, H. H. (1980c). Success and failure in time-limited psychotherapy: Further evidence (Comparison 4). *Archives of General Psychiatry, 37,* 947–954.

Strupp, H. H. (1989). My career as a researcher and psychotherapist. In W. Dryden & L. Spurling (Eds.), *On becoming a psychotherapist* (pp. 101–115). New York: Tavistock/Routledge.

Strupp, H. H. (1990). Time-limited dynamic psychotherapy. In J. K. Zeig & W. M. Munion (Eds.), *What is psychotherapy? Contemporary perspectives* (pp. 64–67). San Francisco: Jossey-Bass.

Strupp, H. H. (1991). Reflections on my career in clinical psychology. In C. E. Walker (Ed.), *The history of clinical psychology in autobiography* (Vol. 1, pp. 293–329). Pacific Grove, CA: Brooks/Cole.

Strupp, H. H. (1992). The future of psychodynamic psychotherapy. *Psychotherapy, 29,* 21–27.

Strupp, H. H., & Binder, J. L. (1984). *Psychotherapy in a new key: A guide to time-limited dynamic psychotherapy.* New York: Basic Books.

Strupp, H. H., & Bloxom, A. L. (1973). Preparing lower class patients for group psychotherapy: Development and evaluation of a role-induction film. *Journal of Consulting and Clinical Psychology, 41,* 373–384.

Strupp, H. H., Hadley, S. W., & Gomes-Schwartz, B. (1977). *Psychotherapy for better or worse.* New York: Aronson.

Sue, S., McKinney, H. L., & Allen, D. B. (1976). Predictors of the duration of therapy for clients in the community mental health system. *Community Mental Health Journal, 12,* 365–375.

Sullivan, H. S. (1953). *The interpersonal theory of psychiatry.* New York: Norton.

Sussman, M. B. (1992). *A curious calling: Unconscious motivations for practicing psychotherapy.* Northvale, NJ: Aronson.

Swift, W. J., & Wonderlich, S. (1993). House of games: A cinematic study of countertransference. *American Journal of Psychotherapy, 47*(1), 38–57.

Szasz, T. S. (1974). *The myth of mental illness.* New York: Harper & Row.

Taub-Bynum, E. B., Hersh, J. B., Poey, K., & Spring, R. Z. (1991). Supervision in short-term psychotherapy. *Clinical Supervisor, 9*(2), 7–18.

Taube, C. A., Burns, B. J., & Kessler, L. (1984). Patients of psychiatrists and psychologists in office-based practice: 1980. *American Psychologist, 39,* 1435–1447.

Taylor, C. B., & Arnow, B. (1988). *The nature and treatment of anxiety disorders.* New York: Free Press.

Tennov, D. (1975). *Psychotherapy: The hazardous cure.* Garden City, NY: Anchor Books.

Teyber, E. (1992). *Interpersonal process in psychotherapy: A guide for clinical training* (2nd ed.). Pacific Grove, CA: Brooks/Cole.

Thoits, P. (1985). Negative outcome: The influence of factors outside therapy. In D. T. Mays & C. M. Franks (Eds.), *Negative outcome in psychotherapy and what to do about it* (pp. 249–263). New York: Springer.

Thompson, A. (1983). *Ethical concerns in psychotherapy and their legal ramifications.* Lanham, MD: University Press of America.

Thompson, J. R. (1987). *The process of psychotherapy: An integration of clinical experience and empirical research.* Lanham, MD: University Press of America.

Thompson, L. W., Gallagher, D., & Breckenridge, J. S. (1987). Comparative effectiveness of psychotherapies for depressed elderlies. *Journal of Consulting and Clinical Psychology, 55*, 385–390.

Thorbeck, J. (1992). The development of the psychodynamic psychotherapist in supervision. *Academic Psychiatry, 16*(2), 72–82.

Tollinton, H. J. (1973). Initial expectations and outcome. *British Journal of Medical Psychology, 46*, 251–257.

Tomlinson, T. M., & Hart, J. T. (1962). A validation study of the process scale. *Journal of Consulting Psychology, 26*, 74–78.

Torrey, E. F. (1986). *Witchdoctors and psychiatrists*. Northvale, NJ: Aronson.

Truax, C. B., & Carkhuff, R. R. (1964). Significant developments in psychotherapy research. *Progress in Clinical Psychology, 6*, 124–155.

Truax, C. B., Carkhuff, R. R., & Douds, J. (1964). Toward an integration of the didactic and experiential approaches to training in counseling and psychotherapy. *Journal of Counseling Psychology, 11*, 240–247.

Truax, C. B., & Wargo, D. G. (1969). Effects of vicarious therapy pretraining and alternative sessions on outcome in group psychotherapy with outpatients. *Journal of Consulting and Clinical Psychology, 33*, 440–447.

Truax, C. B., Wargo, D. G., Frank, J. D., Imber, S. D., Battle, C. C., Hoehn-Saric, R., Nash, E. H., & Stone, A. R. (1966). Therapist empathy, genuineness, and warmth and patient therapeutic outcome. *Journal of Consulting Psychology, 30*, 395–401.

Uhlenhuth, E. H., & Duncan, D. B. (1968). Subjective change with medical student therapists: Course of relief in psychoneurotic outpatients. *Archives of General Psychiatry, 18*, 428–438.

Ungersma, A. J. (1961). *The search for meaning*. Philadelphia: Westminister.

Volkan, V. D. (1987). *Six steps in the treatment of borderline personality organization*. Northvale, NJ: Aronson.

Warren, N. C., & Rice, L. N. (1972). Structuring and stabilizing of psychotherapy for low-prognosis clients. *Journal of Consulting and Clinical Psychology, 39*, 173–181.

Watkins, C. E. (1992). Psychotherapy supervision and the separation-individuation process: Autonomy versus dependency issues. *Clinical Supervisor, 10*(1), 111–121.

Watkins, C. E. (1993). Development of the psychotherapy supervisor: Concepts, assumptions, and hypotheses of the supervisor complexity model. *American Journal of Psychotherapy, 47*(1), 58–74.

Watkins, J. T., Leber, W. R., Imber, S. D., Collins, J. F., Elkin, I., Pilkonis, P. A., Sotsky, S. M., Shea, M. T., & Glass, D. R. (1993). Temporal course of change of depression. *Journal of Consulting and Clinical Psychology, 61*, 858–864.

Weissman, M. M. (1979). The psychological treatment of depression: Evidence for the efficacy of psychotherapy alone, in comparison with, and in combination with pharmacotherapy. *Archives of General Psychiatry, 36*, 1261–1269.

Weissman, M. M., Klerman, G. L., Prusoff, B. A., Sholomskas, D. R., & Padian, N. (1981). Depressed outpatients: Results one year after treatment with drugs and/or interpersonal psychotherapy. *Archives of General Psychiatry, 38*, 51–55.

Weissman, M. M., Prusoff, B. A., DiMascio, A., Neu, C., Goklaney, M., & Klerman, G. L. (1979). The efficacy of drugs and psychotherapy in the treatment of acute depressive episodes. *American Journal of Psychiatry, 13*, 555–558.

Welt, S. R., & Herron, W. G. (1990). *Narcissism and the psychotherapist*. New York: Guilford Press.

Wessler, R. L. (1990). Cognitive appraisal therapy. In J. K. Zeig & W. M. Munion (Eds.), *What is psychotherapy? Contemporary perspectives* (pp. 155–159). San Francisco: Jossey-Bass.

Wessler, R. L., & Ellis, A. (1983). Supervision in counseling: Rational-emotive therapy. *The Counseling Psychologist, 11*, 43–49.

Whitehorn, J. C., & Betz, B. J. (1954). A study of psychotherapeutic relationships between physicians and schizophrenic patients. *American Journal of Psychiatry, 3*, 321–331.

Wiener, A. (1955). The effects of two experimental counseling techniques on performance impaired by induced stress. *Journal of Abnormal and Social Psychology, 51*, 565–572.

Wierzbicki, M., & Pekarik, G. (1993). A meta-analysis of psychotherapy dropout. *Professional Psychology: Research and Practice, 24*, 190–195.

Wilkins, W. (1973). Expectancy of therapeutic gain: An empirical and conceptual critique. *Journal of Consulting and Clinical Psychology, 40*, 69–77.

Williams, J. M. (1984). *The psychological treatment of depression.* New York: Free Press.

Wilson, G. T., & Thomas, M. G. W. (1973). Self- versus drug-produced relaxation and the effects of instructional set in standardized systematic desensitization. *Behavior Research and Therapy, 11*, 279–288.

Winnicott, D. W. (1965). *The maturational process and the facilitating environment.* New York: International Universities Press.

Wiser, S., & Goldfried, M. R. (1993). Comparative study of emotional experiencing in psychodynamic-interpersonal and cognitive-behavioral therapies. *Journal of Consulting and Clinical Psychology, 61*, 892–895.

Wolberg, L. R. (1954). *The technique of psychotherapy.* New York: Grune & Stratton.

Woldenberg, L. (1976). Psychophysiological changes in feeling therapy. *Psychological Reports, 39*, 1059–1062.

Wolowitz, H. M. (1975). Therapist warmth: Necessary or sufficient condition in behavioral desensitization? *Journal of Clinical and Consulting Psychology, 42*, 584.

Woody, G., McLellan, A. T., Luborsky, L., & O'Brien, C. P. (1981). Psychotherapy for opiate addiction: Some preliminary results. *Annals of the New York Academy of Sciences, 362*, 91–100.

Woody, R. H., Hansen, J. C., & Rossberg, R. H. (1989). *Counseling psychology: Strategies and services.* Pacific Grove, CA: Brooks/Cole.

Worthington, E. L., Jr., & Roehlke, H. J. (1979). Effective supervision as perceived by beginning counselors-in-training. *Journal of Counseling Psychology, 26*(1), 64–73.

Yalom, I. D. (1975). *The theory and practice of group psychotherapy* (2nd ed.). New York: Basic Books.

Yalom, I. D. (1980). *Existential psychotherapy.* New York: Basic Books.

Yalom, I. D. (1989). *Love's executioner and other tales of psychotherapy.* New York: Basic Books.

Yerushalmi, H. (1992). On the concealment of the interpersonal therapeutic reality in the course of supervision. *Psychotherapy, 29*(3), 438–446.

Yogev, S. (1982). An eclectic model of supervision: A developmental sequence for beginning psychotherapy students. *Professional Psychology, 13*, 236–243.

Young, M. E., Feller, F., & Witmer, J. M. (1989). *Eclecticism: New foundation for recasting the counseling profession.* Unpublished manuscript. Available from Mark Young, Graduate Programs in Counseling and Therapy, Stetson University, P.O. Box 8365, DeLand, FL 32720.

Zastrow, C. (1992). *The practice of social work* (4th ed.). Belmont, CA: Wadsworth.

Zastrow, C. (1993). *Introduction to social work and social welfare* (5th ed.). Pacific Grove, CA: Brooks/Cole.

Zeig, J. K., & Munion, W. M. (Eds.). (1990). *What is psychotherapy? Contemporary perspectives.* San Francisco: Jossey-Bass.

Zetzel, E. (1956). Current concepts of transference. *International Journal of Psycho-Analysis, 37,* 369–376.

Zilbergeld, B. (1983). *The shrinking of America: Myths of psychological change.* Boston: Little, Brown.

Zinker, J. (1977). *Creative process Gestalt therapy.* New York: Brunner/Mazel.

Zook, A., II, & Walton, J. M. (1989). Theoretical orientations and work settings of clinical and counseling psychologists: A current perspective. *Professional Psychology: Research and Practice, 20,* 23–31.

NAME INDEX

Abeles, N., 132
Abraham, K., 221
Abramowitz, C. U., 56
Abramowitz, S. I., 56
Alexander, F., 114, 118, 147, 162, 234, 246–248
Alexander, L. B., 127
Allen, D. B., 135, 278
Allport, G. W., 119
Altekruse, M. K., 70
Altucher, N., 68
American Psychiatric Association, 193–194
Andrews, G., 97
Angelone, E. O., 73
Appelbaum, A. H., 194, 208–209, 228
Applebaum, S. A., 116
Ard, B. N., 60
Arizmendi, T. G., 12, 173
Arlow, J., 37
Arnkoff, D. B., 36
Arnow, B., 223
Aronson, H., 135, 137
Atthowe, J., 81
Auerbach, A. H., 101, 105, 151, 157, 248
Auerswald, M. C., 141–142
Austin, B., 70
Autry, J. H., 106–107, 112
Aveline, M., 49, 65, 73

Bachrach, H. M., 151, 248
Bandura, A., 138
Barber, J. P., 292
Barker, C. B., 142, 145
Barnat, M., 49–50
Barrabee, E. I., 83, 93
Barrett, J. E., 187
Barrett-Lennard, G. T., 129–130, 143

Bartlett, W. E., 49, 72–73
Basch, M. F., 222
Bascue, L. O., 65
Bass, D., 104
Battler, C. C., 132, 137, 199–200
Bauer, B. P., 205, 234, 237, 256
Baumgardner, P., 211
Beck, A. T., 36, 39, 91, 101–102, 106, 117, 143, 157, 159–160, 164, 177, 206, 238, 251–252, 273, 284, 291, 297
Beck, J., 157, 238, 251–252, 297
Becker, E., 19, 247
Beckham, E. E., 160
Bedrosian, R. C., 206, 284
Bell, G. E., 70
Bellak, L., 31, 177, 181
Benson, J. J., 299
Bergan, J., 256
Berger, D. M., 232
Berger, S. S., 48–49, 72, 75
Bergin, A. E., 80, 86–87, 92, 94, 126, 132, 173, 225, 298
Bergman, D. V., 141
Berman, J. S., 89, 103
Bettelheim, B., 117
Betz, B. J., 132
Beutler, L. E., 12, 27, 74, 112, 125, 132, 173, 185, 244, 256, 259, 278, 292, 298
Bibring, E., 238
Bienvenu, J. P., 138
Bierenbaum, H., 149
Binder, J. L., 159–160, 210, 217
Blanck, G., 37
Blanck, R., 37
Bloch, S., 97
Blocher, D. H., 60
Bloxom, A. L., 138, 217

SUBJECT INDEX

Abandonment issues, of therapist, 231
Abreaction, 114, 247
Abuse, history of, 226–227
  initial assessment, in, 179, 190–191, 240
  of therapist, 9–12
Accountability of the profession, 291, 294
Active listening, 120, 228, 268, 286–287, 294
  as a balance, 275–276, 286
  cognitive therapy and, 273
  defined, 268–273, 286
  flexibility of therapist, 269–271, 275–276, 286
  hypothesis development, 225–228, 271
  novice therapists, 273–274
  orientation, role of therapist's, 35–36
  power issues, of therapist, 14–15
  uncertainty, of therapist, 275–276
  as unobtrusive, 269, 272–273
Adlerian therapy, 128
Adolescence, identity issues during, 55
Advice, 219–223
  cognitive therapy in, 223
  and emotions, 246
  necessity of, 222–223
  pitfalls of, 220–222, 255
  supportive relationship, impact on, 222
Affect. *See* Emotions
Affection, 267–268
Agape, 277
Aggression, 250, 260. *See also* Emotions
Alcohol, 191–192
Alexithymia, 257, 261
Alliance rupture, 169
Allport, and empathy, 119
Aloneness issues, of therapist, 16–22, 171
  empathy, 162
  personal illustration of, 64–69

Aloneness issues, of therapist *(continued)*
  responsibility, 18
  in supervision, 52–53
Alpha level, 104, 107
Altruistic motives for entering profession, 5–6, 204. *See also* Helping tendencies, of therapists
Amitriptyline hydrochloride, 91
Analogue studies
  cognitive insight, 143
  emotions, 147
  outcome studies, 97
Analytic pact, 200
Anhedonia, 193
Anticipatory socialization, 199
Anxiety
  of beginning therapists, 47–49, 61
  change, as part of, 266
  of seasoned therapists, 22
  and therapists' styles, 54–59
  in supervision, 49–54, 62–63
Anxiety induction techniques, 149–150
Art of counseling and psychotherapy, 294–298
  hypothesis development, 230, 235, 239
  in practice, role of, 294–295
  integration with science, 295–298
Assessment. *See* Initial assessment
Authentic engagement, 275
Autonomy, 18, 52, 153, 299. *See also* Responsibility
  advice-giving, 223
  client's emotions, 249, 258–262
  client's search for, 46
  socialization, 210–213
  termination, 280–281, 283, 285
  therapist's search for, 46–47, 54, 60

Cognitive therapy *(continued)*
emotions, role of, 251–254, 266
empathy, 160
hypotheses, role of, 224–225, 235, 238, 241
initial assessment, 178, 180–181
pharmacotherapy, comparisons with, 91, 106–109
research. *See* Comparative studies
science and art of therapy, 297
socializing clients to therapy, 201, 207–209, 212
stereotypes of, 37, 252–253, 273
supportive relationship, role of, 117
termination, 284
therapeutic relationship, role of, 117, 157, 159
varying styles of, 36
Common factors. *See also* Process variables
common-factors eclecticism, 27, 298
Comparative studies, 98–109, 111–112, 292, 298
commentaries on, 103–105
global versus symptomatic measures, 101–102, 107, 112
individual studies, 100–102
Luborsky, Singer, and Luborsky (1975), 99
Manuals, use of, 101–102, 105, 106, 196
Methodological rigor of, 83, 90, 94, 105
National Institute of Mental Health Collaborative Study, 106–109
orientation, researchers' allegiance to, 100–101
review articles, 102–103, 106, 109
Confidentiality, 179, 216
Confrontations and emotions, 246
Consciousness, altered state, 116
Constructivist perspective, 223
Coping-skills therapy, 36
Corrective emotional experience, 162–164, 246
cognitive therapy, 254
supportive relationship, 114, 116–117, 162–164, 167
theory, 114, 116
Counselor. *See* Therapist issues
Countertransference, 118, 204. *See also* Therapist issues
hypothesis development, 231–234
Crime and Punishment, 255
Cyclotherapy, 278

Death
and aloneness issues, of therapist, 19
mourning, 257–258

Delusions, 194
Depression, 91, 100, 102, 106–109, 182–183, 186, 192, 244, 258–261, 291
anger, relationship to, 259
Diagnosis, 183, 194–195
Diagnostic and Statistical Manual of Mental Disorders (DSM-IV), 193–194
Directive interventions
versus being, 225
personal illustration, 270–271
responsibility issues, 133, 270–271
Dodo bird, 99, 103–104, 107, 113–114, 116, 123, 128, 292
Drive theory, 37
Duration of therapy, 278
Dynamic therapy. *See* Psychodynamic psychotherapy

Eclectic therapy, 24–29
common-factors eclecticism, 27, 298
critics of, 26–27
defined, 27–29
versus flexibility, 40–41
integration, 27–40
number of therapists practicing, 25–26, 28, 298
research on, 88, 292, 298
technical eclecticism, 28–43
theoretical eclecticism, 27–28, 43
Education. *See* Training, of therapists
Effectiveness of therapy. *See* Outcome research
Ego, 39
Ego alliance, 158
Ego-dystonic, 238
Ego theory, 37
Emotional insight, 247
Emotions, 121–122, 131, 146–152. *See also* Empathy
anger, of client, 205, 209–210, 249–250, 258–261, 264
anger and depression, relationship between, 259
anxiety induction techniques, 149–150
catharsis, 113, 118, 146–150, 238, 258
as a circular process, 246–247
clarifications, 256–258
cognitions following, 245
cognitions preceding, 253
conflicting, 258
corrective emotional experience, 114, 116, 162–164, 246, 254
emotive psychotherapy, 147–149

CREDITS

This page constitutes an extension of the copyright page. We have made every effort to trace the ownership of all copyrighted material and to secure permission from copyright holders. In the event of any question arising as to the use of any material, we will be pleased to make the necessary corrections in future printings. Thanks are due to the following authors, publishers, and agents for permission to use the material indicated.

Chapter 2: 52, journal excerpt adapted from "On Maybe Becoming a Psychotherapist, Perhaps," by H. E. Book, 1973, *Canadian Psychiatric Association Journal, 18,* 487–493. Copyright © 1973 Canadian Psychiatric Association. Adapted by permission. **52,** journal excerpt, copyright © 1992 Haworth Press, Inc., Binghampton, NY. *Clinical Supervisor,* "Learning from Anxiety: A Transtheoretical Dimension of Supervision and Its Administration," *10*(2), 29–55, by T. G. Frantz. **55,** journal excerpt adapted from "Transference, Countertransference and Identification in Supervision," by G. Bush, 1969, *Contemporary Psychoanalysis, 5,* 158–162. Copyright © 1969 William Alanson White Psychoanalytic Institute. Adapted by permission. **59,** journal excerpt adapted from "Approaching Supervision from a Developmental Perspective: The Counselor Complexity Model," by C. D. Stoltenberg, 1981, *Journal of Counseling Psychology, 28,* 59–65. Copyright © 1981 American Psychological Association. Adapted by permission. **61,** journal excerpt from C. Loganbill, E. Hardy, & U. Delworth, *The Counseling Psychologist,* "Supervision: A Conceptual Model," *10*(1), pp. 3–42, copyright © 1983 by Sage Publications, Inc. Reprinted by permission of Sage Publications, Inc. **69,** journal excerpt adapted from "The Influence of the Supervision of Psychotherapy upon Being Therapeutic. I: Introduction and Background to the Supervisory Relationship. II: Modes of Influence of the Supervisory Relationship," by S. E. Greben, 1979, *Canadian Journal of Psychiatry, 24,* 499–513. Copyright © 1979 Canadian Psychiatric Association. Adapted by permission.
   Chapter 4: 104, journal excerpt adapted from "Are All Psychotherapies Equivalent?" by W. B. Stiles, D. A. Shapiro, & R. Elliott, 1986,

Chapter 6: 137, journal excerpt reprinted with permission from *Journal of Psychiatric Research, 2,* 267–281. R. Hoehn-Saric, J. D. Frank, S. D. Imber, E. H. Nash, A. R. Stone, & C. C. Battle, "Systematic Preparation of Patients for Psychotherapy—I. Effects on Therapy Behavior and Outcome," 1964, Elsevier Science Ltd., Pergamon Imprint, Oxford, England.

TO THE OWNER OF THIS BOOK:

We hope that you have found *Process Variables: Four Common Elements of Counseling and Psychotherapy* useful. So that this book can be improved in a future edition, would you take the time to complete this sheet and return it? Thank you.

School and address: ————————————————————————————————

Department: ————————————————————————————————————

Instructor's name: ——————————————————————————————————

1. What I like most about this book is: ————————————————————

——

——

2. What I like least about this book is: ————————————————————

——

——

3. My general reaction to this book is: —————————————————————

——

4. The name of the course in which I used this book is: ———————————

——

5. Were all of the chapters of the book assigned for you to read? ——————

   If not, which ones weren't? ——————————————————————————

6. In the space below, or on a separate sheet of paper, please write specific suggestions for improving this book and anything else you'd care to share about your experience in using the book.

——

——

——

——

——

Optional:

Your name: _____ Date: _____

May Brooks/Cole quote you, either in promotion for *Process Variables: Four Common Elements of Counseling and Psychotherapy* or in future publishing ventures?

Yes: _____ No: _____

Sincerely,

Frederick S. Walborn

Brooks/Cole Publishing is dedicated to publishing quality books for the helping professions. If you would like to learn more about our publications, please use this mailer to request our catalogue.

Name: _____

Street Address: _____

City, State, and Zip: _____